508 ONE-STORY HOME PLANS

W9-CFI-323

TABLE OF CONTENTS

CREATIVE HOMEOWNER®

COPYRIGHT © 2000
CREATIVE HOMEOWNER®
A Division of Federal Marketing Corp.
Upper Saddle River, NJ

Library of Congress
Catalogue Card No.: 99-068501   ISBN: 1-58011-035-5

Creative Homeowner A Division of Federal Marketing Corp.
24 Park Way, Upper Saddle River, NJ 07458

Manufactured in the United States of America

Current Printing (last digit) 10 9 8 7 6 5 4 3 2

Cover Photography by Donna & Ron Kolb Exposures Unlimited

Perfect for a View

The deck and the screen porch in the rear of the home will allow you to take maximum advantage of a lot with a rear view. Identical his and her closets in the master bedroom will allow plenty of space for both spouses.

Design by The Garlinghouse Company

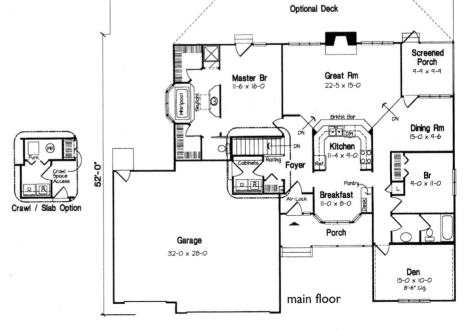

Crawl / Slab Option

66'-0"

Optional Deck

Master Br
11-6 x 16-0

Great Rm
22-5 x 15-0

Screened Porch
9-9 x 9-9

Brkfst Bar

Dining Rm
15-0 x 9-6

Kitchen
11-4 x 9-0

Foyer

Br
9-0 x 11-0

Cabinets   Railing

Pantry

Breakfast
11-0 x 8-0

Air-Lock

52'-0"

Porch

Garage
32-0 x 28-0

Den
15-0 x 10-0
8'-6" Clg.

main floor

Photography by John Ehrenclou

Partial walls create opportunities for creative decorating while giving rooms an open airy atmosphere.

Enjoy the surrounding vistas from the spacious rear deck. Take in the beauty of the outdoors; enjoy a relaxing cup of coffee watching the sunrise.

Plan info

Main Floor	1,738 sq. ft.
Basement	1,083 sq. ft.
Garage	796 sq. ft.
Bedrooms	Two
Baths	2(full)
Foundation	Basement, Slab or Crawl space

3

Woodland Cabin

Vaulted ceilings throughout this quaint cabin create a feeling of spaciousness. The bay in the living room would be a perfect place for reading and a window seat. The screened porch allows you a place to sit bug free at night.

Design by The Meredith Corporation

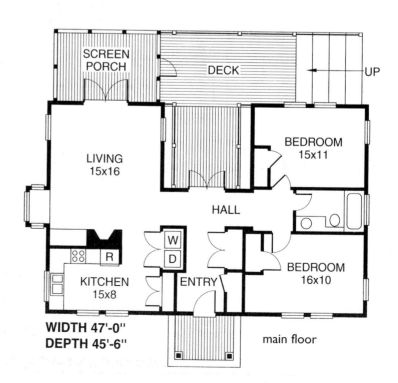

SCREEN PORCH

DECK

UP

LIVING 15x16

BEDROOM 15x11

HALL

W D

R

KITCHEN 15x8

ENTRY

BEDROOM 16x10

WIDTH 47'-0"
DEPTH 45'-6"

main floor

Photography courtesy of The Meredith Corporation

Two cozy bedrooms are separated by a full bath in this comfortable home.

This screen porch allows you to enjoy the outdoors through three seasons. Even at dusk you can enjoy a cool breeze on the porch mosquito free.

Plan info

Main Floor	1,112 sq. ft.
Basement	484 sq. ft.
Deck	280 sq. ft.
Porch	152 sq. ft.
Bedrooms	Two
Baths	1 (full)
Foundation	Basement, Crawl space

Wonderful Street Presence

Classic columns, circle top windows and a bow window study give this stucco home a wonderful street presence. The formal living and dining rooms are straight ahead providing one with a captivating first impression of elegance. Two secondary suites round out the wing. Each suite has full bathrooms. The master wing hosts a convenient study and ample sleeping area, as well as, his and her wardrobe closets and an alluring bath. No materials list is available for this plan.

Design by Sater Design Group

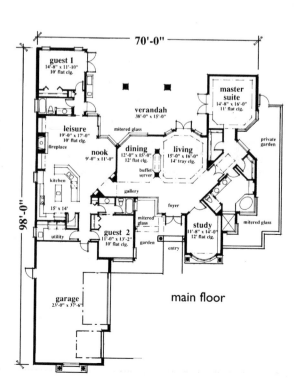

main floor

Photography supplied by Sater Design

The wall where the fireplace is located allows enough space for built-in bookshelves and cabinets, effectively adding to the convenience.

Plan info

Main Floor	2,794 sq. ft.
Garage	883 sq. ft.
Porch	572 sq. ft.
Bedrooms	Three
Baths	3(full)
Foundation	Slab

Not one but two islands expand the work surfaces in this kitchen. The larger island doubles as a snack bar.

Executive Home

An elegant exterior plus lively interior spaces combine to make this home a winner. Plenty of space for outdoor living has been designed into this plan too. The need for storage has not been compromised either.

Design by Donald A. Gardner Architects, Inc.

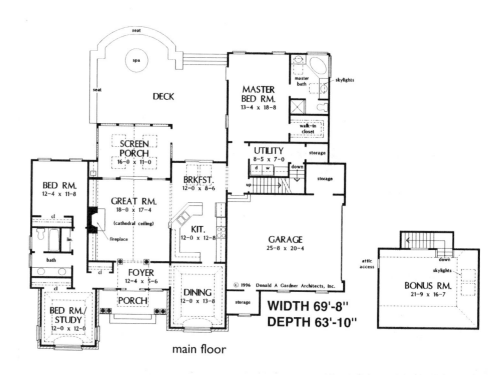

seat

spa

seat

DECK

SCREEN PORCH
16-0 x 11-0

BED RM.
12-4 x 11-8

cl

GREAT RM.
18-0 x 17-4

(cathedral ceiling)

fireplace

bath

lin.

cl

FOYER
12-4 x 5-6

cl

BED RM./
STUDY
12-0 x 12-0

PORCH

DINING
12-0 x 13-8

BRKFST.
12-0 x 8-6

KIT.
12-0 x 12-8

up

MASTER
BED RM.
13-4 x 18-8

master
bath

skylights

walk-in
closet

UTILITY
8-5 x 7-0

storage

d   w

down

storage

GARAGE
25-8 x 20-4

storage

© 1996 Donald A Gardner Architects, Inc.

WIDTH 69'-8"
DEPTH 63'-10"

attic
access

skylights

BONUS RM.
21-9 x 16-7

down

main floor

by Jon Riley, Riley & Riley Photography

The elegant formal dining room enjoys natural illumination from the front arched window and architectural interest has been added by the crowning tray ceiling.

The Master Suite includes a lavish skylit bath with a relaxing whirlpool tub.

Plan info

Main Floor	1,977 sq. ft.
Bonus	430 sq. ft.
Garage	610 sq. ft.
Bedrooms	Three
Baths	2(full)
Foundation	Crawl space

Turret Study

An angled garage, raised entry and a turret study help create a visually exciting and unique streetscape. The angled theme is present throughout the design and is useful in view orientation. A double sided fireplace is shared with the master suite to the right, a wetbar easily serves the living room, dining room and lanai and makes this home perfect for family gatherings or entertaining on a grand scale. An island kitchen easily serves all informal family areas.

Design by Sater Design Group

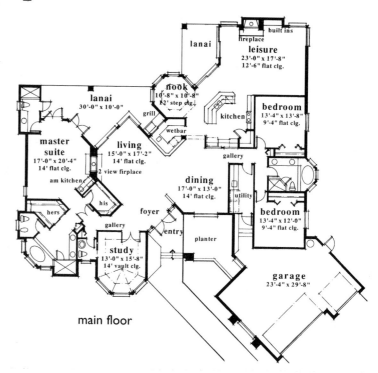

main floor

Photography supplied by Sater Design

This spacious island kitchen is accented by plant shelves and flows into the leisure room. There is plenty of counter space for preparing dinner.

Sunny and bright, the leisure room enjoys a fireplace with built-ins and an abundance of sunlight.

Plan info

Main Floor	3,477 sq. ft.
Garage	771 sq. ft.
Porch	512 sq. ft.
Bedrooms	Three
Baths	2(full), 1 3/4, and 1 1/2
Foundation	Slab

Country Cottage

Not an inch was wasted in the interior of this spacious dormered country cottage. Cathedral ceilings add height and truly please the eye. The garage is connected by the porch to the home and has a bonus room above it for storage or as an office.

Design by Donald A. Gardner Architects, Inc.

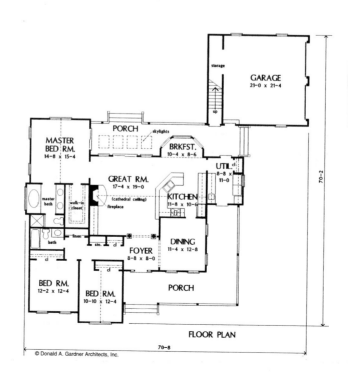

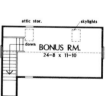

GARAGE
21-0 x 21-4

storage

up

BONUS RM.
24-8 x 11-10

attic stor.

skylights

down

PORCH   skylights

BRKFST.
10-4 x 8-6

MASTER
BED RM.
14-8 x 15-4

UTIL.
8-8 x 11-0

GREAT RM.
17-4 x 19-0

(cathedral ceiling)

fireplace

KITCHEN
11-8 x 10-6

master
bath

walk-in
closet

bath

linen

sto.

DINING
11-4 x 12-8

FOYER
8-8 x 8-0

BED RM.
12-2 x 12-4

BED RM.
10-10 x 12-4

PORCH

FLOOR PLAN

70-2

70-8

© Donald A. Gardner Architects, Inc.

Jon Riley, Riley & Riley Photography

Country-styled front porch gives an old-fashioned feeling to this home. Enjoy a cool glass of lemonade while rocking in a porch rocker.

The Great room has been given added volume with a cathedral ceiling and style by the use of arched openings.

Plan info

Main Floor	**1,815 sq. ft.**
Bonus	**336 sq. ft.**
Garage	**522 sq. ft.**
Bedrooms	**Three**
Baths	**2(full)**
Foundation	**Crawl space**

Photography by Jon Riley, Riley & Riley Photography

Grand Impression

This spectacular front elevation which includes brick, siding and palladian windows makes quite an impression. This home has the option of placing the garage doors to the front or the side based upon your preference.

Design by Donald A. Gardner Architects, Inc.

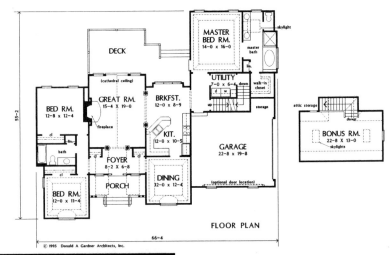

FLOOR PLAN

© 1995 Donald A Gardner Architects, Inc.

Plan info

Main Floor	1,879 sq. ft.
Bonus	360 sq. ft.
Garage	485 sq. ft.
Bedrooms	Three
Baths	2(full)
Foundation	Crawl space

Photography by Jon Riley, Riley & Riley Photography

Compact Three Bedroom

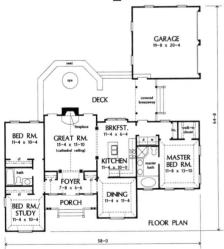

FLOOR PLAN

© 1990 Donald A. Gardner Architects, Inc.

Plan info

Main Floor	1,452 sq. ft.
Garage	427 sq. ft.
Bedrooms	Three
Baths	2(full)
Foundation	Crawl space

This compact three bedroom country charmer doesn't skimp on details, it's open, contemporary interior punctuated by elegant columns. The foyer leads to the dramatic Great room with cathedral ceiling and fireplace. The Great room opens to the island kitchen with breakfast area and accesses a spacious rear deck. Tray ceilings add interest to the bedroom/study, dining room, and master bedroom. The luxurious master suite features a walk-in closet, and a bath with dual vanity, separate shower and whirlpool tub.

Design by Donald A. Gardner Architects, Inc.

15

Plan no.
92630
price code **C** BL ZIP
total living area: 1,782 sq. ft.

Photography by Donna & Ron Kolb Exposures Unlimite

Charming Ranch Style

The appeal of this Ranch-style home is not only in its charm and exterior style. The Great room and the dining room, accented by a sloped ceiling, columns and custom moldings, work together with the corner fireplace, to create an outstanding space. People will naturally want to gather in this breakfast area where the sloped ceiling continues, and the light permeates through the rear windows and the French doors, which lead to the spacious screened porch. No materials list is available for this plan.

Design by Studer Residential Design, Inc.

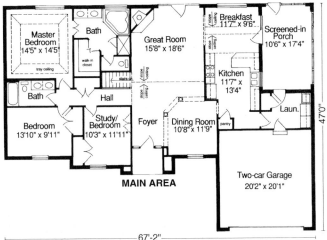

MAIN AREA

Plan info	
Main area	**1,782 sq. ft.**
Basement	**1,735 sq. ft.**
Garage	**407 sq. ft.**
Bedrooms	**Three**
Baths	**2(full)**
Foundation	**Basement**

Photography supplied by Studer Residential Design, Inc.

Warmth and Character

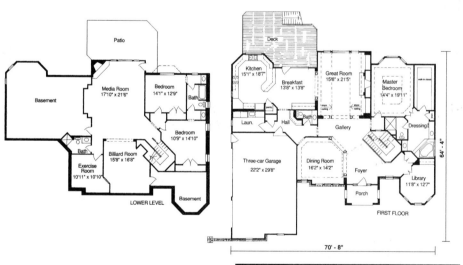

Detailed stucco and stone accents provide warmth and character to the exterior of this one-level home. An arched entry introduces you to the interior where elegant window styles and dramatic ceiling treatments create an impressive showplace. The extra large gourmet kitchen and breakfast room offer a spacious area for chores and family gatherings; while providing a striking view through the great room to the fireplace wall. For convenience, a butler's pantry is located in the hall leading to the sunken dining room. No materials list is available for this plan.

Design by Studer Residential Design, Inc.

Plan info

First Floor	2,582 sq. ft.
Lower Floor	1,746 sq. ft.
Basement	871 sq. ft.
Bedrooms	Three
Baths	2(full), 1 3/4, 1 1/2
Foundation	Basement

17

Photography by Jon Riley, Riley & Riley Photography

Classic Country

Dual porches, gables, and circle top windows give this home a special country charm. Closets and storage locations all around the home and garage provide you with ample storage options. The bonus room is ready to be finished for whatever purpose you desire.

Design by Donald A. Gardner Architects, Inc.

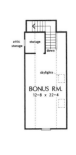

Plan info	
Main Floor	1,832 sq. ft.
Bonus	425 sq. ft.
Garage	562 sq. ft.
Bedrooms	Three
Baths	2(full)
Foundation	Crawl space

Photography by Jon Riley, Riley & Riley Photography

Charm and Personality

DECK

spa

MASTER BED RM.
13–4 x 14–8

lin.

master bath

skylights

fireplace

BED RM.
11–4 x 12–4

GREAT RM.
15–4 x 19–8
(cathedral ceiling)

BRKFST.
11–4 x 8–0

down

w
d

walk-in closet

storage

cl

lin.

bath

KIT.
11–4 x 10–4

GARAGE
20–0 x 19–8

FOYER
8–2 x 6–2

BED RM./ STUDY
11–4 x 11–4

PORCH

DINING
11–4 x 12–4

storage

(optional door location)

FLOOR PLAN

4–0

49–8

64–6

© 1996 Donald A Gardner Architects, Inc.

Charm and personality radiate from this country home. Interior columns dramatically open the foyer and kitchen to the spacious Great room, which boasts an impressive cathedral ceiling and a fireplace. The master suite, with tray ceiling accesses the rear deck through sliding glass doors. The skylit bath has all the amenities you would expect in a quality home. Two generous bedrooms share a second full bath. Tray ceilings with roundtop picture windows bring special elegance to the dining room and front swing room.

Design by Donald A. Gardner Architects, Inc.

Plan info

Main Floor	**1,655 sq. ft.**
Garage	**434 sq. ft.**
Bedrooms	**Three**
Baths	**2(full)**
Foundation	**Crawl space**

Cute and Compact

Cute and compact this Ranch has it all. Find many great features usually reserved for homes much larger in size. This home is the perfect starting place for a young family.

Design by The Garlinghouse Company

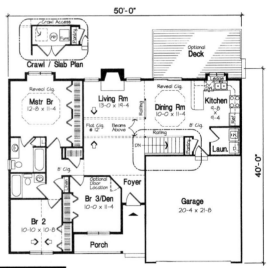

main floor

Plan info

Main Floor	1,312 sq. ft.
Basement	1,293 sq. ft.
Garage	459 sq. ft.
Bedrooms	**Three**
Baths	**2(full)**
Foundation	**Basement, Slab or Crawl space**

Affordable Start

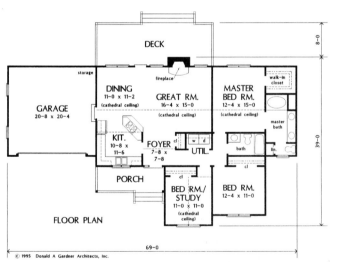

DECK

8–0

storage

DINING
11–0 x 11–2
(cathedral ceiling)

fireplace

GREAT RM.
16–4 x 15–0

(cathedral ceiling)

MASTER
BED RM.
12–4 x 15–0
(cathedral ceiling)

walk–in
closet

GARAGE
20–8 x 20–4

master
bath

KIT.
10–8 x
11–6

FOYER
7–8 x
7–8

w d

UTIL.

cl

bath

lin.

39–0

cl

PORCH

cl

BED RM./
STUDY
11–0 x 11–0
(cathedral ceiling)

BED RM.
12–4 x 11–0

FLOOR PLAN

69–0

© 1995 Donald A Gardner Architects, Inc.

This handsome home contains many popular design features and has been designed to be affordable to build. Cathedral ceilings found throughout the home add a dimension of space and volume. Use the bedroom/study for a private retreat or as a guest room when needed.

Design by Donald A. Gardner Architects, Inc.

Plan info

Main Floor	1,417 sq. ft.
Garage	441 sq. ft.
Bedrooms	Three
Baths	2(full)
Foundation	Crawl space

Country Charm

Country charm and Ranch convenience combine in this three bedroom home. The open design pulls Great room, kitchen, and breakfast bay into one common area, and cathedral ceilings give a feeling of spaciousness. A deck at the rear expands living and entertaining space, while the dining room provides a quiet place for relaxed family dinners or elegant dinner parties. The master suite is elegantly appointed with a cathedral ceiling, walk-in closet, and bath with a whirlpool tub, a shower, and a dual vanity.

Design by Donald A. Gardner Architects, Inc.

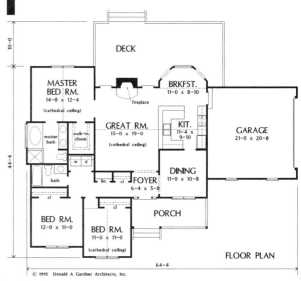

© 1995 Donald A Gardner Architects, Inc.

Plan info

Main Floor	1,512 sq. ft.
Garage	455 sq. ft.
Bedrooms	**Three**
Baths	**2(full)**
Foundation	**Crawl space**

22

Optional Door Location

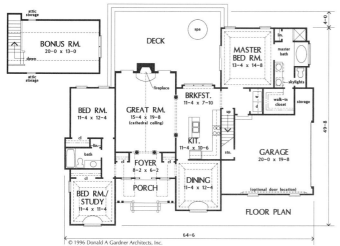

attic storage

BONUS RM.
20–0 x 13–0

down

attic storage

DECK

spa

MASTER BED RM.
13–4 x 14–8

lin.

master bath

skylights

fireplace

BED RM.
11–4 x 12–4

GREAT RM.
15–4 x 19–8
(cathedral ceiling)

BRKFST.
11–4 x 7–10

w
d

walk-in closet

storage

lin.

bath

KIT.
11–4 x 10–6

up

sto.

GARAGE
20–0 x 19–8

FOYER
8–2 x 6–2

BED RM./ STUDY
11–4 x 11–4

PORCH

DINING
11–4 x 12–4

(optional door location)

FLOOR PLAN

64–6

49–8

4–0

© 1996 Donald A Gardner Architects, Inc.

This versatile plan offers you an option for the location of the garage door. Place it to the front or on the side depending on what you prefer or what your lot will accommodate. Inside the home find varied ceiling treatments that add height, volume, and interest.

Design by Donald A. Gardner Architects, Inc.

Plan info	
Main Floor	**1,699 sq. ft.**
Bonus	**336 sq. ft.**
Garage	**498 sq. ft.**
Bedrooms	**Three**
Baths	**2(full)**
Foundation	**Crawl space**

Plan no.
99810

price code **D** | BL ✗ zip ℞R | total living area: 1,685 sq. ft.

Dramatic Dormers

Plenty of options await your decision in how to use the multi functional rooms in this home. A bedroom, a study or a living room can be created in the front of the home. A bonus room over the garage could become a home theatre.

Design by Donald A. Gardner Architects, Inc.

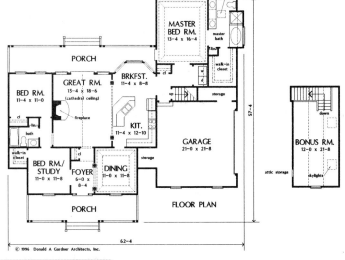

© 1996 Donald A Gardner Architects, Inc.

Plan info	
Main Floor	1,685 sq. ft.
Bonus	331 sq. ft.
Garage	536 sq. ft.
Bedrooms	Three
Baths	2(full)
Foundation	Crawl space

Triple Dormers

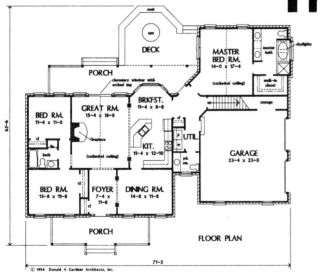

Located steps away from the master bedroom is the rear deck which has the option of a spa for a relaxing soak. Additional storage space is provided in the garage as well as above it in the form of a bonus room.

Design by Donald A. Gardner Architects, Inc.

Plan info	
Main Floor	**1,954 sq. ft.**
Bonus	**436 sq. ft.**
Garage	**649 sq. ft.**
Bedrooms	**Three**
Baths	**2 1/2**
Foundation	**Crawl space**

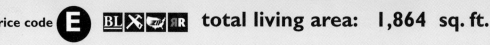

© 1993 Donald A. Gardner Architects, Inc.

Quaint and Cozy

Quaint and cozy on the outside this home surprises with an open floor plan featuring the Great room with a cathedral ceiling. The rear porch opens onto a deck with a spa that could be omitted to make it more spacious.

Design by Donald A. Gardner Architects, Inc.

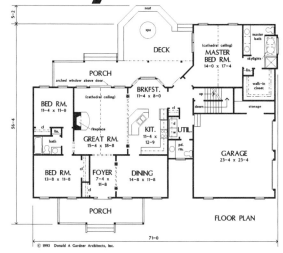

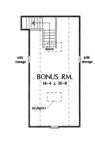

© 1993 Donald A. Gardner Architects, Inc.

Plan info

Main Floor	1,864 sq. ft.
Bonus	420 sq. ft.
Garage	614 sq. ft.
Bedrooms	Three
Baths	2 1/2
Foundation	Crawl space

Design of Distinction

Porch

Dining Area
11'6" x 14'2"

Kitchen
18' x 10'10"

Great Room
16'6" x 17'

Master Bedroom
14' x 11'9"

Bath

47'

Two-car Garage
20' x 22'

Laun.

Foyer

Bath

Hall

Porch

Bedroom
10'6" x 10'6"

Bedroom
11' x 10'6"

main floor

60'

This distinctive design sets itself apart due to its tremendous style. Be the only family on your block to have such a unique looking home. Inside find that all of your needs have been accounted for. This home provides functionality without sacrificing style.

Design by Studer Residential Design, Inc.

Plan info

Main Floor	1,508 sq. ft.
Basement	1,439 sq. ft.
Garage	440 sq. ft.
Bedrooms	Three
Baths	2(full)
Foundation	Basement

Plenty of Room

This design is a great family home that has enough space for everyone and even includes bonus space for growth. Style is definitely not sacrificed for convenience in this home. Many beautiful architectural features are included throughout the home.

Design by Donald A. Gardner Architects, Inc.

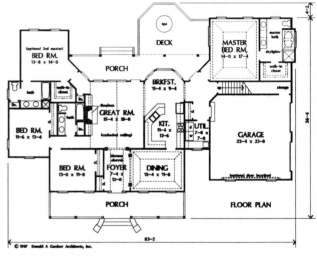

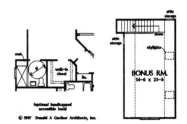

Plan info

Main Floor	2,349 sq. ft.
Bonus	435 sq. ft.
Garage	615 sq. ft.
Bedrooms	Four
Baths	3(full)
Foundation	Crawl space

South Hampton-Style

main floor

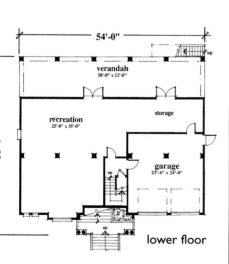

lower floor

Plan info

Main Floor	2,349 sq. ft.
Basement	1,402 sq. ft.
Garage	560 sq. ft.
Bedrooms	Three
Baths	2(full)
Foundation	Pier/Post

The dramatic arched entry of this South Hampton-style cottage borrows freely from its Southern Coastal past. A muted tropical palette with artful details preserves its Atlantic heritage, creating a combination of casual and traditional. The foyer and central hall open to the grand room. The heart of the home is served by a well-crafted kitchen with hard-working amenities. A wrapping counter space, a casual eating bar and a corner walk-in pantry please the cook, while the adjacent morning nook welcomes the entire family. No materials list is available for this plan.

Design by The Sater Design Group

Epitome of Country

Тhis single-level design is the
epitome of Country styling. Sit
a spell on the covered porch that
extends the entire width of the home.
Inside, the casual Country atmosphere
continues with large rooms and open
spaces.

Design by The Garlinghouse
Company

main floor

Plan info	
Main Floor	**1,792 sq. ft.**
Basement	**818 sq. ft.**
Garage	**857 sq. ft.**
Bedrooms	**Three**
Baths	**2(full)**
Foundation	**Basement**

total living area: 1,346 sq. ft. BL X zip R price code C

Plan no. 99826

You will want to have family gatherings in your new home to show it off. The floor plan is open and will accommodate a crowd with the option of also spreading out to the rear deck. For convenience, the laundry room is located close to the bedrooms.

Design by Donald A. Gardner Architects, Inc.

Plan info

Main Floor	1,346 sq. ft.
Garage	462 sq. ft.
Bedrooms	Three
Baths	2(full)
Foundation	Crawl space

---

total living area: 1,372 sq. ft. BL X zip R price code C

Plan no. 99830

This compact plan with a garage in the rear is the perfect starter home for a couple looking towards retirement. A fireplace and a bright front window warm the Great room. The washer and dryer are conveniently located near the bedrooms.

Design by Donald A. Gardner Architects, Inc.

Plan info

Main Floor	1,372 sq. ft.
Garage	537 sq. ft.
Bedrooms	Three
Baths	2(full)
Foundation	Crawl space

31

total living area: 1,590 sq. ft. [BL] [X] [R]   price code **D**   Plan no. **99850**

Country on the outside and contemporary on the inside, this three-bedroom charmer celebrates Country life with a wrap-around porch and a large rear deck. The master suite is privately located at the rear, while two front bedrooms share a second full bath.

Design by Donald A. Gardner Architects, Inc.

Plan info

Plan info	
Main Floor	1,590 sq. ft.
Garage	506 sq. ft.
Bedrooms	Three
Baths	2(full)
Foundation	Crawl space

total living area: 1,561 sq. ft. [BL] [X] [ZIP] [R] price code **D**   Plan no. **96417**

This laid back Country styled home has an elegant quality to it. The exterior detailing coupled with many interesting interior architectural features give this home a feeling of casual elegance. This home is sure to be a hit with your family and neighbors.

Design by Donald A. Gardner Architects, Inc.

Plan info

Plan info	
Main Floor	1,561 sq. ft.
Garage	346 sq. ft.
Bedrooms	Three
Baths	2(full)
Foundation	Crawl space

Design by The Garlinghouse Company

Compact Cabin

■ *Total living area 768 sq. ft.* ■ *Price Code A* ■

No. 84020 BL

■ This plan features:

– Three bedrooms

– One full bath

■ The open Living Room leads into an efficient Kitchen

■ One Bedroom one can be used as the Dining Room

■ All Bedrooms have ample closets and share the full hall Bath

■ No materials list is available for this plan

Main floor — 768 sq. ft.

Slab/Crawlspace Option

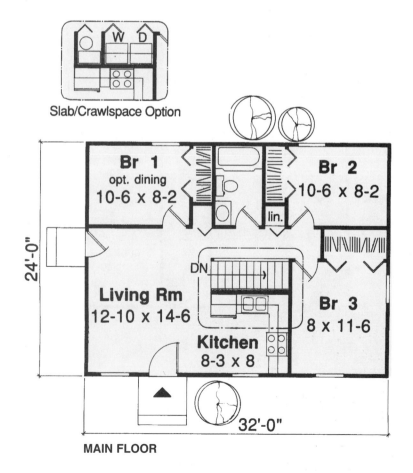

MAIN FLOOR

Easy Maintenance

Design by Marshall Associates

■ *Total living area 786 sq. ft.* ■ ■ *Price Code A* ■

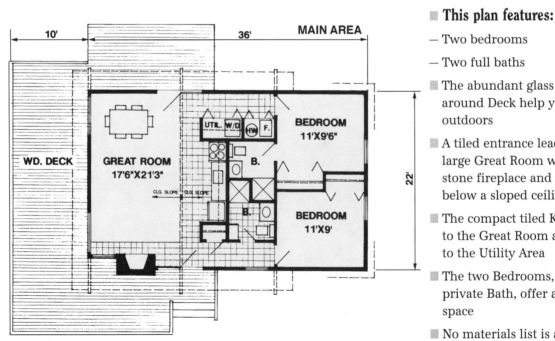

MAIN AREA

10'   36'

WD. DECK

GREAT ROOM
17'6"X21'3"

CLG. SLOPE ◄ ► CLG. SLOPE

UTIL. W/D HW F.

B.

B.

BEDROOM
11'X9'6"

BEDROOM
11'X9'

22'

No. 94307

■ **This plan features:**

— Two bedrooms

— Two full baths

■ The abundant glass and wrap-around Deck help you enjoy the outdoors

■ A tiled entrance leads into the large Great Room with a field-stone fireplace and Dining Area below a sloped ceiling

■ The compact tiled Kitchen opens to the Great Room and is adjacent to the Utility Area

■ The two Bedrooms, one with a private Bath, offer ample closet space

■ No materials list is available for this plan

Main floor — 786 sq. ft.

A Nest for Empty-Nesters

■ *Total living area 884 sq. ft.* ■ *Price Code A* ■

No. 90934 BL ✗

■ This plan features:

— Two bedrooms

— One full bath

■ The covered Sun Deck adds to outdoor living space

■ The Mudroom/Laundry Area inside the side door, traps dirt before it enters the house

■ An open layout is between the Living Room with fireplace, the Dining Room and the Kitchen

Main floor — 884 sq. ft.

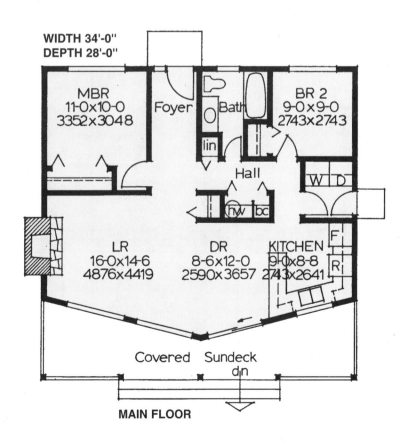

WIDTH 34'-0"
DEPTH 28'-0"

MBR
11-0x10-0
3352x3048

Foyer

Bath

BR 2
9-0x9-0
2743x2743

lin

Hall

W D

hw bc

LR
16-0x14-6
4876x4419

DR
8-6x12-0
2590x3657

KITCHEN
9-0x8-8
2743x2641

F

R

Covered Sundeck
dn

MAIN FLOOR

Duplex Delight

Total living area 914 sq. ft. ■ *Price Code G* ■

No. 91333

■ **This plan features:**

— Two bedrooms

— One full bath

■ Each unit has a single-car Garage

■ A fireplace will warm the Living Room on cold nights

■ The galley Kitchen leads into the Dining Room

■ The Bathroom contains a dual vanity

■ No materials list is available for this plan

Main floor — 914 sq. ft (Each unit)

MAIN FLOOR

WIDTH 78'-0"
DEPTH 36'-0"

Cabin in the Country

■ *Total living area 928 sq. ft.* ■ *Price Code A* ■

No. 90433 BL ✕

■ **This plan features:**

— Two bedrooms

— One full and one half baths

■ The screened Porch is included for enjoyment of your outdoor surroundings

■ The combination Living and Dining Areas include a cozy fireplace

■ The efficient Kitchen with the built-in Pantry is included

■ Two large Bedrooms are located at the rear of the home

■ An optional slab or crawlspace foundation — please specify when ordering

Main floor — 928 sq. ft.
Screened porch — 230 sq. ft.
Storage — 14 sq. ft.

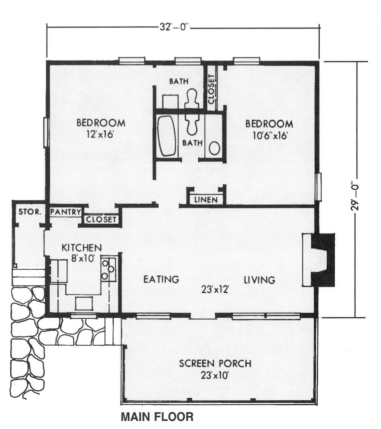

MAIN FLOOR

Champagne Style

No. 24302

This plan features:

— Three bedrooms

— Two full baths

Multiple gables, arched windows, and unique exterior set this delightful Ranch apart in any neighborhood

The Living and Dining Rooms are open to each other creating a very roomy feeling

Sliding doors lead from the Dining Room to the covered Patio

The Master Bedroom has a private Bath

Main floor — 984 sq. ft.
Basement — 988 sq. ft.
Garage — 280 sq. ft
Optional 2-car garage — 384 sq. ft.

Total living area 984 sq. ft. **Price Code A**

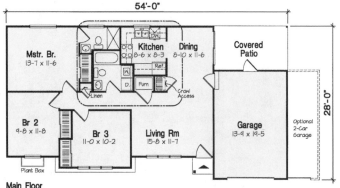

Main Floor

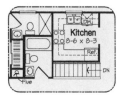

Optional Basement Plan

Large Living in a Small Space

No. 24304

This plan features:

— Three bedrooms

— Two full baths

The sheltered entrance leads into an open Living Room with a corner fireplace and a wall of windows

The well-equipped Kitchen features a peninsula counter with the Nook, the Laundry and clothes closet, and the built-in Pantry

The Master Bedroom has a private Bath

The two additional Bedrooms share a full hall Bath

Main floor — 993 sq. ft.
Garage — 390 sq. ft.
Basement — 987 sq. ft.

Total living area 993 sq. ft. **Price Code A**

Main Floor

Basement Option

Flexible Plan With Options

■ *Total living area 1,016 sq. ft.* ■ *Price Code A* ■

No. 90324

■ **This plan features:**

— Two bedrooms with optional third bedroom/den

— Two full baths

■ The Great Room features a vaulted ceiling, fireplace, and built-in bookcase

■ The eat-in Kitchen opens onto the partially enclosed Deck through sliding doors

■ The L-shaped Kitchen provides for easy meal preparation

■ The Master Bedroom has a private Bath, large walk-in closet, and window seat

Main floor — 1,016 sq. ft.

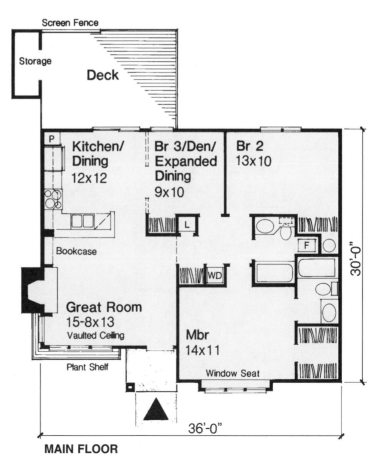

Screen Fence

Storage

Deck

Kitchen/
Dining
12x12

Br 3/Den/
Expanded
Dining
9x10

Br 2
13x10

L

P

Bookcase

WD

F

Great Room
15-8x13
Vaulted Ceiling

Mbr
14x11

Plant Shelf

Window Seat

30'-0"

36'-0"

MAIN FLOOR

Vacation Retreat

■ *Total living area 1,024 sq. ft.* ■ *Price Code A* ■

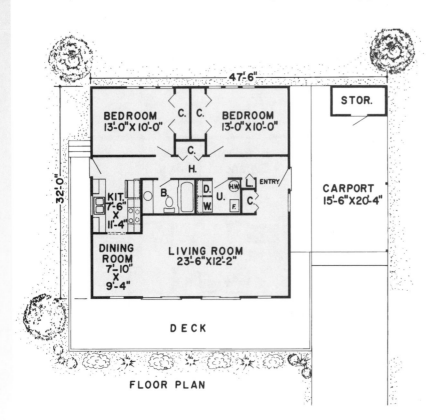

FLOOR PLAN

No. 1078

■ **This plan features:**

— Two bedrooms

— One full bath

■ The long hallway divides the Bedrooms and living areas and assures privacy

■ The Utility Room and the Bath are centrally located

■ The open Living/Dining Room features exposed beams, sloping ceilings and an optional fireplace

Main floor — 1,024 sq. ft.
Carport & storage — 387 sq. ft.
Deck — 411 sq. ft.

Quaint Starter Home

■ *Total living area 1,050 sq. ft.* ■ *Price Code A* ■

No. 92400 **BL**

■ **This plan features:**

— Three bedrooms

— Two full baths

■ The vaulted ceiling gives an airy feeling to the Dining and Living Rooms

■ This plan has a streamlined Kitchen with a comfortable work area, a double sink and ample cabinet space

■ The Living Room has a cozy fireplace

■ The Master Suite with a large closet and private Bath has French doors leading to the Patio

■ The two additional Bedrooms share a full Bath

■ No materials list is available for this plan

Main area — 1,050 sq. ft.
Garage — 261 sq. ft.

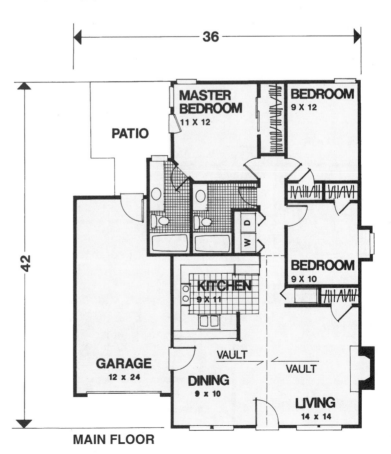

MAIN FLOOR

Perfect First Home

Design by Larry Garnett and Associates, Inc.

■ *Total living area 1,078 sq. ft.* ■ *Price Code A* ■

No. 92704 BL

■ **This plan features:**

— Three bedrooms

— Two full baths

■ This plan has a front Porch with turned posts and railing

■ The large Living Room has an eleven-foot ceiling, sloping towards the sliding glass doors to the rear yard

■ The Dining Area, with its cathedral ceiling, has views of the Porch through an elegant window

■ The corner double sink is below the corner box window in the efficient Kitchen

■ The secluded Master Bedroom includes a private Bath

■ No materials list is available for this plan

Main floor — 1,078 sq. ft.
Garage — 431 sq. ft.

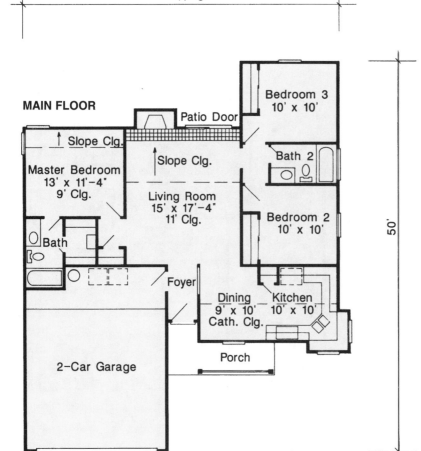

MAIN FLOOR

41'-8"

50'

↑ Slope Clg.

Master Bedroom
13' x 11'-4"
9' Clg.

Slope Clg.

Patio Door

Bedroom 3
10' x 10'

Bath 2

Living Room
15' x 17'-4"
11' Clg.

Bedroom 2
10' x 10'

Bath

Foyer

Dining
9' x 10'
Cath. Clg.

Kitchen
10' x 10'

2-Car Garage

Porch

A Special Kind of Coziness

■ *Total living area 1,089 sq. ft.* ■ *Price Code A* ■

No. 98805 **BL**

■ This plan features:

— Three bedrooms

— One full and one half baths

■ The open rail staircase compliments the central Foyer

■ The Living Room with its warm fireplace combines with the Dining Area

■ The Kitchen is highlighted by a desk, the Pantry, and a serving bar

■ The Laundry is conveniently located near the Bedrooms

■ The Master Suite includes a private half Bath

■ The two secondary Bedrooms have ample closet space

■ No materials list is available for this plan

Main floor — 1,089 sq. ft.
Basement — 1,089 sq. ft.
Garage — 462 sq. ft.

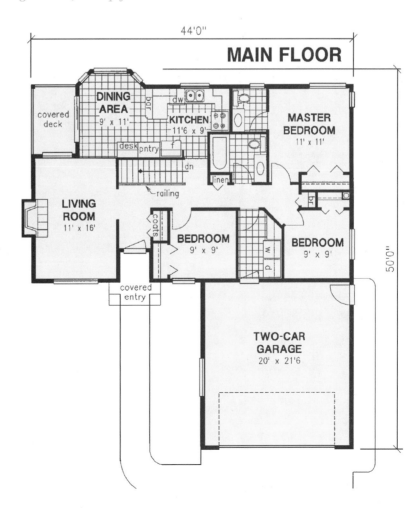

MAIN FLOOR

44'0"

covered deck

DINING AREA
9' x 11'

KITCHEN
11'6 x 9'

desk pntry

MASTER BEDROOM
11' x 11'

LIVING ROOM
11' x 16'

railing

dn

linen

coats

BEDROOM
9' x 9'

BEDROOM
9' x 9'

covered entry

TWO-CAR GARAGE
20' x 21'6

50'0"

Decorative Ceilings Inside

Design by Frank Betz Associates, Inc.

No. 98468 BL

Total living area 1,104 sq. ft. ■ *Price Code A* ■

46'-6"

41'-0"

M. Bath

TRAY CLG.

Master Suite
14⁰x12⁰

W.i.c.

FPL.

Breakfast

Vaulted
Family Room
16⁰x16⁰

SERVING
BAR

Kit.
RANGE

Bath

FRENCH
DOOR

Storage

REF.

OPT. STAIRS
TO BASEMENT

Vaulted
Bedroom
10⁰x10⁰

Bedroom
10⁰x10⁰

Garage
19⁵x19⁵

FLOOR PLAN

copyright © 1991 frank betz associates, inc.

GARAGE LOCATION W/BASEMENT

■ **This plan features:**

— Three bedrooms

— Two full baths

■ The Family Room has a vaulted ceiling, a corner fireplace, and a French door to the rear yard

■ The Breakfast Nook is brightened by windows on two of its walls

■ The galley Kitchen has a Pantry, and a serving bar extending into the Family Room

■ The Master Suite has a tray ceiling, a walk-in closet, and a private Bath

■ The two secondary Bedrooms have ample closet space, bright front wall windows, and one has a vaulted ceiling

■ This home has a two-car Garage with storage space

■ No materials list is available for this plan

■ An optional basement, slab or crawlspace foundation — please specify when ordering

Main floor — 1,104 sq. ft.
Basement — 1,104 sq. ft.
Garage — 400 sq. ft.

Home Sweet Home

Design by The Garlinghouse Company

No. 24723 BL

Total living area 1,112 sq. ft. ■ *Price Code A* ■

33'-0"

MBr
13-8 x 11-0
Clg. @ 4'

Kitchen
9-0 x 11-0

Flat Clg.
@ 4'

Util.

Storage

12"
Serving
Center

Dining
10-5 x 11-7

Flat Clg.
@ 8'

Living
16-9 x 14-2

Garage
21-9 x 20-2

Br 2
10-3 x 9-2

Br 3
10-11x 10-8

T.V. Built-in

MAIN FLOOR

Porch

64'-0"

■ **This plan features:**

— Three bedrooms

— Two full baths

■ A single-level format allows for step-saving convenience

■ The large Living Room, highlighted by a fireplace and built-in entertainment center, adjoins the Dining Room

■ Skylights, a ceiling fan, and room defining columns, accent the Dining Room

■ A serving bar can be found in the Dining Room, and there is ample counter and cabinet space in the Kitchen

■ There are decorative ceiling treatments over the Master Bedroom and the private Master Bath

■ The two secondary Bedrooms have easy access to the full Bath in the hall

■ No materials list is available for this plan

Main floor — 1,112 sq. ft.
Garage — 563 sq. ft.

Design by The Garlinghouse Company

Practical Layout

No. 84330

This plan features:

- Three bedrooms
- One full bath
- ■ The Living Room is enhanced by a fireplace and bright front window
- ■ The U-shaped Kitchen has plenty of counter space for ease in meal preparation
- ■ The Breakfast Nook is adjacent to the Kitchen and has a sliding door to the rear Deck
- ■ All three Bedrooms have large closets
- ■ A full Bath is located in the hall
- ■ No materials list is available for this plan

Main floor — 1,114 sq. ft.

Total living area 1,114 sq. ft. ■ Price Code A

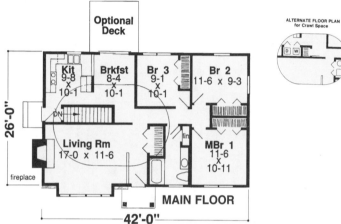

Design by Georgia Toney Lesley

Modern 'Savior Faire'

No. 99504

This plan features:

- Three bedrooms
- Two full baths
- ■ The spacious Country Kitchen has a built-in Pantry, ample storage and workspace
- ■ The Great Room is crowned in a vaulted ceiling and decorated by a fireplace, and has convenient access to the Kitchen
- ■ The Master Bedroom is highlighted by a private, full Bath and a walk-in closet
- ■ An optional crawl space or slab foundation — please specify when ordering
- ■ No materials list is available for this plan

Main floor — 1,127 sq. ft.
Garage — 257 sq. ft.

Total living area 1,127 sq. ft. ■ Price Code A

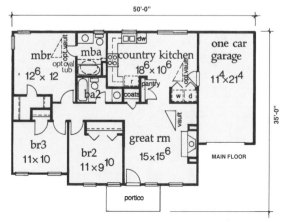

Open Spaces

Design by Frank Betz Associates, Inc.

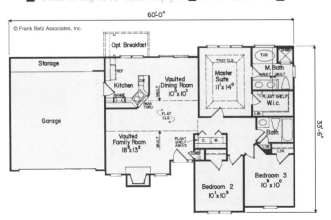

Total living area 1,135 sq. ft. ■ Price Code A

FLOOR PLAN

No. 98498 BL

■ **This plan features:**

— Three bedrooms

— Two full baths

■ There is an open floor plan between the Family Room and the Dining Room

■ Vaulted ceilings add volume and there is a fireplace in the Family Room

■ There are three Bedrooms and the Master Suite has a five-piece private Bath

■ The convenient Laundry Center is located outside the Bedrooms

■ No materials list is available for this plan

Main floor — 1,135 sq. ft.
Garage — 460 sq. ft.

Traditional Brick Home

Design by Larry E. Belk

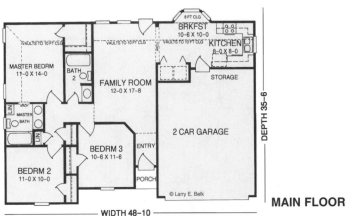

Total living area 1,136 sq. ft. ■ Price Code A

MAIN FLOOR

No. 93019 BL

■ **This plan features:**

— Three bedrooms

— Two full baths

■ A Traditional brick elevation is accented with quoins

■ The Family Room has a vaulted ten-foot ceiling giving a larger feel to the room

■ The Breakfast Room has a sunny bay window

■ The efficient, compact Kitchen is entered through an arched opening

■ The Master Suite has a large walk-in closet, double vanity and a built-in linen cabinet

■ The two additional Bedrooms share a full Bath

■ No materials list is available for this plan

Main floor — 1,136 sq. ft.
Garage — 434 sq. ft.

Quoin Accents

Design by Larry E. Belk

No. 93017 BL

■ **This plan features:**

− Three bedrooms

− Two full baths

■ A Traditional brick elevation has quoin accents

■ The large Family Room has a corner fireplace and direct access to the outside

■ An arched opening leads to the Breakfast Area

■ A bay window illuminates the Breakfast Area with natural light

■ The efficiently designed, U-shaped Kitchen has ample cabinet and counter space

■ The Master Suite has a private Master Bath

■ The two additional Bedrooms share a full hall Bath

■ No materials list is available for this plan

Main floor − 1,142 sq. ft.
Garage − 428 sq. ft.

Total living area 1,142 sq. ft. ■ *Price Code A*

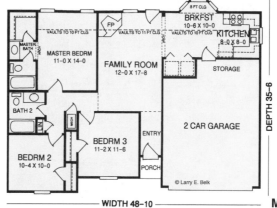

MAIN FLOOR

A Compact Home

Design by Larry E. Belk

No. 93018 BL

■ **This plan features:**

− Three bedrooms

− Two full baths

■ Siding with brick wainscoting distinguishes the elevation

■ The large Family Room has a corner fireplace and direct access to the outside

■ An arched opening leads to the Breakfast Area

■ A bay window illuminates the Breakfast Area with natural light

■ The efficiently designed, U-shaped Kitchen has ample cabinet and counter space

■ The Master Suite has a private Master Bath

■ The two additional Bedrooms share a full hall Bath

■ No materials list is available for this plan

Main floor − 1,142 sq. ft.
Garage − 428 sq. ft.

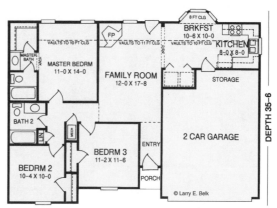

Total living area 1,142 sq. ft. ■ *Price Code A*

MAIN FLOOR

Delightful, Compact Home

Design by The Garlinghouse Company

■ *Total living area 1,146 sq. ft.* ■ *Price Code A* ■

slab/crawlspace option

Floor Plan

No. 34003

■ **This plan features:**

— Three bedrooms

— Two full baths

■ The Living Room, with its fireplace, is brightened by a wonderful picture window

■ The counter island features a double sink separating the Kitchen and Dining Areas

■ The Master Bedroom includes the private Master Bath and a double closet

■ The two additional Bedrooms have ample closet space and share a full Bath

Main floor — 1,146 sq. ft.

Timeless Appeal

■ *Total living area 1,170 sq. ft.* ■ *Price Code A* ■

No. 93075 BL

■ This plan features:

— Three bedrooms

— Two full baths

■ The ten-foot ceiling gives the Living Room an open feel

■ A cozy corner fireplace and access to the rear yard highlight the Living Room

■ The Dining Area is enhanced by a sunny bay window

■ The Bedrooms are conveniently grouped and include roomy closets

■ The Master Bedroom features a private Bath

■ An optional crawl space or slab foundation — please specify when ordering

■ No materials list is available for this plan

Main floor — 1,170 sq. ft.
Garage — 478 sq. ft.

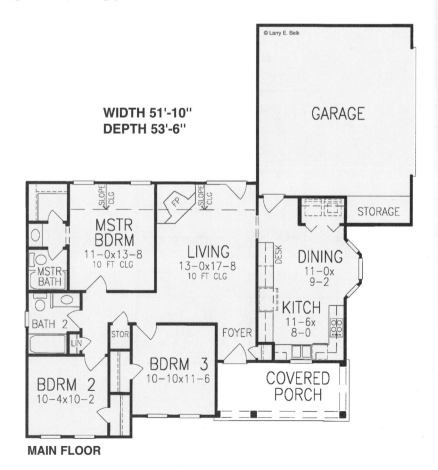

WIDTH 51'-10"
DEPTH 53'-6"

© Larry E. Belk

GARAGE

STORAGE

MSTR BDRM
11-0x13-8
10 FT CLG

LIVING
13-0x17-8
10 FT CLG

DINING
11-0x
9-2

MSTR BATH

BATH 2

LIN

STOR

DESK

KITCH
11-6x
8-0

FOYER

BDRM 2
10-4x10-2

BDRM 3
10-10x11-6

COVERED PORCH

MAIN FLOOR

Beautiful Bungalow

Design by Donald A. Gardner Architects, Inc.

© 1996 Donald A. Gardner Architects, Inc.

B. NATHAN

■ *Total living area 1,182 sq. ft.* ■ *Price Code C* ■

DECK

KIT.
8-4 x 8-8

w
d

pan.

MASTER
BED RM.
11-8 x 12-0

DINING
12-0 x 8-8

walk-in
closet

lin.

master
bath

GREAT RM.
20-4 x 14-4

(cathedral ceiling)

bath

fireplace

cl

closet

FOYER
6-0 x
8-8

BED RM./
STUDY
11-8 x 10-0

GARAGE
14-0 x 20-0

PORCH

FLOOR PLAN

39-5

10-0

53-0

© 1996 Donald A Gardner Architects, Inc.

No. 98075 BL

■ This plan features

— Two bedrooms

— Two full baths

■ The charming front Porch is covered

■ The Great Room has a fireplace and a high ceiling

■ The Dining Room has a pass-through from the Kitchen

■ The U-shaped Kitchen is well appointed

■ The Master Suite includes a walk-in closet and a private Bath

■ The Deck in the rear completes the design

Main floor — 1,182 sq. ft.
Garage — 295 sq. ft.

Quaint and Cozy Ranch

■ *Total living area 1,185 sq. ft.* ■ *Price Code A* ■

No. 98461

■ This plan features:

- Three bedrooms

- Two full baths

- The Great Room includes a vaulted ceiling and cozy fireplace with windows to either side

- The galley Kitchen is efficiently arranged and is open to the Eating Area

- The covered Porch expands living space to the outdoors

- The Master Suite has a tray ceiling over the Bedroom and a vaulted ceiling over a private Bath

- An optional basement or crawl space foundation — please specify when ordering

- No materials list is available for this plan

Main floor — 1,185 sq. ft.
Basement — 1,185 sq. ft.
Garage — 425 sq. ft.

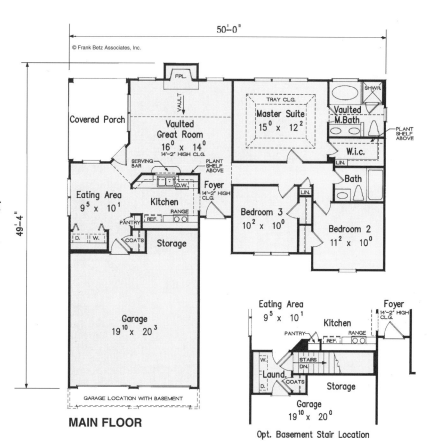

MAIN FLOOR

Opt. Basement Stair Location

Vaulted Ceilings

Design by Frank Betz Associates, Inc.

No. 97256 BL

■ **This plan features:**

— Four bedrooms

— Two full baths

■ The Family Room of this home is topped by a vaulted ceiling and opens to the Dining Area

■ A vaulted ceiling tops the Dining Area and the efficient L-shaped Kitchen

■ The Master Suite is designed with a tray ceiling over the Bedroom and a vaulted ceiling over a Master Bath

■ The two additional Bedrooms share a full Bath in the hall

■ The Laundry Center is located in the hall next to the Garage entrance

■ An optional basement or crawl space foundation — please specify when ordering

■ No materials list is available for this plan

Main floor — 1,198 sq. ft.
Basement — 1,216 sq ft.
Garage — 410 sq ft.

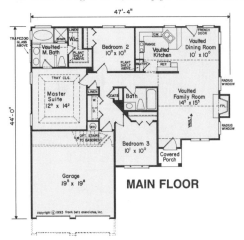

Total living area 1,198 sq. ft. ■ *Price Code A* ■

MAIN FLOOR

Cozy Three Bedroom

Design by W.D. Farmer F.A.I.B.D.

No. 94800 BL X

■ **This plan features:**

— Three bedrooms

— Two full baths

■ The covered Entry leads into the Activity Room highlighted by a double window and a vaulted ceiling

■ The efficient Kitchen has a work island and opens to the Dining Area with access to the Deck

■ The plush Master Bedroom offers a decorative ceiling, walk-in closet and whirlpool tub

■ The two additional Bedrooms, one with a vaulted ceiling, share a full Bath

■ The Garage entry serves as the Mud Room into the Laundry Room

■ An optional basement, slab or crawlspace foundation — please specify when ordering

Main floor — 1,199 sq. ft.
Basement — 1,119 sq. ft.
Garage — 287 sq. ft.

Total living area 1,199 sq. ft. ■ *Price Code A* ■

WIDTH 51'-8"
DEPTH 34'-2"

ALT. PART FLOOR PLAN
(OMITTING BASEMENT STAIR)

MAIN FLOOR

Design by Larry E. Belk

No. 93073 **BL**

■ **This plan features:**

— Three bedrooms

— Two full baths

■ The large covered front Porch opens to the Foyer with a nine-foot ceiling

■ The Kitchen has a built-in desk, sunny window over the sink and Dining Area with a bay window

■ The Living Room has a corner fireplace and a ten-foot ceiling

■ The Bedrooms are grouped for homeowner convenience

■ The Master Suite is topped by a sloped ceiling and includes a private Bath and walk-in closet

■ The two-car Garage, located at the rear of the home, has an optional door location

■ An optional slab or crawl space foundation — please specify when ordering

■ No materials list is available for this plan

Main floor — 1,202 sq. ft.
Garage — 482 sq. ft.

■ *Total living area 1,202 sq. ft.* ■ *Price Code A* ■

MAIN FLOOR

Width 51'-10"
Depth 43'-10"

Design by Perfect Plan

No. 90630 **BL** ✕

■ **This plan features:**

— Three bedrooms

— Two full baths

■ The Living Room has a cathedral ceiling with exposed beams and a stone wall with a heat-circulating fireplace

■ Three sliding glass doors lead from the Living Room to the large Deck

■ The built-in Dining Area separates the Kitchen from the far end of the Living Room

■ The Master Suite has dual closets and a private Bath

■ The two additional Bedrooms, one double sized, share a full hall Bath

Main floor — 1,207 sq. ft.

■ *Total living area 1,207 sq. ft.* ■ *Price Code A* ■

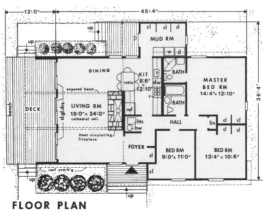

FLOOR PLAN

Great Room is Center of Activity
Design by Rick Garner

Total living area 1,208 sq. ft. ■ Price Code A

FLOOR PLAN

No. 92520

■ **This plan features:**

— Three bedrooms

— Two full baths

■ The sheltered Entry leads into the open Foyer and Great Room beyond

■ The spacious Great Room has a raised, brick hearth fireplace with bin and access to the back Porch

■ The formal Dining Room adjoins the Great Room and Kitchen for easy entertaining

■ The efficient Kitchen has the Laundry Alcove and Garage entrance

■ The Master Bedroom has an arched transom window and a private Bath and walk-in closet

■ The two additional Bedrooms have ample closet space and share a full Bath

■ An optional crawl space or slab foundation — please specify when ordering

Main floor — 1,208 sq. ft.

Drive-Under Garage
Design by Jannis Vann & Associates, Inc.

Total living area 1,208 sq. ft. ■ Price Code A

WIDTH 48'-0''
DEPTH 29'-0''

MAIN FLOOR

No. 98915

■ **This plan features:**

— Three bedrooms

— Two full baths

■ The sheltered entry leads into the Living Area with its inviting fireplace and vaulted ceiling

■ The convenient Dining Area opens to the Living Room, Kitchen and Sun Deck

■ The efficient, U-shaped Kitchen is adjacent to the Dining Area and has access to the Deck

■ The luxurious Master Bedroom has a vaulted ceiling, two closets and a double vanity Bath

■ The two additional Bedrooms share a full Bath with a convenient Laundry Center

Main floor — 1,208 sq. ft.
Basement — 728 sq. ft.
Garage — 480 sq. ft.

No. 94913

■ This plan features:

— Two bedrooms

— Two full baths

■ The recessed entry below the keystone arch adds a distinctive detail to the elevation

■ The spacious Great Room has a large fireplace between transom windows and built-in shelves

■ The Breakfast Area has access to the rear yard and is easily served by a snack bar counter in the step-saving Kitchen

■ The Laundry Room and the Kitchen are accessible from the Garage

■ The Master Bedroom features a large walk-in closet and a double vanity Bath

■ The second Bedroom is next to a full Bath and Linen closet

Main floor — 1,212 sq. ft.
Basement — 1,212 sq. ft.
Garage — 448 sq. ft.

Uncomplicated Living Space

■ *Total living area 1,212 sq. ft.* ■ *Price Code A* ■

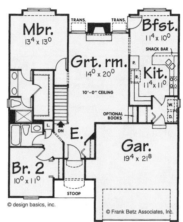

WIDTH 40'-0"
DEPTH 47'-8"

MAIN FLOOR

© design basics, inc.
© Frank Betz Associates, Inc.

Charming Three-Bedroom

No. 97259

BL

■ This plan features:

— Three bedrooms

— Two full baths

■ The covered Porch leads into the Foyer with plant shelves and the Family Room with a vaulted ceiling

■ The efficient Kitchen with Pantry and Laundry area has a pass-thru opening to the Breakfast Area

■ The private Master Suite has a vaulted ceiling, walk-in closet and a plush Master Bath

■ The two secondary Bedrooms have spacious closets and share a full Bath in the hall

■ An optional basement or crawlspace foundation — please specify when ordering

■ No materials list is available for this plan

Main floor — 1,222 sq. ft.
Basement — 1,218 sq. ft.
Garage — 410 sq. ft.

■ *Total living area 1,222 sq. ft.* ■ *Price Code A* ■

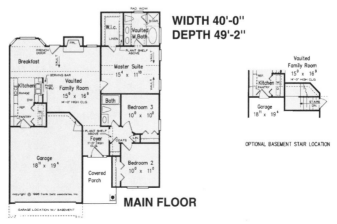

WIDTH 40'-0"
DEPTH 49'-2"

OPTIONAL BASEMENT STAIR LOCATION

MAIN FLOOR

copyright © 1996 frank betz associates, inc.

55

Spectacular Traditional

Design by Rick Garner

■ *Total living area 1,237 sq. ft.* ■ *Price Code A* ■

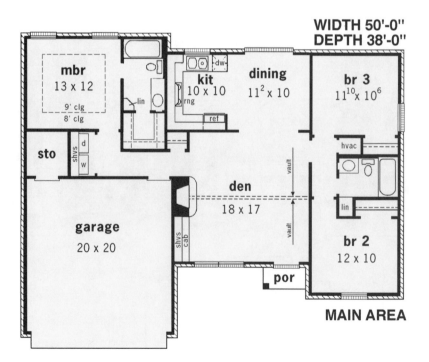

WIDTH 50'-0"
DEPTH 38'-0"

mbr
13 x 12
9' clg
8' clg

kit
10 x 10
rng

dining
11² x 10

br 3
11¹⁰ x 10⁶

sto

den
18 x 17

garage
20 x 20

br 2
12 x 10

por

MAIN AREA

No. 92502 BL ✕

■ This plan features:

— Three bedrooms

— Two full baths

■ The use of gables and the blend of stucco and brick form a spectacular exterior

■ There is a high vaulted ceiling and a cozy fireplace with built-in cabinets in the Den

■ The efficient, U-shaped Kitchen has an adjacent Dining Area

■ The Master Bedroom, with a raised ceiling, includes a private Bath and a walk-in closet

■ The two family Bedrooms share a full hall Bath

■ An optional crawlspace or slab foundation — please specify when ordering

Main area — 1,237 sq. ft.
Garage — 436 sq. ft.

■ *Total living area 1,243 sq. ft.* ■ *Price Code A* ■

No. 90682 BL ✕

■ **This plan features:**

— Three bedrooms

— Two full baths

■ The large and spacious Living Room adjoins the Dining Room for easy entertaining

■ The Bedrooms are conveniently grouped for privacy

■ The Master Bedroom has dual closets and a private Bath

■ The efficient Kitchen has the walk-in Pantry

Main floor — 1,243 sq. ft.
Basement — 1,103 sq. ft.
Garage — 490 sq. ft.

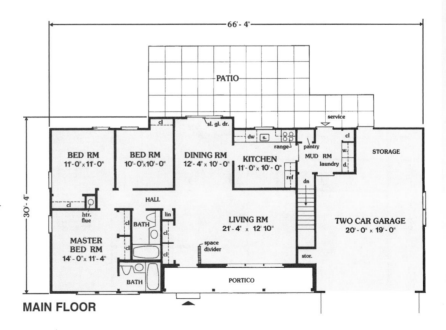

MAIN FLOOR

Split Bedroom Floor Plan

Design by Vaughn A. Lauban Designs

■ *Total living area 1,243 sq. ft.* ■ *Price Code A* ■

No. 96519   BL

■ **This plan features:**

— Three bedrooms

— Two full baths

■ The split bedroom floor plan gives the Master Bedroom ultimate privacy

■ The Great Room is highlighted by a fireplace and a vaulted ten-foot ceiling

■ A snack bar peninsula counter is one of the many conveniences of the Kitchen

■ The Patio is accessed from the Dining Room

■ No materials list is available for this plan

Main floor — 1,243 sq. ft.
Garage — 523 sq. ft.

Delightful Duplex

Total living area 1,245 sq. ft. ■ *Price Code G* ■

No. 94703

■ **This plan features:**

— Three bedrooms

— Two full baths

■ Arched windows and clean lines highlight the exterior

■ The Kitchen has easy access to the Dining Room

■ The Great Room has a door to the back yard

■ The Master Bedroom has a private Bath

■ The two secondary Bedrooms share a full Bath

Main floor — 1,245 sq. ft. (per unit)

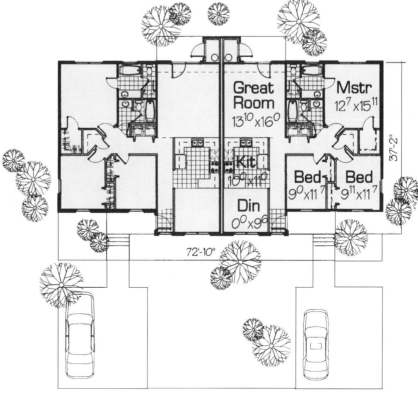

Great Room 13¹⁰x16⁰

Mstr 12⁷x15¹¹

Kit 10⁰x10⁰

Bed 9⁰x11⁷

Bed 9¹¹x11⁷

Din 10⁰x9⁰

37'-2"

72'-10"

MAIN FLOOR

Illusion of Spaciousness

Design by Donald A. Gardner Architects, Inc.

© 1997 Donald A. Gardner Architects, Inc.

■ Total living area 1,246 sq. ft. ■ Price Code C ■

FLOOR PLAN

© 1997 Donald A Gardner Architects, Inc.

No. 96484

■ **This plan features:**

— Three bedrooms

— Two full baths

■ Open living spaces and vaulted ceilings create an illusion of spaciousness

■ Cathedral ceilings maximize space in the Great Room and the Dining Room

■ The Kitchen features a skylight and a breakfast bar

■ The well-equipped Master Suite is privately located

■ The two additional Bedrooms share a full Bath

Main floor — 1,246 sq. ft.
Garage — 420 sq. ft.

Tremendous Curb Appeal

© 1995 Donald A Gardner Architects, Inc.

■ *Total living area 1,246 sq. ft.* ■ *Price Code C* ■

No. 99806 BL ✕ ЯR

■ This plan features:

– Three bedrooms

– Two full baths

■ The Great Room is topped by a cathedral ceiling and enhanced by a fireplace

■ The Great Room, Dining Room and Kitchen are open to each other

■ A Pantry, skylight and peninsula counter add to the comfort and efficiency of the Kitchen

■ A cathedral ceiling crowns the Master Suite with walk-in and linen closets, and a luxurious private Bath

■ One of the two other rooms has a cathedral ceiling and can be used as a Study

Main floor — 1,246 sq. ft.
Garage — 420 sq. ft.

DECK

KIT.
9-0 x
11-0

skylight

master
bath

MASTER
BED RM.
11-8 x 14-4
(cathedral ceiling)

GARAGE
19-4 x 20-4

SCREEN
PORCH
10-0 X 11-0

pantry

DINING RM.
11-8 X 9-4

UTIL.
d w lin.

walk-in
closet

cl   cl

fireplace

GREAT RM.
15-8 X 15-0
(cathedral ceiling)

BED RM.
13-4 x 10-0

bath
skylight

PORCH

BED RM./
STUDY
11-0 X 11-4
(cathedral ceiling)

60-0

60-0

FLOOR PLAN

© 1995 Donald A Gardner Architects, Inc.

One-Floor Living

Design by Vaughn A. Lauban Designs

No. 96511 BL ✕

■ This plan features:

— Three bedrooms

— Two full baths

■ The covered front Porch is supported by columns and accented by balusters

■ The Living Room features a cozy fireplace and a ceiling fan

■ The Kitchen is distinguished by an angled serving bar

■ The Dining Room is convenient to the Kitchen and has access to the rear Porch

■ The two secondary Bedrooms share a Bath in the hall

■ The Master Bedroom has a walk-in closet and a private Bath

■ The two-car Garage with storage space is located in the rear of the home

Main Floor —1,247 sq. ft.
Garage — 512 sq. ft.

■ Total living area 1,247 sq. ft. ■ Price Code A ■

MAIN FLOOR

U-Shaped Kitchen

Design by Donald A. Gardner Architects, Inc.

No. 99858 BL ✕ 🗺 R

■ This plan features:

— Three bedrooms

— Two full baths

■ The continuous cathedral ceiling in the Great Room, Kitchen, and Dining Room adds to the spacious feel of this efficient plan

■ The efficient Kitchen has a skylight, plant shelf and opens to the Dining Area

■ The Master Bedroom has a cathedral ceiling and contains walk-in and linen closets and a private Bath with garden tub and dual vanity

■ A cathedral ceiling is is featured in the front Bedroom/Study

Main floor — 1,253 sq. ft.
Garage & Storage — 420 sq. ft.

© 1995 Donald A Gardner Architects, Inc.

■ Total living area 1,253 sq. ft. ■ Price Code C ■

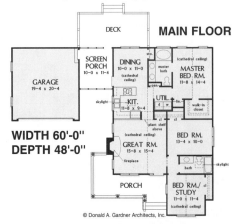

MAIN FLOOR

WIDTH 60'-0"
DEPTH 48'-0"

© Donald A. Gardner Architects, Inc.

Efficient and Compact

No. 93449

■ **This plan features:**

— Three bedrooms

— Two full baths

■ The covered front Porch adds style to the exterior

■ A sloped ceiling and fireplace are in the Family Room

■ The U-shaped Kitchen opens to the Dining Room

■ The Laundry Room is conveniently located

■ The Bedrooms have walk-in closets

■ The two-car Garage features extra storage space

■ No materials list is available for this plan

Main floor — 1,253 sq. ft.
Garage — 486 sq. ft.
Porch — 208 sq. ft.

■ *Total living area 1,253 sq. ft.* ■ *Price Code A* ■

MAIN FLOOR

Rear Porch
16 x 5/9

Master
14 x 12
8' Clg.

Dining
10/9 x 11
8' clg.

Kitchen
9 x 11

Pant.

Bedroom #3
10/4 x 10/7
8' Clg.

Garage
20 x 22

Pass
Thru

W
D

Stor.

Family Room
14 x 16/8
11'-4" Clg.

Bedroom #2
10 x 10/8
8' Clg.

Sloped Ceiling

Foyer

WIDTH 61'-3"
DEPTH 40'-6"

Porch
34/8 x 6

Stylish Bay Window

No. 93004

■ **This plan features:**

— Three bedrooms

— Two full baths

■ A stylish bay window and the covered Porch highlight the exterior elevation

■ The Great Room has a corner fireplace and a ten-foot ceiling

■ The Breakfast Bay is brightened by three windows

■ The Kitchen is a convenient U-shape and features the walk-in Pantry

■ The large Master Bedroom has its own Bath and a walk-in closet with built-in shelves

■ The two additional Bedrooms share a full Bath in the hall.

■ No materials list is available for this plan

Main floor —1,260 sq. ft.

■ *Total living area 1,260 sq. ft.* ■ *Price Code A* ■

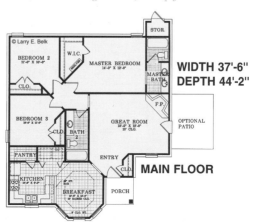

© Larry E. Belk

STOR.

BEDROOM 2
11'-0" X 10'-0"

W.I.C.

MASTER BEDROOM
14'-0" X 12'-0"

MASTER
BATH

WIDTH 37'-6"
DEPTH 44'-2"

CLO.

BEDROOM 3

CLO.

BATH
2

GREAT ROOM

F.P.

OPTIONAL
PATIO

PANTRY

ENTRY

CLO.

KITCHEN

BREAKFAST

PORCH

MAIN FLOOR

Two-Car Garage

Design by Rick Garner

No. 92559 BL ✕

This plan features:

— Three bedrooms

— Two full baths

■ The covered front Porch opens to the Foyer

■ The Den has a sloped ceiling and a fireplace

■ The Dining Room is adjacent to the Kitchen

■ The galley Kitchen has access to the Garage and the Utility Room

■ The Bedrooms are all on one side of the home

■ The Master Bedroom has a raised ceiling and a walk-in closet

■ An optional slab or crawl space foundation — please specify when ordering

Main floor — 1,265 sq. ft.

Garage — 523 sq. ft.

■ Total living area 1,265 sq. ft. ■ Price Code A ■

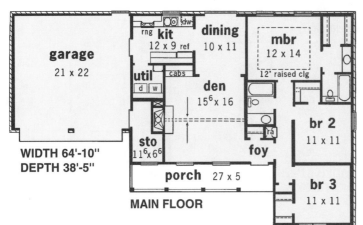

garage 21 x 22

rng **kit** 12 x 9 **ref**

dining 10 x 11

mbr 12 x 14
12' raised clg

util **d** **w** **cabs**

den 15⁶ x 16

sto 11⁶x6⁶

foy

br 2 11 x 11

WIDTH 64'-10"
DEPTH 38'-5"

porch 27 x 5

br 3 11 x 11

MAIN FLOOR

Relaxed Style

Design by Design Basics, Inc.

No. 94985 BL ✕ Я

This plan features:

— Three bedrooms

— Two full and one half baths

■ The lovely covered Porch is a great place to relax and enjoy a cool breeze at the end of the day

■ This plan features one Bedroom for an empty nest lifestyle, with an option for two additional Bedrooms in the Basement

■ The Kitchen, Breakfast Area, and Great Room are open to each other for ease in every day living

■ A cathedral ceiling tops the Great Room and a fireplace adds atmosphere

Main floor — 1,279 sq. ft.
Bonus — 984 sq. ft.
Garage — 509 sq. ft.

■ Total living area 1,279 sq. ft. ■ Price Code A ■

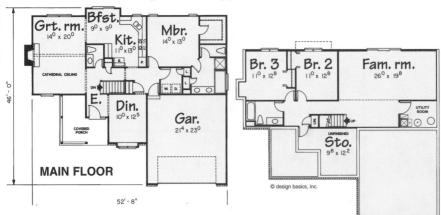

Grt. rm. 14⁰ x 20⁰
CATHEDRAL CEILING

Bfst. 9⁰ x 9⁰

Kit. 11⁰ x 13⁰

Mbr. 14⁰ x 13⁰

Din. 10⁰ x 12⁵

Gar. 21⁴ x 23⁰

46' - 0"

COVERED PORCH

E.

DN

MAIN FLOOR

52' - 8"

Br. 3 11⁰ x 12⁸

Br. 2 11⁰ x 12⁸

Fam. rm. 26⁰ x 19⁸

UTILITY ROOM

UNFINISHED

Sto. 9⁸ x 12²

UP

© design basics, inc.

BONUS

Design by Landmark Design, Inc.

No. 98747 BL ✖

This plan features:

— Three bedrooms

— Two full baths

■ This plan has attractive wood siding and a large L-shaped covered Porch

■ The front Entry leads to the generous Living Room with a vaulted ceiling

■ The large two-car Garage has access through the Utility Room

■ The roomy secondary Bedrooms share a full Bath in the hall

■ The Kitchen is highlighted by the built-in Pantry and a garden window

■ A vaulted ceiling adds volume to the Dining Room

■ The Master Suite is enhanced by abundant closet space, separate vanity and linen storage

Main floor — 1,280 sq. ft.

■ Total living area 1,280 sq. ft. ■ Price Code A ■

WIDTH 52'-0"
DEPTH 47'-0"

An Open Concept Home

Design by Larry E. Belk

No. 93021 BL

This plan features:

— Three bedrooms

— Two full baths

■ The angled Entry creates the illusion of space

■ Two square columns flank the bar and separate the Kitchen from the Living Room

■ The Dining Room is suitable for both formal and informal occasions

■ The Master Bedroom has a large walk-in closet

■ The large Master Bath has a double vanity, linen closet and a whirlpool tub/shower combination

■ The two additional Bedrooms share a full Bath

■ No materials list is available for this plan

Main floor — 1,282 sq. ft.
Garage — 501 sq. ft.

■ Total living area 1,282 sq. ft. ■ Price Code A ■

MAIN FLOOR

WIDTH 48'-10"
DEPTH 52'-6"

Tidewater Comfort

Design by Sater Design Group

■ *Total living area 1,288 sq. ft.* ■ *Price Code A* ■

MAIN FLOOR

No. 94263   BL

■ **This plan features:**

— Two bedrooms

— Two full baths

■ The Foyer is separated from the Dining Room by a half wall

■ The Kitchen shares an eating bar with the Great Room

■ Both the Dining Room and Great Room have access to the covered Porch through French doors

■ The Master Suite is isolated on one side of the home

■ No materials list is available for this plan

Main Floor — 1,288 sq. ft.

Design by Jannis Vann & Associates, Inc.

Welcoming Entry

■ *Total living area 1,292 sq. ft.* ■ *Price Code A* ■

No. 93222

■ This plan features:

— Three bedrooms

— Two full baths

■ The covered entrance provides shelter to visitors

■ The expansive Living Room is enhanced by the large front window

■ The Dining Room has a bay window and direct access to the Sun Deck and the Living Room for easy entertaining

■ The efficient, galley Kitchen is equipped with a double sink

■ The informal Breakfast Room has direct access to the Deck

■ The large Master Suite has a full private Bath

Main floor — 1,276 sq. ft.
Finished staircase — 16 sq. ft.
Basement — 392 sq. ft.
Garage — 728 sq. ft.

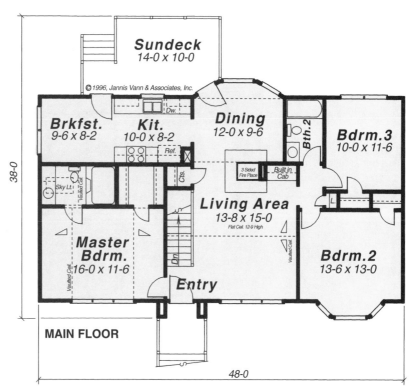

© 1996, Jannis Vann & Associates, Inc.

Sundeck
14-0 x 10-0

Brkfst.
9-6 x 8-2

Kit.
10-0 x 8-2

Dining
12-0 x 9-6

Dw.

Ref.

Bth. 2

Bdrm. 3
10-0 x 11-6

Sky Lt.

3 Sided Fire Place

Built in Cab

Master Bdrm.
16-0 x 11-6

Living Area
13-8 x 15-0
Flat Ceil. 12-9 High

Dn

Bdrm. 2
13-6 x 13-0

Entry

38-0

48-0

MAIN FLOOR

Private Master Suite

Design by Rick Garner

■ *Total living area 1,293 sq. ft.* ■ *Price Code A* ■

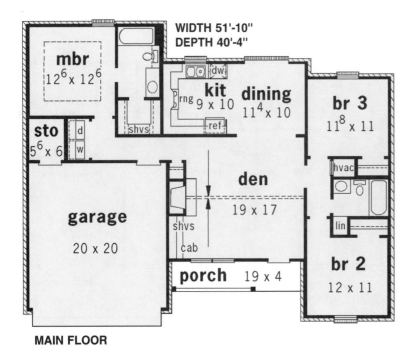

MAIN FLOOR

WIDTH 51'-10"
DEPTH 40'-4"

mbr 12⁶ x 12⁶

sto 5⁶ x 6

garage 20 x 20

kit rng 9 x 10

dining 11⁴ x 10

den 19 x 17

br 3 11⁸ x 11

br 2 12 x 11

porch 19 x 4

shvs / cab / shvs / ref / dw / hvac / lin / d / w

No. 92523

■ **This plan features:**

— Three bedrooms

— Two full baths

■ The spacious Great Room is enhanced by a vaulted ceiling and fireplace

■ The well-equipped Kitchen has a double sink below a window

■ The secluded Master Suite has a decorative ceiling, private Master Bath and walk-in closet

■ The two additional Bedrooms share a hall Bath

■ An optional crawl space or slab foundation — please specify when ordering

Main floor — 1,293 sq. ft.
Garage — 433 sq. ft.

Total living area 1,295 sq. ft. ■ Price Code A ■

No. 91021

■ This plan features:

— Three bedrooms

— Two full baths

■ The wrap-around Porch features the Traditional Entry and sliding glass doors into the Dining Room

■ The Living Room is enhanced by a fireplace

■ The efficient Kitchen opens to both the Dining and Living Rooms

■ The Master Suite has a walk-in closet and private Master Bath

■ An optional basement, slab or crawl space foundation — please specify when ordering

Main floor — 1,295 sq. ft.
Garage — 400 sq. ft.

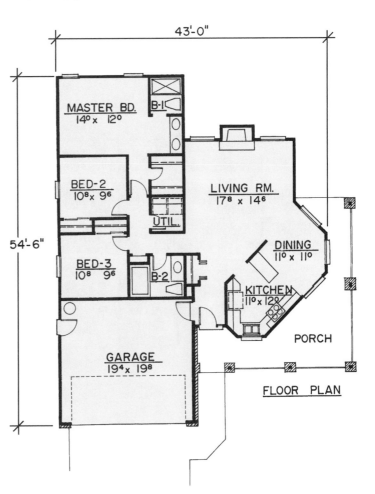

FLOOR PLAN

Design by Donald A. Gardner Architects, Inc.

© 1995 Donald A. Gardner Architects, Inc.

■ *Total living area 1,298 sq. ft.* ■ *Price Code C* ■

No. 99828

■ **This plan features:**

— Three bedrooms

— Two full baths

■ Double gables and the covered Porch add charm to the exterior

■ The common living areas are in an open format and have cathedral ceilings

■ The front Bedroom, doubling as the Study, is topped by a cathedral ceiling and accented by a picture window with circle top

■ The Master Bedroom is crowned in a cathedral ceiling and has a lavish Bath

Main floor — 1,298 sq. ft.
Garage — 287 sq. ft.

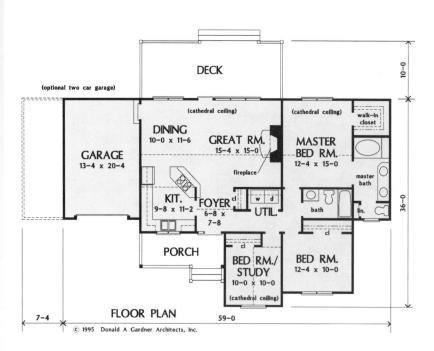

FLOOR PLAN

© 1995 Donald A Gardner Architects, Inc.

A Comfortable Informal Design

■ *Total living area 1,300 sq. ft.* ■ *Price Code A* ■

No. 94801

■ This plan features:

— Three bedrooms

— Two full baths

■ This plan has a Country front Porch with wood details

■ The spacious Activity Room is enhanced by a pre-fab fireplace

■ The open and efficient Kitchen/ Dining Area is highlighted by a bay window and is adjacent to the Laundry and the Garage entry

■ The corner Master Bedroom offers a luxurious Bath with a garden tub

■ The two additional Bedrooms have ample closets and share a full Bath

■ An optional crawl space or slab foundation — please specify when ordering

Main floor — 1.300 sq. ft.
Garage — 576 sq. ft.

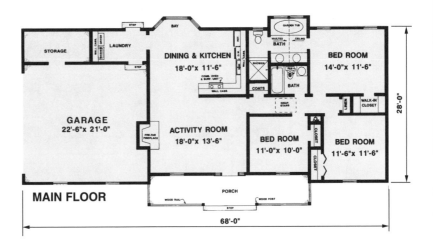

For the Young at Heart

Design by Lifestyle Home Design

■ *Total living area 1,307 sq. ft.* ■ *Price Code A* ■

Floor Plan

No. 99324

■ **This plan features:**

— Three bedrooms

— Two full baths

■ This plan has arched transom windows, divided-light windows, bay windows and the covered Porch entry

■ The Great Room has a vaulted ceiling, a fireplace and a transom window

■ The Kitchen has a vaulted ceiling and the Breakfast Area with sliding glass doors to the Deck

■ The Master Suite has ample closet space and a private full Bath

Main floor — 1,307 sq. ft.
Basement — 1,307 sq. ft.
Garage — 374 sq. ft.

Delightful Doll House

■ *Total living area 1,307 sq. ft.* ■ *Price Code A* ■

No. 20161

■ **This plan features:**

— Three bedrooms

— Two full baths

■ The Living Room has a sloped ceiling and a focal point fireplace

■ The efficient Kitchen has a peninsula counter and the built-in Pantry

■ The Dining Room has a decorative ceiling and sliding glass doors to the Deck

■ The Master Suite has a decorative ceiling, ample closet space and a private full Bath

■ The two additional Bedrooms share a full hall Bath

Main floor — 1,307 sq. ft.
Basement — 1,298 sq. ft.
Garage — 462 sq. ft.

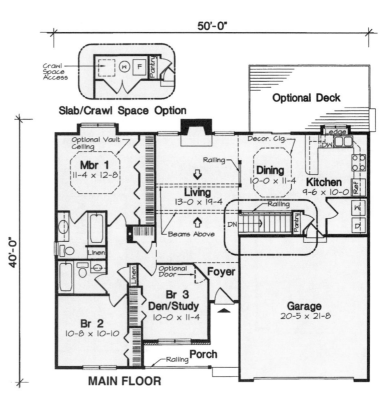

50'-0"

Crawl Space Access

W F Pantry

Slab/Crawl Space Option

40'-0"

Optional Vault Ceiling

Mbr 1
11-4 x 12-8

Optional Deck

Decor. Clg.

Ledge

Dining
10-0 x 11-4

Kitchen
9-6 x 10-0

Ref

Railing

Living
13-0 x 19-4

Railing

DN

Pantry

W

D

Beams Above

Linen

Optional Door

Linen

**Br 3
Den/Study**
10-0 x 11-4

Foyer

Garage
20-5 x 21-8

Br 2
10-8 x 10-10

Railing

Porch

MAIN FLOOR

■ *Total living area 1,310 sq. ft.* ■ *Price Code A* ■

No. 93048 BL

■ **This plan features:**

— Three bedrooms

— Two full baths

■ The efficiently designed Kitchen has a corner sink, ample counter space and a peninsula counter

■ The sunny Breakfast Room has the convenient hide-away Laundry Center

■ The expansive Living Room includes a corner fireplace and direct access to the rear yard

■ The private Master Suite has a walk-in closet and a double vanity Bath

■ No materials list is available for this plan

Main floor — 1,310 sq. ft.
Garage — 449 sq. ft.

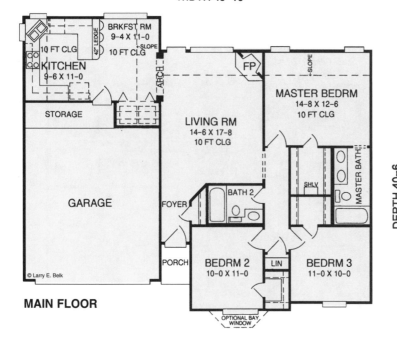

WIDTH 49–10

BRKFST RM
9-4 X 11-0
10 FT CLG

42" LEDGE

10 FT CLG
SLOPE

KITCHEN
9-6 X 11-0

STORAGE

ARCH

FP

SLOPE

MASTER BEDRM
14-8 X 12-6
10 FT CLG

LIVING RM
14-6 X 17-8
10 FT CLG

GARAGE

FOYER

BATH 2

SHLV

MASTER BATH

DEPTH 40–6

PORCH

BEDRM 2
10-0 X 11-0

LIN

BEDRM 3
11-0 X 10-0

© Larry E. Belk

OPTIONAL BAY WINDOW

MAIN FLOOR

Design by Donald A. Gardner Architects, Inc.

Compact Country Cottage

© 1991 Donald A. Gardner Architects, Inc.

■ *Total living area 1,310 sq. ft.* ■ *Price Code C* ■

No. 99856 BL X Я R

■ **This plan features:**

— Three bedrooms

— Two full baths

■ The Foyer opens to the large Great Room with a fireplace and a cathedral ceiling

■ There is an efficient U-shaped Kitchen with peninsula counter

■ Two front Bedrooms, one with a bay window, the other with a walk-in closet, share a full Bath in the hall

■ The Master Suite is located to the rear with a walk-in closet and a private Bath with a double vanity

■ A partially covered Deck with skylights is accessible from the Dining Room, Great Room and the Master Bedroom

Main floor — 1,310 sq. ft.
Garage & storage — 455 sq. ft.

MASTER BED RM.
11-4 x 14-0

DECK

covered deck

skylights

GREAT RM.
15-4 x 18-4

(cathedral ceiling)

fireplace

master bath

walk-in closet

walk-in closet

GARAGE
21-4 x 20-4

DINING
11-4 x 11-0

BED RM.
11-4 x 10-0

w d

cl

FOYER
6-0 x 6-8

KITCHEN
11-4 x 8-4

51-5

cl

bath

BED RM.
11-4 x 12-9

PORCH

FLOOR PLAN

61-0

© 1991 Donald A Gardner Architects, Inc.

Easy to Build

Design by Westhome Planners, Ltd.

Total living area 1,313 sq. ft. ■ **Price Code A** ■

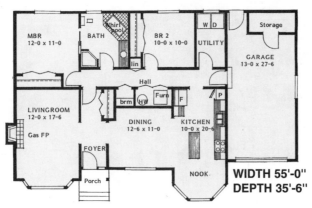

WIDTH 55'-0"
DEPTH 35'-6"

MAIN FLOOR

No. 90865 BL

■ **This plan features:**

— Two bedrooms

— One full bath

■ The covered Entry leads into the Foyer, and the Living and Dining Rooms

■ A focal-point fireplace and bay window enhance the Living Room

■ The Country style Kitchen is open to the Dining Room, Nook, Utility Room and Garage

■ The Master Bedroom features an oversized closet and private access to a full Bath with whirlpool tub

■ The second Bedroom has an oversized closet and access to a full Bath

Main floor — 1,313 sq. ft.
Garage — 385 sq. ft.

Stylish Simplicity

Design by Studer Residential Design, Inc.

Total living area 1,315 sq. ft. ■ **Price Code A** ■

No. 97731 BL

■ **This plan features:**

— Three bedrooms

— Two full baths

■ A mix of materials adds style to the exterior

■ The covered front Porch shelters the Entry to the home

■ A sloped ceiling and fireplace add charm to the Great Room

■ The L-shaped Kitchen is designed for convenience

■ The Master Bedroom has a private Bath

■ The split Bedroom design has the secondary Bedrooms located on one side of the home

■ No materials list is available for this plan

Main floor — 1,315 sq. ft.
Basement — 1,315 sq. ft.
Garage — 488 sq. ft.
Porch — 75 sq. ft.

Design by Studer Residential Design, Inc.

No. 97730

Drive Under Garage

This plan features:

- Three bedrooms
- Two full baths
- This plan has the Basement with a drive-under Garage
- The Master Bedroom has a tray ceiling and Deck access
- Volume is added to the Great Room by the sloped ceiling
- The L-shaped Kitchen is open to the Dining space
- The secondary Bedrooms share a full Bath
- No materials list is available for this plan

Main floor — 1,315 sq. ft.
Basement — 1,315 sq. ft.
Porch — 155 sq. ft.

■ *Total living area 1,315 sq. ft.* ■ *Price Code A* ■

Design by Donald A. Gardner Architects, Inc.

No. 99849

Economical Three Bedroom

This plan features:

- Three bedrooms
- Two full baths
- Dormers above the covered Porch cast light into the Foyer
- Columns punctuate the entrance to the open Great Room/Dining Room with a shared cathedral ceiling and a bank of operable skylights
- The Kitchen has a breakfast counter and is open to the Dining Area
- The private Master Bedroom has a tray ceiling and luxurious bath featuring a double vanity, separate shower, and skylights over a whirlpool tub

Main floor — 1,322 sq. ft.
Garage & Storage — 413 sq. ft.

© 1993 Donald A. Gardner Architects, Inc.

■ *Total living area 1,322 sq. ft.* ■ *Price Code C* ■

© 1993 Donald A Gardner Architects, Inc.

One-Level Family Living

Design by Wein,aster Home Design

■ *Total living area 1,326 sq. ft.* ■ *Price Code A* ■

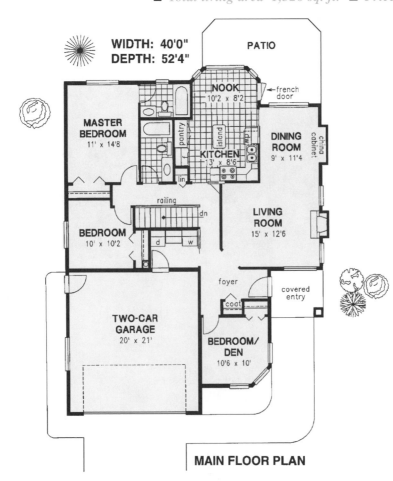

WIDTH: 40'0"
DEPTH: 52'4"

PATIO

NOOK
10'2 x 8'2

← french door

MASTER
BEDROOM
11' x 14'8

pantry

DINING
ROOM
9' x 11'4

china cabinet

KITCHEN
13' x 8'6

island

p w

lin

railing

dn

LIVING
ROOM
15' x 12'6

BEDROOM
10' x 10'2

d   w

foyer

covered entry

coat

TWO-CAR
GARAGE
20' x 21'

BEDROOM/
DEN
10'6 x 10'

MAIN FLOOR PLAN

No. 98808   BL

■ **This plan features:**

— Three bedrooms

— Two full baths

■ The covered Entry leads to the Foyer

■ The secluded Den or third Bedroom is to the left of the Foyer

■ A cozy fireplace highlights the Living Room while built-in china cabinet space is featured in the Dining Room

■ The tiled Kitchen/Nook Area has a built-in Pantry, a work island and a French door to the Patio

■ The Master Bedroom has a private Bath

■ No materials list is available for this plan

Main floor — 1,326 sq. ft.
Basement — 1,302 sq. ft.
Garage — 442 sq. ft.

■ *Total living area 1,330 sq. ft.* ■ *Price Code A* ■

No. 24709 **BL**

■ **This plan features:**

— Two or three bedrooms

— Two full baths

■ The Living Room, enhanced by triple windows and a cozy fireplace, opens to the Dining Room through graceful columns

■ The quiet Study, with convenient built-ins and a sloped ceiling, can convert to a third Bedroom

■ The formal Dining Room is highlighted by a glass alcove and an atrium door to rear yard

■ The U-shaped Kitchen has a laundry closet, Garage entry and extended counter/eating bar

■ The corner Master Bedroom has a double vanity Bath

■ No materials list is available for this plan

Main area— 1,330 sq. ft.
Garage — 523 sq. ft.

OPT. GUEST ROOM
12-4 x 11-8

Corner Lot Design

Design by Greg Marquis & Associates

■ *Total living area 1,333 sq. ft.* ■ *Price Code A* ■

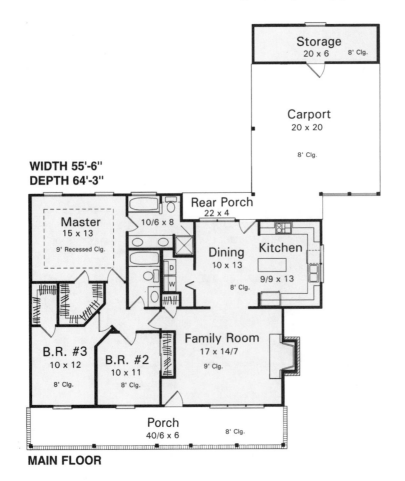

WIDTH 55'-6"
DEPTH 64'-3"

Storage
20 x 6   8' Clg.

Carport
20 x 20

8' Clg.

Rear Porch
22 x 4

Master
15 x 13

9' Recessed Clg.

10/6 x 8

Dining
10 x 13

Kitchen
9/9 x 13

8' Clg.

B.R. #3
10 x 12

8' Clg.

B.R. #2
10 x 11

8' Clg.

Family Room
17 x 14/7

9' Clg.

Porch
40/6 x 6   8' Clg.

MAIN FLOOR

No. 93453

■ **This plan features:**

— Three bedrooms

— Two full baths

■ The covered front Porch is enhanced by columns

■ The Den has a sloped ceiling and a fireplace

■ The Dining Room is adjacent to the Kitchen

■ The galley Kitchen has access to the Garage and the   Utility Room

■ The Master Bedroom has a raised ceiling and a walk-in closet

■ An optional slab or crawl space foundation — please specify when ordering

■ No materials list is available for this plan

Main floor — 1,333 sq. ft.
Carport/Storage — 520 sq. ft.

Design by L. M. Brunier & Associates, Inc.

Easy Living Design

■ *Total living area 1,345 sq. ft.* ■ *Price Code A* ■

No. 91342 BL✗

■ This plan features:

- — Three bedrooms

- — Two full baths

- ■ A handicapped accessible Master Bath plan is available with this plan

- ■ There are vaulted ceilings in the Great Room, the Dining Room and the Kitchen Areas

- ■ The high-tech Kitchen is angled for efficiency and offers an abundance of counters and cabinets

- ■ The Master Bedroom has an ample sized wardrobe, access to the covered Deck, and private a Bath

Main floor — 1,345 sq. ft.

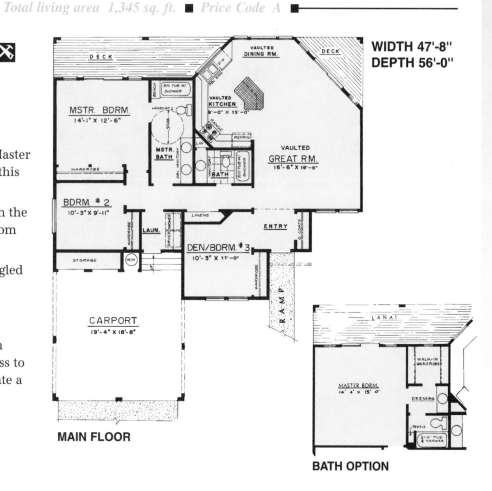

WIDTH 47'-8"
DEPTH 56'-0"

DECK

VAULTED DINING RM.

DECK

VAULTED KITCHEN
9'-0" X 15'-0"

MSTR. BDRM.
14'-1" X 12'-6"

MSTR. BATH

VAULTED GREAT RM.
16'-6" X 19'-8"

WARDROBE

BATH

BDRM. #2
10'-3" X 9'-11"

LINENS

ENTRY

WARDROBE

LAUN.

DEN/BDRM. #3
10'-3" X 11'-0"

RAMP

STORAGE

W/H

CARPORT
19'-4" X 18'-8"

MAIN FLOOR

LANAI

WALK-IN WARDROBE

MASTER BDRM.
14' 4" X 15' 0"

DRESSING

TOWELS

5'-0" TUB W/ SHOWER

BATH OPTION

Simply Cozy

Design by Jannis Vann & Associates, Inc.

■ Total living area 1,325 sq. ft. ■ Price Code A ■

No. 98912 BL ✕

■ **This plan features:**

— Three bedrooms

— Two full baths

■ The quaint front Porch shelters the Entry into the Living Area which is showcased by a massive fireplace and built-ins below a vaulted ceiling

■ The formal Dining Room is accented by a bay of glass with Deck access

■ The efficient, galley Kitchen has the Breakfast Area, Laundry facilities and outdoor access

■ The secluded Master Bedroom offers a roomy walk-in closet and plush Bath with two vanities and a garden, window tub

■ Two additional Bedrooms have ample closets and share a full Bath with a skylight

Main floor — 1,325 sq. ft.
Basement — 556 sq. ft.
Garage — 724 sq. ft.

MAIN FLOOR

Expansive Living Room

Design by Frank Betz Associates, Inc.

■ Total living area 1,346 sq. ft. ■ Price Code A ■

No. 98434 BL ✕

■ **This plan features:**

— Three bedrooms

— Two full baths

■ A vaulted ceiling crowns the spacious Living Room highlighted by a fireplace

■ The built-in Pantry and direct access from the Garage add to the conveniences of the Kitchen

■ A walk-in closet and the private Bath are featured in the Master Suite

■ The secondary Bedrooms share a full Bath in the hall

■ An optional basement, slab or crawl space foundation — please specify when ordering

Main floor — 1,346 sq. ft.
Garage — 385 sq. ft.
Basement — 1,358 sq. ft.

WIDTH 39'-0"
DEPTH 51'-0"

MAIN FLOOR

© Frank Betz Associates, Inc.

Design by Donald A. Gardner Architects, Inc.

For a Narrow Lot

No. 99868

■ This plan features:

— Three bedrooms

— Two full baths

■ The Great Room is topped by a cathedral ceiling and accented by a fireplace

■ A convenient pass-through opens from the Kitchen to the Great Room

■ The Master Suite is loaded with luxuries, including a walk-in closet and a private Bath with a separate shower and garden tub

■ Two additional Bedrooms share a full Bath

Main floor — 1,350 sq. ft.
Garage & storage — 309 sq. ft.

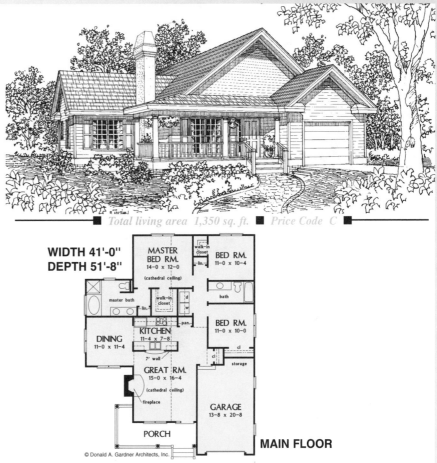

■ *Total living area 1,350 sq. ft.* ■ *Price Code C* ■

Family Favorite

Design by The Garlinghouse Company

No. 20156

■ This plan features:

— Three bedrooms

— Two full baths

■ An open layout with the Dining Room makes the Living Room seem more spacious

■ Windows and a sliding glass door highlight the Dining Room

■ The efficient, compact Kitchen has the built-in Pantry and peninsula counter

■ The Master Suite has a romantic window seat, a private Bath and a walk-in closet

■ Two additional Bedrooms share a full hall closet

Main floor — 1,359 sq. ft.
Basement — 1,359 sq. ft.
Garage — 501 sq. ft.

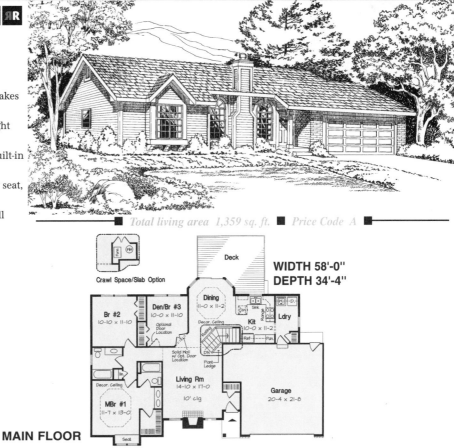

■ *Total living area 1,359 sq. ft.* ■ *Price Code A* ■

One-Floor Convenience

Design by Frank Betz Associates, Inc.

■ *Total living area 1,359 sq. ft.* ■ *Price Code A* ■

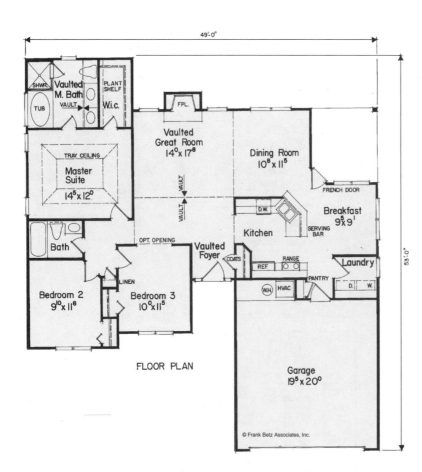

FLOOR PLAN

© Frank Betz Associates, Inc.

No. 98443 BL

■ **This plan features:**

— Three bedrooms

— Two full baths

■ The vaulted Foyer blends with the vaulted Great Room giving a larger feeling to the home

■ The formal Dining Room opens into the Great Room

■ The Kitchen includes a serving bar and a bright Breakfast Area

■ The Master Suite is topped by a decorative tray ceiling and features a vaulted ceiling in the Master Bath

■ An optional slab or crawl space foundation — please specify when ordering

■ No materials list is available for this plan

Main floor — 1,359 sq. ft.
Garage — 439 sq. ft.

Ranch Living

■ Total living area 1,360 sq. ft. ■ Price Code A ■

No. 90354 BL ✗

■ **This plan features:**

— Three bedrooms

— Two full baths

■ The Great Room includes a vaulted ceiling, a fireplace and access to the Deck

■ There is a double door entrance into the Den/third Bedroom

■ The Kitchen/Breakfast Area has a vaulted ceiling and an efficient layout

■ The Master Suite is crowned by a vaulted ceiling and pampered by a private Bath and Dressing Area

■ The full hall Bath serves the two additional Bedrooms

Main area — 1,360 sq. ft.

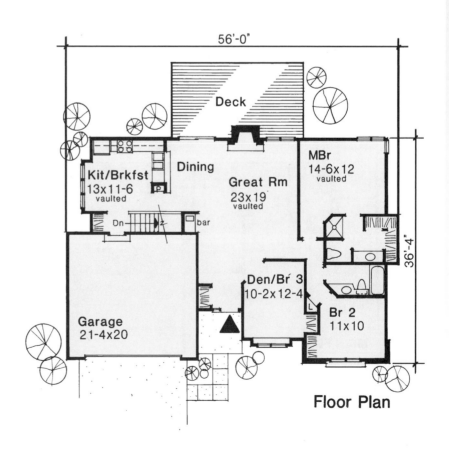

56'-0"

Deck

Kit/Brkfst
13x11-6
vaulted

Dining

Great Rm
23x19
vaulted

MBr
14-6x12
vaulted

Dn

bar

36'-4"

Garage
21-4x20

Den/Br 3
10-2x12-4

Br 2
11x10

Floor Plan

Step Saving

■ *Total living area 1,360 sq. ft.* ■ *Price Code A* ■

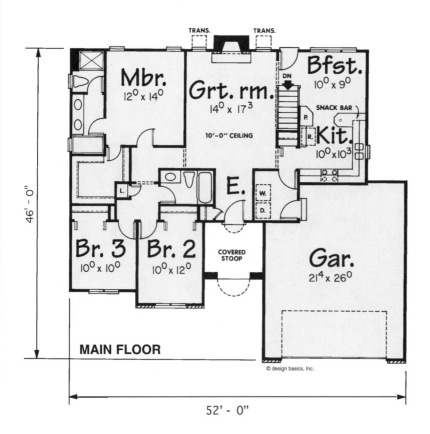

MAIN FLOOR

© design basics, Inc.

46' - 0"

52' - 0"

Mbr.
12⁰ x 14⁰

Grt. rm.
14⁰ x 17³

10'-0" CEILING

Bfst.
10⁰ x 9⁰

SNACK BAR

Kit.
10⁰ x 10³

Br. 3
10⁰ x 10⁰

Br. 2
10⁰ x 12⁰

COVERED STOOP

Gar.
21⁴ x 26⁰

TRANS.   TRANS.

DN

E.

No. 94982

■ **This plan features:**

— Three bedrooms

— One full and one three-quarter baths

■ The covered Porch leads to the Entry and a convenient coat closet

■ The fireplace has transom windows on to either side highlighting the Great Room

■ The Kitchen/Breakfast Area features the Pantry, an extended counter/snack bar, and a double sink

■ The Laundry Room doubles as the Mud Room next to the Kitchen and the Garage

■ The Master Suite includes a private Bath and a large walk-in closet

Main floor — 1,360 sq. ft.
Garage — 544 sq. ft.

Secluded Suite

■ *Total living area 1,361 sq. ft.* ■ *Price Code A* ■

No. 97600 **BL**

■ **This plan features:**

— Three bedrooms

— Two full baths

■ This home has a low maintenance stucco exterior

■ A high ceiling in the Foyer continues into the Family Room with a vaulted ceiling

■ A French door is set beside the fireplace in the Family Room

■ All the Bedrooms have walk-in closets

■ The Master Suite is secluded in the rear of the home

■ No materials list is available for this plan

■ An optional basement or crawl space foundation — please specify when ordering

Main floor — 1,361 sq. ft.
Basement — 1,359 sq. ft.
Garage — 530 sq. ft.

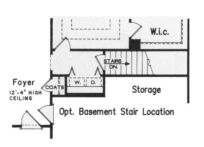

Foyer
12'-4" HIGH CEILING

W.i.c.

STAIRS DN.

W. | D.

COATS

Storage

Opt. Basement Stair Location

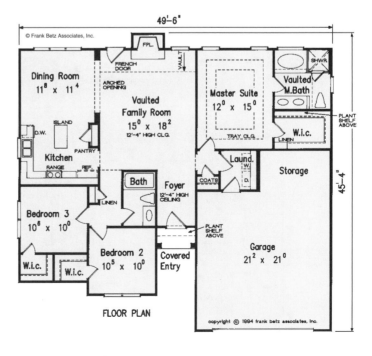

© Frank Betz Associates, Inc.

49'-6"

45'-4"

FPL

FRENCH DOOR

VAULT

Dining Room
11⁸ x 11⁴

ARCHED OPENING

Vaulted Family Room
15⁰ x 18²
12'-4" HIGH CLG.

Master Suite
12⁰ x 15⁰

TRAY CLG.

Vaulted M.Bath

SHWR

PLANT SHELF ABOVE

ISLAND

D.W.

PANTRY

Kitchen

RANGE

REF.

LINEN

W.i.c.

Laund.
W.
D.

Storage

COATS

Bath

Foyer
12'-4" HIGH CEILING

LINEN

Bedroom 3
10⁸ x 10⁰

Bedroom 2
10⁵ x 10⁰

Covered Entry

PLANT SHELF ABOVE

Garage
21² x 21⁰

W.i.c.

W.i.c.

FLOOR PLAN

copyright © 1994 frank betz associates, inc.

Economical Home

Design by Donald A. Gardner Architects, Inc.

No. 99870 BL ✗ Я R

■ This plan features:

— Three bedrooms

— Two full baths

■ The spacious Great Room is complete with cathedral ceiling and a strategically placed fireplace

■ The efficient, U-shaped Kitchen opens to the well-planned Dining Area

■ The Deck off the Kitchen creates additional outdoor living space

■ The Master Bedroom includes a luxurious private Bath

■ Two additional Bedrooms share a second full Bath in the hall

Main floor — 1,362 sq. ft.
Garage & Storage — 297 sq. ft.

Total living area 1,362 sq. ft. ■ Price Code C

MASTER BED RM. 13-8 x 12-0
BED RM. 11-0 x 10-0
DECK
walk-in closet
bath
KITCHEN 12-0 x 10-0
master bath
UTIL.
BED RM. 11-0 x 10-0
DINING 10-0 x 11-4
GREAT RM. 15-0 x 18-4 (cathedral ceiling)
fireplace
storage
GARAGE 13-4 x 20-0
PORCH

FLOOR PLAN
41-8
51-4

© 1996 Donald A Gardner Architects, Inc.

Vaulted Ceilings

Design by Frank Betz Associates, Inc.

No. 97224 BL

■ This plan features:

— Three bedrooms

— Two full baths

■ There is an open layout with vaulted ceilings in the Foyer, the Great Room and the Breakfast Area

■ The Kitchen with a pass-thru and the Pantry, efficiently serves the bright Breakfast Area, the Great Room and the formal Dining Room

■ The luxurious Master Suite features a tray ceiling, two walk-in closets and a double vanity Bath

■ Two secondary Bedrooms share a full Bath

■ No materials list is available for this plan

Main floor — 1,363 sq. ft.
Basement — 715 sq. ft.
Garage — 677 sq. ft.

Total living area 1,363 sq. ft. ■ Price Code A

© Frank Betz Associates, Inc.

47'-0"

FPL.
Vaulted M. Bath
SHWR
TRAY CLG.
W.i.c.
FRENCH DOOR
Vaulted Breakfast
DRIVE UNDER
LINEN
PLANT SHELF ABOVE
W.i.c.
Master Suite 12⁰ x 15⁸
Vaulted Great Room 13⁹ x 19⁸
Kitchen
RANGE
PASS THRU
DW REF
PAN.
Bath
Vaulted Foyer
Bedroom 2 10⁰ x 10⁰
COATS
Bedroom 3 11⁶ x 10⁰
Covered Porch
Dining Room 11' x 10⁰

35'-4"

FLOOR PLAN

Design by Rick Garner

No. 92528

■ **This plan features:**

— Three bedrooms

— Two full baths

■ The Den has a cozy fireplace and a vaulted ceiling

■ The well-equipped Kitchen has a double sink and a built-in Pantry

■ The spacious Master Bedroom has a private Bath and a walk-in closet

■ An optional crawl space or slab foundation — please specify when ordering

Main floor — 1,363 sq. ft.
Garage — 434 sq. ft.

Warm and Inviting

■ *Total living area 1,363 sq. ft.* ■ *Price Code A* ■

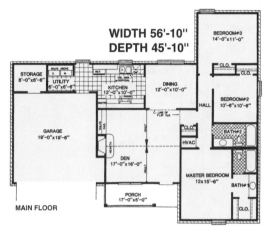

WIDTH 56'-10"
DEPTH 45'-10"

MAIN FLOOR

Design by Perfect Plan

No. 99639

■ **This plan features:**

— Three bedrooms

— Two full baths

■ The Living Room is enhanced by a high ceiling sloping down to a heat-circulating fireplace and Terrace access

■ The efficient Kitchen adjoins the bright Dining Room

■ The Dinette Area provides for informal eating in the Kitchen and access to the Terrace

■ The Master Suite is arranged with a Dressing Area that has a walk-in closet plus two linear closets

■ Two family Bedrooms share a full Bath in the hall

Main area — 1,367 sq. ft.
Basement — 1,267 sq. ft.
Garage — 431 sq. ft.

One-Story Country Home

■ *Total living area 1,367 sq. ft.* ■ *Price Code A* ■

FLOOR PLAN

High Impact Angles

Design by Lifestyle Home Design

No. 90357

■ **This plan features:**

— Three bedrooms

— Two full baths

■ Soaring ceilings give this house a spacious, contemporary feeling

■ The Great Room adjoins the Dining Area and shares an inviting fireplace

■ The convenient Kitchen has sliding glass doors to the Patio

■ The Master Suite has a vaulted ceiling and a private Bath

■ The Den/third Bedroom also has sliding glass doors to the Patio

Main floor — 1,368 sq. ft.

■ *Total living area 1,368 sq. ft.* ■ *Price Code A* ■

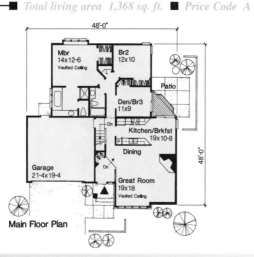

Main Floor Plan

Nostalgia Returns

Design by Lifestyle Home Design

No. 99321

■ **This plan features:**

— Three bedrooms

— Two full baths

■ A half-round transom window with quarter-round detail and a vaulted ceiling are found in the Great Room

■ A cozy corner fireplace brings warmth to the Great Room and the Dining Area

■ A vaulted ceiling is included in the Kitchen/Breakfast Area

■ The Master Suite has a walk-in closet and a private Master Bath

■ Two additional Bedrooms share a full hall Bath

Main area — 1,368 sq. ft.
Basement — 1,368 sq. ft.
Garage — 412 sq. ft.

■ *Total living area 1,368 sq. ft.* ■ *Price Code A* ■

Floor Plan

Design by Ahmann Design, Inc.

No. 97148

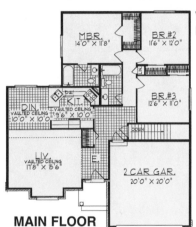

Vaulted Ceilings

This plan features:

– Three bedrooms

– Two full baths

■ A box window and vaulted ceiling highlight the Living Room

■ Tile floors are found in the Entry, the Kitchen, and the Dining Area

■ The Master Bedroom has its own Bath and a walk-in closet

■ There are two ample sized secondary Bedrooms that share a full Bath

■ No materials list is available for this plan

Main floor — 1,370 sq. ft.

■ *Total living area 1,370 sq. ft.* ■ *Price Code A* ■

WIDTH 44'-0"
DEPTH 50'-4"

MAIN FLOOR

Design by Weinmaster Home Design

No. 98804

Compact Design Packs Much In

This plan features:

– Three bedrooms

– Two full baths

■ The covered, front Porch leads into the Foyer that contains a coat closet

■ The U-shaped Kitchen has it all, including a corner double sink, the Pantry, a desk, and the Nook with a bay window

■ The Living Room features loads of windows, access to the rear Deck, and adjoins the Dining Room

■ The Master Bedroom has double closets, a private Bath, and a French door to the Deck

■ Two Bedrooms, identical in size share a Bath in the hall

■ The Laundry/Utility Room also provides access to the two-car Garage

■ No materials list is available for this plan

Main floor — 1,372 sq. ft.
Basement — 1,372 sq. ft.
Garage — 484 sq. ft.

■ *Total living area 1,372 sq. ft.* ■ *Price Code A* ■

MAIN FLOOR

WIDTH 51'-0"
DEPTH 50'-0"

Charming Style

Design by Vaughn A. Lauban Designs

■ Total living area *1,372 sq. ft.* ■ *Price Code A* ■

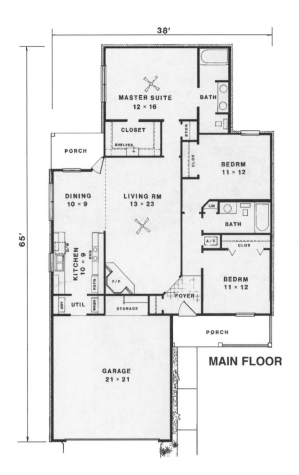

38'

65'

MASTER SUITE
12 × 16

BATH

CLOSET

SHELVES

STOR

PORCH

CLOS

BEDRM
11 × 12

DINING
10 × 9

LIVING RM
13 × 23

LIN

BATH

A/C CLOS

KITCHEN
10 × 9

D/W

RNG

REFRG

F/P

WASH

DRY UTIL

STORAGE

FOYER

BEDRM
11 × 12

PORCH

MAIN FLOOR

GARAGE
21 × 21

No. 96510

■ **This plan features:**

— Three bedrooms

— Two full baths

■ The tiled Foyer gives way to the welcoming Living Room highlighted by a cozy fireplace

■ The Living Room and the Dining Area are joined to create the feeling of more space

■ The efficient, galley-styled Kitchen has direct access to the Utility Room and the Garage

■ The private Master Suite contains a walk-in closet, and a private, double vanity Bath

■ Two additional Bedrooms are located in close proximity to a full Bath in the hall

Main floor — 1,372 sq. ft.
Garage — 465 sq. ft.

Style and Convenience

■ Total living area 1,373 sq. ft. ■ Price Code A ■

No. 98411

■ This plan features:

— Three bedrooms

— Two full and one half baths

■ Large front windows, dormers and an old-fashioned Porch give a pleasing style to the home

■ A vaulted ceiling tops the Foyer and continues into the Family Room that is highlighted by a fireplace

■ The efficient Kitchen is enhanced by the Pantry and a pass-through to the Family Room

■ A decorative tray ceiling, a private Bath, and a walk-in closet are located in the Master Suite

■ An optional basement or crawl space foundation — please specify when ordering

Main floor — 1,373 sq. ft.
Basement — 1,386 sq. ft.

WIDTH 50'-4"
DEPTH 45'-0"

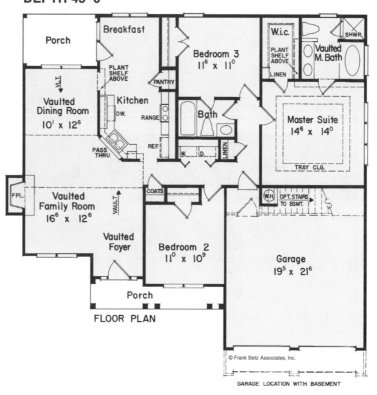

FLOOR PLAN

© Frank Betz Associates, Inc.

GARAGE LOCATION WITH BASEMENT

Charming Bow Window

Design by Wickes Lumber Company

■ *Total living area 1,373 sq. ft.* ■ *Price Code A* ■

No. 35003

■ This plan features:

— Three bedrooms

— Two full baths

■ The inviting Porch leads into the Foyer and the Living Room which has a bow window and a sloping ceiling

■ The open Kitchen provides easy access to the Dining Room, the Deck/Patio, the Laundry and the Garage

■ The private Master Bedroom offers two walk-in closets and a full Bath

■ Two additional Bedrooms have large closets and share a full Bath in the hall

Main floor — 1,373 sq. ft.
Garage — 400 sq. ft.

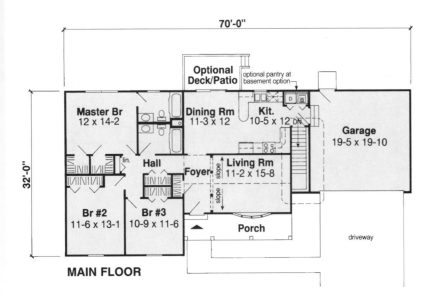

70'-0"

32'-0"

Optional Deck/Patio

optional pantry at basement option

Master Br
12 x 14-2

Dining Rm
11-3 x 12

Kit.
10-5 x 12

D | W

Garage
19-5 x 19-10

lin.

Hall

Foyer

slope

Living Rm
11-2 x 15-8

DN

Br #2
11-6 x 13-1

Br #3
10-9 x 11-6

Porch

driveway

MAIN FLOOR

Multiple Gables and Dormers

B. NATHAN

© 1998 Donald A. Gardner, Inc.

■ *Total living area 1,377 sq. ft.* ■ *Price Code C* ■

No. 98029

■ This plan features:

— Three bedrooms

— Two full baths

■ Distinguished details inside and out make this modest home very appealing

■ A Cathedral ceiling, a cozy fireplace, built-in shelves and a wall of windows with Porch access enhance the Great Room, the Dining Area and the open Kitchen

■ The quiet, corner Master Bedroom features a cathedral ceiling, a walk-in closet and a plush Bath

■ Two additional Bedrooms, with ample closets, share a hall Bath and Laundry facilities

■ The Bonus Room over Garage provides options for a growing family

Main floor — 1,377 sq. ft.
Bonus room — 383 sq. ft.
Garage & storage — 597 sq. ft.

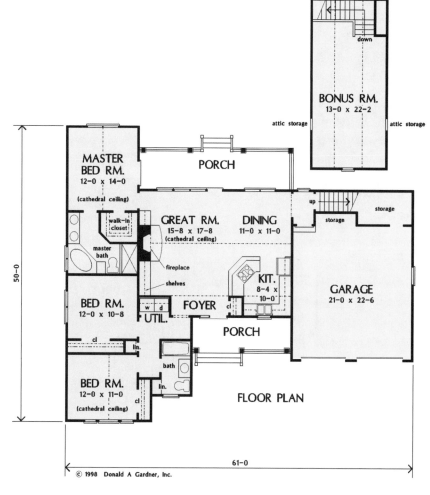

BONUS RM.
13-0 x 22-2

attic storage   attic storage

MASTER BED RM.
12-0 x 14-0
(cathedral ceiling)

PORCH

walk-in closet

master bath

GREAT RM.
15-8 x 17-8
(cathedral ceiling)

DINING
11-0 x 11-0

up

storage   storage

storage

fireplace

shelves

KIT.
8-4 x 10-0

GARAGE
21-0 x 22-6

BED RM.
12-0 x 10-8

w d
UTIL.

FOYER

cl

PORCH

bath

BED RM.
12-0 x 11-0
(cathedral ceiling)

cl

lin.

FLOOR PLAN

50-0

61-0

© 1998 Donald A Gardner, Inc.

Sunny Dormer Brightens Foyer

Design by Donald A. Gardner Architects, Inc.

© 1996 Donald A Gardner Architects, Inc.

■ Total living area 1,386 sq. ft. ■ Price Code C ■

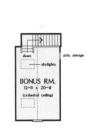

FLOOR PLAN

© 1996 Donald A Gardner Architects, Inc.

No. 99812 BL ✕ ✈ ЯR

■ **This plan features:**

— Three bedrooms

— Two full baths

■ The open layout of the Great Room, the Dining Room, and the Kitchen is topped by a cathedral ceiling and emphasizes the feeling of space

■ The adjoining Deck provides extra living and entertaining space in the pleasant weather

■ The Master Bedroom is crowned by a cathedral ceiling, and pampered by a private Bath with garden tub, dual vanity and a walk-in closet

■ The skylit Bonus Room above the Garage offers flexibility and an opportunity for growth

Main floor — 1,386 sq. ft.
Garage — 517 sq. ft.
Bonus room — 314 sq. ft.

Decorative Ceilings

Design by Ahmann Design

■ Total living area 1,387 sq. ft. ■ Price Code A ■

WIDTH 50'-0"
DEPTH 49'-0"

MAIN FLOOR PLAN

No. 93134 BL

■ **This plan features:**

— Three bedrooms

— Two full baths

■ The sheltered entrance and tiled Foyer lead into the spacious Living Room with a cathedral ceiling and a hearth fireplace

■ The formal Dining Room opens to the Living Room and accesses the rear yard

■ An efficient, eat-in Kitchen is handy to the Dining Room, the Laundry, and the Garage entrance

■ The Master Bedroom Suite is accented by a tray ceiling, a walk-in closet and a private Bath

■ Two additional Bedrooms share a full Bath, and have ample closets, and window seats

■ No materials list is available for this plan

Main floor — 1,387 sq. ft.
Basement — 1,387 sq. ft.
Garage — 482 sq. ft.

Design by Homeplanners

No. 90288 BL X

This plan features:

— Two bedrooms (with optional third bedroom)

— Two full baths

■ The sunny Master Suite has a sloping ceiling, private Terrace, and luxurious garden Bath with an adjoining Dressing Room

■ The Gathering Room has a fireplace and opens to the Study and formal Dining Room

■ The convenient pass-through adds to the efficiency of the galley Kitchen and the adjoining Breakfast Room

Main area — 1,387 sq. ft.
Garage — 440 sq. ft.

■ Total living area 1,387 sq. ft. ■ Price Code A ■

MAIN AREA

Design by Greg Marquis & Associates

No. 93454 BL

This plan features:

— Three bedrooms

— Two full baths

■ Three windows brighten the Kitchen and the Dining Room

■ The center island is a bonus in the Kitchen

■ A sloped ceiling is found in the Family Room

■ A convenient access door to the rear yard is found in the Garage

■ A recessed ceiling adds character to the Master Suite

■ A boxed bay window graces the front of Bedroom number three

■ No materials list is available for this plan

■ An optional slab or a crawl space foundation — please specify when ordering

Main floor — 1,388 sq. ft.
Garage — 492 sq. ft.

■ Total living area 1,388 sq. ft. ■ Price Code A ■

WIDTH 66'-2"
DEPTH 34'-6"

MAIN FLOOR

Open Spaces

Design by Jannis Vann & Associates, Inc.

■ *Total living area 1,388 sq. ft.* ■ *Price Code A* ■

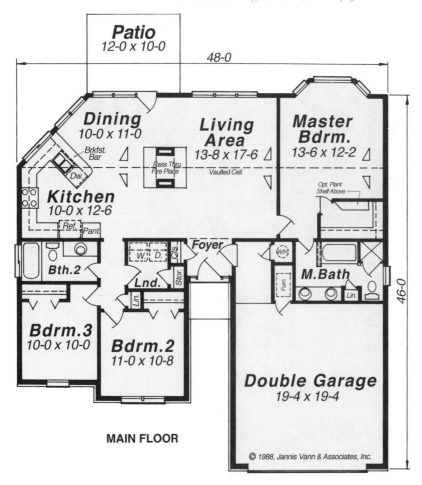

Patio
12-0 x 10-0

48-0

Dining
10-0 x 11-0

Brkfst. Bar

Dw.

Living Area
13-8 x 17-6
Vaulted Ceil.

Pass Thru. Fire Place

Master Bdrm.
13-6 x 12-2

Opt. Plant Shelf Above

Kitchen
10-0 x 12-6

Ref. Pant

W. D.

Cts.

Foyer

W/H

Bth.2

Lnd.

Stor.

Lin.

Fun.

M.Bath

Lin.

Bdrm.3
10-0 x 10-0

Bdrm.2
11-0 x 10-8

46-0

Double Garage
19-4 x 19-4

MAIN FLOOR

© 1988, Jannis Vann & Associates, Inc.

No. 93279

■ **This plan features:**

— Three bedrooms

— Two full baths

■ The Family Room, Kitchen and Breakfast Area all connect to form a great space

■ A central, double fireplace adds warmth and atmosphere to the Family Room, the Kitchen and the Breakfast Area

■ The efficient Kitchen is highlighted by a peninsula counter which doubles as a snack bar

■ The Master Suite includes a walk-in closet, a double vanity, separate shower and tub Bath

■ An optional crawl space or slab foundation — please specify when ordering

Main floor — 1,388 sq. ft.
Garage — 400 sq.

Elegant Brick Exterior

■ *Total living area 1,390 sq. ft.* ■ *Price Code A* ■

No. 92557 BL ✗

■ This plan features:

— Three bedrooms

— Two full baths

■ Detailing and accent columns highlight the covered front Porch

■ The Den is enhanced by a corner fireplace and adjoins the Dining Room

■ The efficient well-appointed Kitchen has easy access to the Utility/Laundry Room

■ The Master Bedroom is topped by a vaulted ceiling and features a private Bath and a walk-in closet

■ An optional slab or crawl space foundation — please specify when ordering

Main floor — 1,390 sq. ft.
Garage — 590 sq. ft.

WIDTH 67'-4"
DEPTH 32'-10"

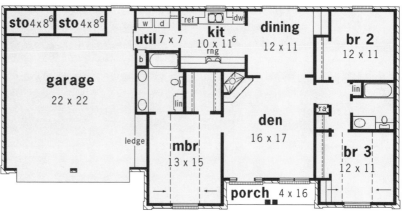

MAIN FLOOR

Affordable Energy-Saver

Design by Perfect Plan

No. 90680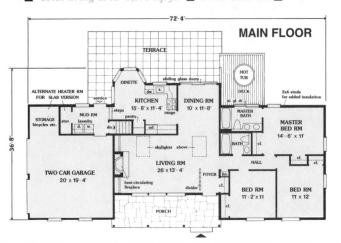

This plan features:

— Three bedrooms

— Two full baths

■ The covered Porch leads into the open Foyer and Living/Dining Room with skylights

■ The efficient Kitchen has a Dinette Area with a bay window, and a walk-in Pantry adjacent to the Mud Room and Garage Area

■ The private Master Bedroom has a luxurious Bath leading to the private Deck complete with a hot tub

■ The two additional Bedrooms have access to a full hall Bath

Main floor — 1,393 sq. ft.
Basement — 1,393 sq. ft.
Garage — 542 sq. ft.

Total living area 1,393 sq. ft. ● Price Code A

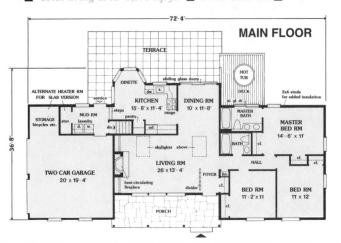

Cute Cottage

Design by Greg Marquis & Associates

No. 93414 BL

This plan features:

— Three bedrooms

— Two full baths

■ The cute covered front Porch adds character to this cottage plan

■ The large Living Room has a ten-foot ceiling and a side wall fireplace

■ The Kitchen is equipped with a center cooktop island and a planning desk

■ The convenient Laundry Room is adjacent to the Kitchen

■ This plan also has a detached two-car Garage

■ No materials list is available for this plan

Main floor — 1,393 sq. ft.
Garage — 528 sq. ft.

Total living area 1,393 sq. ft. ● Price Code A

MAIN FLOOR

Design by The Garlinghouse Company

No. 34054 BL ✕ 🛠 🇺🇸 ᴙ

■ This plan features:

— Three bedrooms

— Two full baths

■ The Dining Room has sliding glass doors to the backyard

■ The two-car Garage is accessed through the Laundry Room

■ The Master Bedroom has a private full Bath

Main floor — 1,400 sq. ft.
Basement — 1,400 sq. ft.
Garage — 528 sq. ft.

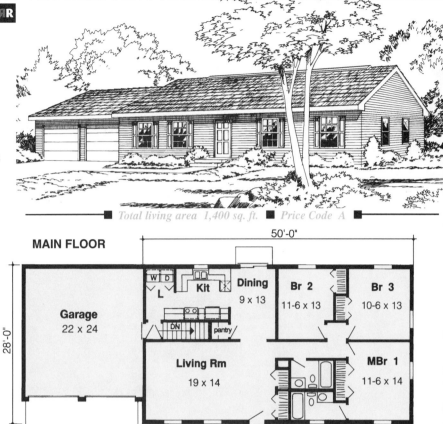

Total living area 1,400 sq. ft. ■ *Price Code A*

MAIN FLOOR

50'-0"

28'-0"

Garage
22 x 24

W D
L
Kit
Dining
9 x 13
Br 2
11-6 x 13
Br 3
10-6 x 13

DN
pantry

Living Rm
19 x 14

MBr 1
11-6 x 14

Design by Larry E. Belk

No. 93026 BL

■ This plan features:

— Three bedrooms

— Two full baths

■ The large Living Room has a ten-foot ceiling

■ The Dining Room has a distinctive bay window

■ The Breakfast Room is located off the Kitchen

■ The Kitchen has an angled Eating Bar that opens to the Living Room

■ The Master Suite features a ten-foot ceiling and dual vanity, a combination whirlpool tub and shower, plus a huge walk-in closet

■ No materials list is available for this plan

Main floor — 1,402 sq. ft.
Garage — 437 sq. ft.

Total living area 1,402 sq. ft. ■ *Price Code A*

WIDTH 59–10

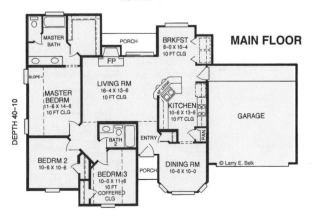

MASTER BATH

PORCH

BRKFST
8-0 X 10-4
10 FT CLG

MAIN FLOOR

FP

SLOPE

MASTER BEDRM
11-6 X 14-6
10 FT CLG

LIVING RM
16-4 X 13-6
10 FT CLG

KITCHEN
10-6 X 13-6
10 FT CLG

GARAGE

DEPTH 40–10

BATH 2

ENTRY

PAN

BEDRM 2
10-6 X 10-6

BEDRM 3
10-0 X 11-6
10 FT COFFERED CLG

PORCH

DINING RM
10-6 X 10-0

© Larry E. Belk

101

An Affordable Floor Plan

Design by DDI Architecture

■ Total living area 1,410 sq. ft. ■ Price Code A ■

MAIN FLOOR

No. 91807 BL⚒

■ **This plan features:**
— Three bedrooms
— Two full baths

■ This plan includes the covered Porch entry

■ An old-fashioned hearth fireplace is featured in the vaulted ceiling Living Room

■ The efficient Kitchen, with U-shaped counter, is accessible from the Dining Room

■ The Master Bedroom has a large walk-in closet and private Bath

■ An optional slab or crawl space foundation — please specify when ordering

Main floor — 1,410 sq. ft.
Garage — 484 sq. ft.

One-Story Farmhouse

Design by Perfect Plan

■ Total living area 1,412 sq. ft. ■ Price Code A ■

FLOOR PLAN

No. 99669 BL⚒

■ **This plan features:**
— Three bedrooms
— Two full baths

■ The elliptical topped Dinette window, large window areas and trim accents create great curb appeal

■ The Great Room is accented by a fireplace and a high ceiling

■ The Dining Room and Living Room have direct access to the rear wood Deck via two six-foot sliding glass doors

■ The Master Suite contains a five-piece Bath and three closets

Main floor — 1,412 sq. ft.
Basement — 1,412 sq. ft.
Garage — 441 sq. ft.

Many Amenities

No. 97124

■ **This plan features:**

— Three bedrooms

— Two full baths

■ The tiled Foyer has a vaulted ceiling and leads to the Great Room

■ A corner fireplace and a wall of windows distinguish the Great Room

■ The Dining Room has a cathedral ceiling and an access door to the rear yard

■ Wrap-around counters provide working convenience in the Kitchen

■ The Master Bedroom is secluded and has an enormous walk-in closet

■ The secondary Bedrooms are located on the opposite side of the home

■ This plan also features a two-car Garage

■ No material list is available for this plan

Main floor — 1,416 sq. ft.
Basement — 1,430 sq. ft.

■ *Total living area 1,416 sq. ft.* ■ *Price Code A* ■

MAIN FLOOR

Classic Columns Accent Porch

No. 94729

■ **This plan features:**

— Three bedrooms

— Two full baths

■ Classic columns accent the entry Porch of this home

■ An open floor plan incorporates twelve-foot ceilings in the main living rooms

■ Sliding glass doors open to the rear Patio for expanded living space

■ The large Kitchen includes a peninsula counter/Eating Bar, convenient for meals on the go

■ The Master Suite is designed with a large walk-in closet

■ The Master Bath has a garden tub and a double vanity

■ The two additional Bedrooms share a full family Bath

Main floor — 1,417 sq. ft.
Garage — 522 sq. ft.

■ *Total living area 1,417 sq. ft.* ■ *Price Code A* ■

MAIN FLOOR

Great Starter

Design by Alan Mascord Design Associates

■ *Total living area 1,420 sq. ft.* ■ *Price Code A* ■

◀ **40'** ▶

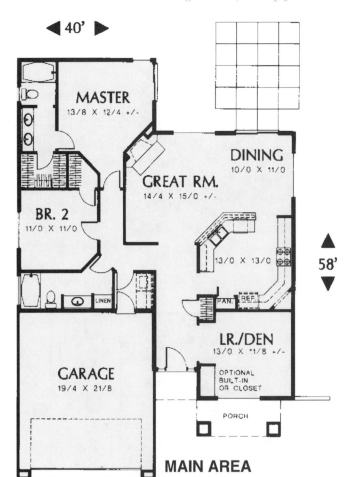

MASTER
13/8 X 12/4 +/-

BR. 2
11/0 X 11/0

GREAT RM.
14/4 X 15/0 +/-

DINING
10/0 X 11/0

13/0 X 13/0

LINEN

PAN.   REF.

LR./DEN
13/0 X 11/8 +/-

GARAGE
19/4 X 21/8

OPTIONAL
BUILT-IN
OR CLOSET

PORCH

▲
58'
▼

MAIN AREA

No. 91545

■ **This plan features:**

— Two bedrooms

— Two full baths

■ The front room can be a formal
Living Room or a cozy Den

■ The efficient Kitchen has ample
counter and storage space

■ The formal Dining Room is
situated next to the Kitchen and is
open to the Great Room

■ A corner fireplace highlights the
Great Room

■ A walk-in closet and a private
double vanity Bath are located in
the Master Suite

■ The additional Bedroom has easy
access to the full hall Bath

Main area — 1,420 sq. ft.

Captivating Sun-Catcher

■ *Total living area 1,421 sq. ft.* ■ *Price Code A* ■

No. 99303

■ **This plan features:**

— Two bedrooms

— Two full baths

■ The glass-walled Breakfast Room adjoins the vaulted-ceiling Kitchen

■ The Living Room, with fireplace and vaulted ceiling, is open to the Dining Room

■ A greenhouse window is featured over the tub in the luxurious Master Bath

■ Two walk-in closets and sliding glass doors are located in the Master Bedroom

Main area — 1,421 sq. ft.
Garage — 400 sq. ft.

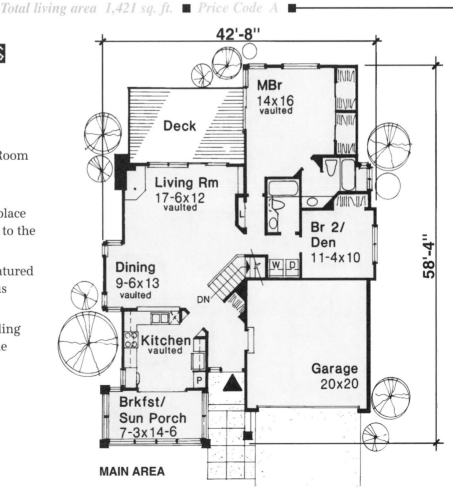

42'-8"

58'-4"

MBr
14x16
vaulted

Deck

Living Rm
17-6x12
vaulted

Br 2/
Den
11-4x10

Dining
9-6x13
vaulted

W D

DN

Kitchen
vaulted

Garage
20x20

P

Brkfst/
Sun Porch
7-3x14-6

MAIN AREA

Comfort and Style

Design by Wesplan Building Design

■ *Total living area 1,423 sq. ft.* ■ *Price Code A* ■

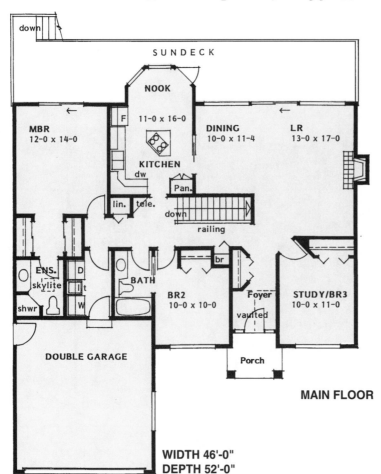

MAIN FLOOR

WIDTH 46'-0"
DEPTH 52'-0"

No. 90990

■ **This plan features:**

— Two bedrooms with a possible third bedroom/den

— Two full baths

■ An unfinished daylight basement provides future space for family recreation

■ The Master Suite is complete with a private Bath with skylight

■ The large Kitchen includes an Eating Nook

■ The Sun Deck is easily accessible from the Master Suite, the Eating Nook and the Living/Dining Area

Main floor — 1,423 sq. ft.
Basement — 1,423 sq. ft.
Garage — 399 sq. ft.

Split-Bedroom Floor Plan

■ *Total living area 1,425 sq. ft.* ■ *Price Code A* ■

No. 92056 BL ✕

■ This plan features:

– Three bedrooms

– One full and one three-quarter bath

■ The outstanding Living Room has a cathedral ceiling and a boxed bay window

■ The combination Kitchen and Dining Room has a raised peninsula counter/snack bar

■ The wood rear Deck expands living space to the outdoors

■ The secluded Master Suite has a private three-quarter Bath

■ The two additional Bedrooms have ample closet space

Main floor — 1,425 sq. ft.
Basement — 1,425 sq. ft.

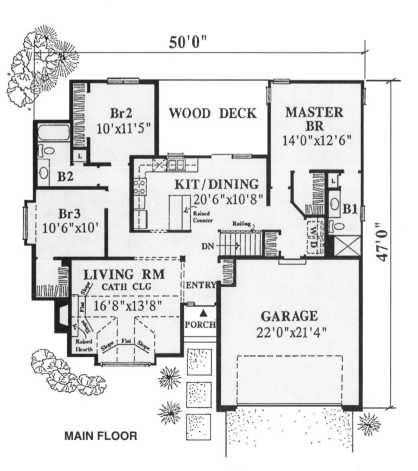

50'0"

Br2
10'x11'5"

WOOD DECK

MASTER
BR
14'0"x12'6"

B2

KIT/DINING
20'6"x10'8"

Br3
10'6"x10'

Raised
Counter

B1

Railing

DN

LIVING RM
CATH CLG
16'8"x13'8"

ENTRY

W/D

47'0"

PORCH

GARAGE
22'0"x21'4"

Raised
Hearth

MAIN FLOOR

Rustic Simplicity

Design by Donald A. Gardner Architects, Inc.

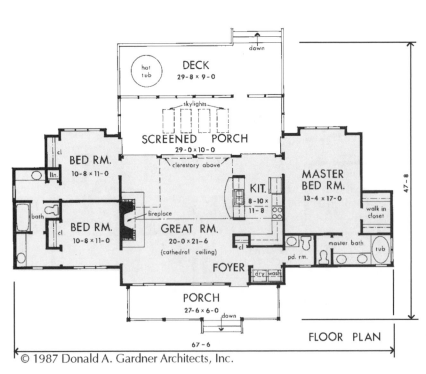

© 1987 Donald A. Gardner Architects, Inc.

■ *Total living area 1,426 sq. ft.* ■ *Price Code C* ■

DECK
29-8 × 9-0

hot tub

down

skylights

SCREENED PORCH
29-0 × 10-0

clerestory above

BED RM.
10-8 × 11-0

cl

lin.

bath

BED RM.
10-8 × 11-0

fireplace

KIT.
8-10 ×
11-8

MASTER
BED RM.
13-4 × 17-0

walk in closet

GREAT RM.
20-0 × 21-6
(cathedral ceiling)

cl

master bath

tub

pd. rm.

FOYER

dry wash

PORCH
27-6 × 6-0

down

67-6

47-8

FLOOR PLAN

© 1987 Donald A. Gardner Architects, Inc.

No. 99864

■ This plan features:

— Three bedrooms

— Two full and one half baths

■ The central living area features a cathedral ceiling, exposed wood beams and a clerestory window

■ The long screened Porch has a bank of skylights

■ The open Kitchen contains a convenient serving and eating counter

■ The generous Master Suite opens to the screened Porch, and is enhanced by a walk-in closet and a whirlpool tub

■ The two additional Bedrooms share a second full Bath

Main floor — 1,426 sq. ft.

© 1998 Donald A. Gardner, Inc.

■ *Total living area 1,428 sq. ft.* ■ *Price Code C* ■

No. 98059 **BL**

■ **This plan features:**

— Three bedrooms

— Two full baths

■ The front and side Porches add outdoor living space

■ The Great Room has a fireplace set between built-in shelves

■ Columns separate the Dining Room from the Great Room

■ The Kitchen is conveniently set-up for the family cook

■ The Master Bedroom has a tray ceiling

■ No materials list is available for this plan

Main floor — 1,428 sq. ft.
Bonus — 313 sq. ft.
Garage — 453 sq. ft.

master bath

MASTER BED RM.
14-0 x 14-0

walk-in closet

BED RM.
11-0 x 11-8

bath

UTIL.

KIT.
10-0 x 12-8

DINING
11-0 x 12-8

PORCH

lin.

storage

up

optional door

BED RM./ STUDY
11-0 x 11-0

cl

fireplace

GREAT RM.
18-0 x 14-8
(cathedral ceiling)

GARAGE
20-0 x 20-0

PORCH

52-4

52-8

FLOOR PLAN

© 1998 Donald A Gardner, Inc.

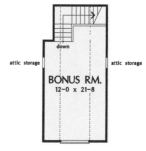

down

attic storage

attic storage

BONUS RM.
12-0 x 21-8

Split Bedroom Plan

Design by Frank Betz Associates, Inc.

No. 98415 BL ✕

■ **This plan features:**

—Three bedrooms

—Two full baths

■ The Master Bedroom has a tray ceiling and a vaulted ceiling tops the five-piece Master Bath

■ A full Bath is located between the secondary Bedrooms

■ A corner fireplace and a vaulted ceiling highlight the Family Room

■ A wetbar, serving bar to the Family Room and a built-in Pantry add to the convenience of the Kitchen

■ The formal Dining Room is crowned in an elegant high ceiling

■ An optional basement, slab or crawl space foundation — please specify when ordering

Main floor — 1,429 sq. ft.
Basement — 1,429 sq. ft.
Garage — 438 sq. ft.

■ Total living area 1,429 sq. ft. ■ Price Code A ■

Small Yet Stylish

Design by Fillmore Design Group

No. 98549 BL

■ **This plan features:**

— Three bedrooms

— Two full baths

■ The Living Room is topped by a ten-foot ceiling and highlighted by a fireplace and a built-in entertainment center

■ The Kitchen and the Dining Room are open to each other and topped by cathedral ceilings

■ A walk-in Pantry is located in the Utility Room for added storage

■ A walk-in closet and a five-piece Bath enhance the Master Suite

■ No material list is available for this plan

Main floor — 1,431 sq. ft.
Garage — 410 sq. ft.

■ Total living area 1,431 sq. ft. ■ Price Code A ■

Floor Plan

No. 98354 BL ✗

This plan features:

— Two bedrooms

— Two full baths

■ A large arched window in the Living Room highlights both the interior and exterior of this design

■ A bay window enhances the Den

■ The formal Dining Room and the Living Room adjoin for a spacious feeling

■ The efficiently arranged Kitchen includes a Breakfast Area topped by a vaulted ceiling

■ The Patio is accessed from the Dining Room or the Breakfast Area

■ The Master Suite is topped by a coffered ceiling and features two walk-in closets and a private, five-piece Bath

■ The additional Bedroom has easy access to the full Bath in the hall

Main floor — 1,431 sq. ft.
Basement — 1,431 sq. ft.
Garage — 410 sq. ft.

Exceptional Windows

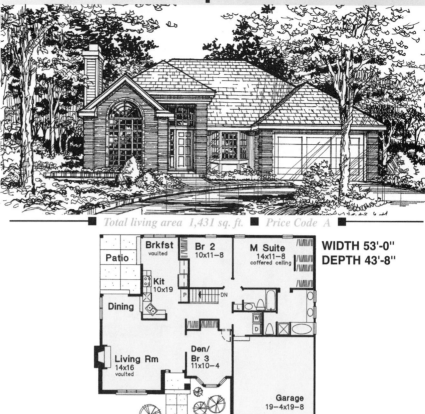

■ *Total living area 1,431 sq. ft.* ■ *Price Code A* ■

WIDTH 53'-0"
DEPTH 43'-8"

MAIN FLOOR

No. 97274 BL ✗

This plan features:

— Three bedrooms

— Two full baths

■ Windows and exterior detailing create a striking elevation

■ The Foyer has a twelve-foot ceiling

■ The Dining Room has a front window wall and arched openings

■ The secondary Bedrooms are in their own wing and share a Bath

■ The Great Room has a vaulted ceiling and a fireplace

■ The Breakfast Bay is open to the galley Kitchen

■ The Master Suite features a tray ceiling, a walk-in closet and a private Bath

■ An optional basement or crawl space foundation — please specify when ordering

Main floor — 1,432 sq. ft.
Basement — 1,454 sq. ft.
Garage — 440 sq. ft.

Striking Style

■ *Total living area 1,432 sq. ft.* ■ *Price Code A* ■

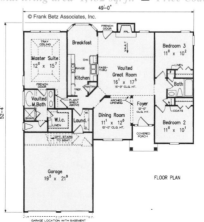

© Frank Betz Associates, Inc.

FLOOR PLAN

Country Charmer

Design by Vaughn A. Lauban Designs

No. 96509 BL ✕

■ **This plan features:**

— Three bedrooms

— Two full baths

■ The quaint front Porch is perfect for sitting and relaxing

■ The Great Room opens into the Dining Area and Kitchen

■ The corner Deck in the rear of home is accessed from the Kitchen and the Master Suite

■ The Master Suite has a private Bath, walk-in closet and built-in shelves

■ The two large secondary Bedrooms in the front of the home share a hall Bath

■ The two-car Garage is located in the rear of the home

Main floor — 1,438 sq. ft.
Garage — 486 sq. ft.

Total living area 1,438 sq. ft. ■ Price Code A

MAIN FLOOR

GARAGE
22 × 22

DECK

DINING
12 × 11

KITCHEN
12 × 10

BATH

MASTER SUITE
13 × 15

BATH

SHELVES

CLOSET

GREAT RM
17 × 18

BEDRM
14 × 11

BEDRM
11 × 13

PORCH

54'

57'

Well Designed

Design by Donald A. Gardner Architects, Inc.

No. 99833

■ **This plan features:**

— Three bedrooms

— Two full baths

■ An optional Garage can be built in the rear

■ The Dining Room is separated from the Great Room by columns

■ The Bedrooms are all located at one end of the home

■ The U-shaped Kitchen has ample cabinet space

Main floor — 1,440 sq. ft.
Garage — 570 sq. ft.

Total living area 1,440 sq. ft. ■ Price Code C

(optional)
GARAGE
20-8 × 22-0

storage

MASTER
BED RM.
14-0 × 12-4

master bath

walk-in
closet

KITCHEN
13-4 × 9-0

DINING
13-9 × 10-8

walk-in
closet

BED RM.
10-4 × 11-0

BED RM.
10-4 × 11-0

FOYER
6-0 ×
5-8

GREAT RM.
13-4 × 13-10

PORCH

FLOOR PLAN

46-11

© 1996 Donald A. Gardner Architects, Inc.

Design by Studer Residential Design, Inc.

No. 92685 BL

This plan features:

— Three bedrooms

— Two full baths

■ The Great Room combines with the Breakfast Area to form a spacious gathering place

■ A sloped ceiling tops the Great Room and reaches a twelve-foot height

■ Windows across the rear of home provide a favorable indoor/outdoor relationship

■ A step-saving Kitchen has ample counter space, cabinets and a Pantry

■ The Master Suite includes a walk-in closet and a full Bath

■ The two additional Bedrooms share the full Bath in the hall

■ No materials list is available for this plan

Main floor — 1,442 sq. ft.
Basement — 1,442 sq. ft.
Garage — 421 sq. ft.

Compact One-Level Home

Total living area 1,442 sq. ft. ■ *Price Code A*

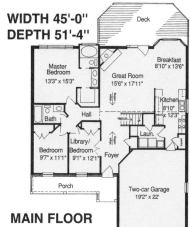

WIDTH 45'-0"
DEPTH 51'-4"

Deck

Master Bedroom 13'3" x 15'3"

Breakfast 8'10" x 13'6"

Great Room 15'6" x 17'11"

Kitchen 8'10" x 12'3"

Bath

Hall

Laun.

Bedroom 9'7" x 11'1"

Library/ Bedroom 9'1" x 12'1"

Foyer

Porch

Two-car Garage 19'2" x 22'

MAIN FLOOR

Design by The Garlinghouse Company

No. 24718 BL

This plan features:

— Three bedrooms

— Two full baths

■ The Breakfast Area overlooks the Porch and is easily served by an extended counter in the Kitchen

■ The Dining Room and the Great Room are highlighted by a two-sided fireplace, enhancing the temperature as well as the atmosphere

■ The roomy Master Suite is enhanced by a whirlpool Bath, a double vanity and a walk-in closet

■ The two secondary Bedrooms feature walk-in closets

■ No materials list is available for this plan

Main floor — 1,452 sq. ft.
Garage — 584 sq. ft.

Gazebo Porch

Total living area 1,452 sq. ft. ■ *Price Code A*

67'-0"

47'-0"

Master Br 14-5 x 12-0

Great Rm 14-0 x 16-7

Porch 11-5 x 7-0

FURN. W.H.

Dining 11-5 x 9-3

2-SIDED F.P.

Garage 23-8 x 23-4

Br 2 11-0 x 10-0

SERVING

Kitchen 11-7 x 10-1

Brkfst 11-7 x 7-9

Br 3 10-2 x 10-0

Porch

MAIN FLOOR

One Floor Convenience

Design by Design Basics, Inc.

■ *Total living area 1,453 sq. ft.* ■ *Price Code A* ■

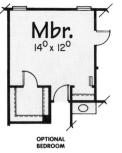

Mbr.
14⁰ x 12⁰

OPTIONAL BEDROOM

MAIN FLOOR

Bfst.
12⁰ x 10⁰

Grt. rm.
15⁰ x 18⁰
10'-0" CEILING

Mbr.
14⁰ x 14⁴

TRANS. TRANS.

PANT.

Kit.
12⁰ x 11⁴

DN

R.

Gar.
21⁴ x 21⁸

E.

Br. 3
10⁰ x 10⁰

Br. 2
10⁰ x 11²

W. D.

L.

COVERED PORCH

44' - 0"

48' - 8"

© design basics, inc.

No. 94914

■ This plan features:

— Three bedrooms

— Two full baths

■ The cozy front Porch invites sitting and shelters the Entry

■ The fabulous Great Room is accented by a focal point fireplace and transom windows

■ The efficient Kitchen has an island workspace, built-in Pantry and a bright Breakfast Area with access to the back yard

■ The comfortable Master Bedroom Suite has a double vanity Bath and option for two closets

■ The two additional Bedrooms share a full Bath and Laundry facilities

Main floor — 1,453 sq. ft.
Basement — 1,453 sq. ft.
Garage — 481 sq. ft.

No Wasted Space

■ *Total living area 1,454 sq. ft.* ■ *Price Code A* ■

No. 90412 BL ✕

■ This plan features:

— Three bedrooms

— Two full baths

■ This plan has a centrally located Great Room with a cathedral ceiling, exposed wood beams, and a wall of windows

■ The Living and Dining Areas are separated by a massive stone fireplace

■ The secluded Master Suite has a walk-in closet and a private Bath

■ The efficient Kitchen has a convenient Laundry Area

■ An optional basement, slab or crawl space foundation — please specify when ordering

Main area — 1,454 sq. ft.

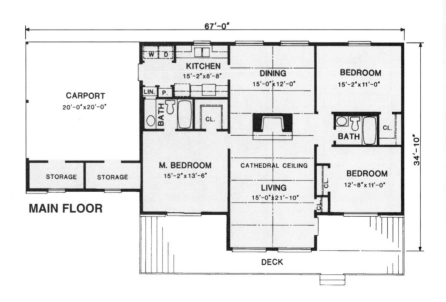

MAIN FLOOR

67'-0"

CARPORT
20'-0"x20'-0"

W D

KITCHEN
15'-2"x8'-8"

DINING
15'-0"x12'-0"

BEDROOM
15'-2"x11'-0"

LIN. P.

BATH

CL.

BATH

CL.

STORAGE   STORAGE

M. BEDROOM
15'-2"x13'-6"

CATHEDRAL CEILING

BEDROOM
12'-8"x11'-0"

LIVING
15'-0"x21'-10"

CL.

34'-10"

DECK

Easy Living

■ *Total living area 1,456 sq. ft.* ■ *Price Code A* ■

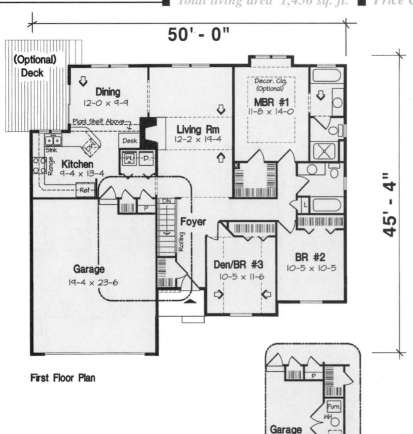

First Floor Plan

Slab/Crawl Space Option

No. 20164 BL X ZIP ЯR

■ **This plan features:**

— Three bedrooms

— Two full baths

■ The Living Room has a dramatic sloped ceiling and a massive fireplace

■ The Dining Room is enhanced by a sloped ceiling, a plant shelf and sliding glass doors to the Deck

■ The U-shaped Kitchen has abundant cabinets, a window over the sink, and a walk-in Pantry

■ The Master Suite has a full, private Bath, a decorative ceiling and a walk-in closet

■ The two additional Bedrooms share a full Bath

First floor — 1,456 sq. ft.
Basement — 1,448 sq. ft.
Garage — 452 sq. ft.

Country Front Porch

■ *Total living area 1,458 sq. ft.* ■ *Price Code A* ■

No. 96516 BL ✕ R

■ This plan features:

— Three bedrooms

— Two full baths

■ A ten-foot high ceiling and a cozy fireplace accent the expansive Great Room

■ The Kitchen and the Dining Room adjoin for a feeling of more space

■ The split Bedroom floor plan is perfect for families with older children

■ The Master Suite is near the Garage entrance for a quick change of clothes after work

■ The rear Porch expands living space to the outside

Main floor — 1,458 sq. ft.
Garage — 452 sq. ft.

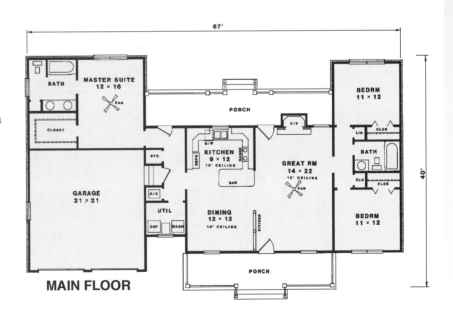

MAIN FLOOR

High Ceilings

Design by Frank Betz Associates, Inc.

■ *Total living area 1,459 sq. ft.* ■ *Price Code A* ■

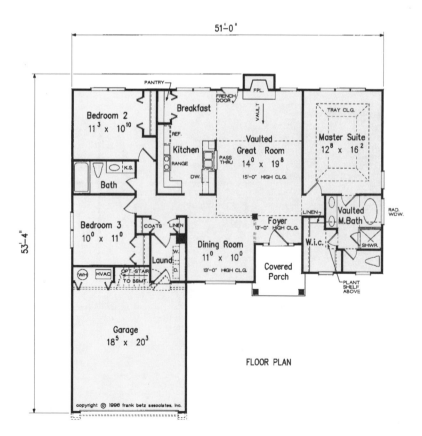

51'-0"

53'-4"

PANTRY

Bedroom 2
11³ x 10¹⁰

Breakfast

FRENCH DOOR

FPL.

VAULT

TRAY CLG.

REF.

Kitchen

RANGE

Vaulted
Great Room
14⁰ x 19⁸
15'-0" HIGH CLG.

Master Suite
12⁸ x 16²

PASS THRU

DW.

K.S.

Bath

LINEN

Vaulted
M.Bath

RAD. WDW.

Bedroom 3
10⁰ x 11⁰

COATS

LINEN

W.

Foyer
13'-0"
HIGH CLG.

W.ic.

SHWR.

Laund.
D.

Dining Room
11⁰ x 10⁰
13'-0" HIGH CLG.

Covered
Porch

WH

HVAC

OPT. STAIR
TO BSMT.

PLANT
SHELF
ABOVE

Garage
18⁵ x 20³

FLOOR PLAN

No. 97601

■ **This plan features:**

— Three bedrooms

— Two full baths

■ High ceilings permeate the main living space

■ An arched window in the Dining Room compliments the design of the Porch

■ The large Pantry increases the Kitchen storage space

■ A tray ceiling beautifies the Master Bedroom

■ A rear wall fireplace warms the Great Room

■ No materials list is available for this plan

■ An optional basement or crawl space foundation — please specify when ordering

Main floor — 1,459 sq. ft.
Basement — 1,466 sq. ft.
Garage — 390 sq. ft.

© Donald A. Gardner Architects, Inc.

■ Total living area 1,460 sq. ft. ■ Price Code C ■

No. 98096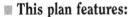

■ This plan features:

— Three bedrooms

— Two full baths

■ The covered Porch leads into the Entry and a coat closet

■ The Kitchen has a well-planned work triangle

■ The Living and Dining Rooms share a voluminous cathedral ceiling

■ The Great Room has a fireplace and built-ins

■ The Master Suite has a tray ceiling and a private Bath

■ The Deck in the rear is a great place to relax

Main floor — 1,460 sq. ft.
Garage — 490 sq. ft.
Deck — 128 sq. ft.
Porch — 100 sq. ft.

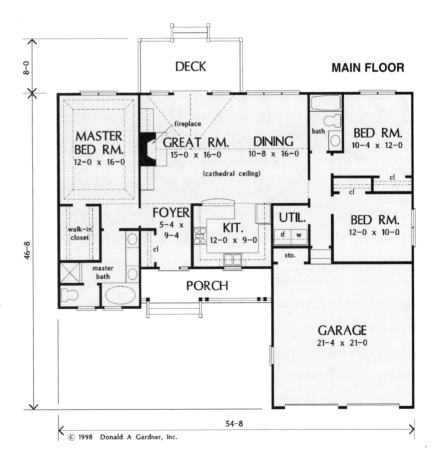

MAIN FLOOR

DECK

8-0

MASTER
BED RM.
12-0 x 16-0

fireplace

GREAT RM.
15-0 x 16-0

DINING
10-8 x 16-0

(cathedral ceiling)

bath

BED RM.
10-4 x 12-0

cl

cl

walk-in
closet

FOYER
5-4 x
9-4

cl

KIT.
12-0 x 9-0

UTIL.

d   w

sto.

BED RM.
12-0 x 10-0

master
bath

PORCH

46-8

GARAGE
21-4 x 21-0

54-8

© 1998   Donald A Gardner, Inc.

119

Country Flair

Design by Ahmann Design, Inc.

No. 97137 BL

■ This plan features:

— Three bedrooms

— Two full baths

■ The inviting front Porch leads into a tiled Entry and the Great Room with a focal point fireplace

■ The open layout of the Great Room, Dining Area, Deck, and Kitchen easily accommodates a busy family

■ The Master Bedroom, set in a quiet corner, offers a huge walk-in closet and a double vanity Bath

■ The two additional Bedrooms, one an optional Den, share the full hall Bath

■ No materials list is available for this plan

Main floor — 1,461 sq. ft.
Basement — 1,461 sq. ft.
Garage — 458 sq. ft.

Total living area 1,461 sq. ft. ■ *Price Code A*

MAIN FLOOR

Gingerbread Charm

Design by Vaughn A. Lauban Designs

No. 96517 BL X

■ This plan features:

— Three bedrooms

— Two full baths

■ Gingerbread details add charm to the front Porch

■ The Foyer includes ample space for coats

■ A vaulted ceiling and a paddle fan highlight the Family Room

■ The Kitchen is convenient to the Dining Room

■ The Master Bedroom overlooks the rear Porch

■ One of the secondary Bedrooms has a walk-in closet

■ The Garage has been placed in the rear of the home

Main floor — 1,463 sq. ft.
Garage — 468 sq. ft.
Porch — 382 sq. ft.

Total living area 1,463 sq. ft. ■ *Price Code A*

MAIN FLOOR

Rustic Exterior

No. 99662

This plan features:

- Three bedrooms
- Two full baths
- The covered front Porch shelters the Entry
- A bay window and corner fireplace accent the Living Room
- The formal Dining Room and the Dinette adjoin the Kitchen
- The Terrace expands the living space outdoors
- Extra storage space is found in the rear of the Garage
- The Master Bedroom features a walk-in closet and a full Bath
- A secondary Bedroom can be used as a Study

Main floor — 1,466 sq. ft.
Basement — 1,466 sq. ft.
Garage — 477 sq. ft.

■ Total living area 1,466 sq. ft. ■ Price Code A ■

56'-4"

whirlpool tub

B.R. 10'-4" x 10'
B.R. 13'-4" x 10'
M.B.R. 14'-10" x 14'-4"
W.I.C.
KIT. 19'8" x 9'
D'NET.
TERR.
L.R. 21'-6" x 14'-10'
D.R. 10' x 11'
M.R.
STOR.
2-CAR GAR. 20' x 22'-8" AVE.
PORCH

49'-8"

FLOOR PLAN

Magical Ceilings

No. 97262

This plan features:

- Three bedrooms
- Two full baths
- Beautiful windows complement a low maintenance stucco exterior
- High ceilings add volume to the Family and Dining Rooms
- A tray ceiling adds charm in the Master Suite
- There is a convenient pass-through from the Kitchen
- The secondary Bedrooms feature large closets
- No materials list is available for this plan
- An optional basement or crawl space foundation —please specify when ordering

Main floor — 1,467 sq. ft.
Basement — 1,515 sq. ft.
Garage — 410 sq. ft.

■ Total living area 1,467 sq. ft. ■ Price Code A ■

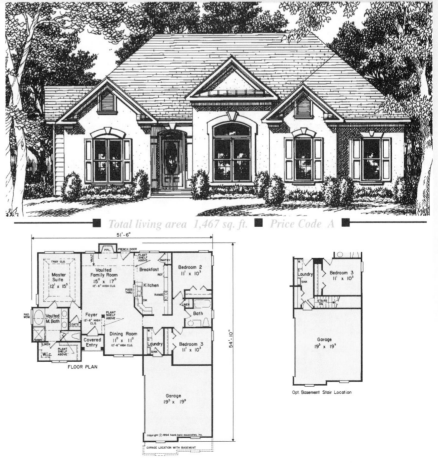

51'-6"

Master Suite 12' x 15'
Vaulted M. Bath
W.I.C.
Vaulted Family Room 15'0 x 17'0
Breakfast
Kitchen
Pantry
Bedroom 2 11' x 10'3
Foyer
Dining Room 11' x 11'
Covered Entry
Bath
Laundry
Bedroom 3 11' x 10'3
Garage 19'9 x 19'9

54'-10"

FLOOR PLAN

Laundry
Bedroom 3 11' x 10'3
Garage 19'9 x 19'9

Opt. Basement Stair Location

GARAGE LOCATION WITH BASEMENT

Brick Details Add Class

Design by Ahmann Design, Inc.

No. 93165 **BL**

■ This plan features:

— Three bedrooms

— Two full baths

■ A keystone entrance leads into the easy care, tile Entry with a plant ledge and a convenient closet

■ The expansive Great Room has a cathedral ceiling over a triple window and a corner gas fireplace

■ The hub Kitchen, accented by arches and columns, is open to the Great Room and Dining Areas

■ The adjoining Dining Area has lots of windows and access to the rear yard and the screened Porch

■ The private Master Suite has a walk-in closet, and plush Bath with a corner whirlpool tub

■ No materials list is available for this plan

Main floor — 1,472 sq. ft.
Basement — 1,472 sq. ft.
Garage — 424 sq. ft.

Total living area 1,472 sq. ft. ■ Price Code A

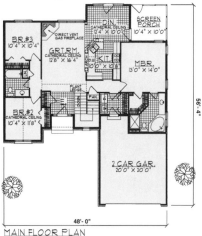

MAIN FLOOR PLAN

Lakeside or Mountain Retreat

Design by Corley Plan Service

No. 90479 **BL** ✕

■ This plan features:

— Three bedrooms

— Two full baths

■ The large screened Porch allows for peaceful evening entertaining or relaxation

■ The Living/Dining Room has a cathedral ceiling and a fireplace

■ The U-shaped Kitchen has a serving counter and a Pantry

■ The Master Bedroom has a walk-in closet and a private Bath, and access to the Deck

■ The two additional Bedrooms share a full Bath

■ The Porch is located off the Utility Room in the rear of the home

■ An optional crawl space or slab foundation — please specify when ordering

Main floor — 1,472 sq. ft.

Total living area 1,472 sq. ft. ■ Price Code A

MAIN FLOOR

Design by Donald A. Gardner Architects, Inc.

Form and Function

No. 98081

■ This plan features:

— Three bedrooms

— Two full baths

■ A column accents this open floor plan

■ A cathedral ceiling adds volume to the Great Room

■ A perfect view of the fireplace is seen from the Kitchen

■ The Master Bedroom is set apart from the rest of the sleeping quarters

■ The Bonus Room over the Garage is ready to be finished

■ The Deck in the rear compliments the home quite well

Main floor — 1,473 sq. ft.
Bonus — 297 sq. ft.
Garage — 501 sq. ft.
Deck — 94 sq. ft.
Porch — 156 sq. ft.

■ Total living area 1,473 sq. ft. ■ Price Code C ■

Design by Greg Marquis & Associates

Easy Living

No. 93447

■ This plan features:

— Three bedrooms

— Two full baths

■ The covered front Porch shelters the Entry to this home

■ The Family Room is enlarged by a vaulted ceiling and has a fireplace

■ The L-shaped Kitchen includes a center island

■ The Dining Room is open to the Kitchen for maximum convenience

■ A covered walkway leads to the two-car Garage

■ The Master Bedroom has a private Bath

■ The secondary Bedrooms have walk-in closets

■ No material list is available for this plan

Main Floor — 1,474 sq. ft.
Garage — 454 sq. ft.

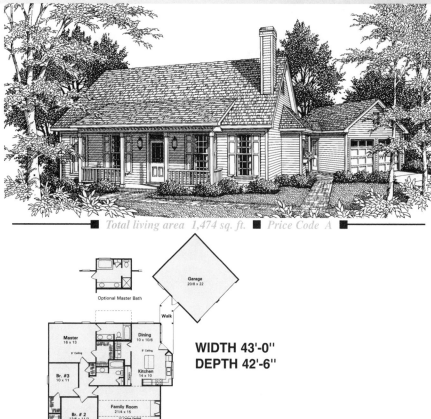

■ Total living area 1,474 sq. ft. ■ Price Code A ■

WIDTH 43'-0''
DEPTH 42'-6''

MAIN FLOOR

Center Island Kitchen

Design by Greg Marquis & Associates

■ *Total living area 1,475 sq. ft.* ■ *Price Code A* ■

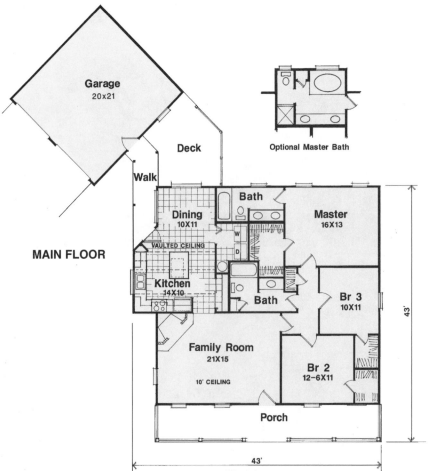

Garage
20x21

Deck

Optional Master Bath

Walk

MAIN FLOOR

Dining
10X11

Bath

Master
16X13

VAULTED CEILING

W
D

Kitchen
14X10

Bath

Br 3
10X11

43'

Family Room
21X15

10' CEILING

Br 2
12-6X11

Porch

43'

No. 93416

■ This plan features:

— Three bedrooms

— Two full baths

■ This well designed floor plan easily supports a busy family's lifestyle

■ The large Kitchen, with a center island, facilitates quick meal preparation

■ The Family Room has a corner fireplace

■ The Master Bedroom has walk-in closets and a double vanity Bath

■ The Deck connects the home to Garage

■ No materials list is available for this plan

Main floor — 1,475 sq. ft.
Garage & Storage — 455 sq. ft

Exciting Ceilings Add Appeal

©1994 Donald A. Gardner Architects, Inc.

■ *Total living area 1,475 sq. ft.* ■ *Price Code C* ■

No. 96452

■ **This plan features:**

– Three bedrooms

– Two full baths

■ An open design is enhanced by cathedral and tray ceilings above arched windows

■ The Foyer with columns leads into the Great Room with a central fireplace and Deck access

■ A cooktop island in the Kitchen provides great cooks with convenience and company

■ The ultimate Master Suite offers a walk-in closet, a tray ceiling, and a whirlpool Bath

■ The Front Bedroom/Study offers multiple uses with a tray ceiling and an arched window

Main floor — 1,475 sq. ft.
Garage & storage — 478 sq. ft.

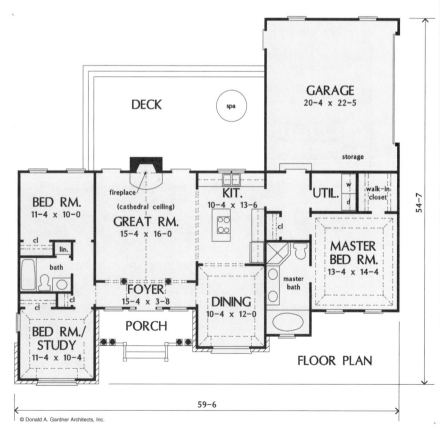

FLOOR PLAN

© Donald A. Gardner Architects, Inc.

Efficient Design

Design by Donald A. Gardner Architects, Inc.

© 1998 Donald A. Gardner, Inc.

■ *Total living area 1,476 sq. ft.* ■ *Price Code C* ■

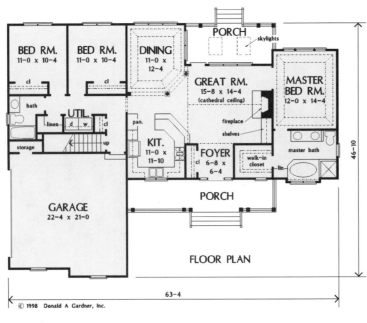

FLOOR PLAN

© 1998 Donald A Gardner, Inc.

63-4

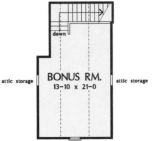

No. 98026

■ This plan features:

— Three bedrooms

— Two full baths

■ This efficient design provides a spacious feeling in modest proportions

■ The Great Room has a cathedral ceiling, an inviting fireplace and built-in cabinets, and access to a rear Porch

■ This plan has an open layout for the Great Room, the Dining Area, and the Kitchen

■ The compact Kitchen is easy to work in with a Pantry and angled breakfast bar

■ The secluded Master Bedroom features an elegant tray ceiling and a lavish Bath

Main floor — 1,476 sq. ft.
Bonus room — 340 sq. ft.
Garage & storage — 567 sq. ft.

Dining in a Greenhouse Bay

■ *Total living area 1,476 sq. ft.* ■ *Price Code A* ■

No. 90620

■ This plan features:

– Three bedrooms

– Two full baths

■ A covered entrance leads into the bright Foyer highlighted by a skydome

■ The formal Living Room is accented by a heat-circulating fireplace and sliding glass doors to the Terrace

■ This plan features a Greenhouse in the Dining Room

■ The efficient Kitchen has a peninsula counter and a bay window Dinette Area convenient to the Laundry and the Garage

Main floor — 1,476 sq. ft.
Basement — 1,476 sq. ft.
Garage — 506 sq. ft.

Formal Balance

Design by Perfect Plan

Total living area 1,476 sq. ft. ■ Price Code A

No. 90689

■ **This plan features:**

— Three bedrooms

— Two full baths

■ The Living Room has a cathedral ceiling and a cozy heat-circulating fireplace

■ A bow window in the Dining Room adds elegance as well as natural light

■ The well-equipped Kitchen serves both the Dinette and the formal Dining Room efficiently

■ The Master Bedroom has three closets and a private Master Bath with sliding glass doors to the Deck with a hot tub

Main floor — 1,476 sq. ft.
Basement — 1,361 sq. ft.
Garage — 548 sq. ft.

MAIN FLOOR

Spacious Feeling

Design by Vaughn A. Lauban Designs

Total living area 1,481 sq. ft. ■ Price Code A

No. 96508

■ **This plan features:**

— Three bedrooms

— Two full baths

■ There is a definite feeling of spaciousness in the Living Room

■ An angled serving bar in the Kitchen is accessible from the Dining Room

■ The secondary Bedrooms have their own wing and share a full Bath

■ The Master Suite has a tray ceiling and dual walk-in closets

■ The Master Bath contains a whirlpool tub

Main floor — 1,481 sq. ft.
Garage — 477 sq. ft.
Porch — 40 sq. ft.

MAIN FLOOR

Large Family Favorite

No. 35005

This plan features:

— Three bedrooms

— One full and one three-quarter baths

■ The cute covered front Porch welcomes you home

■ The formal Living Room opens into the Dining Room which is perfect for entertaining

■ The Family Room has a fireplace and access to the rear Deck

■ This plan features a compact and efficient U-shaped Kitchen

■ The large Master Bedroom features a closet and an attached three-quarter Bath

■ The secondary Bedrooms share a full Bath in the hall

■ The Laundry is conveniently located near all of the Bedrooms

Main floor — 1,484 sq. ft.
Garage — 480 sq. ft.

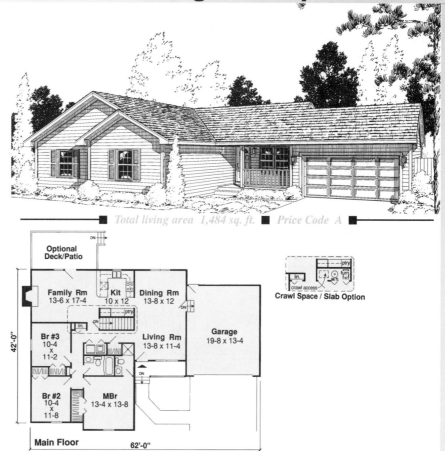

Total living area 1,484 sq. ft. ■ Price Code A

Design by The Garlinghouse Company

Master Retreat

No. 34154

This plan features:

— Three bedrooms

— Two full baths

■ The Foyer opens into an huge Living Room with a fireplace, sloped ceiling and Deck access

■ The efficient Kitchen has a Pantry, serving counter, Dining Area, Laundry Closet and Garage entry

■ The corner Master Bedroom offers a walk-in closet and a luxurious Bath with a raised tub

■ Two more Bedrooms, one could be a Den , share a full Bath

Main area — 1,486 sq. ft.
Garage — 462 sq. ft.

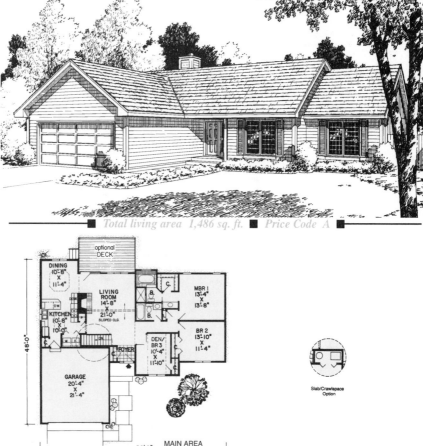

Total living area 1,486 sq. ft. ■ Price Code A

Southwestern Influence

Design by Weinmaster Home Design

■ *Total living area 1,487 sq. ft.* ■ *Price Code A* ■

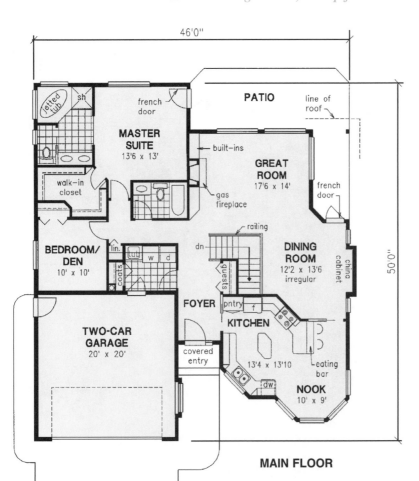

MAIN FLOOR

No. 98807 BL

■ **This plan features:**

— Two bedrooms

— Two full baths

■ The covered Entry leads into the formal Foyer

■ The Great Room is highlighted by a gas fireplace and built-in shelves

■ The Kitchen has a center island, built-in Pantry and sunny Eating Nook

■ The Master Suite has a French door to the rear Patio and a plush Bath

■ No material list is available for this plan

Main floor — 1,487 sq. ft.
Basement — 1,480 sq. ft.
Garage — 427 sq. ft.

Easy Living One-Level

■ *Total living area 1,488 sq. ft.* ■ *Price Code A* ■

No. 97724

■ This plan features:

— Three bedrooms

— Two full baths

■ The Great Room is open to the Dining Area for a spacious effect

■ A French door leads to a raised Deck to create a favorable indoor/ outdoor relationship

■ The Master Bedroom has a large walk-in closet and a deluxe Bath

■ The rear walkout Basement has an opportunity for increased living space

■ No material list is available for this plan

Main floor —1,488 sq. ft.
Basement — 1,488 sq. ft.
Garage — 417 sq. ft.

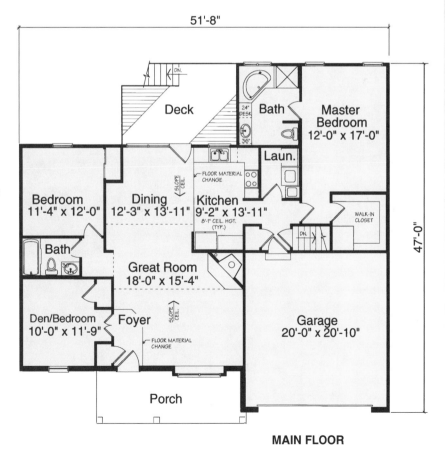

51'-8"

47'-0"

Deck

Bath

Master Bedroom
12'-0" x 17'-0"

Laun.

Bedroom
11'-4" x 12'-0"

Dining
12'-3" x 13'-11"

Kitchen
9'-2" x 13'-11"
8'-1" CEIL. HGT.
(TYP.)

WALK-IN CLOSET

Bath

Great Room
18'-0" x 15'-4"

Den/Bedroom
10'-0" x 11'-9"

Foyer

Garage
20'-0" x 20'-10"

FLOOR MATERIAL CHANGE

Porch

MAIN FLOOR

Brick Tradition

Design by Donald A. Gardner Architects, Inc.

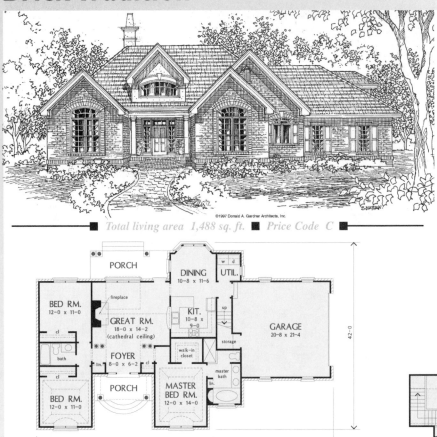

©1997 Donald A. Gardner Architects, Inc.

S-NATHAN

■— Total living area 1,488 sq. ft. ■ Price Code C —■

No. 98000

■ **This plan features:**

— Three bedrooms

— Two full baths

■ This plan features a beautiful brick exterior

■ Dormers provide light to the Great Room which has a cathedral ceiling

■ Two Bedrooms have tray ceilings

■ The Dining Room is lengthened by a bay window

■ The Kitchen has a well-planned work space

■ The Bonus Room is over the Garage

Main floor — 1,488 sq. ft.
Bonus — 338 sq. ft.
Garage — 534 sq. ft.
Porch — 192 sq. ft.

attic access

BONUS RM.
18–10 x 13–8

attic access

Affordable Style

Design by Landmark Designs, Inc.

■— Total living area 1,490 sq. ft. ■ Price Code A —■

No. 91753 **BL**

■ **This plan features:**

— Three bedrooms

— Two full baths

■ A Country Porch welcomes you to the Entry hall with a convenient closet

■ The well-appointed Kitchen features a double sink, ample counter and storage space, a peninsula eating bar and a built-in hutch

■ The terrific Master Suite includes a private Bath and a walk-in closet

■ The Dining Room flows from the Great Room into the Kitchen that includes sliding glass doors to the Deck

■ The Great Room has a cozy fireplace that can also be enjoyed from the Dining Area

■ No materials list is available for this plan

Main area— 1,490 sq. ft.
Covered porch — 120 sq. ft.
Basement — 1,490 sq. ft.
Garage — 579 sq. ft.

WIDTH 58'-0"
DEPTH 61'-0"

MAIN AREA

Design by Frank Betz Associates, Inc.

Accented Detailing

No. 98472 BL

■ **This plan features:**

— Three bedrooms

— Two full baths

■ The columned front Porch, keystones, and shutters accent the exquisite detail of this home

■ The Foyer has a fourteen-foot high ceiling that continues into the Great Room

■ The Great Room has a vaulted ceiling and a rear wall fireplace set between windows

■ The Dining Room and the Breakfast Nook both have window walls to let in sunlight

■ The Kitchen is conveniently arranged and adjacent to the Breakfast Nook

■ The Master Suite has a tray ceiling, a plant shelf, a walk-in closet, and a French door into the Bath

■ The two-car Garage has extra storage space

■ No materials list is available for this plan

■ An optional basement or crawl space foundation — please specify when ordering this plan

Main floor — 1,492 sq. ft.
Garage — 465 sq. ft.

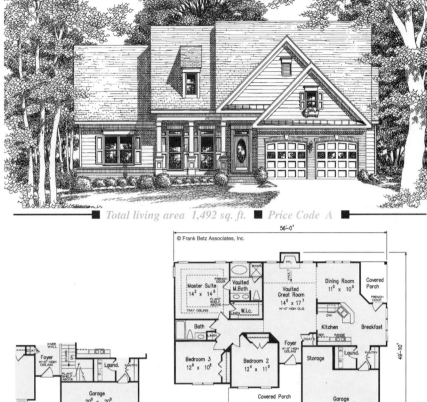

Total living area 1,492 sq. ft. ■ *Price Code A* ■

© Frank Betz Associates, Inc.

FIRST FLOOR PLAN

OPT. BASEMENT STAIR LOCATION

Design by The Garlinghouse Company

Elegant Window Treatment

No. 34150 BL

■ **This plan features:**

— Two bedrooms (optional third)

— Two full baths

■ A huge, arched window floods the front room with natural light

■ This plan features a homey, well-lit Office or Den

■ The efficient Kitchen has easy access to the Dining Room

■ The fireplaced Living Room has a sloped ceiling and a window wall

■ The Master Bedroom has a private Bath with a roomy walk-in closet

Main floor — 1,492 sq. ft.
Basement — 1,486 sq. ft.
Garage — 462 sq. ft.

Total living area 1,492 sq. ft. ■ *Price Code A* ■

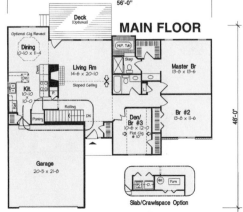

MAIN FLOOR

Slab/Crawlspace Option

133

Especially Surprising

Design by Ahmann Design, Inc.

■ *Total living area 1,495 sq. ft.* ■ *Price Code A* ■

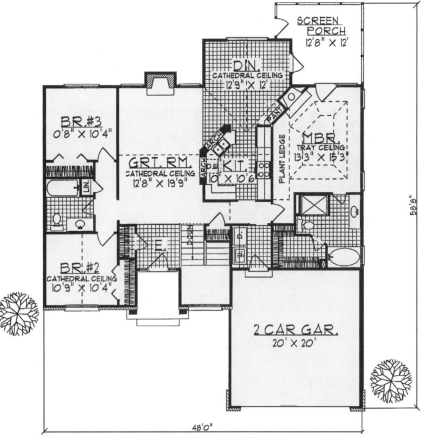

SCREEN PORCH 12'8" X 12'

DIN.
CATHEDRAL CEILING
12'9" X 12'

BR. #3
0'8" X 10'4"

GRT. RM.
CATHEDRAL CEILING
12'8" X 19'9"

KIT.
10' X 10'6"

MBR.
TRAY CEILING
13'3" X 15'3"

PLANT LEDGE

ARCH

BR. #2
CATHEDRAL CEILING
10'9" X 10'4"

DOWN

2 CAR GAR.
20' X 20'

58'8"

48'0"

MAIN FLOOR PLAN

No. 99106 [BL]

■ **This plan features:**

— Three bedrooms

— Two full baths

■ Graceful columns support the covered Entry

■ The tiled Foyer leads directly into the Great Room with a rear wall fireplace and cathedral ceiling

■ The Kitchen has an arched pass-through to the Great Room and is open to the Dining Room

■ The Master Suite has a plant ledge, a fireplace, a tray ceiling, a walk-in closet, and a fully appointed Bath

■ No materials list is available for this plan

Main floor — 1,495 sq. ft.
Basement — 1,495 sq. ft.

For Family on a Budget

© 1996 Donald A. Gardner Architects, Inc.

■ *Total living area 1,498 sq. ft.* ■ *Price Code C* ■

No. 99860

■ **This plan features:**

— Three bedrooms

— Two full baths

■ Columns punctuate an open one-level floor plan

■ The front Porch and the large, rear Deck extend living space outdoors

■ This plan has tray ceilings in the Master Bedroom, Dining Room and Bedroom/Study

■ The private Master Bath has a garden tub, double vanity, separate shower and skylights

Main floor — 1,498 sq. ft.
Garage & storage — 427 sq. ft.

© 1996 DONALD A. GARDNER ARCHITECTS, INC.

Inexpensive Ranch Design

Design by The Garlinghouse Company

No. 20062

■ **This plan features:**

— Three bedrooms

— Two full baths

■ A large picture window brightens the Breakfast Area

■ This plan features a well planned Kitchen

■ The Living Room is accented by an open beam across the sloping ceiling and a wood burning fireplace

■ The Master Bedroom has an extremely large Bath Area

Main floor — 1,500 sq. ft.
Basement — 1,500 sq. ft.
Garage — 482 sq. ft.

■ Total living area 1,500 sq. ft. ■ Price Code A ■

MAIN FLOOR

Sophisticated Homeowner

Design by Larry E. Belk

No. 93027 BL

■ **This plan features:**

— Three bedrooms

— Two full baths

■ The formal Dining Room opens off the Foyer and has a classic bay window

■ The Kitchen is notable for its angled eating bar that opens to the Living Room

■ A cozy fireplace in the Living Room can be enjoyed from the Kitchen

■ The Master Suite includes a whirlpool tub/shower combination and a walk-in closet

■ Ten-foot ceilings are found in the major living areas including the Master Bedroom

■ No materials list is available for this plan

Main area — 1,500 sq. ft.
Garage — 437 sq. ft.

■ Total living area 1,500 sq. ft. ■ Price Code A ■

WIDTH 59-10

MAIN AREA

High Ceilings

■ *Total living area 1,502 sq. ft.* ■ *Price Code B* ■

No. 98441 **BL**

■ This plan features:

— Three bedrooms

— Two full baths

■ The Dining Room and the Sitting Room in the Master Suite are filled with natural light from large arched windows

■ The Kitchen has a convenient pass-through to the Great Room and also has a serving bar

■ The Great Room is topped by a vaulted ceiling

■ Decorative columns define the entrance to the Dining Room

■ No materials list is available for this plan

■ An optional basement or crawl space foundation — please specify when ordering

Main floor — 1,502 sq. ft.
Basement — 1,555 sq. ft.
Garage — 448 sq. ft.

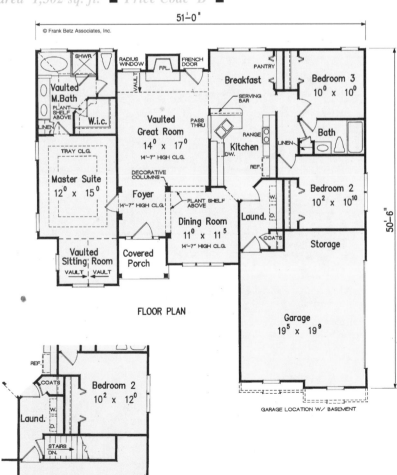

FLOOR PLAN

OPT. BASEMENT STAIR LOCATION

Craftsman Character

Design by Donald A. Gardner Architects, Inc.

■ *Total living area 1,511 sq. ft.* ■ *Price Code D* ■

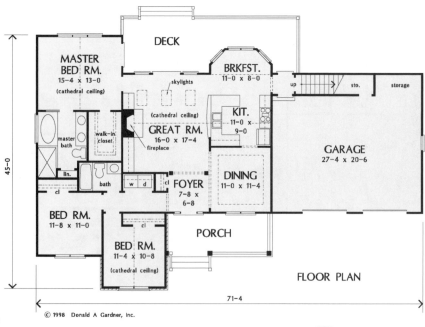

DECK

MASTER BED RM.
15-4 x 13-0
(cathedral ceiling)

skylights

BRKFST.
11-0 x 8-0

up

sto.

storage

KIT.
11-0 x 9-0

(cathedral ceiling)

GREAT RM.
16-0 x 17-4
fireplace

master bath

walk-in closet

GARAGE
27-4 x 20-6

lin.

bath

cl

w d

FOYER
7-8 x 6-8

DINING
11-0 x 11-4

BED RM.
11-8 x 11-0

cl

BED RM.
11-4 x 10-8
(cathedral ceiling)

PORCH

45-0

71-4

FLOOR PLAN

© 1998 Donald A Gardner, Inc.

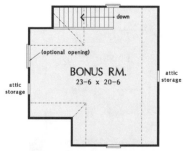

down

(optional opening)

BONUS RM.
23-6 x 20-6

attic storage

attic storage

No. 98083

■ This plan features:

— Three bedrooms

— Two full baths

■ The Great Room includes a cathedral ceiling, a fireplace, and convenient built-in shelves

■ A trio of skylights let the sun shine into the Great Room

■ The Master Suite has Deck access and a cathedral ceiling

■ The oversized Garage allows for ample storage

■ The large Bonus Room above the Garage is ready for future expansion

Main floor — 1,511 sq. ft.
Garage — 655 sq. ft.
Bonus — 549 sq. ft.

Efficient Country Cottage

■ *Total living area 1,512 sq. ft.* ■ *Price Code D* ■

No. 96420

■ This plan features:

— Three bedrooms

— Two full baths

■ The Foyer opens to formal the Dining Room and the large Great Room with a fireplace, cathedral ceiling and a wall of windows

■ The Kitchen is convenient to the Dining Room, the Breakfast Alcove, the Utility Room, and the Garage

■ The Master Bedroom wing has Deck access and a plush Master Bath

■ The secondary Bedrooms have ample closets and share another full Bath

Main floor — 1,512 sq. ft.
Garage & storage — 516 sq. ft.

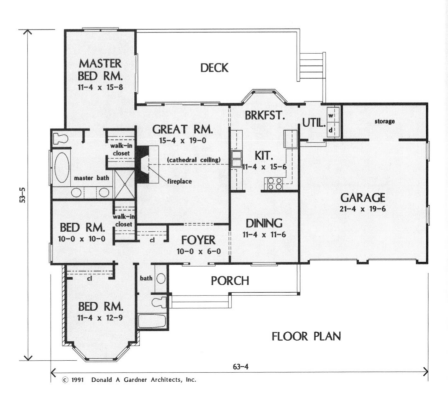

MASTER BED RM.
11-4 x 15-8

DECK

GREAT RM.
15-4 x 19-0

BRKFST.

UTIL.

storage

walk-in closet

(cathedral ceiling)

KIT.
11-4 x 15-6

master bath

fireplace

GARAGE
21-4 x 19-6

BED RM.
10-0 x 10-0

walk-in closet

DINING
11-4 x 11-6

cl

FOYER
10-0 x 6-0

53-5

cl

bath

PORCH

BED RM.
11-4 x 12-9

FLOOR PLAN

63-4

© 1991 Donald A Gardner Architects, Inc.

139

Private Master Suite

Design by Donald A. Gardner Architects, Inc.

© 1997 Donald A. Gardner Architects, Inc.

B. NATHAN

■ *Total living area 1,515 sq. ft.* ■ *Price Code D* ■

FLOOR PLAN

© 1997 Donald A Gardner Architects, Inc.

No. 99835

■ This plan features:

— Three bedrooms

— Two full baths

■ The Kitchen with a work island is open to the Great Room with its vaulted ceiling and a fireplace

■ Clerestory dormers allow light into the Great Room

■ The Dining Room and Master Bedroom are enhanced by tray ceilings

■ The Bonus Space has two skylights

■ A private Master Suite has its own Bath and an expansive walk-in closet

Main floor — 1,515 sq. ft.
Bonus — 288 sq. ft.
Garage — 476 sq. ft.

Design by Vaughn A. Lauban Designs

Cozy Three-Bedroom

No. 96522 BL ✕

■ This plan features:

– Three bedrooms

– Two full baths

■ The expansive Great Room is accented by a cozy gas fireplace

■ The efficient Kitchen includes an eating bar and is open to the Great Room

■ The Master Bedroom is highlighted by a walk-in closet and a whirlpool Bath

■ The secondary Bedrooms share the full Bath in the hall

■ The triple arched front Porch adds to the curb appeal of the home

■ An optional crawl space or slab foundation — please specify when ordering this plan

Main floor — 1,515 sq. ft.
Garage — 528 sq. ft.

■ Total living area 1,515 sq. ft. ■ Price Code B ■

Design by Donald A. Gardner Architects, Inc.

Compact Country Home

No. 98004 BL ✕ �R

■ This plan features:

– Three bedrooms

– Two full baths

■ This home has an economical squared off design with gables and arches

■ The welcoming front Porch leads into the Foyer, the Great Room and the Deck beyond

■ A comfortable gathering area is created by the open layout of the Great Room, the Dining Area and the Kitchen

■ The Master Suite provides privacy, an elegant tray ceiling, a walk-in closet and a lavish Bath with two vanities

■ Two more Bedrooms, with ample closets, share a double vanity Bath

■ The Laundry facility has access to the Bonus Room with a skylight

Main floor — 1,517 sq. ft.
Bonus Room — 287 sq. ft.
Garage — 447 sq. ft.

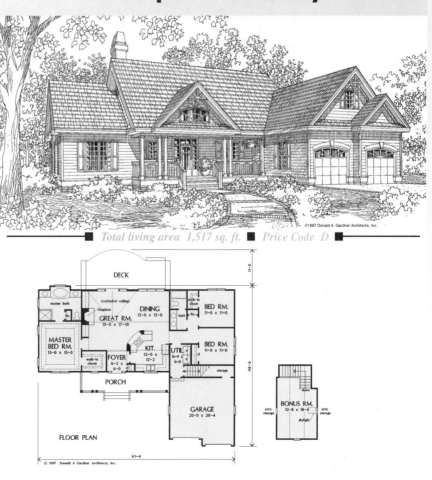

■ Total living area 1,517 sq. ft. ■ Price Code D ■

©1997 Donald A. Gardner Architects, Inc.

141

Easy One Floor Living

Design by Homeplanners

Total living area 1,521 sq. ft. ■ Price Code B

MAIN AREA

51'-4"

52'-4"

No. 99216 BL ✕

■ **This plan features:**

— Three bedrooms

— Two full baths

■ The living areas are conveniently grouped on one side of the home for everyday activities

■ The Gathering Room has a sloped ceiling and a fireplace

■ The Kitchen is designed for easy cooking with a closet Pantry and plenty of counter space and cupboards

■ The third Bedroom makes a perfect home Office or Study

Main area — 1,521 sq. ft.
Basement — 1,521 sq. ft.

Brick Abounds

Design by Fillmore Design Group

Total living area 1,528 sq. ft. ■ Price Code B

Floor Plan

40'-0"

60'-8"

No. 98522 BL

■ **This plan features:**

— Three bedrooms

— Two full baths

■ The covered front Porch opens into the Entry with a ten-foot ceiling and a coat closet

■ The large Living Room is distinguished by a fireplace and a front window wall

■ The Dining Room has a ten-foot ceiling and access to the rear covered Patio

■ The angled Kitchen has a Pantry and a cooktop island

■ The Master Bedroom is located in the rear for privacy and has a triangular shaped walk-in closet and a private Bath

■ Two more Bedrooms have large closets and share a hallway Bath

■ The two-car Garage is accessed through the Utility Room

■ No materials list is available for this plan

Main floor — 1,528 sq. ft.
Garage — 440 sq. ft.

Open Layout

■ *Total living area 1,537 sq. ft.* ■ *Price Code B* ■

No. 99167 BL

■ This plan features:

— Three bedrooms

— Two full baths

■ This Ranch design has a dramatic open layout

■ A vaulted ceiling adds dimension to the Living Room

■ The Kitchen is designed in a convenient U-shape

■ Extra storage space is provided in the rear of the Garage

■ The Master Bedroom has a walk-in closet and a private Bath

■ No materials list is available for this plan

Main floor — 1,537 sq. ft.
Basement — 1,537 sq. ft.
Garage — 989 sq. ft.

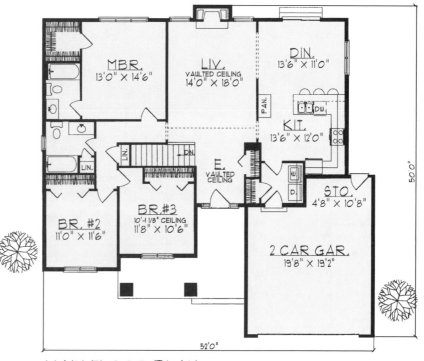

MAIN FLOOR PLAN

Extravagant Luxury

Design by Donald A. Gardner Architects, Inc.

©1994 Donald A. Gardner Architects, Inc.

■ *Total living area 1,537 sq. ft.* **■** *Price Code D* **■**

DECK

spa

GARAGE
20-0 x 20-8

fireplace

UTIL.
d
w

KIT.
10-4 x 13-6

lin.

cl

BED RM.
13-4 x 10-4

cl

master bath

GREAT RM.
15-4 x 16-0
(cathedral ceiling)

walk-in
closet

cl

BED RM.
13-4 x 10-4

bath

MASTER
BED RM.
11-4 x 15-0

FOYER
15-4 x 3-8

DINING
10-4 x 12-0

FLOOR PLAN

55-0

59-2

© 1994 Donald A Gardner Architects, Inc.

No. 96454

■ This plan features:

— Three bedrooms

— Two full baths

■ Tray, cathedral, and nine-foot
ceilings, found throughout the
home, provide vertical drama

■ An open layout creates an
expansive living area

■ The Kitchen has a curved counter
serving both the Great Room and
the Dining Area

■ Secondary Bedrooms are
separated from the Master Suite
to give complete privacy

■ A dual vanity, whirlpool tub, and
separate shower are found in the
Master Bath

Main floor — 1,537 sq. ft.
Garage & storage — 434 sq. ft.

Design by Studer Residential Design, Inc.

Total living area 1,537 sq. ft. ■ Price Code B ■

No. 92694 BL

■ This plan features:

— Three bedrooms

— Two full baths

■ The open Foyer is accented by a wood railed staircase

■ The open Great Room has a corner fireplace

■ The Dining Area has a sloped ceiling and access to the rear Porch

■ The L-shaped Kitchen has a center island

■ The large Master Bedroom has access to the rear Porch, a walk-in closet, and a private Bath

■ No materials list is available for this plan

Main floor — 1,537 sq. ft.
Basement — 1,537 sq. ft.
Garage — 400 sq. ft.

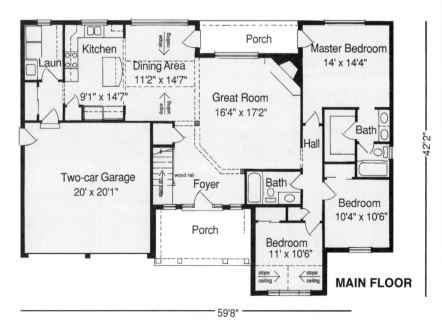

145

Ranch with Country Appeal

Design by The Garlinghouse Company

■ *Total living area 1,539 sq. ft.* ■ *Price Code B* ■

MAIN AREA

45'-4"

50'-0"

Deck

Dining
17-3 x 9-9

Breakfast Bar

Kitchen
13-5 x 9-8

Pantry

Garage
19-5 x 23-6

Shelves

Desk

Living Rm
12-2 x 19-4

Flat Clg.
@ 11'-0"

Flat Clg.
@ 8'-0" TYP

Hall

Foy

Den/Br 3
10-5 x 11-6

Porch

MBr 1
11-8 x 14-0

Decor
Clg.

Flue

Br 2
10-6 x 12-3

No. 24721

■ **This plan features:**

— Three bedrooms

— Two full baths

■ A sloped ceiling tops the Living Room and is accented by a fireplace

■ Built-in shelves and an arched opening separate the Living Room and the Dining Room

■ The Efficient U-shaped Kitchen is highlighted by a breakfast bar

■ The French door accesses the rear Deck from the Dining Area

■ The Master Suite is crowned with a decorative ceiling

■ No materials list is available for this plan

Main area — 1,539 sq. ft.
Basement — 1,530 sq. ft.
Garage — 460 sq. ft.

Hip Roof Ranch

■ *Total living area 1,540 sq. ft.* ■ *Price Code B* ■

No. 93161   BL ✕ ⚒

■ **This plan features:**

— Three bedrooms

— Two full baths

■ The cozy front Porch leads into the Entry accented with a vaulted ceiling and sidelights

■ The open Living Room is enhanced by a cathedral ceiling, a wall of windows and corner fireplace

■ The large and efficient Kitchen has an extended counter and a bright Dining Area with access to the screened Porch

■ The convenient Utility Area has access to the Garage and Storage Area

■ The spacious Master Bedroom has a walk-in closet and private Bath

Main floor — 1,540 sq. ft.
Basement — 1,540 sq. ft.

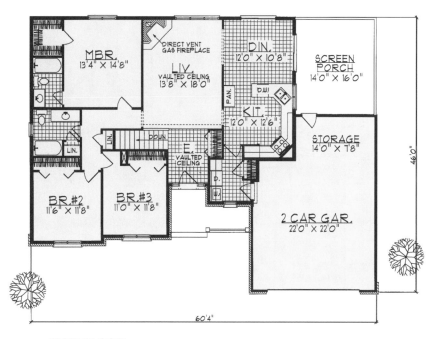

MAIN FLOOR

A Much Larger Feeling

Design by Donald A. Gardner Architects, Inc.

© 1991 Donald A. Gardner Architects, Inc.

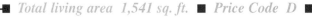

Total living area 1,541 sq. ft. ■ *Price Code D* ■

MAIN FLOOR

© 1991 Donald A Gardner Architects, Inc.

No. 96419 BL ✕ ЯR

■ **This plan features:**

— Three bedrooms

— Two full baths

■ Arched windows, dormers, front and side Porches, rear Deck, and an open interior give this home a spacious atmosphere

■ Elegant columns is defined by the Dining Room

■ The open Great Room has a cathedral ceiling and arched window above the sliding glass door

■ An optional basement or crawl space foundation — please specify when ordering this plan

Main floor — 1,541 sq. ft.
Garage & Storage — 446 sq. ft.

©1997 Donald A. Gardner Architects, Inc.

■ *Total living area 1,542 sq. ft.* ■ *Price Code D* ■

No. 98005 BL ✗ R

■ This plan features:

— Three bedrooms

— Two full baths

■ Privacy and openness are balanced in this house designed with expansion in mind

■ The combined Great Room and Dining Area have a cathedral ceiling, a fireplace, and access to the Deck

■ The efficient, U-shaped Kitchen is convenient to the Dining and Utility Areas

■ The Master Bedroom has a tray ceiling, a walk-in closet and fully appointed Bath

Main floor — 1,542 sq. ft.
Bonus — 352 sq. ft.
Garage — 487 sq. ft.

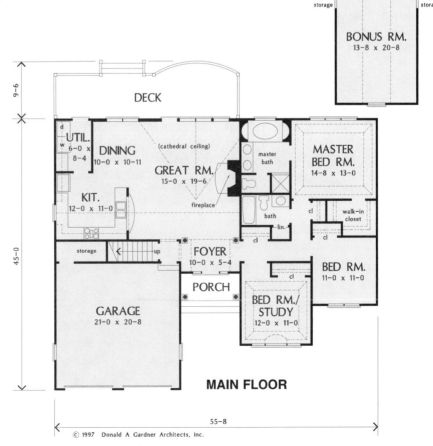

attic storage

down

attic storage

BONUS RM.
13-8 x 20-8

DECK

UTIL.
6-0 x 8-4

DINING
10-0 x 10-11

(cathedral ceiling)

GREAT RM.
15-0 x 19-6

master bath

MASTER BED RM.
14-8 x 13-0

KIT.
12-0 x 11-0

fireplace

bath

lin.

cl

walk-in closet

cl

storage

up

FOYER
10-0 x 5-4

cl

GARAGE
21-0 x 20-8

PORCH

BED RM./STUDY
12-0 x 11-0

cl

BED RM.
11-0 x 11-0

MAIN FLOOR

9-6

45-0

55-8

© 1997 Donald A Gardner Architects, Inc.

European Flair

Design by Frank Betz Associates, Inc.

No. 98460

■ **This plan features:**

— Three bedrooms

— Two full baths

■ A large fireplace serves as an attractive focal point for the vaulted Family Room

■ Decorative columns define the elegant Dining Room

■ The Kitchen has a serving bar and a Breakfast Area

■ The Master Suite is topped by a tray ceiling over the Bedroom and a vaulted ceiling over the plush Bath

■ There is an optional Bonus Room for future expansion

■ An optional basement or crawl space foundation — please specify when ordering

■ No materials list is available for this plan

Main floor — 1,544 sq. ft.
Bonus room — 284 sq. ft.
Basement — 1,544 sq. ft.
Garage — 440 sq. ft.

Total living area 1,544 sq. ft. ■ Price Code B

© Frank Betz Associates, Inc.

Economical Home

Design by Donald A. Gardner Architects, Inc.

No. 98027

■ **This plan features:**

— Three bedrooms

— Two full baths

■ This plan has appealing character with gables, pediments and an inviting front Porch

■ A tray ceiling and columns enhance the Dining Area open to the Great Room for comfortable gatherings

■ The Great Room has a cathedral ceiling, a fireplace between built-in shelves and access to the Deck

■ The open Kitchen keeps the cook part of all activities

■ The corner Master Bedroom offers two walk-in closets and a double vanity Bath

■ The two additional Bedrooms have ample closets and share a full Bath in the hall

■ The Bonus Room over the Garage provides options for a growing family

Main floor — 1,544 sq. ft.
Bonus room — 320 sq. ft.
Garage & storage — 478 sq. ft.

Total living area 1,544 sq. ft. ■ Price Code D

MAIN FLOOR

© 1998 Donald A Gardner, Inc.

Design by James Fahy Design

No. 94116 BL ✕

■ This plan features:

— Three bedrooms

— Two full baths

■ The Great Room adjoins the Dining Room for ease in entertaining

■ The Kitchen is highlighted by a peninsula counter/snack bar extending the work space conveniently

■ The Split Bedroom plan ensures privacy for the Master Suite with its private Bath and walk-in closet

■ The two additional Bedrooms share the full Bath in the hall

■ The Garage entry is convenient to the Kitchen

Main floor — 1,546 sq. ft.
Basement — 1,530 sq. ft.
Garage — 440 sq. ft.

Small, But Not Lacking

■ *Total living area 1,546 sq. ft.* ■ *Price Code B* ■

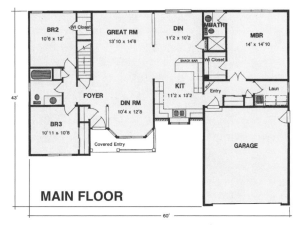

MAIN FLOOR

Design by Greg Marquis & Associates

No. 93455 BL

■ This plan features:

— Three bedrooms

— Two full baths

■ Porches provide outdoor living space front and rear

■ The Family Room has a high ceiling and a fireplace

■ The snack bar is adjacent to the Family and Dining rooms

■ An island adds convenience to the Kitchen

■ The three large Bedrooms are located in their own wing

■ No materials list is available for this plan

Main floor — 1,550 sq. ft.
Garage — 548 sq. ft.

Wrapping Porch

■ *Total living area 1,550 sq. ft.* ■ *Price Code B* ■

MAIN FLOOR

WIDTH 68'-3"
DEPTH 73'-8"

Ceiling Treatments Add Interest

Design by Frank Betz Associates, Inc.

No. 98412 BL ✕

■ This plan features:

— Three bedrooms

— Two full baths

■ A vaulted ceiling crowns the Family Room and a tray ceiling tops the Master Suite

■ Decorative columns accent the entrance to the Dining Room

■ The Great Room has a pass-through from the Kitchen, a fireplace framed by a window and a French door

■ A built-in Pantry and desk add convenience to the Kitchen

■ An optional basement, slab or crawl space foundation — please specify when ordering

Main floor — 1,553 sq. ft.
Basement — 1,605 sq. ft.
Garage — 434 sq. ft.

Total living area 1,553 sq. ft. ■ Price Code B

© Frank Betz Associates, Inc.

52'-0"

49'-6"

TRAY CLG.
Master Suite
14'x14'

PANTRY
DESK
Breakfast
FRENCH DOOR
FPL.

RANGE
Kitchen
PASS THRU

Vaulted Family Room
15'x17'

Bedroom 3
11'x11'

TUB
M.Bath
VAULT

Bath

W.I.C.
W D

DECORATIVE COLUMNS
Foyer
HIGH CLG.

OPT. STAIRS TO BASEMENT

Dining Room
11'x11'

Bedroom 2
11'x11'

Garage

Main floor

Covered Porches

Design by The Garlinghouse Company

No. 24738 BL

■ This plan features:

— Three bedrooms

— Two full baths

■ Covered Porches are found in both the front and the rear of this home

■ A slit Bedroom design adds privacy to the Master Suite

■ The Dining and Great Rooms are open and accented by columns

■ An eating bar provides a casual dining option

■ A fireplace warms the center of the home

■ No material list is available for this plan

Main floor — 1,554 sq. ft.
Basement — 1,402 sq. ft.
Garage — 541 sq. ft.
Porch — 219 sq. ft.

Total living area 1,554 sq. ft. ■ Price Code B

60'-3"

55'-6"

Covered Porch

Brkfst
11-8 x 7-1

M. Br.
11-8 x 15-1

Kitchen
11-0 x 8-0

Great Rm
11-8 x 15-1

Br 2
11-8 x 10-4

Ldry

Dining Rm
11-4 x 14-3

Br 3
11-8 x 10-2

Garage
21-5 x 23-8

Covered Porch

MAIN FLOOR

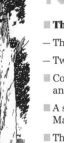

Varied Ceilings

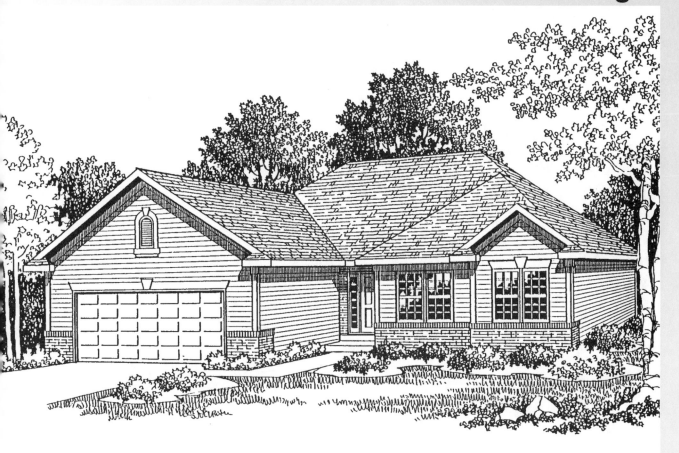

■ *Total living area 1,557 sq. ft.* ■ *Price Code B* ■

No. 99152 [BL]

■ This plan features:

— Three bedrooms

— Two full baths

■ Varied ceilings add beauty and dimension to this home

■ The Great Room has an inviting fireplace and a cathedral ceiling

■ The Dining Room has access to the rear yard

■ The U-shaped Kitchen has easy access to the Laundry and Garage

■ This plan has a tiled Entry

■ No materials list is available for this plan

Main floor — 1,557 sq. ft.
Basement — 1,557 sq. ft.
Garage — 440 sq. ft.

DIN.
13'0" X 10'0"

GREAT RM.
CATHEDRAL CEILING
14'8" X 21'0"

MBR.
TRAY CEILING
15'4" X 15'0"

KIT.
12'8" X 10'10"

SHELVES

LIN.

DN.

BR. #3
11'10" X 10'0"

BR. #2
12'0" X 10'4"

2 CAR GAR.
21'4" X 20'8"

49'0"

MAIN FLOOR

53'0"

Cute Starter Home

Design by Ahmann Design, Inc.

■ *Total living area 1,557 sq. ft.* ■ *Price Code B* ■

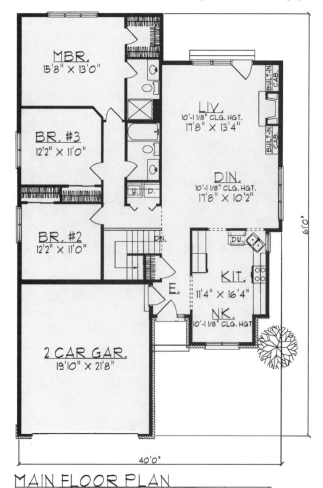

MBR.
15'8" X 13'0"

BR. #3
12'2" X 11'0"

BR. #2
12'2" X 11'0"

LIV.
10'-1 1/8" CLG. HGT.
17'8" X 13'4"

BUILT-IN CAB.

BUILT-IN CAB.

DIN.
10'-1 1/8" CLG. HGT.
17'8" X 10'2"

W D

DN.

DW

KIT.
11'4" X 16'4"

E.

NK.
10'-1 1/8" CLG. HGT

2 CAR GAR.
19'10" X 21'8"

61'0"

40'0"

MAIN FLOOR PLAN

No. 97152

■ **This plan features:**

— Three bedrooms

— Two full baths

■ A simple design with quality details provides charm inside and out

■ The spacious Living/Dining Room allows comfortable gatherings and includes multiple windows and outdoor access to the outdoors

■ The open Kitchen/Nook has easy access to the Dining Area, the Laundry closet and the Garage

■ The corner Master Bedroom offers a full view of the rear yard, a walk-in closet and a private Bath

■ No materials list is available for this plan

Main floor — 1,557 sq. ft.
Basement — 1,557 sq. ft.
Garage — 400 sq. ft.

Southern Traditional Flavor

■ *Total living area 1,567 sq. ft.* ■ *Price Code B* ■

No. 99641 BL X

■ **This plan features:**

— Three bedrooms

— Two full baths

■ The Living Room is enhanced by a nine foot ceiling and a fireplace and built-in bookcases

■ French doors lead from the Dining Room to the Terrace

■ Plenty of counter and storage space is found in the wrap-around Kitchen

■ The Laundry Area serves as a Mud Room between the Garage and the Kitchen

■ The Master Suite has a large walk-in closet and a double vanity Bath

First floor — 1,567 sq. ft.
Bonus — 338 sq. ft.
Basement — 1,567 sq. ft.
Garage — 504 sq. ft.

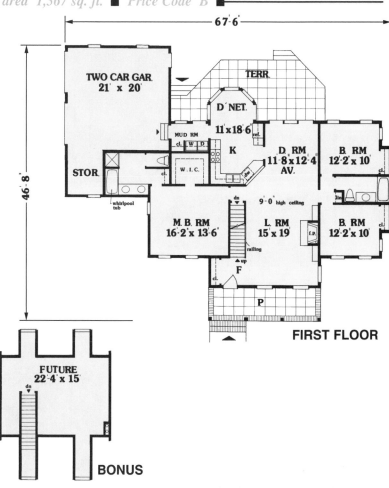

67'-6"

46'-8"

TWO CAR GAR.
21' x 20'

STOR.

TERR.

D´NET.
11' x 18-6"

MUD RM
cl. W D

K

WIC.

D. RM
11-8 x 12-4
AV.

B. RM
12-2' x 10'

ref.

whirlpool
tub

M. B. RM
16-2' x 13-6'

9'-0" high ceiling

L. RM
15' x 19'

f.p.

B. RM
12-2' x 10'

railing

up

F

dn

FIRST FLOOR

P

FUTURE
22-4' x 15'

dn

BONUS

Traditional Ranch

Design by The Garlinghouse Company

■ *Total living area 1,568 sq. ft.* ■ *Price Code B* ■

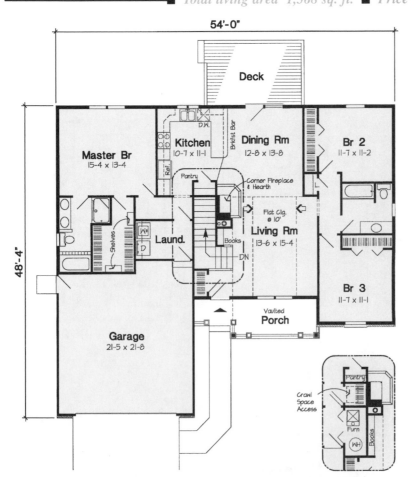

54'-0"

Deck

Master Br
15-4 x 13-4

Kitchen
10-7 x 11-1

Dining Rm
12-8 x 13-8

Br 2
11-7 x 11-2

D.W.

Ref

Pantry

Brkfst Bar

Corner Fireplace & Hearth

Flat Clg. @ 10'

Living Rm
13-6 x 15-4

48'-4"

Shelves

Laund.

Books

DN

Br 3
11-7 x 11-1

Garage
21-5 x 21-8

Vaulted
Porch

Crawl
Space
Access

Pantry

Furn

WH

Books

Main Floor

No. 20220

■ **This plan features:**

— Three bedrooms

— Two full baths

■ A large front palladium window gives this home great curb appeal

■ A vaulted ceiling in the Living Room adds to the architectural interest and the spacious feel of the room

■ Sliding glass doors in the Dining Room lead to a wood Deck

■ A built-in Pantry, double sink and Breakfast Bar are found in the efficient Kitchen

■ The Master Suite includes a walk-in closet and a private Bath with a double vanity

Main floor —1,568 sq. ft.
Basement — 1,568 sq. ft.
Garage — 509 sq. ft.

Design by Frank Betz Associates, Inc.

Total living area 1,575 sq. ft. ■ Price Code B

No. 98479

■ This plan features:

— Three bedrooms

— Two full baths

■ The Foyer, the Family Room, and the Dining Room have fifteen-foot, eight-inch ceilings

■ The Breakfast Room and the Master Bath have vaulted ceilings

■ The Master Suite is topped by a tray ceiling

■ This plan features arched openings to the Dining Room from the Family Room and the Foyer

■ An optional basement or crawl space foundation — please specify when ordering

■ No materials list is available for this plan

First floor — 1,575 sq. ft
Basement — 1,612 sq. ft.
Garage — 456 sq. ft.

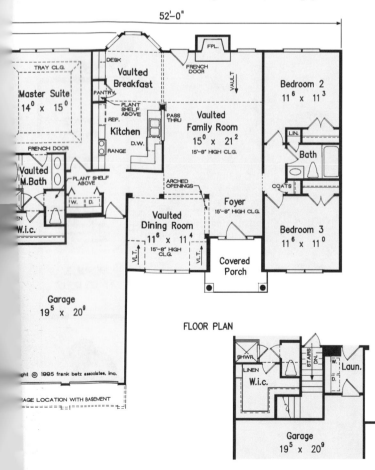

FLOOR PLAN

Opt. Basement Stair Location

Design by The Garlinghouse Company

Foyer Isolates Bed...

A

■ *Total living area 1,568 sq. ft.* ■ *Price Code B* ■

No. 20087

■ This plan features:

- Three bedrooms

- Two full baths

- ■ The Living Room is complete with windows on either side of a massive fireplace

- ■ The Dining Room has a recessed ceiling and a pass-through to the kitchen for convenience

- ■ The Master Suite has Deck access and a luxurious Bath

- ■ The spacious Kitchen has built-ins and access to the two-car Garage

Main floor —1,568 sq. ft.
Basement — 1,568 sq. ft.
Garage — 484 sq. ft.

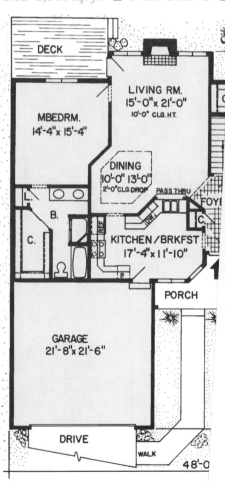

DECK

LIVING RM.
15'-0" x 21'-0"
10'-0" CLG. HT.

MBEDRM.
14'-4" x 15'-4"

DINING
10'-0" 13'-0"
2'-0" CLG. DROP

PASS THRU

FOY

B.

C.

REF

KITCHEN / BRKFST
17'-4" x 11'-10"

P.

PORCH

GARAGE
21'-8" x 21'-6"

52'-6"

DRIVE

WALK

48'-0

One-Level with a Twist

■ *Total living area 1,575 sq. ft.* ■ *Price Code B* ■

No. 20083

■ **This plan features:**

— Three bedrooms

— Two full baths

■ The wide-open, active areas are centrally-located

■ This plan has spacious Dining, Living, and Kitchen Areas

■ The Master Suite is found at the rear of the house with a full Bath

■ Two additional Bedrooms share a full hall Bath and a quiet atmosphere

Main floor — 1,575 sq. ft.
Basement — 1,575 sq. ft.
Garage — 475 sq. ft.

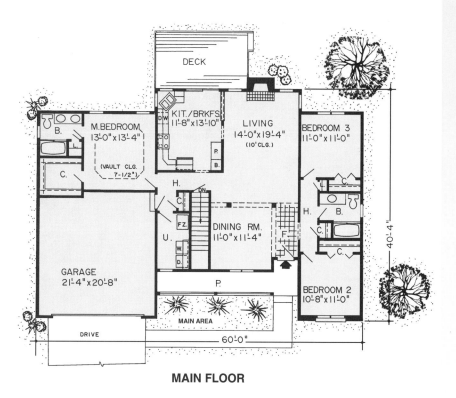

MAIN FLOOR

Three Bedroom Ranch

Design by Frank Betz Associates, Inc.

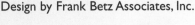

No. 98414 BL ✕

■ **Total living area 1,575 sq. ft.** ■ **Price Code B** ■

■ **This plan features:**

— Three bedrooms

— Two full baths

■ The formal Dining Room is enhanced by a plant shelf and a side window

■ A wetbar is located between the Kitchen and the Dining Room

■ A built-in Pantry, a double sink and a snack bar highlight the Kitchen

■ The Breakfast Room includes a radius window and a French door to the rear yard

■ A large cozy fireplace is framed by windows in the Great Room

■ The Master Suite has a vaulted ceiling over the Sitting Area, a Master Bath and a walk-in closet

■ The two additional Bedrooms share the full Bath in the hall

■ An optional basement or crawl space foundation — please specify when ordering

Main floor — 1,575 sq. ft.
Basement — 1,658 sq. ft.
Garage — 459 sq. ft.

Didn't Waste An Inch of Space

Design by Donald A. Gardner Architects, Inc.

No. 99834 BL ✕ ЯR

■ **Total living area 1,575 sq. ft.** ■ **Price Code D** ■

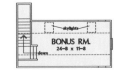

■ **This plan features:**

— Three bedrooms

— Two full baths

■ The Great Room with fireplace and built-in cabinetsand the angled Kitchen both have cathedral ceilings

■ The separate Dining Room allows for more formal entertaining

■ The Master Bedroom is topped by a cathedral ceiling, walk-in closet, and well appointed Bath

■ The front and rear covered Porches encourage relaxation

■ The skylit Bonus Room will make a great Recreation Room or Office in the future

Main floor — 1,575 sq. ft.
Bonus — 276 sq. ft.
Garage — 536 sq. ft.

Design by Donald A. Gardner Architects, Inc.

Traditional Beauty

No. 99802 BL ✈ 🗺 ℛ

This plan features:

- Three bedrooms

- Two full baths

■ Large arched windows, stately columns, covered Porch, and brick veneer create an appealing exterior

■ Clerestory dormers above the covered Porch highlight the Foyer

■ A cathedral ceiling enhances the Great Room along with a cozy fireplace

■ The open Kitchen with a Breakfast Area accesses the large Deck which offers an optional spa

■ Columns that define open spaces beautifully

■ Tray ceilings are found in the Master Bedroom, Dining Room and the Bedroom/Study

■ A double vanity, a separate shower, and a whirlpool tub are located in the Master Bath

Main floor — 1,576 sq. ft.
Garage — 465 sq. ft.

© 1993 Donald A Gardner Architects, Inc.

■ Total living area 1,576 sq. ft. ■ Price Code D ■

© 1993 Donald A Gardner Architects, Inc.

MAIN FLOOR

Design by The Garlinghouse Company

Cozy Country Ranch

No. 24708 BL ✈ 🗺

This plan features:

- Three bedrooms

- Two full baths

■ The front Porch shelters outdoor visiting and entrance into Living Room

■ The expansive Living Room is highlighted by a boxed window and hearth fireplace between built-ins

■ Columns frame the entrance to the Dining which as access to the back yard

■ Efficient, U-shaped Kitchen has direct access to the Screened Porch and the Dining Room

■ The Master Bedroom wing is enhanced by a large walk-in closet and a double vanity Bath with a whirlpool tub

■ Two additional Bedrooms with large closets share a double vanity Bath with Laundry Center

Main floor — 1,576 sq. ft.
Basement — 1,454 sq. ft.
Garage — 576 sq. ft.

■ Total living area 1,576 sq. ft. ■ Price Code B ■

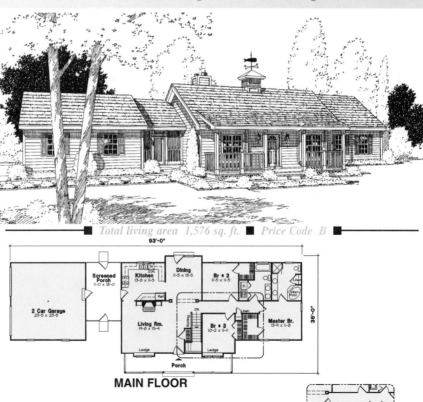

MAIN FLOOR

Alternate Crawl/Slab Plan

Impressive Two-Sided Fireplace

Design by Design Basics, Inc.

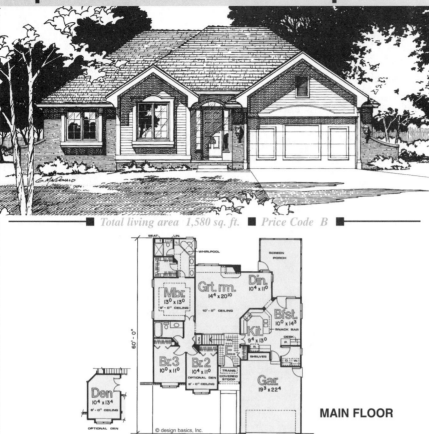

Total living area 1,580 sq. ft. ■ Price Code B ■

MAIN FLOOR

No. 94972 BL ✕

■ **This plan features:**

– Three bedrooms

– Two full baths

■ The Great Room is enhanced by an impressive two-sided fireplace

■ The Formal Dining Area is open to the Great Room offering a view of the fireplace

■ French doors off the Entry provide access to the Kitchen which has a planning desk, a snack bar, and built-in Pantry

■ The Breakfast Area accesses a large comfortable screened Porch

■ The Laundry Room is strategically located off the Kitchen and provides direct access to the Garage.

■ The Master Suite is accessed by French doors, topped by an elegant, decorative ceiling and highlighted by a pampering Bath

Main floor — 1,580 sq. ft.
Garage — 456 sq. ft.

For Today and Tomorrow

Design by The Garlinghouse Company

Total living area 1,583 sq. ft. ■ Price Code B ■

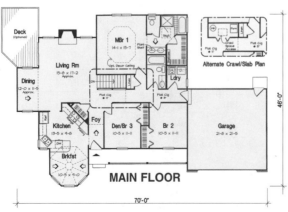

MAIN FLOOR

No. 34043 BL ✕ ▱ ℛ

■ **This plan features:**

– Three bedrooms

– Two full baths

■ An intriguing Breakfast Nook is adjacent to the Kitchen

■ The wide open Living Room has a cozy fireplace and glass sliders to an optional Deck

■ A step-saving arrangement of the Kitchen is located between the Breakfast Area and the formal Dining Room

■ A handsome Master Bedroom has a sky-lit, luxurious Bath

Main area — 1,583 sq. ft.
Basement — 1,573 sq. ft.
Garage — 484 sq. ft.

Design by United Design Associates

Elegant Columns

No. 94724

■ **This plan features:**

— Three bedrooms

— Two full baths

■ Columns support the covered front Porch

■ The spacious Dining Room is perfect for entertaining

■ A fireplace warms the adjacent Great Room

■ The Master Bedroom is located away from the active areas

■ The Garage has plenty of storage space

■ An optional slab or crawl space foundation — please specify when ordering

Main floor — 1,589 sq. ft.
Garage — 410 sq. ft.

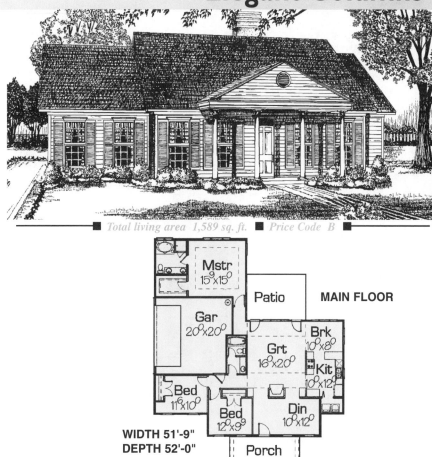

■ *Total living area 1,589 sq. ft.* ■ *Price Code B* ■

WIDTH 51'-9"
DEPTH 52'-0"

Design by Perfect Plan

Romantic Charm

No. 90684

■ **This plan features:**

— Three bedrooms

— Two full and one half baths

■ The spacious Living Room and formal Dining Room combination is perfect for entertaining

■ The Family Room has a large fireplace and a wall of windows that overlooks the Patio

■ The efficient Kitchen has a peninsula counter dividing it from the Family Room

■ The Master Bedroom has dual closets and a private Bath

■ The secondary bedrooms share the full Bath in the hall

Main floor — 1590 sq. ft.
Basement — 900 sq. ft.

■ *Total living area 1,590 sq. ft.* ■ *Price Code B* ■

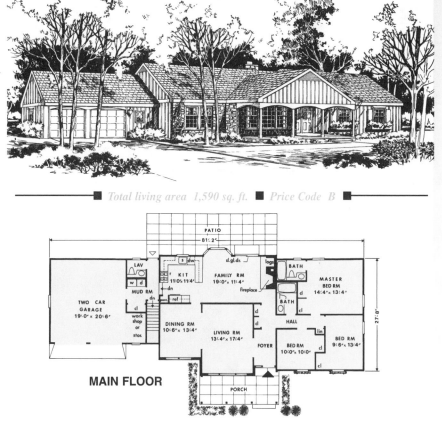

MAIN FLOOR

Easy Living Ranch

Design by National Home Planning Service

Total living area 1,590 sq. ft. ■ Price Code B ■

MAIN FLOOR

No. 99081 BL

■ **This plan features:**

— Three bedrooms

— Two full baths

■ This plan has distinct exterior features including vinyl siding, a series of gables, an arched window, and a protected front door with sidelights

■ The Dining Room has a fourteen foot ceiling over an arched window

■ The Kitchen has a Serving Bar

■ The Dinette has easy access to the Great Room

■ The Master Bedroom is crowned with a tray ceiling

■ The Master Bath includes a large walk-in closet, a separate shower and a garden tub

■ No material list is available for this plan

Main floor — 1,590 sq. ft.

Luxury in One-Story Plan

Design by W. D. Farmer F.A.I.B.D.

Total living area 1,595 sq. ft. ■ Price Code B ■

MAIN FLOOR

No. 94827 BL X

■ **This plan features:**

— Three bedrooms

— Two full baths

■ The covered stoop leads into a dynamic Activity Room with a fireplace, a recessed ceiling, and adjacent to the Dining Room and Sun Deck

■ The Open Kitchen/Breakfast Room offers loads of counter space with a nearby Pantry, the Laundry and the Garage

■ The plush Bedroom Suite has a tray ceiling, a walk-in closet, and a garden bath tub

■ Two additional Bedrooms share a full Bath

■ An optional basement, slab or crawl space foundation — please specify when ordering

Main floor — 1,595 sq. ft.
Basement — 1,595 sq. ft.
Garage — 491 sq. ft.

■ *Total living area 1,597 sq. ft.* ■ *Price Code B* ■

No. 90697

■ **This plan features:**

— Three bedrooms

— Two full baths

■ The corner fireplace adds warmth to the sunny Living Room

■ Skylights are located in the high sloping ceiling of the Family Room, which also has a greenhouse bay window and a heat-circulating fireplace

■ The elegant formal Dining Room has a window alcove

■ The Master Bedroom has a private Bath and two closets

■ Two additional Bedrooms share the full Bath in the hall

Main floor — 1,597 sq. ft.
Basement — 1,512 sq. ft.

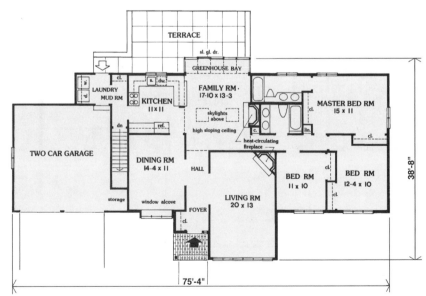

MAIN FLOOR

Carefree Convenience

Design by The Garlinghouse Company

■ *Total living area 1,600 sq. ft.* ■ *Price Code B* ■

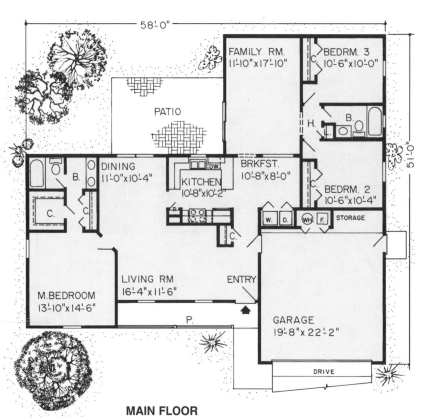

MAIN FLOOR

No. 10674

■ **This plan features:**

— Three bedrooms

— Two full baths

■ The galley Kitchen is centrally located between the Dining, the Breakfast and the Living Room Areas

■ The huge Family Room exits onto the Patio

■ The Master Suite has two closets and a double vanity

■ Two additional Bedrooms share a full Bath in the hall

Main floor — 1,600 sq. ft.
Garage — 465 sq. ft.

Columns and Arches

■ *Total living area 1,600 sq. ft.* ■ *Price Code B* ■

No. 99163 **BL**

■ **This plan features:**

— Three bedrooms

— Two full baths

■ The tiled Entry has a high ceiling

■ The Great Room and the Dining Area have arched openings

■ The Master Bedroom has an immense walk-in closet and a private Bath

■ The third Bedroom has a cathedral ceiling and can also serve as a Den

■ The U-shaped Kitchen has a work island and adjoins the Laundry and the Garage

■ No materials list is available for this plan

Main floor — 1,600 sq. ft.
Basement — 1,600 sq. ft.
Garage — 406 sq. ft.
Deck — 118 sq. ft.

WD. DECK
9'10" X 12'0"

KIT.
10'0" X 11'8"

DIN.
10'0" X 12'0"

MBR.
TRAY CEILING
14'8" X 12'8"

GRT. RM.
10'-1 1/8" CEILING
14'0" X 19'4"

2 CAR GAR.
20'8" X 19'8"

E.
10'-1 1/8"
CEILING

ARCH SOFFIT

BR. #3/ DEN
CATHEDRAL CEILING
11'0" X 11'10"

BR. #2
10'8" X 11'0"

45'0"

54'8"

MAIN FLOOR PLAN

Exciting Facade

Design by Studer Residential Design, Inc.

■ *Total living area 1,601 sq. ft.* ■ *Price Code B* ■

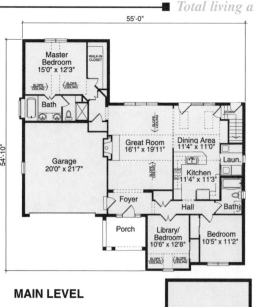

MAIN LEVEL

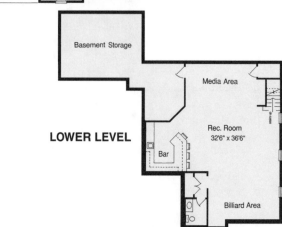

LOWER LEVEL

No. 97702

■ This plan features:

— Three bedrooms

— Two full baths

■ Brick, stone, and siding combine to create an exciting facade

■ The covered Porch shelters the front entrance

■ A sloping ceiling and fireplace are featured in the impressive Great Room

■ Skylights and outdoor access highlight the Dining Area

■ The Master Bedroom has a large walk-in closet and a comfortable Bath

■ The lower level offers future Recreation Space

■ No materials list is available for this plan

Main level — 1,601 sq. ft
Lower level — 1,601 sq. ft
Garage — 426 sq. ft

■ *Total living area 1,604 sq. ft.* ■ *Price Code B* ■

No. 94986 BL ✗

■ **This plan features:**

— Three bedrooms

— Two full baths

■ The Great Room is highlighted by a fireplace set between windows

■ A see-through wetbar is found between the Breakfast Area and the Dining Room

■ A decorative ceiling treatment adds elegance to the Dining Room

■ The fully equipped Kitchen has a planning desk and a Pantry

■ The roomy Master Bedroom has a plant shelf, a walk-in closet, a double vanity and a whirlpool tub

■ The secondary Bedrooms have ample closets and share a convenient, hall Bath

Main floor — 1,604 sq. ft.
Garage — 466 sq. ft.

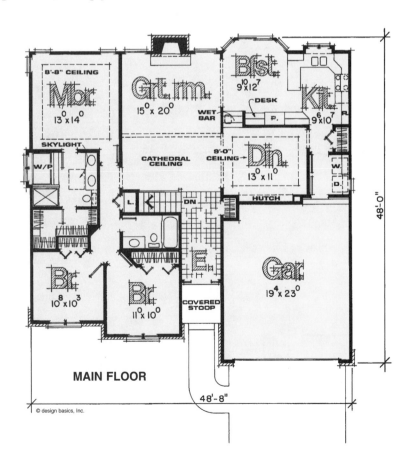

MAIN FLOOR

© design basics, Inc.

Outdoor Living Options

Design by Donald A. Gardner Architects, Inc.

Total living area 1,609 sq. ft. ■ _Price Code D_ ■

© 1997 Donald A. Gardner Architects, Inc.

MAIN FLOOR

No. 96489 BL ✕ ℞R

■ **This plan features:**

– Three bedrooms

– Two full baths

■ Living areas are open and casual

■ The Great Room is crowned by a cathedral ceiling which continues out to the screened Porch

■ The Kitchen opens to a bright Breakfast Bay and is adjacent to the formal Dining Room

■ The Master Suite is topped by a tray ceiling and enhanced by an indulgent Bath with a roomy walk-in closet

■ Two additional Bedrooms share a full Bath

Main floor — 1,609 sq. ft.
Garage & storage — 500 sq. ft.

Varied Roof Heights

Design by Perfect Plan

Total living area 1,613 sq. ft. ■ _Price Code B_ ■

MAIN FLOOR

No. 90601 BL ✕

■ **This plan features:**

– Three bedrooms

– Two full and one half baths

■ The spacious Family Room has a heat-circulating fireplace visible from the Foyer

■ The large Kitchen has a cooktop island, and opens into the Dinette Bay

■ The Master Suite has two closets and a private Master Bath

■ Two additional Bedrooms share a full, hall Bath

■ The formal Dining and Living Rooms flow into each other for easy entertaining

Main floor — 1,613 sq. ft.
Basement — 1,060 sq. ft.
Garage — 461 sq. ft.

Design by Wesplan Building Design

Rooms with a View

No. 90954

■This plan features:

— Three bedrooms

— Two full and one half baths

■ The vaulted Foyer offers access to every area of the house

■ The Kitchen has a built-in Pantry and desk, and a bay Nook for informal meals

■ The Master Suite has private access to the Deck

Main floor — 1,617 sq. ft.
Basement — 1,617 sq. ft.
Garage — 471 sq. ft.

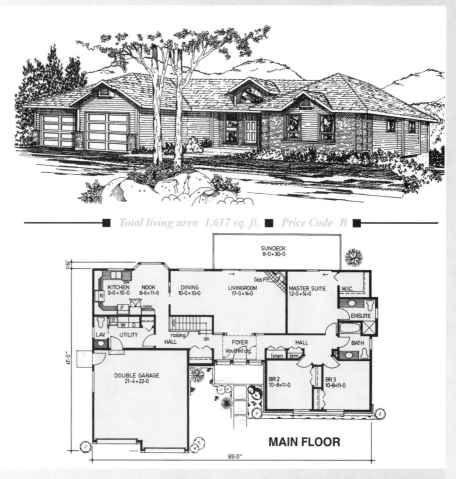

■ Total living area 1,617 sq. ft. ■ Price Code B ■

MAIN FLOOR

Design by The Garlinghouse Company

Bright Living Spaces

No. 24317

■This plan features:

— Three bedrooms

— Two full baths

■ The generous use of windows throughout the home, create a bright living space

■ A center work island and a built-in Pantry are found in the Kitchen

■ The plan features a sunny Eating Nook for informal eating and a formal Dining Room for entertaining

■ The large Living Room has a cozy fireplace to add atmosphere to the room as well as warmth

■ The Master Bedroom has a private Bath and double closets

■ Two additional Bedrooms share a full, hall Bath

Main floor — 1,620 sq. ft.

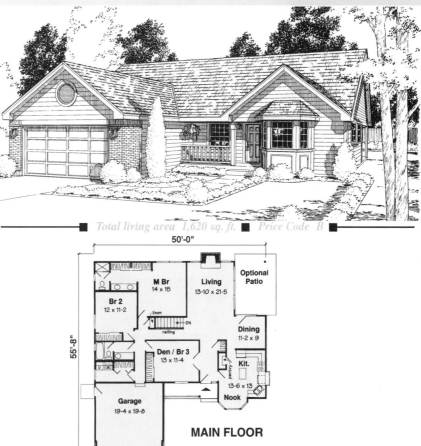

■ Total living area 1,620 sq. ft. ■ Price Code B ■

MAIN FLOOR

Heart of the Home

Design by Georgia Toney Lesley

No. 99503

■ This plan features:

— Three bedrooms

— Two full baths

■ The Great Room has a cathedral ceiling, a fireplace, and a wall of windows

■ The Dining Area has a cathedral ceiling above an arched window

■ The U-shaped Country Kitchen has plenty of counter space and room for a Kitchen table

■ The screened Porch in the rear is accessed from the Great Room and the Master Bedroom

■ The Master Bedroom has a vaulted ceiling, a plant shelf, a walk-in closet and a private Bath

■ Two additional Bedrooms have ample closet space and share a full Bath

■ The two-car Garage has a Bonus Room above

■ No materials list is available for this plan

Main floor — 1,620 sq. ft.
Bonus room — 290 sq. ft.
Garage — 547 sq. ft.

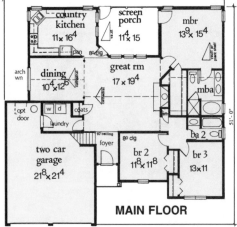

Total living area 1,620 sq. ft. Price Code B

MAIN FLOOR

OPTION

Convenient Floor Plan

Design by The Garlinghouse Company

No. 24701

■ **This plan features:**

— Three bedrooms

— Two full baths

■ The Central Foyer leads to the Den/Guest Room with an arched window below vaulted ceiling, and the Living Room with a two-sided fireplace

■ The efficient, U-shaped Kitchen has a peninsula counter/Breakfast Bar serving the Dining Room, and an adjacent Utility/Pantry

■ The Master Suite features a large walk-in closet, and the private Bath with double vanity and a whirlpool tub

■ Two additional Bedrooms have ample closet space, and share a full Bath

Main floor — 1,625 sq. ft.
Basement — 1,625 sq. ft.
Garage — 455 sq. ft.

Total living area 1,625 sq. ft. Price Code B

MAIN FLOOR

Alternate Foundation Plan

Design by Donald A. Gardner Architects, Inc.

Cathedral Ceilings

© 1992 Donald A. Gardner Architects, Inc.

■ *Total living area 1,625 sq. ft.* ■ *Price Code D* ■

No. 99854 BL X R

■ This plan features:

— Three bedrooms

— Two full baths

■ Cathedral ceilings add volume to the high activity areas of this home

■ A storage space is located in the rear of the Garage

■ The Great Room has a fireplace set between built-ins and access to the Porch and Deck

■ Bay windows are featured in both Dining Areas

■ The Kitchen has a great work triangle

■ The Bedrooms have ample closet space

■ The Master Bath provides a luxurious retreat for its occupants

Main floor — 1,625 sq. ft.
Garage — 532 sq. ft.

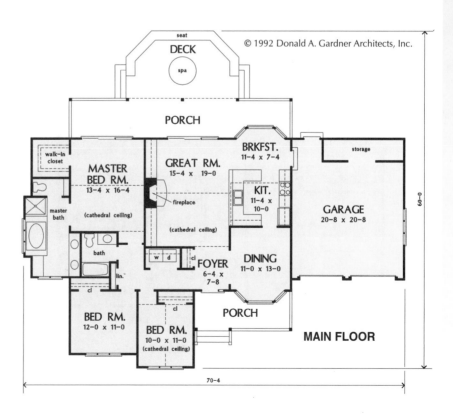

■ *Total living area 1,628 sq. ft.* ■ *Price Code B* ■

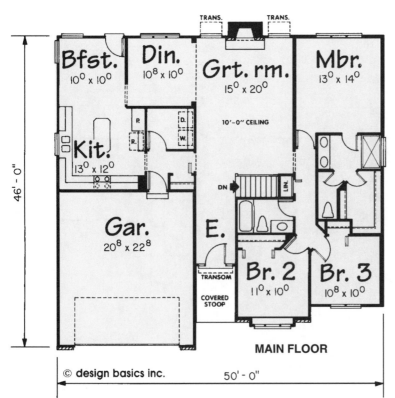

TRANS.   TRANS.

Bfst.
10⁰ x 10⁰

Din.
10⁸ x 10⁰

Grt. rm.
15⁰ x 20⁰

Mbr.
13⁰ x 14⁰

10'-0" CEILING

P.

D.

R.

W.

Kit.
13⁰ x 12⁰

DN

LIN.

46'-0"

Gar.
20⁸ x 22⁸

E.

Br. 2
11⁰ x 10⁰

Br. 3
10⁸ x 10⁰

TRANSOM

COVERED
STOOP

MAIN FLOOR

© design basics inc.   50'-0"

No. 97445

■ **This plan features:**

— Three bedrooms

— Two full baths

■ The covered stoop shelters the front entrance to the home

■ Windows with transoms above, flank the cozy fireplace in the Great Room

■ A box window highlights one of the secondary Bedrooms

■ The Master Bedroom has a private Bath

■ The Kitchen has a center work island and a bright Breakfest Area

■ The Dining Room opens to the Great Room

Main floor — 1,628 sq. ft.
Garage — 487 sq. ft.

Unity Distinguishes Plan

■ *Total living area 1,630 sq. ft.* ■ *Price Code B* ■

No. 90398 BL X

■ **This plan features:**

— Three bedrooms

— Two full baths

■ A vaulted ceiling and a cozy fireplace are located in the Living Room

■ Columns divide the Living and Dining Rooms, and a half-wall separates the Kitchen and Breakfast Room

■ The luxurious Master Suite has a Sitting Area with a private sky-lit Bath, double vanity and a generous walk-in closet

Main floor —1,630 sq. ft.

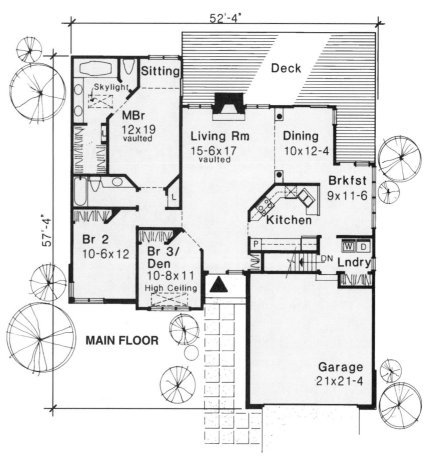

52'-4"

Sitting

Deck

Skylight

MBr
12x19
vaulted

Living Rm
15-6x17
vaulted

Dining
10x12-4

Brkfst
9x11-6

Kitchen

57'-4"

Br 2
10-6x12

Br 3/
Den
10-8x11
High Ceiling

P

W D

DN

Lndry

MAIN FLOOR

Garage
21x21-4

Beautiful From Front to Back

Design by Donald A. Gardner Architects, Inc.

© 1995 Donald A. Gardner Architects, Inc.

B. NATHAN

■ *Total living area 1,632 sq. ft.* ■ *Price Code D* ■

No. 99840

■ **This plan features:**

— Three bedrooms

— Two full baths

■ Porches front and back, gables and dormers provide a special charm

■ The central Great Room has a cathedral ceiling, fireplace, and a clerestory window

■ Columns divide the open Great Room from the Kitchen and the Breakfast Bay

■ A tray ceiling and columns dress up the formal Dining Room

■ The skylit Master Bath has a shower, a whirlpool tub , a dual vanity and a spacious walk-in closet

Main floor — 1,632 sq. ft.
Garage & Storage — 561 sq. ft.

Elegantly Adorned

■ *Total living area 1,633 sq. ft.* ■ *Price Code B* ■

No. 98337

■ **This plan features:**

– Three bedrooms

– Two full baths

■ The large fireplace is flanked by windows enhancing the Living Room

■ Columns accent the entrance into the formal Dining Room

■ The Kitchen is efficiently appointed

■ The Master Suite is designed with an intimate Sitting Area and a private Bath

Main floor — 1,633 sq. ft.
Basement — 1,633 sq. ft.
Garage — 450 sq. ft.

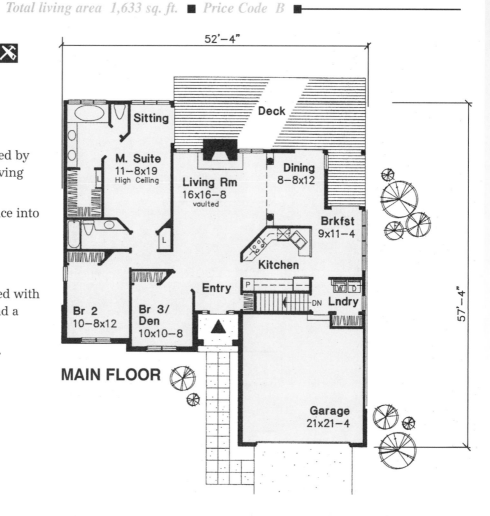

52'–4"

Sitting

M. Suite
11–8x19
High Ceiling

Deck

Dining
8–8x12

Living Rm
16x16–8
vaulted

Brkfst
9x11–4

Kitchen

Br 2
10–8x12

Br 3/
Den
10x10–8

Entry

Lndry

DN

57'–4"

MAIN FLOOR

Garage
21x21–4

Grow In Style

Design by Donald A. Gardner Architects, Inc.

©1995 Donald A. Gardner Architects, Inc.

B. NATHAN

■ *Total living area 1,633 sq. ft.* ■ *Price Code D* ■

MAIN FLOOR

© 1995 Donald A Gardner Architects, Inc.

BONUS

No. 96463

■ **This plan features:**

— Three bedrooms

— Two full baths

■ The open Great Room and Kitchen are enlarged by a cathedral ceiling

■ The wooden rear Deck expands entertaining to the outdoors

■ The cathedral ceiling adds volume and drama to the Master Suite

■ The flexible Bedroom/Study includes a cathedral ceiling and a double window with an arched top

■ The second floor Bonus space may be finished as two more Bedrooms

Main floor — 1,633 sq. ft.
Garage & storage — 512 sq. ft.
Bonus — 595 sq. ft.

Brick and Fieldstone

■ *Total living area 1,640 sq. ft.* ■ *Price Code B* ■

No. 98580 BL

■ This plan features:

— Three bedrooms

— Two full baths

■ The stately appearance of entrance and arched windows gives style to this modest plan

■ The Great Room opens to the Study, the Covered Patio and the Dining Area/Kitchen

■ The efficient Kitchen features a Pantry, serving ledge and bright Dining Area

■ The Master Bedroom wing offers access to a covered Patio, a huge walk-in closet and a whirlpool Bath

■ No materials list is available for this plan

Main floor — 1,640 sq. ft.
Garage — 408 sq. ft.

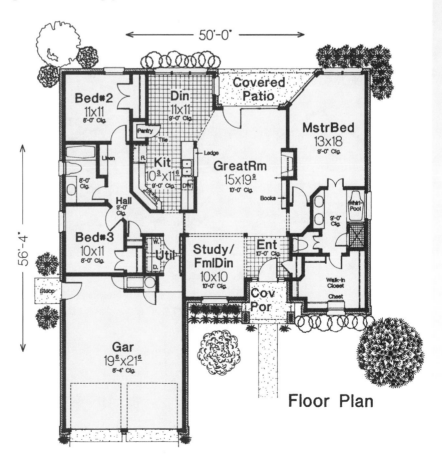

Floor Plan

Flexible Floor Plan

Design by Perfect Plan

No. 99657 BL ✗

■ **This plan features:**

— Three bedrooms

— Two full baths

■ The Sheltering entrance Porch leads into the open Foyer, Living and Dining Rooms

■ The comfortable Dining Room has an elegant bow window

■ The spacious Living Room is enhanced by skylight, inviting fireplace, and Terrace access

■ The Country-size Kitchen offers a bright Dining Area with Terrace access, Laundry closet and Garage entry

■ The corner Master Bedroom offers a large walk-in closet and deluxe bath with a whirlpool tub

■ Two additional Bedrooms share a double vanity Bath

■ The convenient Den can be easily converted to an Office or fourth Bedroom

Main floor — 1,641 sq. ft.
Garage — 427 sq. ft.
Basement — 1,667 sq. ft.

Total living area 1,641 sq. ft. ■ Price Code B

Keystones, Arches and Gables

Design by Ahmann Design, Inc.

No. 93171 BL

■ **This plan features:**

— Three bedrooms

— Two full and one half baths

■ The tiled Entry opens to the Living Room with focal point fireplace

■ An U-shaped Kitchen has a built-in Pantry, Eating Bar and nearby Laundry/Garage entry

■ The comfortable Dining Room has a bay window and French doors for access to the screened Porch which expands the living area outdoors

■ The corner Master Bedroom offers a great walk-in closet and private Bath

■ Two additional Bedrooms have ample closets, double windows and share a full Bath

■ No materials list is available for this plan

Main floor — 1,642 sq. ft.
Basement — 1,642 sq. ft.

Total living area 1,642 sq. ft. ■ Price Code B

Design by Barclay Home Designs, Inc.

No. 90502

■ This plan features:

— Three bedrooms

— Two full baths

■ The sheltered Entry opens to an airy Living/Dining Room with an inviting fireplace

■ The central Family Room has another fireplace and opens to the Nook with access to covered the Patio

■ The open Kitchen is convenient to the Dining Area, Nook and Patio beyond

■ French doors open to Master Suite with Patio access and a private Bath

■ Two additional Bedrooms have ample closets and share a full Bath

Main floor — 1,642 sq. ft.

Stucco Captures Shade

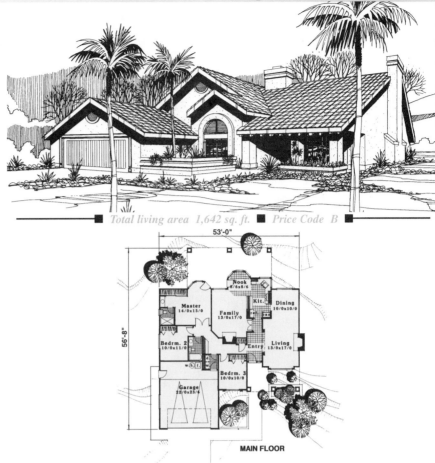

Total living area 1,642 sq. ft. ■ *Price Code B* ■

MAIN FLOOR

Design by The Garlinghouse Company

No. 24717

■ This plan features:

— Three bedrooms

— Two full baths

■ The welcoming front Porch is enhanced by graceful columns and curved windows

■ The Parlor and Dining Room frame the Entry hall

■ The expansive Great Room is accented by a corner fireplace and outdoor access

■ The open and convenient Kitchen has a work island, angled peninsula counter/eating bar, and nearby Laundry and Garage entry

■ The secluded Master Bedroom has a large walk-in closet and luxurious Bath with a dressing table

■ The two additional Bedrooms have ample closets, share a double vanity Bath

■ No materials list is available for this plan

Main floor — 1,642 sq. ft.
Garage — 420 sq. ft.
Basement — 1,642 sq. ft.

Arches are Appealing

Total living area 1,642 sq. ft. ■ *Price Code B* ■

Optional Basement Stairs

Floor Plan

Convenient Single Level

Design by The Garlinghouse Company

No. 84056 BL

■ **This plan features:**

— Three bedrooms

— Two full baths

■ The well-appointed U-shaped Kitchen includes a view of the front yard and a built-in Pantry

■ The expansive Great Room has direct access to the rear yard, expanding the living space

■ The Master Bedroom is equipped with two closets, one a walk-in, and a private Bath

■ The two additional Bedrooms share a full hall Bath

■ No materials list is available for this plan

Main floor — 1,644 sq. ft.
Garage — 576 sq. ft.

■ Total living area 1,644 sq. ft. ■ Price Code B ■

MAIN FLOOR

52'-0"

Optional Garage
24 x 24

Dining/Living
25-8 x 15

Br 1
12 x 15-10

32'-0"

DN pan.

Breakfast
10 x 12-6

Kit
10 x 12-6

Entry

Br 2
10-8 x 11-8

Br 3
12 x 11-8

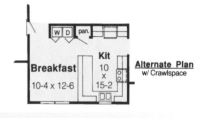

Breakfast
10-4 x 12-6

Kit
10 x 15-2

Alternate Plan
w/ Crawlspace

Split Bedroom Design

Design by Jannis Vann & Associates, Inc.

No. 98920 BL

■ **This plan features:**

— Three bedrooms

— Two full baths

■ Built-in cabinets are set between the fireplace in the Living Room

■ A bay window extends the Dining Room

■ This plan features a well-planned Kitchen

■ The Master Bedroom has a tray ceiling

■ The secondary Bedrooms have walk-in closets

■ No materials list is available for this plan

■ An optional slab or crawl space foundation — please specify when ordering

Main floor — 1,646 sq. ft.

■ Total living area 1,646 sq. ft. ■ Price Code B ■

Patio
16-0 x 12-0

Dining
14-2 x 13-6
w/Bay

Vaulted Living Area
17-4 x 17-6

Master Bdrm.
13-6 x 16-2
w/Bay

Kitchen
14-2 x 12-0

Bth.2

M.Bath

Foyer
6-0 x 13-10

Storage

Bdrm.2
10-2 x 11-6

Bdrm.3
10-6 x 11-6

54-0

Double Garage
21-4 x 19-8

MAIN FLOOR

52-0

©1997 Jannis Vann & Associates, Inc.

Modernized Country Theme

No. 96513 BL X

This plan features:

– Three bedrooms

– Two full and one half baths

■ Open living areas are spacious and airy

■ The Great Room is accented by a quaint, corner fireplace and a ceiling fan

■ The Dining Room is open to the Great Room and the Kitchen which is illuminated by an attractive bay window

■ The Kitchen snack bar conveniently serves informal meals on the go

■ The Master Bedroom is secluded in its own separate wing for total privacy

■ Two additional Bedrooms share a full Bath in the hall

Main floor — 1,648 sq. ft.
Garage — 479 sq. ft.

Total living area 1,648 sq. ft. ■ Price Code B

MAIN FLOOR

Family Friendly

No. 97442 BL X

This plan features:

– Three bedrooms

– Two full baths

■ A desk in the Kitchen allows mom to supervise homework

■ A bay window extends the Breakfast Nook

■ The plan features an open rail staircase to the Basement

■ A tray ceiling and hutch space highlight the Dining Room

■ A whirlpool tub is located in the Master Bath

■ Double windows are found in both of the secondary Bedrooms

Main floor — 1,650 sq. ft.
Garage — 529 sq. ft.

Total living area 1,650 sq. ft. ■ Price Code B

© design basics inc.

Brick and Wood Facade

Design by Design Basics, Inc.

No. 94921 [BL] [X]

■ **This plan features:**

— Two or three bedrooms

— Two full baths

■ Covered front and rear Porches expand the living space outside

■ The handy Serving Area is located between the formal Dining Room and expansive Great Room

■ Transom windows frame the hearth fireplace in the Great Room and highlight Breakfast Room

■ The hub Kitchen has a built-in Pantry, snack bar and adjoins Laundry/Garage entry

■ French doors lead into the Den with wetbar

■ The exclusive Master Suite includes decorative ceiling, walk-in closet, twin vanity and a corner whirlpool tub

Main floor — 1,651 sq. ft.
Basement — 1,651 sq. ft.
Garage — 480 sq. ft.

■ Total living area 1,651 sq. ft. ■ Price Code B ■

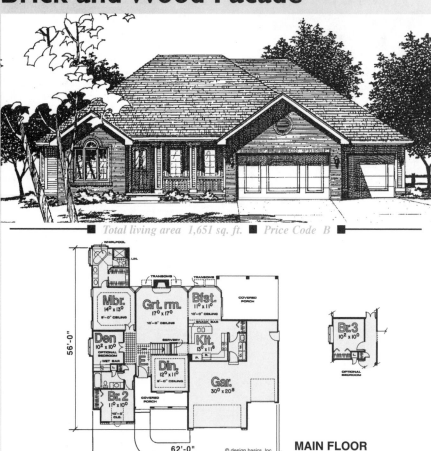

MAIN FLOOR

© design basics, Inc.

Dormer Delight

Design by Donald A. Gardner Architects, Inc.

No. 98058 [BL]

■ **This plan features:**

— Three bedrooms

— Two full baths

■ Tray ceilings can be found in the Dining Room and the Master Suite

■ Skylights brighten the Master Bath and the screened Porch

■ Columns mark the openings of the Dining Room

■ The Great Room has a voluminous cathedral ceiling

■ The Bonus Room is located over the Garage

■ No materials list is available for this plan

Main floor — 1,652 sq. ft.
Bonus — 367 sq. ft.
Garage — 507 sq. ft.

■ Total living area 1,652 sq. ft. ■ Price Code D ■

©1997 Donald A. Gardner Architects, Inc.

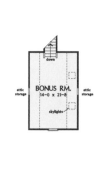

FLOOR PLAN

© 1997 Donald A Gardner Architects, Inc.

Design by Vaughn A. Lauban Designs

No. 96523 BL ✗

■ This plan features:

— Three bedrooms

— Two full baths

■ The spacious Great Room is highlighted by a corner fireplace and accesses the rear Porch

■ The Dining Area has views of the front yard and is separated from the Kitchen by an Eating Bar

■ The private Master Suite is tucked into the rear left corner of the home

■ A tray ceiling, a whirlpool tub and a walk-in closet highlight the Master Suite

■ Two additional Bedrooms are located on the opposite side of the home and share a full Bath

■ An optional slab or crawl space foundation — please specify when ordering this plan

Main floor — 1,652 sq. ft.
Garage — 497 sq. ft.

Total living area 1,652 sq. ft. ■ Price Code B

MAIN FLOOR

Design by Fillmore Design Group

No. 92283 BL

■ This plan features:

— Three bedrooms

— Two full baths

■ A sheltered Porch leads into an easy-care tiled Entry

■ The spacious Living Room offers a cozy fireplace, triple window and access to Patio

■ The efficient Kitchen has a skylight, work island, Dining Area, walk-in Pantry and Utility/Garage entry

■ The secluded Master Bedroom is highlighted by a vaulted ceiling, features a lavish Bath and access to the Patio

■ Two additional Bedrooms, one with a cathedral ceiling, share a full Bath

■ No materials list is available for this plan

Main floor — 1,653 sq. ft.
Garage — 420 sq. ft.

Total living area 1,653 sq. ft. ■ Price Code B

Main Floor

Open Layout

Design by Vaughn A. Lauban Designs

No. 96506 BL ✕

■ **This plan features:**

— Three bedrooms

— Two full and one half baths

■ The Great Room and Master Suite have step-up ceiling treatments

■ A cozy fireplace provides a warm focal point to the Great Room

■ An open layout in the Kitchen, Dining and Great Rooms provides a spacious feeling

■ The five-piece, private Bath and walk-in closet accentuate the Master Suite

■ Two additional Bedrooms are located away from the Master Suite and share the full Bath in the hall

Main floor — 1,654 sq. ft.
Garage — 480 sq. ft.

■ Total living area 1,654 sq. ft. ■ Price Code B ■

WIDTH 68'-0"
DEPTH 46'-0"

9' CEILINGS

MAIN FLOOR

Garage in the Rear

Design by Larry E. Belk

No. 93078 BL

■ **This plan features:**

— Three bedrooms

— Two full baths

■ The Garage has extra storage space

■ Columns are used instead of walls to separate rooms in the family living area

■ A large walk-in Pantry is featured

■ The Master Bedroom and Bath have high ceilings

■ No materials list is available for this plan

Main floor — 1,654 sq. ft.
Garage — 591 sq. ft.

■ Total living area 1,654 sq. ft. ■ Price Code B ■

MAIN FLOOR

WIDTH 54'-10"

Cozy See-Through Fireplace

No. 93426 [BL]

■ This plan features:

– Three bedrooms

– Two full baths

■ The Family Room is enhanced by a see-through fireplace and a pass-through from the Kitchen

■ The Dining Area has access to the outside

■ The Kitchen includes a work island, a double sink and direct access to the Laundry Room

■ The Master Suite is located to the rear of the home and is accessed from the Dining Area

■ A lavish Bath and a walk-in closet highlight the Master Suite

■ Two additional Bedrooms have walk-in closets and easy access to the full Bath in the hall

■ No material list is available for this plan

Main floor — 1,655 sq. ft.
Garage — 484 sq. ft.

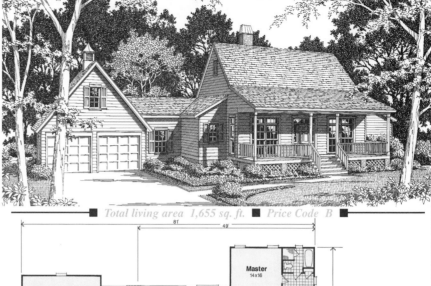

Total living area 1,655 sq. ft. ■ Price Code B

Floor Plan

Open Family Living Space

No. 96518 [BL][X]

■ This plan features:

– Three bedrooms

– Two full baths

■ An open layout in the expansive family living area promotes family interaction

■ A cooktop Eating Bar highlights the Kitchen and the Dining Areas

■ A fireplace adds coziness to the Great Room

■ The Dining Area directly accesses the Porch

■ The Master Suite is crowned in a decorative ceiling and includes a private four-piece Bath

■ Two additional Bedrooms share the full Bath in the hall

Main floor — 1,657 sq. ft.
Garage — 555 sq. ft.

Total living area 1,657 sq. ft. ■ Price Code B

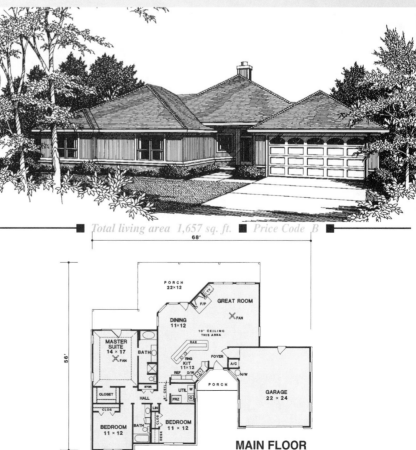

MAIN FLOOR

187

Striking Traditional

Design by Donald A. Gardner Architects, Inc.

No. 98062

■ **This plan features:**

— Three bedrooms

— Two full baths

■ A cathedral ceiling expands the Great Room, Dining Room, and Kitchen; all are open to one another for a casual atmosphere

■ The efficient, U-shaped Kitchen positions sink, stove and refrigerator in perfect proximity

■ The front Bedroom and the Master Bedroom have cathedral ceilings for added spaciousness

■ Both the Great Room and the Master Bedroom allow access to an optional rear Deck or Patio

Main floor — 1,658 sq. ft.
Garage & storage — 522 sq. ft.
Bonus — 359 sq. ft.

Total living area 1,658 sq. ft. ■ Price Code D

©1998 Donald A. Gardner, Inc.

FLOOR PLAN

© 1998 Donald A Gardner, Inc.

Well Proportioned

Design by Perfect Plan

No. 99668

■ **This plan features:**

— Three bedrooms

— Two full baths

■ The Great Room has a corner fireplace

■ The Dining Room accesses a private Terrace

■ A boxed bay window and walk-in closet graces the Master Suite

■ The secondary Bedrooms share a full Bath

■ The Garage is located in the rear of the home

Main floor — 1,658 sq. ft.
Basement — 1,658 sq. ft.
Garage — 473 sq. ft.

Total living area 1,658 sq. ft. ■ Price Code B

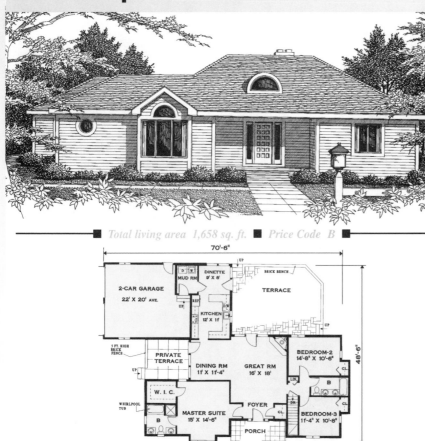

MAIN FLOOR

Design by Rick Garner

No. 92560

■ This plan features:

- Three bedrooms
- Two full baths
- ■ This Traditional Country home features front and rear covered Porches
- ■ A peninsula counter/eating bar for meals on the go is found in the Kitchen
- ■ The formal Dining Room includes a built-in cabinet
- ■ A vaulted ceiling and a cozy fireplace highlight the Den
- ■ The Master Suite located in a private corner features a five-piece Bath
- ■ This split Bedroom plan has two additional Bedrooms that share a full Bath
- ■ An optional slab or crawl space foundation — please specify when ordering

Main floor — 1,660 sq. ft.
Garage — 544 sq. ft.

Total living area 1,660 sq. ft. ■ *Price Code B* ■

MAIN FLOOR

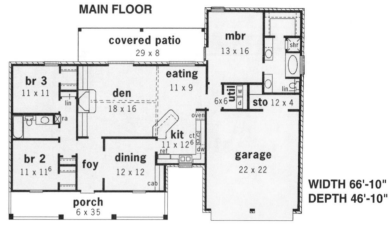

WIDTH 66'-10"
DEPTH 46'-10"

Design by Fillmore Design Group

No. 92238 BL X

■ This plan features:

- Three bedrooms
- Two full baths
- ■ The front entrance is accented by segmented arches, sidelight and transom windows
- ■ The open Living Room has a focal point fireplace, wetbar and access to Patio
- ■ The Dining Area is open to both the Living Room and the Kitchen
- ■ The efficient Kitchen has a cooktop island, walk-in Pantry and Utility Area with a Garage entry
- ■ A large walk-in closet, double vanity Bath and access to Patio are featured in the Master Suite
- ■ Two additional Bedrooms share a double vanity Bath

Main floor — 1,664 sq. ft.
Basement — 1,600 sq. ft.
Garage — 440 sq. ft

Total living area 1,664 sq. ft. ■ *Price Code B* ■

Main Floor

Carefree Comfort

Design by Sun-tel

■ *Total living area 1,665 sq. ft.* ■ *Price Code B* ■

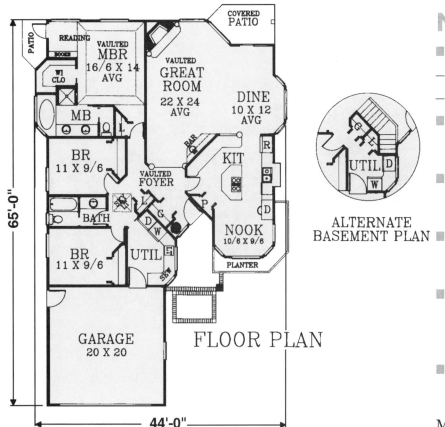

65'-0"

44'-0"

COVERED PATIO

PATIO

READING

BOOKS

VAULTED
MBR
16/6 X 14
AVG

WI
CLO

MB

BR
11 X 9/6

VAULTED
GREAT
ROOM
22 X 24
AVG

DINE
10 X 12
AVG

BAR

KIT

R

VAULTED
FOYER

NOOK
10/6 X 9/6

BATH

UTIL

D

W

SEW

PLANTER

BR
11 X 9/6

GARAGE
20 X 20

FLOOR PLAN

No. 91418 BL ✕

■ **This plan features:**

— Three bedrooms

— Two full baths

■ The Kitchen has a range top island and a sunny eating Nook surrounded by a built-in planter

■ A vaulted ceiling is found in the Great Room which also has a built-in bar and corner fireplace

■ The Dining Room with a bay window combines with the Great Room for a spacious feel

■ The Master Bedroom has a private Reading Nook, vaulted ceiling, walk-in closet, and a well-appointed private Bath

■ An optional basement, crawl space or slab foundation — please specify when ordering

Main floor — 1,665 sq. ft.

UTIL

D

W

ALTERNATE BASEMENT PLAN

Decorative Windows

■ *Total living area 1,666 sq. ft.* ■ *Price Code B* ■

No. 94923

■ **This plan features:**

— Three bedrooms

— Two full baths

■ Brick and stucco enhance the dramatic front elevation and entrance

■ The inviting Entry leads into the expansive Great Room with a hearth fireplace framed by transom windows

■ The Dining Room features a bay window and a decorative ceiling and is convenient to the Great Room and the Kitchen/Breakfast Area

■ The corner Master Suite has a tray ceiling, roomy walk-in closet and a plush Bath with a double vanity and whirlpool window tub

Main floor — 1,666 sq. ft.
Basement — 1,666 sq. ft.
Garage — 496 sq. ft.

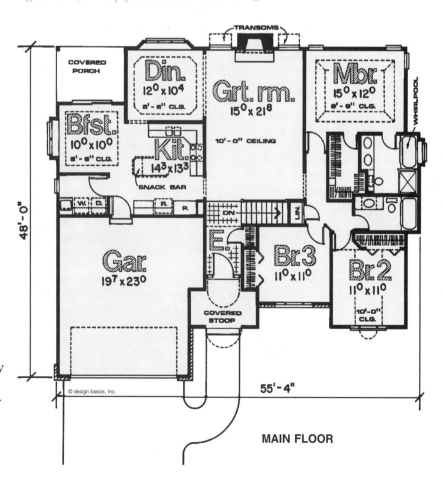

MAIN FLOOR

Rocking Chair Living

Design by Corley Plan Service

No. 90409

- This plan features:
  - Three bedrooms
  - Two full baths
- A massive fireplace separates the Living and Dining Rooms
- The isolated Master Suite has a walk-in closet and private Bath
- The galley-type Kitchen is located between the Breakfast Room and Dining Room
- An optional basement, slab or crawl space foundation — please specify when ordering

Main floor — 1,670 sq. ft.
Basement — 1,670 sq. ft.
Garage — 427 sq. ft.

Total living area 1,670 sq. ft. • *Price Code B*

MAIN FLOOR

Keystones and Arched Windows

Design by Frank Betz Associates, Inc.

No. 98432

- **This plan features:**
  - Three bedrooms
  - Two full baths
- A large arched window in the Dining Room offers eye-catching appeal
- A decorative column helps to define the Dining Room from the Great Room
- A fireplace and French door to the rear yard are found in the Great Room
- The efficient Kitchen includes a serving bar, Pantry and pass-through to the Great Room
- A vaulted ceiling is highlighted over the Breakfast Room
- The plush Master Suite includes a private Bath and a walk-in closet
- An optional basement, slab or crawl space foundation — please specify when ordering

Main floor — 1,670 sq. ft.
Garage — 240 sq. ft.

Total living area 1,670 sq. ft. • *Price Code B*

MAIN FLOOR

Design by Frank Betz Associates, Inc.

No. 98423

■ This plan features:

— Three bedrooms

— Two full baths

■ The spacious Family Room is topped by a vaulted ceiling and has a fireplace for cozy evenings at home

■ A Serving Bar is open to the Family Room and the Dining Room

■ A crowning tray ceiling is featured in the Master Bedroom with a vaulted ceiling in the Master Bath and adjacent Sitting Area

■ A vaulted ceiling is located over the Sitting Room in the Master Bedroom

■ The two additional Bedrooms, roomy in size, share a full Bath in the hall

■ An optional basement, slab or crawl space foundation — please specify when ordering

Main floor — 1,671 sq. ft.
Basement — 1,685 sq. ft.
Garage — 400 sq. ft.

Total living area 1,671 sq. ft. ■ *Price Code B*

MAIN FLOOR

© Frank Betz Associates, Inc.

Design by The Garlinghouse Company

No. 34011

■ This plan features:

— Three bedrooms

— Two full baths

■ The Master Suite has huge dual walk-in closets and a private Bath

■ The second and third Bedrooms have ample closet space

■ The Kitchen is equipped with an island counter, and is adjacent to the Dining and Family Rooms

■ The Laundry Room is conveniently located near all three Bedrooms

■ An optional Garage is also featured

Main floor— 1,672 sq. ft.
Garage — 566 sq. ft.

Total living area 1,672 sq. ft. ■ *Price Code B*

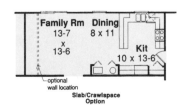

Family Rm
13-7
x
13-6

Dining
8 x 11

Kit
10 x 13-6

optional wall location

Slab/Crawlspace Option

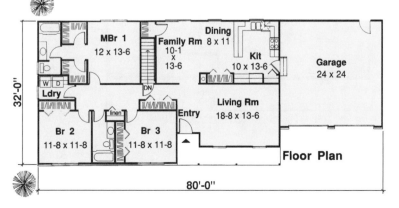

Floor Plan

193

Four Bedrooms

■ *Total living area 1,676 sq. ft.* ■ *Price Code B* ■

No. 96537 🄱🄻

■ **This plan features:**

— Four bedrooms

— Two full baths

■ There is a workbench and storage space in the Garage

■ The huge Great Room has a corner fireplace

■ The galley Kitchen opens into the Dining Room

■ The Master Suite has a ceiling fan

■ One of the secondary Bedrooms can be used as a Study

■ No materials list is available for this plan

Main floor — 1,676 sq. ft.
Garage — 420 sq. ft.

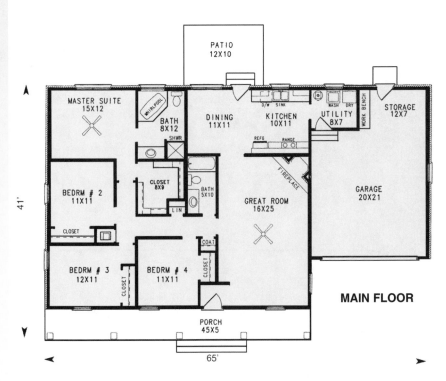

MAIN FLOOR

Design by Donald A. Gardner Architects, Inc.

Cozy Plan

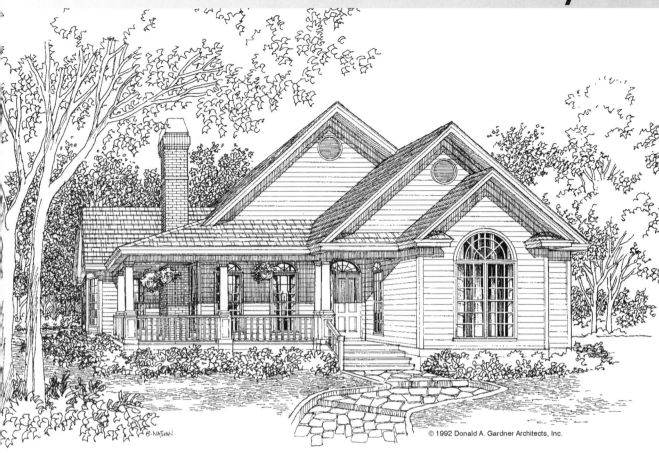

© 1992 Donald A. Gardner Architects, Inc.

■ *Total living area 1,677 sq. ft.* ■ *Price Code D* ■

No. 96482

■ This plan features:

— Three bedrooms

— Two full baths

■ Lovely columns support the covered Porches

■ The covered Breezeway leads to the Garage in the rear

■ The Dining Room has a tray ceiling and a bay window

■ A fireplace warms the Great Room

■ One of the secondary Bedrooms can be used as a Study

■ The Master Bedroom has ample closet space

Main floor — 1,677 sq. ft.
Garage — 504 sq. ft.

FLOOR PLAN

© Donald A. Gardner Architects, Inc.

Secluded Master Suite

Design by Rick Garner

No. 92527 BL X

This plan features:

— Three bedrooms

— Two full baths

This is a convenient one-level design with an open floor plan between the Kitchen, Breakfast Area and Great Room

A vaulted ceiling and a cozy fireplace are featured in the spacious Great Room

The well-equipped Kitchen uses a peninsula counter as an Eating Bar

The Master Suite has a luxurious Master Bath

The two additional Bedrooms share a full hall Bath

An optional slab or crawl space foundation — please specify when ordering

Main floor — 1,680 sq. ft.
Garage — 538 sq. ft.

Total living area 1,680 sq. ft. ■ *Price Code B*

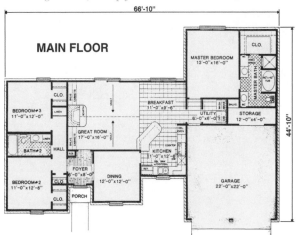

MAIN FLOOR

66'-10"

44'-10"

MASTER BEDROOM
13'-0"x16'-0"

CLO.

BEDROOM #3
11'-0"x12'-0"

GREAT ROOM
17'-0"x16'-0"

BREAKFAST
11'-0"x9'-6"

UTILITY
6'-0"x6'-0"

STORAGE
12'-0"x4'-0"

MASTER BATH

BATH #2

HALL

KITCHEN
11'-0"x12'-0"

FOYER
6'-0"x8'-0"

DINING
12'-0"x12'-0"

GARAGE
22'-0"x22'-0"

CLO.

PORCH

Bright Master Bedroom

Design by The Garlinghouse Company

No. 34029 BL X 🇺🇸 ℝ

This plan features:

— Three bedrooms

— Two full baths

This home features a covered Porch entry

The Foyer separates the Dining Room from the Breakfast Area and Kitchen

The Living Room is enhanced by a vaulted beam ceiling and a fireplace

The Master Bedroom has a decorative ceiling and a skylight in the private Bath

An optional Deck is accessible through sliding glass doors in the Master Bedroom

Main floor — 1,686 sq. ft.
Basement — 1,676 sq. ft.
Garage — 484 sq. ft.

Total living area 1,686 sq. ft. ■ *Price Code B*

61'-0"

54'-0"

Optional Deck

Br #2
14-7 x 11-4

Living Rm
13-5 x 23-4
vaulted Beams

MBR #1
15-6 x 18-6

opt. decor ceiling

skylight above

Br #3
11-1 x 11-4

Ldry

Kit
11-10 x 12-0

Brkfst
8-10 x 10-1

Foy

Dining
10-5 x 12-0

opt. decor ceiling

Garage
21-5 x 21-4

MAIN FLOOR

Crawl Space Access

Furn

Slab/Crawl Space Option

Elegant Ceiling Treatments

Design by Frank Betz Associates, Inc.

No. 97254

■ This plan features:

— Three Bedrooms

— Two full baths

■ The cozy wrap-around front Porch shelters the entrance

■ The Dining Room is defined by entrance columns

■ The Kitchen is highlighted by a peninsula counter/Serving Bar

■ The Breakfast Room is adjacent to the Kitchen

■ A vaulted ceiling highlights the Great Room which also includes a fireplace

■ The Master Suite has a tray ceiling over the Bedroom, a Sitting Room and a plush Master Bath

■ An optional basement or crawl space foundation — please specify when ordering

■ No materials list is available for this plan

Main floor — 1,692 sq. ft.
Bonus room — 358 sq. ft.
Basement — 1,705 sq. ft.
Garage — 472 sq. ft.

■ *Total living area 1,692 sq. ft.* ■ *Price Code B* ■

FLOOR PLAN

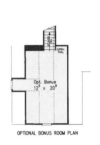

OPTIONAL BONUS ROOM PLAN

Two Separate Dining Areas

Design by L.M. Brunier & Associates, Inc.

No. 91349

■ This plan features:

— Three bedrooms

— Two full baths

■ The Entry has a vaulted ceiling

■ The Living Room has a vaulted ceiling, and is accented by a bay window and an optional fireplace

■ A garden window, Eating Bar, and an abundance of storage space are featured in the efficient Kitchen

■ The Master Bedroom has a private Bath, with a double sink vanity and a walk-in closet

■ The Library has a vaulted ceiling option and a window seat

Main floor — 1,694 sq. ft.

■ *Total living area 1,694 sq. ft.* ■ *Price Code B* ■

MAIN FLOOR

Open Floor Plan

Design by Donald A. Gardner Architects, Inc.

B. NATHAN.

© 1997 Donald A. Gardner Architects, Inc.

■ *Total living area 1,695 sq. ft.* ■ *Price Code D* ■

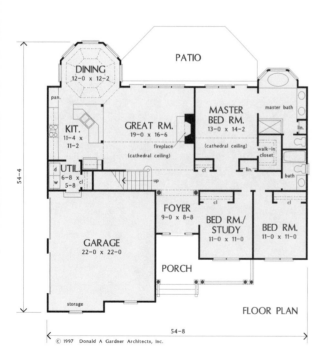

FLOOR PLAN

© 1997 Donald A Gardner Architects, Inc.

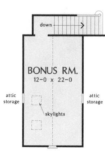

No. 96488

■ **This plan features:**

— Three bedrooms

— Two full and one half baths

■ Cathedral and tray ceilings add vertical volume to home

■ The Great Room has a fireplace and is crowned by a cathedral ceiling

■ The octagonal shaped Dining Room is adjacent to the Great Room and the Kitchen

■ The Kitchen is defined by columns and has a Pantry

■ The Master Suite has a cathedral ceiling, Patio access, a walk-in closet, and a lavish Bath

■ Bonus space above the Garage provides extra room for storage and expansion

Main floor — 1,695 sq. ft.
Bonus room — 287 sq. ft.
Garage & storage — 527 sq. ft.

Good Balance

Total living area 1,699 sq. ft. ■ *Price Code B* ■

No. 98814 **BL**

■ This plan features:

— Three bedrooms

— Two full baths

■ Windows highlight the connected Dining and Living Rooms

■ The Family Room includes a gas fireplace and covered Patio access

■ A bay window adds light to the Breakfast Nook

■ The Kitchen includes a Pantry and planning desk

■ The secondary Bedrooms are identical in size

■ The Master Suite overlooks the rear yard

■ No materials list is available for this plan

Main floor — 1,699 sq. ft.
Garage — 470 sq. ft.

MAIN FLOOR PLAN

WIDTH 50'-0"
DEPTH 56'-0"

European Sophistication

Design by Donald A. Gardner Architects, Inc.

© 1996 Donald A Gardner Architects, Inc.

■ *Total living area 1,699 sq. ft.* ■ *Price Code D* ■

FLOOR PLAN

© 1996 Donald A Gardner Architects, Inc.

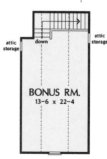

BONUS RM.
13-6 x 22-4

No. 99831

■ **This plan features:**

— Three bedrooms

— Two full baths

■ Keystone arches, gables, and stucco give the exterior a European touch

■ The Large Great Room has a fireplace, and the U-shaped Kitchen has access to the large Utility Room

■ An octagonal tray ceiling adds style to the Dining Room

■ Special ceiling treatments include a cathedral ceiling in the Great Room, and tray ceilings in the Master and front Bedrooms

■ An indulgent Master Bath includes a separate toilet area, a garden tub, shower and dual vanity

■ The Bonus Room adds flexibility

Main floor — 1,699 sq. ft.
Garage — 637 sq. ft.
Bonus — 386 sq. ft.

Design by Donald A. Gardner Architects, Inc.

Stucco and Stone

© Donald A. Gardner Architects, Inc.

■ *Total living area 1,700 sq. ft.* ■ *Price Code D* ■

No. 98086

■ This plan features:

— Three bedrooms

— Two full baths

■ This home has a low maintenance exterior

■ The covered Porch leads into the Foyer

■ The Bedroom off the Foyer would make a great Study

■ A cathedral ceiling adds height to the Great Room

■ The Master Bedroom is located in a private spot

■ The Bonus Room over the Garage expands your options

Main floor — 1,700 sq. ft.
Bonus — 294 sq. ft.
Garage — 464 sq. ft.

DECK

(cathedral ceiling)

fireplace

MASTER BED RM.
13-0 x 15-8

GREAT RM.
22-0 x 16-0

DINING
13-8 x 11-0

FOYER
5-0 x 12-4

KITCHEN
13-8 x 10-4

master bath

BED RM.
11-0 x 12-0

walk-in closet

pan.
lin.

bath

PORCH

BED RM.
11-4 x 12-0

d
w

(optional storage)

FLOOR PLAN

cl
up

GARAGE
20-4 x 20-0

down

attic storage

BONUS RM.
12-8 x 20-2

attic storage

63-8

8-0

50-0

© 1998 Donald A Gardner, Inc.

Magnificent Master Suite

Design by The Garlinghouse Company

Total living area 1,702 sq. ft. ■ **Price Code B** ■

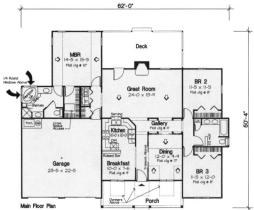

No. 24719 BL

■ **This plan features:**

— Three bedrooms

— Two full baths

■ Soft arches and friendly dormers enhance covered Porch

■ The front Hall between Kitchen and the Dining Room leads to the Gallery and the Great Room beyond

■ The formal Dining Room has a dormer window and pocket doors

■ The expansive Great Room has a cozy fireplace and Deck access

■ The angled and efficient Kitchen has serving counter, extended raised bar and bright Breakfast Area

■ The secluded Master Bedroom has a large walk-in closet and lavish Bath with two vanities and a corner whirlpool tub

■ The two additional Bedrooms have ample closets and share a double vanity Bath

■ No materials list is available for this plan

Main floor — 1,702 sq. ft.
Garage — 540 sq. ft.

Superbly Styled

Design by Fillmore Design Group

Total living area 1,706 sq. ft. ■ **Price Code B** ■

No. 92268 BL

■ **This plan features:**

— Four bedrooms

— Two full baths

■ The covered Porch leads to the Entry which has a nine-foot ceiling

■ The Living Room has a rear wall fireplace and access to the covered Patio

■ The L-shaped Kitchen features a center island and opens into the Dining Room

■ The Master Bedroom has a ten-foot vaulted ceiling plus a private Bath with a cathedral ceiling

■ The two secondary Bedrooms share a hall Bath, while a fourth Bedroom could be used as a Study

■ This plan has a two-car Garage

■ No materials list is available for this plan

Main floor — 1,706 sq. ft.
Garage — 399 sq. ft.

Design by Frank Betz Associates, Inc.

High Ceilings Add Volume

No. 98456 BL ✗

■ **This plan features:**

— Three bedrooms

— Two full baths

■ The covered entry opens to a fourteen-foot high ceiling in the Foyer

■ An arched opening leads into the Great Room which has a vaulted ceiling and a fireplace

■ The Dining Room is brightened by triple windows with transoms above

■ The Kitchen is a gourmet's delight and is open to the Breakfast Nook

■ The Master Suite has a tray ceiling, a vaulted ceiling in the Sitting Area and a private Bath

■ The two Bedrooms on the opposite side of the home share the Bath in the hall

■ An optional basement, slab or crawl space foundation — please specify when ordering

Main floor — 1,715 sq. ft.
Basement — 1,715 sq. ft.
Garage — 450 sq. ft.

■ *Total living area 1,715 sq. ft.* ■ *Price Code B* ■

MAIN FLOOR

Design by Landmark Designs, Inc.

Economy at It's Best

No. 91746 BL ✗

■ **This plan features:**

— Three bedrooms

— Three full baths

■ The attractive Porch adds to the curb appeal of this economical-to-build home

■ A vaulted ceiling tops the Entry and the Living and Dining Rooms

■ A lovely bay window adds sophistication to the Living Room which has direct access to the side Deck

■ The Master Suite has a walk-in closet, and a private Bath with an oversized shower

■ The two additional Bedrooms share a full hall Bath which is topped by a skylight

■ A vaulted ceiling tops the Dining Area which is open to the efficient Kitchen

■ The walk-in Pantry adds to the storage space of the Kitchen, which is equipped with a cooktop island and a double sink with a window above

■ The Garage offers direct entrance to the home

Main area — 1,717 sq. ft.
Garage — 782 sq. ft.

■ *Total living area 1,717 sq. ft.* ■ *Price Code B* ■

WIDTH 80'-0"
DEPTH 42'-0"

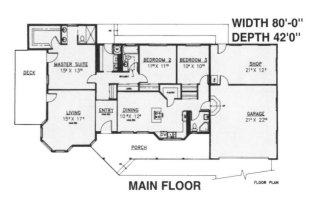

MAIN FLOOR

Surrounded with Sunshine

Design by Wesplan Building Design

No. 90986

This plan features:

— Three bedrooms

— Two full and one half baths

■ This Italianate-style home features columns and tile

■ Tile is used from the Foyer into the Kitchen and Nook, and in the Utility Room

■ A whirlpool tub is located in the elaborate and spacious Master Suite

■ The Great Room has a corner gas fireplace

■ A turreted Breakfast Nook and peninsula counter extend the Kitchen

■ The secondary Bedrooms share the full hall Bath

■ An optional basement or crawl space foundation — please specify when ordering

Main area — 1,731 sq. ft.
Garage — 888 sq. ft.
Basement — 1,715 sq. ft.

Total living area 1,731 sq. ft. ■ *Price Code B* ■

WIDTH 74'-0"
DEPTH 45'0"

MAIN FLOOR

Tray Ceilings

Design by Donald A. Gardner Architects, Inc.

No. 98087

This plan features:

— Three bedrooms

— Two full baths

■ Triple dormers and the covered Porch highlight the front of the home

■ Both the Dining Room and the Master Suite have tray ceilings

■ The centerpiece of the Great Room is the fireplace

■ One of the Bedrooms could be used as an Office or a Study

■ The Master Bath includes a tub and a shower

■ Bonus space is provided over the Garage

Main floor — 1,733 sq. ft.

Total living area 1,733 sq. ft. ■ *Price Code D* ■

FLOOR PLAN

Wide Open and Convenient

No. 20100

This plan features:

- Three bedrooms
- Two full baths

■ This home has vaulted ceilings in the Dining Room and the Master Bedroom

■ A sloped ceiling tops the fireplace in the Living Room

■ A skylight illuminates the Master Bath

■ The large Master Bedroom has a walk-in closet

Main floor — 1,737 sq. ft.
Basement — 1,727 sq. ft.
Garage — 484 sq. ft.

■ *Total living area 1,737 sq. ft.* ■ *Price Code B* ■

MAIN FLOOR

Clever Use of Interior Space

No. 99844

This plan features:

- Three bedrooms
- Two full baths

■ The charming interior has cathedral and tray ceilings to create a feeling of space

■ The Great Room boasts a cathedral ceiling above a cozy fireplace, built-in shelves and columns

■ The octagonal Dining Room and Breakfast Alcove easily access the Porch to the rear

■ The open Kitchen features an island counter sink and a Pantry

■ The Master Bedroom is enhanced by a tray ceiling and plush Bath

Main floor — 1,737 sq. ft.
Garage & storage — 517 sq. ft.

© 1994 Donald A. Gardner Architects, Inc.

■ *Total living area 1,737 sq. ft.* ■ *Price Code D* ■

© Donald A. Gardner Architects, Inc.

FLOOR PLAN

Turret Dining Views

Design by Larry E. Belk

Total living area 1,742 sq. ft. ■ Price Code B

STORAGE 14-0 X 6-0

UTIL 7-0 X 6-8

BRKFST 10-6 X 8-6 10 FT CLG

MAIN FLOOR

FP

GARAGE 22-0 X 20-0

KITCHEN 10-6 X 16-6 10 FT CLG

GREAT ROOM 17-0 X 13-6 10 FT CLG

MASTER BEDRM 15-6 X 12-6 10 FT CLG

MASTER BATH 10 FT CLG

PAN

BATH 2

LIN

© Larry E. Belk

DINING ROOM 10-6 X 13-0

ENTRY

PORCH

BEDRM 3 11-6 X 11-6 10 FT CLG

BEDRM 2 12-6 X 13-0

DEPTH 40-10

WIDTH 78-10

No. 93061 BL

■ This plan features:

— Three bedrooms

— Two full baths

■ The front Porch and Entry lead into the Dining and Great Rooms

■ The expansive Great Room has a focal point fireplace and access to the rear yard

■ The unique Dining Room has an alcove of windows and adjoins the Kitchen

■ An angled counter with an eating bar and a built-in Pantry are located in the Kitchen which is open to the Breakfast Area, the Great Room and the outdoors

■ The comfortable Master Bedroom has a Bath with a corner whirlpool tub, a double vanity and a huge walk-in closet

■ The two additional Bedrooms have oversized closets and share a full Bath

■ An optional slab or crawl space foundation — please specify when ordering

■ No materials list is available for this plan

Main floor — 1,742 sq. ft.
Garage — 566 sq. ft.

Easy Living

Design by Frank Betz Associates, Inc.

Total living area 1,743 sq. ft. ■ Price Code B

53'-6"

© Frank Betz Associates, Inc.

copyright © 1995 frank betz associates, inc.

FPL

FRENCH DOOR

Sitting Area 9⁹ x 10⁰

Master Suite 12⁹ x 15²

TRAY CLG.

VAULT

Vaulted Breakfast

VAULT

Vaulted Great Room 16⁰ x 18⁸ 13'-8" HIGH CLG.

SERVING BAR

RANGE

39'-4"

PLANT SHELF ABOVE

Vaulted M.Bath

COATS

OPEN RAIL

STAIRS DN

DW. Kitchen

REF.

W.i.c.

LINEN

LINEN

Both

Foyer 13'-8" HIGH CLG.

PANTRY

Vaulted Bedroom 2 12⁴ x 11²
17'-0" HIGH CLG.

Bedroom 3 11⁰ x 11²

Dining Room 11⁵ x 12⁰ 11'-0" HIGH CLG.

Laun.

VAULT

MAIN FLOOR

No. 97233 BL

■ This plan features:

— Three bedrooms

— Two full baths

■ Arched windows, keystones, and shutters highlight the exterior

■ The Great Room and the Breakfast Nook feature vaulted ceilings

■ There is direct access from the Dining Room to the Kitchen

■ The Kitchen has a space saving Pantry and ample counter space

■ Both secondary Bedrooms have spectacular front wall windows

■ The Master Suite is enormous and features a glass walled Sitting Area

■ A walk-in closet, a dual vanity and a whirlpool tub highlight the Master Bath

■ This home has a convenient drive-under Garage

■ No materials list is available for this plan

Main Floor — 1,743 sq. ft.
Basement — 998 sq. ft.
Garage — 763 sq. ft.

Design by Studer Residential Design, Inc.

No. 92625

■ **This plan features:**

— Three bedrooms

— Two full baths

■ This home features an attractive, classic brick design, with wood trim, multiple gables, and wing walls

■ A sheltered Porch leads into the Foyer

■ A sloped ceiling adds elegance to the formal Dining Room which opens to into the Great Room

■ A sloped ceiling and a corner fireplace enhance the Great Room

■ The Kitchen has a garden window above the double sink

■ A peninsula counter joins the Kitchen and the Breakfast Room in an open layout

■ The Master Suite is equipped with a large walk-in closet and a private Bath has an oval corner tub, a separate shower and a double vanity

■ The two additional Bedrooms share a full hall Bath

Main area — 1,746 sq. ft.
Basement — 1,560 sq. ft.
Garage — 455 sq. ft.

■ Total living area 1,746 sq. ft. ■ Price Code B ■

MAIN FLOOR

Patio

Breakfast 10'10" x12'

Great Room 16'2" x 18'4"

Master Bedroom 15' x12'10"

Bath

Kitchen 11'8" x 14' 4"

Dining Room 11' x 9'2"

Foyer

Hall

Bath

Laun.

Porch

Bedroom 11' x 12'6"

Bedroom 12'6"x11'11"

Two-car Garage 22' x 20'8"

WIDTH 65'-10"
DEPTH 56'-0"

Design by Studer Residential Design, Inc.

No. 92655

■ **This plan features:**

— Three bedrooms

— Two full baths

■ The front Porch accesses the open Foyer

■ The spacious Dining Room and Great Room both feature sloped ceilings

■ A corner fireplace, windows and an atrium door to the Patio enhance the Great Room

■ The convenient Kitchen has a Pantry and peninsula serving counter for the bright Breakfast Area as well as a nearby Laundry/Garage entry

■ The Master Bath includes a walk-in closet and back yard view

■ The two additional Bedrooms, one with an arched window, share a full Bath

Main floor — 1,746 sq. ft.
Garage — 480 sq. ft.
Basement — 1,697 sq. ft.

■ Total living area 1,746. ft. ■ Price Code B ■

Patio

Breakfast 10'10" x12'

Great Room 16'2" x 18'4"

Master Bedroom 15' x12'10"

Bath

Kitchen 11'8" x 14' 4"

Dining Room 11' x 9'2"

Foyer

Hall

Bath

Laun.

Porch

Bedroom 11' x 12'6"

Bedroom 12'6"x11'11"

Two-car Garage 22' x 20'8"

WIDTH: 65' - 10"
DEPTH: 56' - 0"   **MAIN FLOOR**

Columned Porch

Design by Rick Garner

■ *Total living area 1,754 sq. ft.* ■ *Price Code C* ■

No. 92531

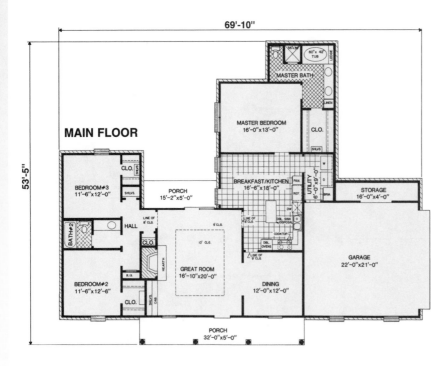

MAIN FLOOR

69'-10"

53'-5"

BEDROOM#3
11'-6"x12'-0"

CLO.

PORCH
15'-2"x5'-0"

MASTER BATH

60"x 42"
TUB

MASTER BEDROOM
16'-0"x13'-0"

CLO.

BATH#2

HALL

CLO.

GREAT ROOM
16'-10"x20'-0"

BREAKFAST/KITCHEN
16'-6"x18'-0"

UTILITY
6'-0"x9'-0"

STORAGE
16'-0"x4'-0"

BEDROOM#2
11'-6"x12'-6"

CLO.

DINING
12'-0"x12'-0"

GARAGE
22'-0"x21'-0"

PORCH
32'-0"x5'-0"

■ This plan features:

— Three bedrooms

— Two full baths

■ The Great Room has a fireplace and a decorative ceiling

■ The large, efficient Kitchen has a Breakfast Area

■ The Master Bedroom has a private Master Bath and a walk-in closet

■ The formal Dining Room is conveniently located near the Kitchen

■ An optional crawl space or slab foundation — please specify when ordering

First floor — 1,754 sq. ft.
Garage — 552 sq. ft.

Appealing Arches

■ *Total living area 1,756 sq. ft.* ■ *Price Code C* ■

No. 92658 BL

■ This plan features:

— Three bedrooms

— Two full baths

■ The brick exterior is accented by quoins and arched windows

■ The Foyer opens to formal the Dining Room and the spacious Great Room

■ A sloped ceiling above the corner fireplace and an atrium door to the Deck enhance the Great Room

■ The efficient Kitchen has a serving counter

■ The secluded Master Bedroom offers a arge walk-in closet

■ No materials list is available for this plan

Main floor — 1,756 sq. ft.
Garage — 485 sq. ft.
Basement — 1,669 sq. ft.

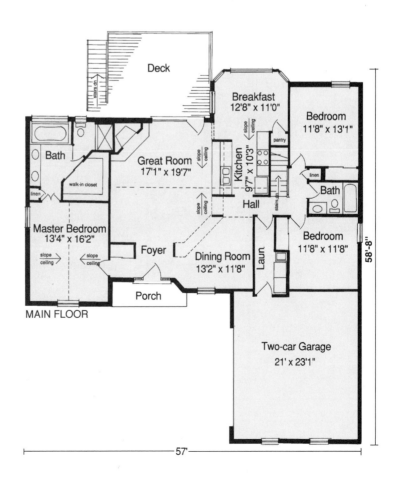

Deck

Breakfast
12'8" x 11'0"

Bedroom
11'8" x 13'1"

Bath

walk-in closet

Great Room
17'1" x 19'7"

Kitchen
9'7" x 10'3"

pantry

linen

Bath

Master Bedroom
13'4" x 16'2"

Hall

slope ceiling

Foyer

Dining Room
13'2" x 11'8"

Laun

Bedroom
11'8" x 11'8"

slope ceiling

Porch

MAIN FLOOR

Two-car Garage
21' x 23'1"

58'-8"

57'

Perfect Plan for Busy Family

Design by Ahmann Design, Inc.

■ *Total living area 1,756 sq. ft.* ■ *Price Code C* ■

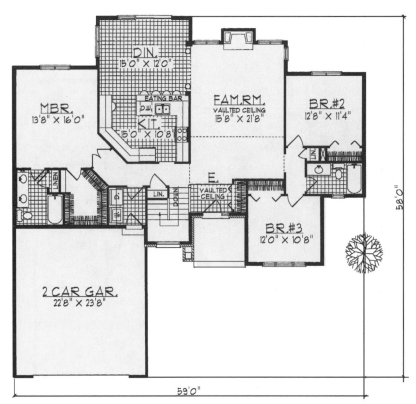

MAIN FLOOR PLAN

No. 93191 BL

■ **This plan features:**

— Three bedrooms

— Two full baths

■ The covered Entry opens to the vaulted Foyer and the Family Room

■ The spacious Family Room has a vaulted ceiling, central fireplace and expansive backyard views

■ The angular and efficient Kitchen has an eating bar

■ The secluded Master Bedroom has a large walk-in closet and double vanity Bath

■ There is plenty of room for a growing family to expand on lower level

■ No materials list is available for this plan

Main floor — 1,756 sq. ft.
Basement — 1,756 sq. ft.

Tandem Garage

■ *Total living area 1,761 sq. ft.* ■ *Price Code C* ■

No. 93133 BL X ⊠ ℞

■ This plan features:

— Three bedrooms

— Two full baths

■ The open Foyer leads into the spacious Living Room highlighted by a wall of windows

■ The Country-sized Kitchen with an efficient, U-shaped counter, work island, and an Eating Nook with back yard access is near the Laundry/Garage Entry

■ French doors open to the pampering Master Bedroom with window alcove, walk-in closet and double vanity Bath

Main floor —1,761 sq. ft.
Garage — 658 sq. ft.
Basement — 1,761

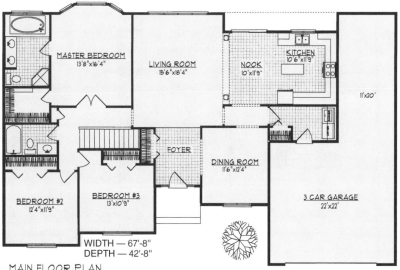

MASTER BEDROOM
13'8"x16'4"

LIVING ROOM
15'6"x18'4"

NOOK
10'x11'9"

KITCHEN
10'6"x11'9"

11'x20'

FOYER

DINING ROOM
11'6"x12'4"

3 CAR GARAGE
22'x22'

BEDROOM #2
12'4"x11'9"

BEDROOM #3
13'x10'9"

WIDTH — 67'-8"
DEPTH — 42'-8"

MAIN FLOOR PLAN

Casual Country Charmer

Design by Donald A. Gardner Architects, Inc.

© Donald A. Gardner Architects, Inc.

■ *Total living area 1,770 sq. ft.* ■ *Price Code E* ■

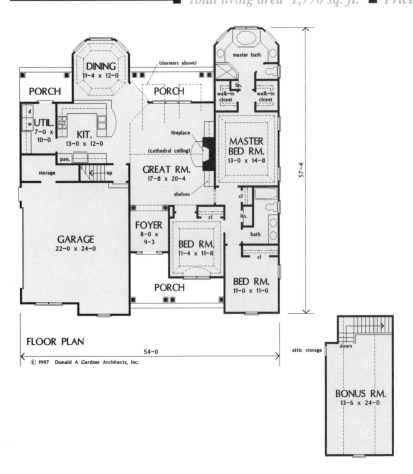

FLOOR PLAN

© 1997 Donald A Gardner Architects, Inc.

No. 96493

■ **This plan features:**

— Three bedrooms

— Two full baths

■ Columns and arches frame the front Porch

■ The open floor plan combines the Great Room, the Kitchen and the Dining Room

■ The Kitchen offers a convenient breakfast bar for meals on the run

■ The Master Suite features a private Bath oasis

■ The secondary Bedrooms share a full Bath with a dual vanity

Main floor — 1,770 sq. ft.
Bonus — 401 sq. ft.
Garage — 630 sq. ft.

Energy Efficient Entry

■ *Total living area 1,771 sq. ft.* ● *Price Code C* ■

No. 24714 BL

■ This plan features:

— Two bedrooms

— Two full baths

■ The attractive covered Porch highlights the curb appeal of this charming home

■ A cozy window seat and a vaulted ceiling enhance the private Den

■ The sunken Great Room is accented by a fireplace between large windows

■ The screened Porch, accessed from the Dining Room, extends the living space to the outdoors

■ The Master Bath features a garden tub, separate shower, dual walk-in closets and a skylight

■ No materials list is available for this plan

Main floor — 1,771 sq. ft.
Basement — 1,194 sq. ft.
Garage — 517 sq. ft.

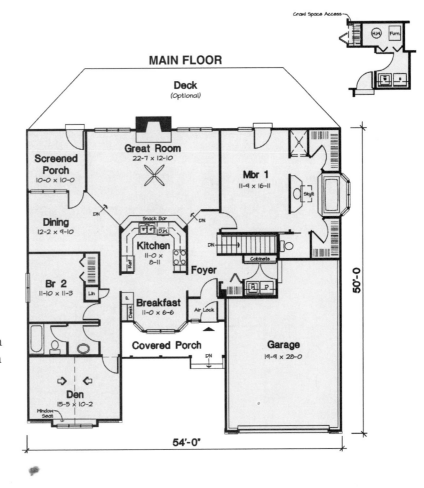

MAIN FLOOR

Curb Appeal

Design by Jannis Vann & Associates, Inc.

No. 98936

■ This plan features:

— Three bedrooms

— Two full baths

■ Triple arches and columns add charm to the front Porch

■ The Laundry closet is located near the Bedrooms

■ The Master Suite contains a Bath and a walk-in closet

■ The Dining Room is separated from the Foyer by columns

■ The Nook and the Kitchen share an angled counter

■ The Living Room has access to the Deck

■ No materials list is available for this plan

Main floor — 1,772 sq. ft.
Basement — 845 sq. ft.
Garage — 888 sq. ft.
Deck — 220 sq. ft.
Porch — 136 sq. ft.

Total living area 1,772 sq. ft. ■ Price Code C

Your Classic Hideaway

Design by Corley Plan Service

No. 90423

■ **This plan features:**

— Three bedrooms

— Two full baths

■ A lovely fireplace in the Living Room is both cozy and a source of heat

■ The efficient Kitchen is handy to the Dining and Utility Rooms

■ A lavish Master Suite is enhanced by a spa, more than ample closet space, and a separate shower

■ The screened Porch and Patio area is accessed from the Kitchen and Dining Rooms for outdoor living

■ An optional basement, slab or crawl space foundation — please specify when ordering

Main area — 1,773 sq. ft.
Screened porch — 240 sq. ft.

Total living area 1,773 sq. ft. ■ Price Code C

Design by Jannis Vann & Associates, Inc.

No. 93261 BL ✗ ✈

A Terrific Front Porch

■ **This plan features:**

— Three bedrooms

— Two full baths

■ The expansive Living Area includes a fireplace

■ The Master Suite has a private Master Bath and a walk-in closet, as well as a bay window with a view of the front yard

■ The efficient Kitchen is convenient to the sunny Breakfast Area and the Dining Room

■ A built-in Pantry and a desk add to the conveniences in the Breakfast Area

■ The additional Bedrooms share the full hall Bath

■ The main floor Laundry Room is convenient to the secondary Bedrooms

Main area — 1,778 sq. ft.
Basement — 1,008 sq. ft.
Garage — 728 sq. ft.

■ Total living area 1,778 sq. ft. ■ Price Code C ■

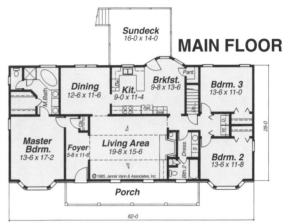

MAIN FLOOR

Design by United Design Associates

No. 94738 BL ✗

Natural Light

■ **This plan features:**

— Three bedrooms

— Two full baths

■ The drive-under Garage and the Basement add to the space of the home

■ Triple dormers and a Porch enhance to this elevation

■ The Master Bedroom is located in the rear for privacy

■ The Laundry is located near the secondary Bedrooms

■ The active area is open and separated only by columns

■ The Great and Keeping Rooms share a see-through fireplace

Main floor — 1,779 sq. ft.
Garage — 545 sq. ft.

■ Total living area 1,779 sq. ft. ■ Price Code C ■

MAIN FLOOR

European Flavor

Design by Frank Betz Associates, Inc.

Total living area 1,779 sq. ft. ■ Price Code C

No. 98464 BL

This plan features:

— Three bedrooms

— Two full baths

■ The covered entry opens to the Foyer with a fourteen-foot ceiling

■ The Family Room has a vaulted ceiling, a fireplace, and a French door to the rear yard

■ The Breakfast Area has a tray ceiling and a bay window that overlooks the backyard

■ The Kitchen has every imaginable convenience including a walk-in Pantry

■ The Dining Room is delineated by columns and has a plant shelf above it

■ The privately located Master Suite has a tray ceiling, a walk-in closet and a private Bath

■ Two other Bedrooms share a full Bath on the opposite side of the home

■ An optional basement or crawl space foundation — please specify when ordering

■ No materials list available for this plan

Main floor — 1,779 sq. ft.
Basement — 1,818 sq. ft.
Garage — 499 sq. ft.

FLOOR PLAN

OPT. BASEMENT STAIR LOCATION

Enticing Design

Design by Design Basics, Inc.

Total living area 1,782 sq. ft. ■ Price Code C

No. 97415 BL ✕

This plan features:

— Three bedrooms

— Two full baths

■ The all brick facade offers the homeowner low exterior maintenance

■ A three-sided fireplace warms both the Great Room and the Hearth Room

■ The Kitchen incorporates a peninsula snack bar that opens to the Great Room and the Hearth Room

■ The private Master Suite has a nine-foot boxed ceiling, a large walk-in closet, a double vanity and a whirlpool tub

■ An optional basement or slab foundation— please specify when ordering

Main floor — 1,782 sq. ft.
Garage — 466 sq. ft.

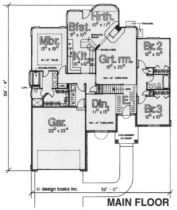

MAIN FLOOR

Circular Living Area

Design by The Garlinghouse Company

No. 10274

■ **This plan features:**

— Three bedrooms

— Two full baths

■ A dramatically positioned fireplace is the focal point for the main living area

■ The Kitchen, the Dining and Living Rooms form a circle for a great open atmosphere

■ The Deck is accessible through sliding glass doors

■ The convenient Laundry Room is located off the Kitchen

■ The double Garage provides excellent storage

Main area — 1,783 sq. ft.
Garage — 576 sq. ft.

■ *Total living area 1,783 sq. ft.* ■ *Price Code C* ■

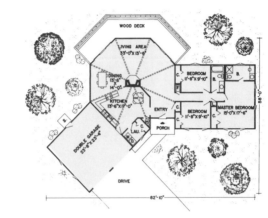

Garden Entry

Design by Sater Design Group

No. 94200 BL

■ **This plan features:**

— Three bedrooms

— Two full baths

■ The garden Entry, with double doors below a decorative transom window, leads into the open Foyer and the Living/Dining Areas

■ An open layout offers air and light in the Dining and Living Areas

■ The spacious Kitchen/Nook has an open counter/snack bar adjacent to the Leisure Area with its wall of sliding doors

■ The private Master Suite has a large walk-in closet, a double vanity, step-in shower, and a window tub

■ The additional Bedrooms have over-sized closets and share a full Bath with a double vanity

■ The convenient Laundry Room is adjacent to the Garage

■ No materials list is available for this plan

Main floor — 1,784 sq. ft.
Garage — 491 sq. ft.

■ *Total living area 1,784 sq. ft.* ■ *Price Code C* ■

WIDTH 58'-0"
DEPTH 64'-8"

MAIN FLOOR

Exciting Three Bedroom

Design by Donald A. Gardner Architects, Inc.

© Donald A. Gardner Architects, Inc.

■ *Total living area 1,787 sq. ft.* ■ *Price Code E* ■

FLOOR PLAN

© 1994 Donald A Gardner Architects, Inc.

No. 99805 BL ✕ ⛫ ℝ

■ **This plan features:**

— Three bedrooms

— Two full baths

■ The Great Room is enhanced by a fireplace, cathedral ceiling, and built-in bookshelves

■ The Kitchen is designed for efficiency with a food preparation island and a Pantry

■ The Master Suite is topped by a cathedral ceiling and has a luxurious Bath and a walk-in closet

■ The additional Bedrooms, one with a cathedral ceiling and a walk-in closet, share a skylit Bath

■ A second floor Bonus Room is perfect for the Study or the Play Area

Main floor — 1,787 sq. ft.
Garage & storage — 521 sq. ft.
Bonus room — 326 sq. ft.

Craftsman Inspired

Design by Donald A. Gardner Architects, Inc.

© 1998 Donald A. Gardner, Inc.

■ *Total living area 1,792 sq. ft.* ■ *Price Code E* ■

FLOOR PLAN

No. 98054 BL ✕

■ **This plan features:**

— Three bedrooms

— Three full baths

■ There are covered Porches in the front and rear of this home

■ Decorative ceilings can be found throughout the home

■ A unique U-shaped counter defines the Kitchen and overlooks the Great Room

■ There are two Bedrooms suitable for use as the Master Suite

■ A Bonus Room is located over the Garage

Main floor — 1,792 sq. ft.
Bonus — 351 sq. ft.
Garage — 513 sq. ft.

Design by Donald A. Gardner Architects, Inc.

No. 98100

A Second Suite

This plan features:

- Three bedrooms
- Three full baths
- The attractive Country-styled Porch shelters the entrance and provides curb appeal
- This home features an open common area separating the two Master Suites
- Three rear Porches extend living space to the outdoors
- Added flexibility is found in the Bedroom/Study and Bonus Room
- The fireplace in the Great Room, combined with the cathedral ceiling, offers atmosphere and warmth

Main floor — 1,792 sq. ft.
Bonus room — 338 sq. ft.
Garage/storage — 504 sq. ft.
Porch — 477 sq. ft.

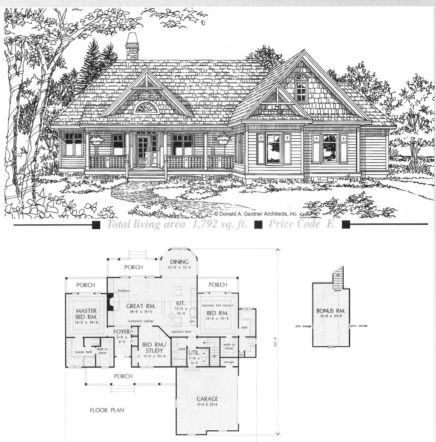

Total living area 1,792 sq. ft. ■ Price Code E

Design by Ahmann Design, Inc.

No. 97108 BL

Classic Ranch

This plan features:

- Three bedrooms
- Two full baths
- The fabulous Great Room has a step ceiling and a cozy fireplace
- An elegant arched soffit connects the Great Room to the Dining Room
- The Kitchen has wrap-around counters, a center island and a Nook
- The Master Bedroom includes a walk-in closet and a private Bath
- The additional Bedrooms with ample closet space share a full Bath
- No materials list is available for this plan

Main floor — 1,794 sq. ft.
Basement — 1,794 sq. ft.

Total living area 1,794 sq. ft. ■ Price Code C

MAIN FLOOR PLAN

Style and Practicality

Design by Donald A. Gardner Architects, Inc.

© 1998 Donald A. Gardner, Inc.

B. NATHA

■ *Total living area 1,795 sq. ft.* ■ *Price Code E* ■

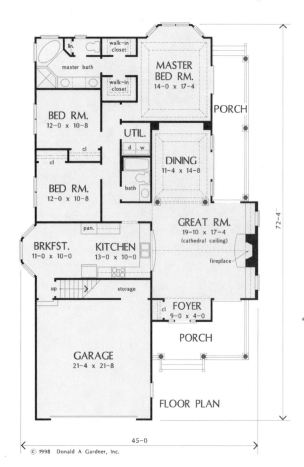

FLOOR PLAN

© 1998 Donald A Gardner, Inc.

No. 98020 BL ✕ Я R

■ This plan features:

— Three bedrooms

— Two full baths

■ This plan easily fits on a narrow lot

■ A cathedral ceiling enhances the Great Room with a fireplace and built-in shelves

■ The optional Loft/Study above the Kitchen overlooks the Great Room

■ Columns frame the entry to the formal Dining Room which is topped by a tray ceiling

■ The complete Master Suite has a tray ceiling, bay window, side porch access, dual walk-in closets, and Bath with garden tub and separate shower

Main floor — 1,795 sq. ft.
Bonus room — 368 sq. ft.
Garage — 520 sq. ft.

Designed For Easy Living

© 1996 Donald A Gardner Architects, Inc.

■ *Total living area 1,800 sq. ft.* ■ *Price Code E* ■

No. 99814

■ **This plan features:**

— Three Bedrooms

— Two full baths

■ A refined, traditional exterior is created by brick, double dormers, and a hip roof

■ The Foyer opens to the generous Great Room with a cathedral ceiling and a fireplace

■ Columns define the entrance to the Kitchen which has a center island

■ The Master Bedroom, the Dining Room, and the front Bedroom/Study have distinctive tray ceilings

Main floor — 1,800 sq. ft.
Garage — 477 sq. ft.

© 1996 Donald A Gardner Architects, Inc.

Distinctive Ranch

Design by Ahmann Design, Inc.

■ Total living area 1,802 sq. ft. ■ Price Code C ■

MAIN FLOOR PLAN

No. 93143

■ **This plan features:**

— Three bedrooms

— Two full baths

■ This hip roofed ranch has an exterior that mixes brick and siding

■ The cozy front Porch leads into a tiled Entry with sidelights and transoms

■ The Great Room has a cathedral ceiling and a rear wall fireplace

■ The Kitchen has a center island and opens into the Nook

■ The Dining Room features a high ceiling and a bright front window

■ The Bedroom wing has three large Bedrooms and two full Baths

■ No materials list is available for this plan

Main floor — 1,802 sq. ft.
Basement — 1,802 sq. ft.

Wonderful One Level Living

Design by Ahmann Design, Inc.

■ Total living area 1,802 sq. ft. ■ Price Code C ■

MAIN FLOOR PLAN

No. 93193 BL

■ **This plan features:**

— Three bedrooms

— Two full and one half baths

■ The charming front Porch accesses the easy-care Entry with archway to Dining Room

■ The central Great Room is enhanced by a cathedral ceiling over a cozy fireplace set in a wall of windows

■ The large and convenient Kitchen has a work island/snackbar, the Nook with a sliding glass door to the backyard, and is near the Laundry/Garage entry

■ The corner Master Bedroom includes a walk-in closet and plush Bath with a double vanity and spa tub

■ The additional Bedrooms with ample closets and double windows, share a full Bath

■ No materials list is available for this plan

Main floor — 1,802 sq. ft.
Basement — 1,802 sq. ft.

Split Bedroom Ranch

Design by Corley Plan Service

No. 90476

■ **This plan features:**

— Three bedrooms

— Two full baths

■ The formal Foyer opens into the Great Room which features a vaulted ceiling and a hearth fireplace

■ The U-shaped Kitchen is located between the Dining Room and the Breakfast Nook

■ The secluded Master Bedroom is spacious and includes amenities such as walk-in closets and a full Bath

■ The secondary Bedrooms have ample closet space and share a full Bath

■ The covered front Porch and rear Deck provide additional space for entertaining

■ An optional basement, slab or a crawl space foundation — please specify when ordering

Main Floor — 1,804 sq. ft.
Basement — 1,804 sq. ft.
Garage — 506 sq. ft.

Total living area 1,804 sq. ft. ■ Price Code C

MAIN FLOOR

French Country Style

Design by Rick Garner

No. 92517

■ **This plan features:**

— Three bedrooms

— Two full baths

■ The sheltered Porch leads into the open Foyer and

■ The Great Room is enhanced by a raised hearth fireplace between book shelves, a vaulted ceiling and access to the Patio

■ The hub Kitchen, with a peninsula counter and Utility/Garage entry, easily serves the Breakfast Area and the formal Dining Room

■ The spacious Master Bedroom has a Sitting Area and a plush Master Bath

■ The additional, roomy Bedrooms with over-sized closets share a double vanity Bath

■ An optional slab or crawl space foundation — please specify when ordering

Main floor — 1,805 sq. ft.
Garage & storage — 524 sq. ft.

Total living area 1,805 sq. ft. ■ Price Code C

MAIN AREA

Columns And Arched Windows
Design by Design Basics, Inc.

© design basics inc.

■ Total living area 1,806 sq. ft. ■ Price Code C ■

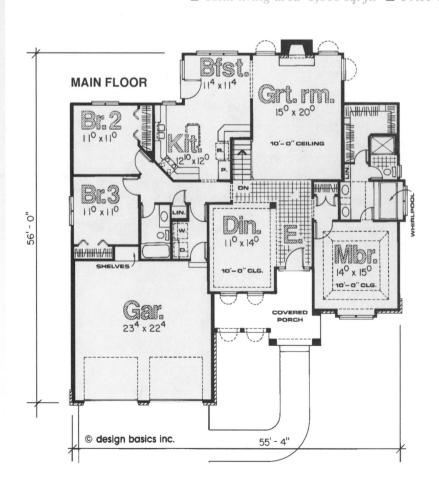

MAIN FLOOR

Bfst.
11⁴ x 11⁴

Grt. rm.
15⁰ x 20⁰
10'-0" CEILING

Br. 2
11⁰ x 11⁰

Kit.
12¹⁰ x 12⁰

Br. 3
11⁰ x 11⁰

R.

P.

DN

LIN.

56' - 0"

SHELVES

LIN.
W.
D.

Din.
11⁰ x 14⁰
10'-0" CLG.

Mbr.
14⁰ x 15⁰
10'-0" CLG.

WHIRLPOOL

Gar.
23⁴ x 22⁴

COVERED PORCH

© design basics inc.

55' - 4"

No. 99487 BL

■ **This plan features:**

— Three bedrooms

— Two full baths

■ The entry is open to the Dining Room and the Great Room

■ A brick fireplace and arched windows are featured in the Great Room

■ The large island Kitchen has an angled range, work island and a built-in Pantry

■ The Master Suite has a whirlpool Bath and a sloped ceiling

■ An optional basement or slab foundation — please specify when ordering

Main floor — 1,806 sq. ft.
Garage — 548 sq. ft.

Country Covered Porches

©1994 Donald A. Gardner Architects, Inc.

B. NATHAN

■ *Total living area 1,807 sq. ft.* ■ *Price Code E* ■

No. 96453 BL ✕ ᴙR

■ This plan features:

— Three bedrooms

— Two full baths

■ The smart, user-friendly Kitchen and a generous Great Room share a cathedral ceiling

■ Both the front Bedroom and the Master Bedroom enjoy cathedral ceilings

■ The Master Suite is privately tucked away with a luxurious Bath, walk-in closet and access to the Porch

■ The spacious Utility Room offers convenience with built-in cabinets

■ The Bonus Room is available for future expansion

Main floor — 1,807 sq. ft.
Garage — 669 sq. ft.
Bonus room — 419 sq. ft.

MASTER BED RM.
14-8 x 15-4

PORCH

skylights

UTILITY
11-8 x 8-4

storage

w d

BRKFST.
10-4 x 8-6

master bath

walk-in closet

GREAT RM.
17-4 x 19-4

(cathedral ceiling)

KITCHEN
11-8 x 10-6

GARAGE
20-10 x 22-4

fireplace

up

52-8

BED RM.
12-4 x 11-0

cl

lin.

cl

FOYER
8-8 x 7-8

DINING
11-4 x 12-8

storage

cl

bath

BED RM.
10-10 x 12-0

PORCH

70-8

FIRST FLOOR PLAN

© Donald A. Gardner Architects, Inc.

attic storage

skylights

BONUS RM.
20-10 x 17-8

attic storage

Convenient Ranch

Design by Patrick Morabito A.I.A.

No. 93311 BL

■ **This plan features:**

— Three bedrooms

— Two full and one half baths

■ A barrel vaulted ceiling is featured in the Foyer

■ A stepped ceiling appears in both the Dinette and the formal Dining Room

■ The expansive Gathering Room has a large focal point fireplace and access to the wood Deck

■ The efficient Kitchen includes a work island and a built-in Pantry

■ The luxurious Master Suite has a private Bath that includes a separate tub and step-in shower

■ The two additional Bedrooms share a full hall Bath

■ No materials list is available for this plan

First floor — 1,810 sq. ft.
Garage — 528 sq. ft.

■ Total living area 1,810 sq. ft. ■ Price Code C ■

Moderate Ranch

Design by Corley Plan Service

No. 90441 BL ✕

■ **This plan features:**

— Three bedrooms

— Two full baths

■ The large Great Room has a vaulted ceiling and a stone fireplace with bookshelves on either side

■ The spacious Kitchen has ample cabinet space conveniently located next to the large Dining Room

■ The Master Suite includes a large Bath with a garden tub, double vanity and a walk-in closet

■ The two other large Bedrooms, each with a walk-in closet, share a full Bath

■ An optional basement, slab or crawl space combination — please specify when ordering

Main floor — 1,811 sq. ft.

■ Total living area 1,811 sq. ft. ■ Price Code C ■

Southern Hospitality

No. 92220

■ **This plan features:**

— Three bedrooms

— Two full baths

■ The welcoming covered Veranda catches the breeze

■ The easy-care, tiled Entry leads into Great Room with fieldstone fireplace and atrium door to another covered Veranda topped by a cathedral ceiling

■ The bright Kitchen/Dining Room includes a stovetop island/ snackbar, built-in Pantry and desk and access to covered Veranda

■ A vaulted ceiling crowns the Master Bedroom which offers a plush Bath and huge walk-in closet

■ The two additional Bedrooms, with ample closets, share a double vanity Bath

Main floor — 1,830 sq. ft.
Garage — 759 sq. ft.

■ *Total living area 1,830 sq. ft.* ■ *Price Code C* ■

MAIN FLOOR

Cozy Traditional

No. 99208

■ **This plan features:**

— Three bedrooms

— Two full baths

■ This plan is a convenient one-level design

■ The galley-style Kitchen shares a snack bar with the spacious Gathering Room

■ An inviting focal point fireplace is featured in the Gathering Room

■ The ample Master Suite has a luxury Bath which includes a whirlpool tub and separate Dressing Room

■ Two additional Bedrooms, one that could double as a Study, are located at the front of the house

Main floor — 1,830 sq. ft.
Basement — 1,830 sq. ft.

■ *Total living area 1,830 sq. ft.* ■ *Price Code C* ■

MAIN FLOOR

Western Ranch House

Design by National Home Planning Service

No. 90007

■ **This plan features:**

— Four bedrooms

— Three full baths

■ This design has authentic Ranch styling with long Loggia, posts and braces, hand-split shake roof and cross-buck doors

■ The Texas-sized hexagonal, sunken Living Room has two solid walls, one with a fireplace, and two ten-foot walls of sliding glass doors

■ The Porch surrounds the Living Room on three sides

■ The Master Suite has a private Master Bath

■ The efficient, well-equipped Kitchen opens to the Family Room

Main floor — 1,830 sq. ft.
Basement — 1,830 sq. ft.
Garage — 540 sq. ft.

Total living area 1,830 sq. ft. ■ Price Code C ■

MAIN FLOOR

Exclusive Master Suite

Design by The Garlinghouse Company

No. 34031

■ **This plan features:**

— Three bedrooms

— Two full and one half baths

■ The Foyer is open to the Living and Dining Rooms

■ A huge fireplace and double window highlight the Living Room

■ The convenient Kitchen has a cooktop island/snackbar, Pantry, and bright Breakfast Area with backyard access

■ The corner Master Bedroom offers a decorative ceiling, walk-in closets and a double vanity Bath

■ The two additional Bedrooms have ample closets and private access to the full Bath

Main floor — 1,831 sq. ft.
Garage — 484 sq. ft.
Basement — 1,831 sq. ft.

Total living area 1,831 sq. ft. ■ Price Code C ■

MAIN FLOOR

No. 91122 BL

This plan features:

— Three bedrooms

— Two full baths

■ Walk-in closets are in all of the Bedrooms

■ A plant ledge can be found above the Entry to the living space

■ The combined Living/Dining Room has a corner fireplace for ambiance

■ A vaulted ceiling adds dimension to the Master Suite

■ The Kitchen has plenty of space for multiple cooks

■ A convenient built-in ironing board can be found in the Laundry Room

■ No materials list is available for this plan

Main floor — 1,838 sq. ft.
Garage — 452 sq. ft.

■ Total living area 1,838 sq. ft. ■ Price Code C ■

MAIN FLOOR

Easy-Flowing Floor Plan

Design by Donald A. Gardner Architects, Inc.

No. 98056 BL

This plan features:

— Three bedrooms

— Two full baths

■ This home has a convenient one-story design with bonus space over the Garage

■ The bedroom wing is located down a short hall, a great arrangement for families with small children

■ A cathedral ceiling tops the Great Room and the Dining Room

■ There is direct access to the rear Porch from the Great Room

■ An optional door arrangement could be used to create a Den from one of the Bedrooms

■ No materials list is available for this plan

First floor - 1,844 sq. ft.
Bonus - 250 sq. ft.
Garage - 635 sq. ft.
Porch - 246 sq. ft.

© Donald A. Gardner Architects, Inc.

■ Total living area 1,844 sq. ft. ■ Price Code E ■

FLOOR PLAN

© 1996 Donald A Gardner Architects, Inc.

Small, Yet Lavishly Appointed

Design by Frank Betz Associates, Inc.

■ *Total living area 1,845 sq. ft.* ■ *Price Code C* ■

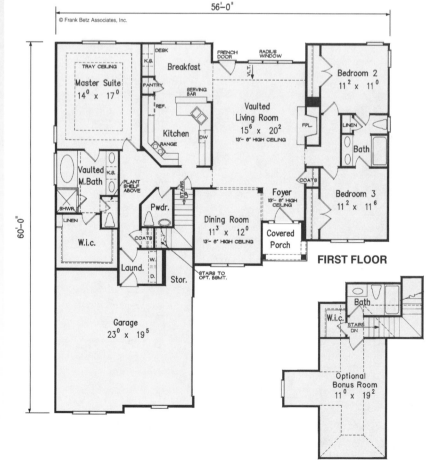

FIRST FLOOR

OPT. BONUS FLOOR PLAN

No. 98425

■ **This plan features:**

– Three bedrooms

– Two full and one half baths

■ The Dining Room, Living Room, Foyer and Master Bath are all topped by high ceilings

■ The Master Bedroom includes a decorative tray ceiling

■ The Kitchen opens to the Breakfast Room

■ The Living Room has a large fireplace and a French door to the rear yard

■ The Master Suite is privately located

■ An optional basement or crawl space foundation — please specify when ordering

Main floor — 1,845 sq. ft.
Bonus — 409 sq. ft.
Basement — 1,845 sq. ft.
Garage — 529 sq. ft.

© Donald A. Gardner Architects, Inc.

B. NATHAN

■ *Total living area 1,845 sq. ft.* ■ *Price Code E* ■

No. 98101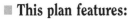

■ This plan features:

— Three bedrooms

— Two full baths

■ Decorative brackets accent the gables of this split-bedroom design

■ Volume ceilings amplify the key rooms

■ Built-ins in the Great Room and the Master Suite make life easier

■ The front and rear Porches extend living space to the outdoors

■ The Utility Room doubles as a Mud Room

Main floor — 1,845 sq. ft.
Bonus room — 317 sq. ft.
Garage/storage — 564 sq. ft.
Porch — 359 sq. ft.

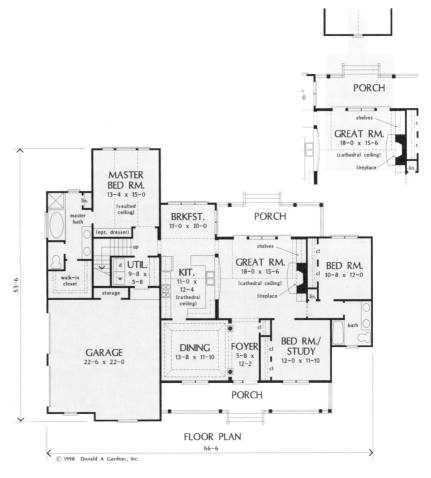

FLOOR PLAN
66-6

© 1998   Donald A Gardner, Inc.

Traditional Ranch

Design by Corley Plan Service

■ *Total living area 1,845 sq. ft.* ■ *Price Code C* ■

No. 90466

■ **This plan features:**

— Three bedrooms

— Two full and two half baths

■ The split Bedroom design is great for families with older children

■ Columns delineate the formal Dining Room

■ The fireplace in the Great Room is set between built-ins

■ Dual walk-in closets and a cathedral ceiling highlight the Master Suite

■ The Garage has storage space in the rear

■ An optional slab or crawl space foundation — please specify when ordering

Main floor — 1,845 sq. ft.
Garage — 512 sq. ft.
Deck — 216 sq. ft.
Porch — 38 sq. ft.

Plush Master Bedroom Wing

■ *Total living area 1,849 sq. ft.* ■ *Price Code C* ■

No. 92705 **BL**

■ This plan features:

— Three bedrooms

— Two full baths

■ The raised, tile Foyer with a decorative window leads into an expansive Living Room featuring a tiled fireplace, framed by French doors

■ The efficient Kitchen has a walk-in Pantry and serving bar adjoining the Breakfast and Utility Areas

■ The private Master Bedroom, crowned by a stepped ceiling, features an atrium door to the outside, a huge, walk-in closet and a luxurious Bath

■ No materials list is available for this plan

Main floor — 1,849 sq. ft.
Garage — 437 sq. ft.

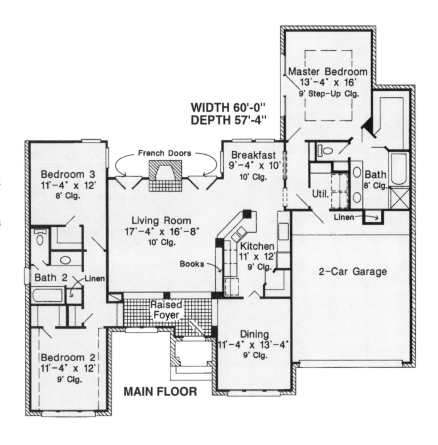

WIDTH 60'-0"
DEPTH 57'-4"

Master Bedroom
13'-4" x 16'
9' Step-Up Clg.

Bath
8' Clg.

Util.

Linen

French Doors

Breakfast
9'-4" x 10'
10' Clg.

Bedroom 3
11'-4" x 12'
8' Clg.

Living Room
17'-4" x 16'-8"
10' Clg.

Kitchen
11' x 12'
9' Clg.

Books

2-Car Garage

Bath 2   Linen

Raised
Foyer

Dining
11'-4" x 13'-4"
9' Clg.

Bedroom 2
11'-4" x 12'
9' Clg.

MAIN FLOOR

Attractive Styling

Design by Greg Marquis & Associates

Total living area 1,849 sq. ft. ■ Price Code C ■

No. 93427 BL

■ **This plan features:**

— Three bedrooms

— Two full baths

■ Tremendous style and presence is created by windows, sidelights and transoms

■ The formal Dining Room, off the Foyer, features a view of the front yard and access to the Family Room

■ A grand fireplace, with windows to either side, serves as a focal point in the Family Room

■ The Breakfast Room/Kitchen is open to the Family Room

■ The secluded Master Suite has a walk-in closet, recessed ceiling and a five-piece Bath

■ The two additional Bedrooms, located at the opposite side of the home, share a full Bath

■ No materials list is available for this plan

Main floor — 1,949 sq. ft.
Garage — 555 sq. ft.

MAIN FLOOR

WIDTH 66'-4"
DEPTH 59'-10"

Sophisticated Stucco

Design by Rick Garner

Total living area 1,856 sq. ft. ■ Price Code C ■

No. 92562 BL

■ **This plan features:**

— Three bedrooms

— Two full baths

■ A raised ceiling in the Master Suite and the Den add architectural interest to the plan

■ The spacious Kitchen serves the Breakfast Area and Dining Room with efficiency and ease

■ The vaulted ceiling in the Dining Room adds elegance to the room

■ The Master Suite has a luxurious Master Bath with a separate tub and shower

■ The secondary Bedrooms are in close proximity to the full Bath in the hall

■ An optional slab or crawl space foundation — please specify when ordering

Main floor — 1,856 sq. ft.
Garage & storage — 521 sq. ft.

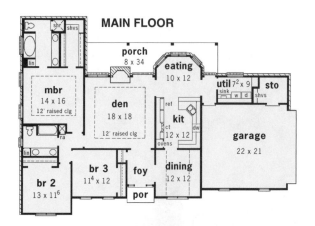

MAIN FLOOR

Design by Frank Betz Associates, Inc.

Porch with Columns

No. 98408

■ **This plan features:**

— Three bedrooms

— Two full baths

■ The Foyer, with twelve-foot ceiling, leads past decorative columns into the Family Room with a center fireplace

■ The Living and Dining Rooms are linked by the Foyer and have windows overlooking the front Porch

■ The Kitchen has a serving bar and is adjacent to the Breakfast Nook which has a French door that opens to the backyard

■ The private Master Suite has a tray ceiling, a vaulted Bath with a double vanity, and a walk-in closet

■ An optional basement, slab, or crawl space foundation — please specify when ordering this plan

Main floor — 1,856 sq. ft.
Garage — 429 sq. ft.
Basement — 1,856

Total living area 1,856 sq. ft. ■ Price Code C

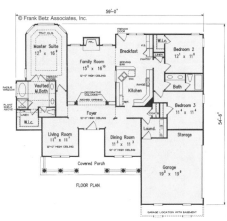

Design by Rick Garner

Classically Appointed

No. 92561

■ **This plan features:**

— Three bedrooms

— Two full baths

■ The recessed front Entry leads into a formal Foyer

■ The Dining Room has a bright front window and direct access to the Kitchen

■ The Kitchen is U-shaped and features a wall oven and an angled counter eating bar with a bay window

■ There is an Eating Area that overlooks the back Porch and is open to the Kitchen

■ The Den has a twelve-foot raised ceiling and a fireplace

■ The Master Suite features a raised ceiling, a full Bath, and a walk-in closet

■ The two large secondary Bedrooms share the Bath in the hall

■ An optional slab or crawl space foundation — please specify when ordering

Main floor — 1,856 sq. ft.
Garage — 521 sq. ft.

Total living area 1,856 sq. ft. ■ Price Code C

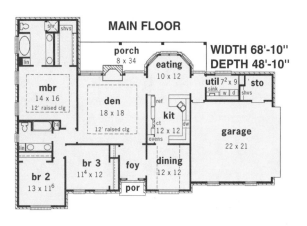

MAIN FLOOR

WIDTH 68'-10"
DEPTH 48'-10"

Country Style Charm

Design by Landmark Designs, Inc.

■ Total living area 1,857 sq. ft. ■ Price Code C ■

WIDTH 51'-6"
DEPTH 65'-0"

No. 91731 BL X

■ **This plan features:**

— Three bedrooms

— Two full baths

■ The outside features brick accents, front facing gable, and railed wrap-around covered Porch

■ The dog-leg shaped Kitchen features a built-in range and oven

■ The Nook has Garage access for convenient unloading of groceries and other supplies

■ A bay window wraps around the front of the formal Living Room

■ The Master Suite has French doors opening to the Deck

Main area — 1,857 sq. ft.
Garage — 681 sq. ft.

Easy Living Plan

Design by Donald A. Gardner Architects, Inc.

■ Total living area 1,864 sq. ft. ■ Price Code E ■

No. 96468 BL X R

■ **This plan features:**

— Three bedrooms

— Two full baths

■ The sunlit Foyer opens into the generous Great Room

■ The Great Room is crowned in a cathedral ceiling and is accented by a fireplace

■ Accent columns add to the open Kitchen and Breakfast Bay

■ The Master Bedroom is topped by a tray ceiling and is highlighted by a well-appointed Master Bath

■ The two additional Bedrooms share a skylit Bath in the hall and create the children's wing

First floor — 1,864 sq. ft.
Bonus room — 319 sq. ft.
Garage — 503 sq. ft.

Design by Donald A. Gardner Architects, Inc.

Victorian Accents

No. 99857

■ **This plan features:**

- Three bedrooms
- Two full baths
- The covered wrap-around Porch connects to the rear Deck
- The Foyer opens into the octagonal Great Room that is warmed by a fireplace
- The Dining Room has a tray ceiling and convenient access to the Kitchen
- The Galley Kitchen opens into the Breakfast Area
- The Master Bedroom has a walk-in closet and a fully appointed Bath
- Two additional Bedrooms complete this plan and share the other full Bath

Main floor — 1,865 sq. ft.
Garage — 505 sq. ft.

Total living area 1,865 sq. ft. ■ Price Code E

MAIN FLOOR

© 1991 Donald A. Gardner Architects, Inc.

Welcoming Front Porch

Design by Rick Garner

No. 92542

■ **This plan features:**

- Three bedrooms
- Two full baths
- The open Foyer leads into the Dining Room, defined by columns, and a spacious Den
- The Den features a cozy fireplace, built-in shelves, a decorative ceiling and sliding glass doors to the rear Porch
- The efficient U-shaped Kitchen has a peninsula snack bar and a bright Breakfast Area
- The secluded Master Suite has a decorative ceiling, a huge walk-in closet and a private Bath
- The two additional Bedrooms have ample closets and share the double vanity Bath
- An optional crawl space or slab foundation — please specify when ordering

Main floor — 1,866 sq. ft.
Garage/Storage — 538 sq. ft.

Total living area 1,866 sq. ft. ■ Price Code C

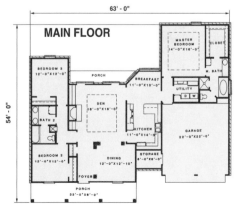

MAIN FLOOR

Charming Brick Home

Design by Ahmann Design, Inc.

■ *Total living area 1,868 sq. ft.* ■ *Price Code C* ■

No. 93107

■ This plan features:

— Three bedrooms

— Two full baths

■ A covered entrance leads into the spacious Living Room

■ The Kitchen with an island opens to the Dining Room

■ The Master Bedroom has a walk-in closet and a plush bath

■ No materials list is available for this plan

Main floor — 1,868 sq., ft,
Basement — 1,868 sq. ft.
Garage — 782 sq. ft.

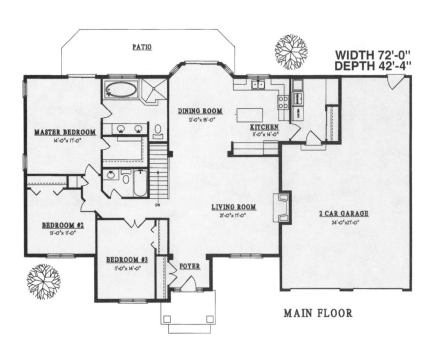

WIDTH 72'-0"
DEPTH 42'-4"

PATIO

DINING ROOM
12'-0" x 15'-0"

KITCHEN
11'-0" x 14'-0"

MASTER BEDROOM
14'-0" x 17'-0"

LIVING ROOM
21'-0" x 17'-0"

2 CAR GARAGE
24'-0" x 21'-0"

BEDROOM #2
13'-0" x 11'-0"

BEDROOM #3
11'-0" x 14'-0"

FOYER

MAIN FLOOR

Country Styled Ranch

■ *Total living area 1,869 sq. ft.* ■ *Price Code C* ■

No. 92677 BL

■ **This plan features:**

— Three bedrooms

— One full and one three-quarter baths

■ The combination Living and Dining Room create an attractive formal area

■ A worktop island divides the Kitchen and the Breakfast Area

■ The Great Room ceiling slopes to a twelve-foot height and offers a comfortable gathering place to relax with family and friends

■ The Master Bedroom has a tray ceiling with the center height of nine-feet and a large walk-in closet

■ No materials list is available for this plan

Main floor - 1,869 sq. ft.
Basement - 1,705 sq. ft.
Garage - 600 sq. ft.

European Styling

Design by Rick Garner

■ *Total living area 1,873 sq. ft.* ■ *Price Code C* ■

No. 92552 BL X

■ **This plan features:**

— Four bedrooms

— Two full baths

■ The exterior features arch topped windows, quoins and shutters

■ The formal Foyer leads to the formal Dining Room and spacious Den

■ The Kitchen is open to into the informal Eating Area

■ The Master Suite is privately located to the rear

■ An optional slab or crawl space foundation — please specify when ordering

Main floor — 1,873 sq. ft.
Garage — 613 sq. ft.
Bonus — 145 sq. ft.

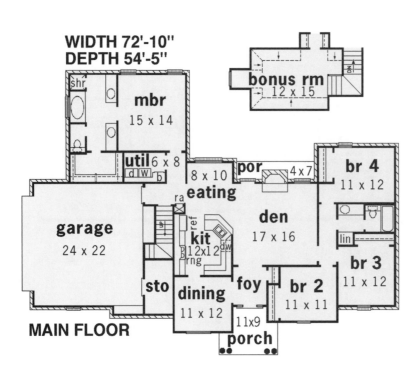

WIDTH 72'-10"
DEPTH 54'-5"

bonus rm 12 x 15

mbr 15 x 14

util 6 x 8

garage 24 x 22

eating 8 x 10

por 4 x 7

br 4 11 x 12

kit 12 x 12

den 17 x 16

br 3 11 x 12

sto

dining 11 x 12

foy

br 2 11 x 11

porch 11x9

MAIN FLOOR

Spectacular Front Window

■ *Total living area 1,875 sq. ft.* ■ *Price Code C* ■

No. 97253 BL

■ This plan features:

— Three bedrooms

— Two full baths

■ The Family Room is crowned in a vaulted ceiling and is accented by a fireplace flanked by windows

■ The Kitchen includes a walk-in Pantry

■ The Master Suite features a tray ceiling over the Bedroom and a vaulted ceiling over the Bath

■ An optional basement, slab, or crawl space foundation — please specify when ordering

■ No materials list is available for this plan

Main floor — 1,875 sq. ft.
Basement — 1,891 sq. ft.
Garage — 475 sq. ft.

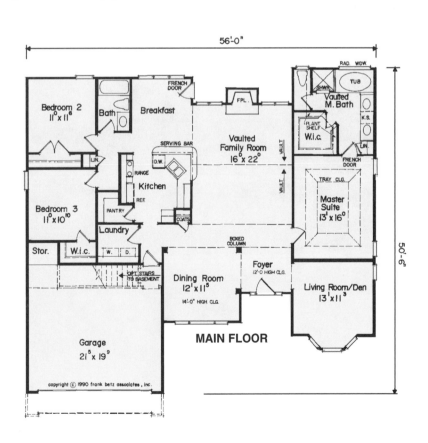

MAIN FLOOR

copyright © 1990 frank betz associates, inc.

Featuring Exposed Beams

Design by Fillmore Design Group

No. 98503 **BL**

This plan features:

— Three bedrooms

— Two full baths

■ The covered Porch shelters the Entry to this home

■ The large Living Room with exposed beams includes a fireplace and built-ins

■ The bright Dining Room is located next to the Kitchen which features a center island

■ The Bedroom Wing features three spacious Bedrooms and two full Baths

■ The two-car Garage has a handy Workshop Area

■ An optional slab or crawl space foundation — please specify when ordering

■ No materials list is available for this plan

Main floor — 1,876 sq. ft.
Garage — 619 sq. ft.

Total living area 1,876 sq. ft. ■ *Price Code C*

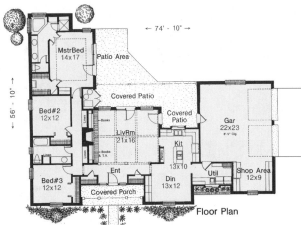

Floor Plan

Skylight Luxury

Design by Landmark Designs, Inc.

No. 99727 **BL** ✕

This plan features:

— Two bedrooms

— Two full baths

■ Five skylights bathe most of the house in soft sunlight

■ A wood stove serves as a centerpiece for the Living Room, Dining Room and the Kitchen

■ The efficient Kitchen has a cooktop peninsula

■ The Master Suite has a walk-in closet, double vanity and huge tub and shower

■ The Patio and Deck surround the house

Main floor — 1,876 sq. ft.
Garage — 624 sq. ft.

Total living area 1,876 sq. ft. ■ *Price Code C*

WIDTH 62'-0"
DEPTH 62'-0"

FLOOR PLAN

Design by Frank Betz Associates, Inc.

No. 98430 BL ✕

This plan features:

- Three bedrooms

- Two full and one half baths

■ A sixteen-foot high ceiling is above the Foyer

■ Arched openings highlight the hallway accessing the Great Room which is further enhanced by a fireplace

■ Another vaulted ceiling tops the Dining Room which is convenient to both the Living Room and the Kitchen

■ The expansive Kitchen features a center work island, a built-in Pantry and a Breakfast Area defined by a tray ceiling

■ The Master Suite also has a tray ceiling treatment and includes a lavish private Bath and a huge walk-in closet

■ The secondary Bedrooms have private access to a full Bath

■ An optional basement, slab, or crawl space foundation — please specify when ordering

Main floor — 1,884 sq. ft.
Basement — 1,908 sq. ft.
Garage — 495 sq. ft.

■ Total living area 1,884 sq. ft. ■ Price Code C ■

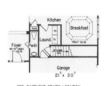

OPT. BASEMENT STAIRS LOCATION

Design by Larry E. Belk

No. 93080 BL

This plan features:

- Three bedrooms

- Two full baths

■ There are ten-foot ceilings in many of the rooms

■ This home has plenty of storage space

■ The Dining Room is open to the Foyer and Living Room

■ A fireplace is set between built-in cabinets in the Living Room

■ The Kitchen is well planned and executed

■ No materials list is available for this plan

Main floor — 1,890 sq. ft.
Garage — 565 sq. ft.

■ Total living area 1,890 sq. ft. ■ Price Code C ■

MAIN FLOOR

French Influenced Design

Design by Larry E. Belk

■ *Total living area 1,890 sq. ft.* ■ *Price Code C* ■

No. 96601

■ **This plan features:**

— Three bedrooms

— Two full baths

■ The interior of the home features a formal Dining Room with a ten-foot coffered, decorative ceiling

■ The oversize Living Room includes built-in bookcases on either side of the fireplace

■ An angled bar separates the Kitchen and Breakfast Room and opens the Kitchen to the Living Room beyond.

■ The Master Bedroom includes a luxurious Master Bath with a huge walk-in closet, dual vanity, and separate whirlpool tub and shower

■ No materials list is available for this plan

Main floor — 1,890 sq. ft.
Garage — 565 sq. ft.

MAIN FLOOR

WIDTH 65'-10"
DEPTH 53'-5"

© Larry E. Belk

One Level Living is a Breeze

Design by The Garlinghouse Company

■ *Total living area 1,899 sq. ft.* ■ *Price Code C* ■

No. 10656

■ **This plan features:**

— Three bedrooms

— Two full and one half baths

■ The Master Bedroom has a full Bath, walk-in closet and Dressing Area with access to the Deck

■ The airy Kitchen is open to the Breakfast Nook and Laundry Area

■ The Great Room has vaulted ceilings, a fireplace, and room for books

Main floor — 1,899 sq. ft.
Basement — 1,890 sq. ft.
Garage — 530 sq. ft.

MAIN FLOOR

One-Story Farmhouse

©1997 Donald A. Gardner Architects, Inc.

B. NASSAN

Design by Donald A. Gardner Architects, Inc.

No. 98006

■ **This plan features:**

– Three bedrooms

– Two full baths

■ The wrap-around Porch surrounds the front of the home

■ The Great Room is crowned in a cathedral ceiling and a dormer window bathes the room in natural light

■ A vaulted ceiling tops the formal Dining Room

■ The screened Porch is entered from the Breakfast Bay

■ The Bonus Room over the Garage provides options for expansion

Main floor — 1,899 sq. ft.
Bonus — 315 sq. ft.
Garage — 530 sq. ft.

■ *Total living area 1,899 sq. ft.* ■ *Price Code E* ■

Open Air Ranch

Design by The Garlinghouse Company

No. 84014

■ **This plan features:**

– Four bedrooms

– Two full baths

■ The stone fireplace, wood storage and bookshelves separate the Living Room from the Family Room

■ The Dining Room features doors to the rear Patio

■ The convenient U-shaped Kitchen is highlighted by a double sink, a Pantry, and ample counter space

■ The Laundry/Utility Room is located off of the two-car Garage

■ Three Bedrooms share a full bath

■ The Master Bedroom has two closets and a private Bath with a dual vanity

■ No materials list is available for this plan

Main floor — 1,901 sq. ft.
Garage — 420 sq. ft.

■ *Total living area 1,901 sq. ft.* ■ *Price Code C* ■

245

Old Cottage Feeling

Design by Fillmore Design Group

No. 98589

■ This plan features:

— Three bedrooms

— Two full and one half baths

■ The Entry and the Gallery have ten-foot ceilings

■ The Great Room is also topped by a ten-foot ceiling and is accented by a fireplace

■ The Kitchen has the added convenience of a serving bar to the Great Room

■ The covered Porch in the front of the home and the covered Patio to the rear expand living space outdoors

■ The private Patio is accessible from the Master Bedroom

■ No materials list is available for this plan

Main floor — 1,902 sq. ft.
Garage — 636 sq. ft.

Total living area 1,902 sq. ft. ■ Price Code C

FLOOR PLAN

Victorian Charm

Design by Donald A. Gardner Architects, Inc.

No. 96405

■ This plan features:

— Four bedrooms

— Two full baths

■ This home combines Victorian charm with today's lifestyle needs

■ Ceilings are vaulted in the Great Room and are ten-feet high in the Foyer, Dining Room, Kitchen/Breakfast Bay and Bedroom/Study

■ The secluded Master Bedroom features a tray ceiling, walk-in closet and private, skylit Bath

■ The two additional Bedrooms, located in separate wing, share a full Bath

■ The front and rear Porches extend living area outdoors

Main floor — 1,903 sq. ft.
Garage & storage — 531 sq. ft.

© Donald A. Gardner Architects, Inc.

Total living area 1,903 sq. ft. ■ Price Code E

FLOOR PLAN

Design by Ahmann Design, Inc.

Total living area 1,906 sq. ft. ■ *Price Code C* ■

No. 99113 **BL**

■ This plan features:

— Three bedrooms

— Two full and one half baths

■ The recessed entrance has an arched transom window over the door and sidelight windows

■ The Living Room boasts a high ceiling and a warm fireplace

■ The large Kitchen Area includes the open Dining Area with a rear bay that accesses the backyard

■ There is a large Utility Room, Garage access, and a half Bath located off of the Kitchen

■ This home has a three-car Garage

■ No materials list is available for this plan

Main floor — 1,906 sq. ft.
Basement — 1,906 sq. ft.

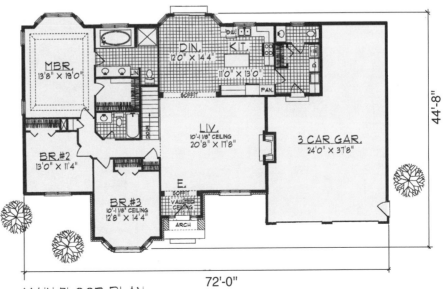

MAIN FLOOR PLAN

72'-0"

44'-8"

Traditional Three Bedroom

Design by Ahmann Design, Inc.

No. 99154 BL

This plan features:

— Three bedrooms

— Two full and one half baths

■ The vaulted Entry and Great Room provide this home's wonderful first impression

■ The large three-stall Garage includes ample storage space for hobby materials and yard equipment

■ The covered Porch, accessed from the Dining Room, expands living space to the outdoors

■ No materials list is available for this plan

Main floor — 1,907 sq. ft.
Basement — 1,907 sq. ft.
Garage — 678 sq. ft.

Total living area 1,907 sq. ft. ■ Price Code C

MAIN FLOOR

Comfort Zone

Design by Ryan & Associates

No. 91105 BL

This plan features:

— Three bedrooms

— Two full baths

■ The stunning brick veneer, arched windows, gabled rooflines and herringbone patterns add plenty of character

■ The efficient Master Bath includes a double vanity with knee space, a corner whirlpool tub, and a separate shower

■ The Bonus Area over the Garage is accessed by a stairway near the Kitchen

■ Extra features include a Kitchen snack bar, the back Porch, an abundance of closets, and the large Living Room

■ No materials list is available for this plan

Main Level — 1,908 sq. ft.
Bonus — 262 sq. ft.
Garage — 562 sq. ft.

Total living area 1,908 sq. ft. ■ Price Code C

MAIN FLOOR

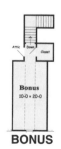

BONUS

Pretty as a Picture

No. 98008

This plan features:

— Three bedrooms

— Two full baths

■ This picture perfect Country-style plan offers space and flexibility

■ The wrap-around front Porch is beautiful and functional at the same time

■ The Great Room has a cathedral ceiling and a fireplace

■ The Dining Room has windows that overlook the front Porch, plus a tray ceiling

■ The Kitchen has a convenient layout with a good work triangle

■ The Master Bedroom is isolated and features a galley Bath that leads into the walk-in closet

■ Two additional Bedrooms are located in their own wing with a full Bath

■ The two-car Garage is conveniently located in the rear of the home

■ There is a Bonus Room over the Garage waiting to be finished to suit your needs

Main floor — 1,911 sq. ft.
Bonus — 406 sq. ft.
Garage — 551 sq. ft.

©1997 Donald A. Gardner Architects, Inc.

■ *Total living area 1,911 sq. ft.* ■ *Price Code E* ■

FLOOR PLAN

© 1997 Donald A Gardner Architects, Inc.

Beautiful Arched Window

No. 94966

This plan features:

—Three bedrooms

—Two full baths

■ Ten-foot ceilings top the Entry and the Great Room

■ A see-through fireplace is shared between the Great Room and the Hearth Room

■ A built-in entertainment center and a bay window highlight the Hearth Room

■ The Breakfast Room and Hearth Room share an open layout separated only by a snack bar in the Kitchen

■ A built-in Pantry and double corner sink enhance efficiency in the Kitchen

■ The split Bedroom plan assures homeowner's privacy in the Master Suite, which includes a decorative ceiling, private Bath and a large walk-in closet

■ Two additional Bedrooms at the opposite side of the home share a full, skylit Bath in the hall

Main floor — 1,911 sq. ft.
Garage — 481 sq. ft.

■ *Total living area 1,911 sq. ft.* ■ *Price Code C* ■

© Design Basics, Inc.

MAIN FLOOR

Great As A Mountain Retreat

Design by Donald A. Gardner Architects, Inc.

No. 99815

This plan features:

— Three bedrooms

— Two full baths

■ Board and batten siding, stone and stucco combine to give this popular plan a casual feel

■ The user-friendly Kitchen has a huge Pantry for ample storage and an island counter

■ Casual family meals are set in the sunny Breakfast Area and formal gatherings are in the columned Dining Area

■ The Master Suite is topped by a deep tray ceiling, a large walk-in closet, an extravagant private Bath and direct access to the back Porch

Main floor — 1,912 sq. ft.
Garage — 580 sq. ft.
Bonus — 398 sq. ft.

Total living area 1,912 sq. ft. ■ *Price Code E* ■

© Donald A. Gardner Architects, Inc.

FLOOR PLAN

© 1996 Donald A Gardner Architects, Inc.

For A Narrow Lot

Design by Donald A. Gardner Architects, Inc.

No. 98034

This plan features:

— Three bedrooms

— Two full baths

■ The wrap-around front Porch, triple gables and arched window add curb appeal to this charming home

■ Columns, a vaulted ceiling and an inviting fireplace accent the Great Room

■ The unusual octagonal Dining Area with Porch access provides elegant setting

■ The open Kitchen easily serves Dining Area, Breakfast Alcove and screened Porch

■ The Master Bedroom offers privacy with two walk-in closets and skylit Bath

■ Two more Bedrooms, with ample closets, share a skylit Bath

■ The Bonus Room upstairs could be a future fourth Bedroom

■ No materials list is available for this plan

Main floor — 1,918 sq. ft.
Bonus room — 307 sq. ft.
Garage — 552 sq. ft.

Total living area 1,918 sq. ft. ■ *Price Code E* ■

© Donald A. Gardner Architects, Inc.

MAIN FLOOR

© Donald A. Gardner Architects, Inc.

WIDTH 48'-8"
DEPTH 89'-4"

Design by Donald A. Gardner Architects, Inc.

Traditional Elegance

No. 98061

■ This plan features:

— Three bedrooms

— Two full baths

■ A smart combination of brick and siding lends traditional elegance to the exterior of this economical to build home

■ A squared off, uncomplicated footprint allows for easy construction

■ Tray ceilings add elegance to the formal Dining Room and the Master Bedroom

■ Soaring cathedral ceilings expand the Great Room and the Kitchen

■ No materials list is available for this plan

Main floor — 1,925 sq. ft.
Bonus room - 386 sq. ft.
Garage/storage - 591 sq. ft.

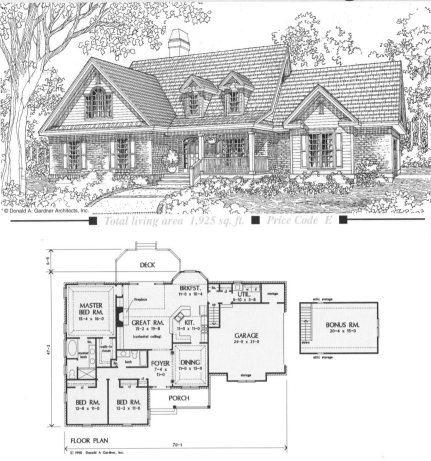

Total living area 1,925 sq. ft. ■ Price Code E

Design by Frank Betz Associates, Inc.

Grand Window

No. 97277

■ This plan features:

— Three bedrooms

— Two full baths

■ The two-story window accenting the front of the home streams natural light into the Dining Room to create an airy atmosphere

■ Vaulted and high ceilings punctuate this home with a feeling of volume and spaciousness

■ The Bonus Room adds possibilities for expansion

■ The private Sitting Area in the Master Suite creates a quiet retreat

■ No materials list is available for this plan

Main floor — 1,927 sq. ft.
Bonus room — 424 sq. t.
Basement — 1,927 sq. ft.
Garage — 494 sq. ft.

Total living area 1,927 sq. ft. ■ Price Code C

Triple Arched Porch

Design by Archival Designs

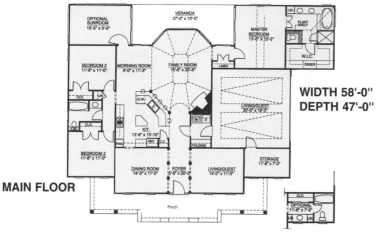

Total living area 1,928 sq. ft. ■ Price Code C

MAIN FLOOR

WIDTH 58'-0"
DEPTH 47'-0"

No. 98238 BL

■ **This plan features:**

— Three bedrooms

— Two full baths

■ Columns accent the Porch and separate living space inside this home without obstructing views

■ The split Bedroom layout assures the Master Suite of privacy

■ The openness of the common space creates the illusion of more space

■ The optional Sun Room expands the living space and is accessed from the Morning Room

■ No materials list is available for this plan

Main floor — 1,928 sq. ft.
Sunroom — 160 sq. ft.
Porch — 315 sq. ft.
Garage — 400 sq. ft.

Double Arches

Design by Larry E. Belk

Total living area 1,932 sq. ft. ■ Price Code C

MAIN FLOOR

© Larry E. Belk

No. 93098 BL

■ **This plan features:**

— Three bedrooms

— Two full baths

■ Double arches form the entrance to this elegantly styled home

■ Two palladian windows add distinction to the elevation and give the home a timeless appeal

■ Ten-foot ceilings in all major living areas give the home an expansive feeling

■ The Kitchen features an angled eating bar and opens to both the Breakfast Room and Living Room

■ The Master Suite includes a Master Bath with all the amenities, including a huge walk-in closet

■ The two additiona Bedrooms are located conveniently nearby and share a Bath

■ No materials list is available for this plan

Main floor — 1,932 sq. ft.
Garage — 552 sq. ft.

Design by Donald A. Gardner Architects, Inc.

Stunning Stone and Stucco

No. 98097

■ **This plan features:**

— Three bedrooms

— Two full baths

■ Unusual gable detailing compliments this design and the grand fieldstone entrance

■ The expansive Great Room offers a cathedral ceiling, fireplace nestled between book shelves and access to the Deck, Dining Area and screened Porch

■ The efficient Kitchen with curved serving counter and Pantry easily accesses the Breakfast and Dining Areas, and Utility and Garage

■ The comfortable Master Bedroom has Deck access, walk-in closet and plush Bath

■ Two additional Bedrooms, with ample closets, share a full Bath in the hall

Main floor — 1,933 sq. ft.
Garage — 526 sq. ft.

© Donald A. Gardner Architects, Inc.

■ *Total living area   1,933 sq. ft.* ■ *Price Code   E* ■

FLOOR PLAN

Design by Frank Betz Associates, Inc.

Outstanding Four Bedroom

No. 98435

■ **This plan features:**

— Four bedrooms

— Two full baths

■ A radius window highlights the exterior and the formal Dining Room

■ A high ceiling tops the Foyer for a grand first impression

■ A vaulted ceiling enhances the Great Room accented by a fireplace that is framed by windows to either side

■ An arched opening leads you to the Kitchen from the Great Room

■ The Breakfast Room is topped by a vaulted ceiling and enhanced by an elegant French door to the rear yard

■ A tray ceiling and a five-piece Bath gives luxurious presence to the Master Suite

■ An optional basement or crawl space foundation — please specify when ordering

Main floor — 1,945 sq. ft.

■ *Total living area   1,945 sq. ft.* ■ *Price Code   C* ■

MAIN FLOOR

253

A Very Distinctive Ranch

Design by Ahmann Design, Inc.

No. 99115

This plan features:

— Three bedrooms

— Two full and one half baths

■ This hip roofed Ranch has an exterior mix of brick and siding

■ The recessed entrance has sidelights which create a formal Entry

■ The formal Dining Room has a Butler's Pantry for added convenience

■ The Great Room features a vaulted ceiling and a fireplace for added atmosphere

■ The large open Kitchen has ample cupboard space and a spacious Breakfast Area

■ The Master Suite includes a walk-in closet, private Bath and an elegant bay window

■ The Laundry Room is on the main floor between the three-car Garage and the Kitchen

■ No materials list is available for this plan

Main floor — 1,947 sq. ft.
Basement — 1,947 sq. ft.

■ Total living area 1,947 sq. ft. ■ Price Code C ■

MAIN FLOOR

Step-Saving Floor Plan

Design by Living Concepts Home Planning

No. 96902

This plan features:

— Three bedrooms

— Two full and one half baths

■ A recessed entrance leads into the Foyer and the Dining Room is defined by columns with the Gathering Room beyond

■ The expansive Gathering Room has an inviting fireplace that opens to the Deck/Terrace and Breakfast/ Kitchen Area for comfortable gatherings

■ An angled serving counter and the Pantry save steps in the Kitchen

■ The corner Master Suite is privately located with a decorative ceiling, a wall of windows, plush Bath and a double walk-in closet

■ The two additional Bedroom Suites, with ample closets, share a full double vanity Bath

■ No materials list is available for this plan

Main floor — 1,950 sq. ft.
Basement — 1,287 sq. ft.
Garage — 466 sq. ft.
Bonus — 255 sq. ft.

■ Total living area 1,950 sq. ft. ■ Price Code C ■

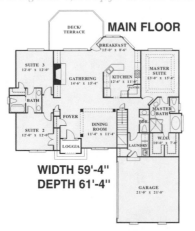

MAIN FLOOR

WIDTH 59'-4"
DEPTH 61'-4"

©1997 Donald A. Gardner Architects, Inc.

■ *Total living area 1,954 sq. ft.* ■ *Price Code E* ■

No. 98009

■ This plan features:

— Four bedrooms

— Two full and one half baths

■ Large top circle windows, stucco, and a tile roof add style to this home

■ The common space of the home is impressive with twelve-foot ceilings and columns

■ The Kitchen is partially enclosed by eight-foot high walls

■ The screened Porch in the rear is perfect for entertaining guests

■ The Master Bedroom has a tray ceiling and a private Bath

■ An optional slab or a crawl space foundation — please specify when ordering

Main floor — 1,954 sq. ft.

SCREEN PORCH
24–11 x 8–7
(12' ceiling)

BRKFST.
11–8 x 9–0
(12' ceiling)

fireplace

MASTER BED RM.
15–0 x 13–4

GREAT RM.
19–0 x 15–0
(12' ceiling)

KIT.
11–8 x 11–8
(12' ceiling)

bath

BED RM.
11–0 x 12–0

(8' high wall)

pan.

master bath

cl

pd. rm.

FOYER
6–0 x 7–4

DINING
11–0 x 12–0
(12' ceiling)

w.
d.

lin.

cl

BED RM.
12–0 x 11–0

walk-in closet

cl

STUDY/ BED RM.
11–4 x 12–0
(10' ceiling)

PORCH

GARAGE
21–8 x 22–10

FLOOR PLAN

58–10

64–10

© 1997 Donald A Gardner Architects, Inc.

(optional full bath)

Compact Plan

Design by Larry E. Belk

■ *Total living area 1,955 sq. ft.* ■ *Price Code C* ■

WIDTH 65–0

© Larry E. Belk

MASTER BEDRM
12-8 X 14-6
10 FT CLG

MASTER BATH
10 FT CLG

BATH 2

LIN

BEDRM 2
11-0 X 13-6

BEDRM 3
12-6 X 13-4

FOYER
10 FT CLG

FP

GREAT ROOM
18-6 X 15-6
10 FT CLG

BRKFST RM
12-0 X 10-0
10 FT CLG

KITCHEN
12-6 X 14-0
10 FT CLG

DINING ROOM
12-2 X 14-0
10 FT CLG

UTIL
6-8 X 8-6

PAN

ARCH

ARCH

ARCH

DEPTH 58–8

PORCH

GARAGE

MAIN FLOOR

No. 93085 BL

■ **This plan features:**

— Three bedrooms

— Two full baths

■ The roomy front Porch adds outdoor living area

■ The Dining Room and Great Room are visible from the Foyer through a series of elegant archways

■ An angled Counter opens to the Great Room from the Kitchen

■ The Master Suite has a luxurious private Bath including a whirlpool tub and a separate shower and an enormous walk-in closet

■ The two additional Bedrooms share a full Bath

■ No materials list is available for this plan

Main floor — 1,955 sq. ft.
Garage — 517 sq. ft.

Elegant Entry Columns

■ *Total living area 1,955 sq. ft.* ■ *Price Code C* ■

No. 93031 ▪ BL

■ This plan features:

— Three bedrooms

— Two full baths

■ This plan has a Traditional Southern elevation with an Entry flanked by large square columns

■ Elegant columns define the Dining Room and the Great Room

■ The Master Suite is privately located away from the other Bedrooms

■ The Kitchen has a Pantry and plenty of cabinet and counter space

■ No materials list is available for this plan

First floor — 1,955 sq. ft.
Garage — 561 sq. ft.
Bonus — 240 sq. ft.

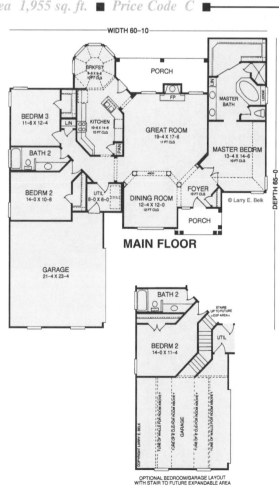

MAIN FLOOR

OPTIONAL BEDROOM/GARAGE LAYOUT
WITH STAIR TO FUTURE EXPANDABLE AREA

Spacious Smaller Home

Design by Landmark Designs, Inc.

No. 98743 BL

■ This plan features:

— Three bedrooms

— Two full baths

■ A vaulted ceiling and a dormer create the spacious Entry

■ The eye-catching Great Room has a vaulted ceiling, a corner fireplace and a bank of windows filling the room with light

■ The efficient U-shaped Kitchen has an angled eating bar, built-in Pantry and a double sink

■ The luxurious Master Suite includes a roomy walk-in closet, access to the Deck, and a private Bath

■ A Mini-Master Suite includes a walk-in closet with a vanity and private access to the hall Bath

■ The third Bedroom shares the use of the hall Bath

■ No materials list is available for this plan

Main floor — 1,958 sq. ft.

Total living area 1,958 sq. ft. ■ _Price Code C_

MAIN FLOOR

WIDTH 58'-0"
DEPTH 68'-6"

Elegant and Efficient

Design by Rick Garner

No. 92515 BL

■ **This plan features:**

— Three bedrooms

— Two full baths

■ A covered entrance into the Foyer leads to a spacious Living Room with a decorative ceiling above a hearth fireplace

■ A decorative window and ceiling highlight the formal Dining Room

■ The Large, Country Kitchen with double ovens, a cooktop and a peninsula snack bar, serves the bright Eating Area

■ The Large Master Bedroom Suite has a decorative ceiling, a walk-in closet, and plush Bath

■ Two additional Bedrooms, with walk-in closets, share a full Bath

■ An optional slab or crawl space foundation — please specify when ordering

Main floor — 1,959 sq. ft.
Garage — 512 sq. ft.

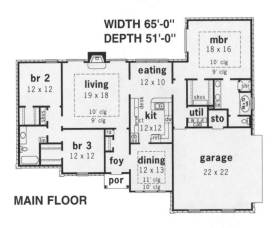

Total living area 1,959 sq. ft. ■ _Price Code D_

WIDTH 65'-0"
DEPTH 51'-0"

MAIN FLOOR

Easy, Economical Building

No. 99813

■ This plan features:

— Three bedrooms

— Two full baths

■ Many architectural elements enhance this efficient and economical design

■ The Great Room is topped by a vaulted ceiling including a arched, window dormer

■ The Open Kitchen with an angled counter easily serves the Breakfast Area

■ Tray ceilings enhance the Dining Room, the front Bedroom and the Master Bedroom

■ The Private Master Bath provides a garden tub, a double vanity and skylight

Main floor — 1,959 sq. ft.
Bonus room — 385 sq. ft.
Garage & storage — 484 sq. ft.

© Donald A. Gardner Architects, Inc.

■ *Total living area 1,959 sq. ft.* ■ *Price Code E* ■

© 1996 Donald A Gardner Architects, Inc.

FLOOR PLAN

Definitely Detailed

No. 97703 BL

■ This plan features:

— Three bedrooms

— Two full baths

■ An artistically detailed brick exterior adds to the appeal of this home

■ The Foyer is separated from the Great Room by columns

■ The Great Room has a wall of windows and a warming fireplace

■ The Dining Room has a sloped ceiling and adjoins the Kitchen

■ The Kitchen is arranged in a U-shape and features a center island plus a walk-in Pantry

■ The Bedrooms are all on one side of the home for privacy

■ An optional plan for the Basement includes a Recreation Room, an Exercise Room, and a Bath

■ No materials list is available for this plan

Main Floor — 1,963 sq. ft.
Basement — 1,963 sq. ft.

■ *Total living area 1,963 sq. ft.* ■ *Price Code C* ■

MAIN FLOOR

BASEMENT

Comfortable and Charming

Design by Studer Residential Design, Inc.

■ Total living area 1,964 sq. ft. ■ Price Code C ■

MAIN FLOOR

55'-8"

55'-2"

No. 92660

■ **This plan features:**

— Three bedrooms

— Two full baths

■ The front entry opens into the Foyer and the spacious Great Room

■ The formal Dining Room has a sloped ceiling and an expansive view of the back yard

■ A cooktop island and Pantry are featured in the Kitchen

■ The corner Master Bedroom offers a sloped ceiling, a walk-in closet, and a plush Bath

■ No materials list is available for this plan

Main floor — 1,964 sq. ft.
Garage — 447 sq. ft.
Basement — 1,807 sq. ft.

Great Room Center Attraction

■ *Total living area 1,972 sq. ft.* ■ *Price Code C* ■

No. 96527 BL X

■ **This plan features:**

— Three bedrooms

— Two full baths

■ The Foyer has a vaulted ceiling to the dormer window

■ The Great Room has a rear wall fireplace, and opens to the rear Porch

■ The Kitchen features an eating bar and opens into the Dining Area

■ The Master Suite has a tray ceiling a whirlpool Bath, and two walk-in closets

■ Two secondary Bedrooms and a Study round out this plan

Main floor — 1,972 sq. ft.
Garage — 462 sq. ft.

MAIN FLOOR

Sizzling with Style

Design by Frank Betz Associates, Inc.

■ *Total living area 1,978 sq. ft.* ■ ● *Price Code C* ●

MAIN FLOOR

GARAGE LOCATION W/ BASEMENT

Opt. Basement Stair Location

No. 97623

■ This plan features:

— Three bedrooms

— Two full and one half baths

■ This floor plan has a Garage entry, cutting down on tracked in dirt

■ The serving bar in the Kitchen expands the workspace and adds a casual dining option

■ The split Bedroom layout assures the Master Suite of privacy

■ The high ceilings throughout the home give added volume and atmosphere to the rooms

■ An optional basement or crawl space foundation — please specify when ordering

■ No materials list is available for this plan

Main floor — 1,978 sq. ft.
Basement — 2,008 sq. ft.
Garage — 406 sq. ft.

Splendid Space

■ *Total living area 1,983 sq. ft.* ■ *Price Code C* ■

No. 91129 BL ЯR

■ This plan features:

- Three bedrooms

- Two full baths

■ The split Bedroom plan allows for privacy

■ Arched entries lead into the Living and Dining Rooms

■ The Sunroom is accessed from the Living and Breakfast Rooms

■ The Breakfast Room has a built-in desk

■ No materials list is available for this plan

Main floor — 1,983 sq. ft.
Garage — 492 sq. ft.

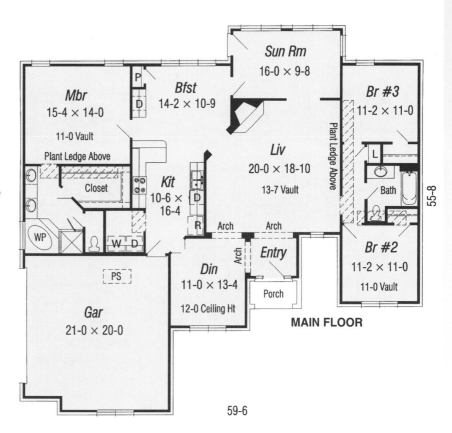

MAIN FLOOR

Brick Detail with Arches

Design by Rick Garner

■ *Total living area 1,987 sq. ft.* ■ *Price Code C* ■

MAIN FLOOR

BEDROOM 4
11'-0"X12'-6"

LIN.

PORCH 6'-0"X29'-8"

MASTER BEDROOM
14'-0"X15'-0"

BREAKFAST
8'-0"X12'-0"

W
D

STO.

DEN
18'-0"X18'-0"

BEDROOM 3
11'-0"X12'-0"

KITCHEN
10'-0"X12'-0"

GARAGE
21'-6"X22'-0"

FOYER

BEDROOM 2
11'-0"X12'-0"

PORCH
6'-0"X16'-0"

DINING
12'-0"X12'-0"

67'-0" Width
49'-0" Depth

No. 92544

■ **This plan features:**

— Four bedrooms

— Two full and one half baths

▨ Front and back Porches expand the living space

▨ The spacious Den has a fireplace flanked by built-in shelves, and double access to the rear Porch

▨ The formal Dining Room has an arched window, and direct access to the Kitchen

▨ The u-shaped Kitchen has a snack bar counter, a Breakfast Area, and an adjoining Laundry and Garage

▨ The secluded Master Suite has a walk-in closet, and a double vanity Bath

▨ An optional slab or crawl space foundation — please specify when ordering

Main floor — 1,987 sq. ft.
Garage/Storage — 515 sq. ft.

Breakfast Bay

■ *Total living area 1,990 sq. ft.* ■ *Price Code C* ■

No. 24743 BL

■ This plan features:

— Three bedrooms

— Two full baths

■ This home has a split Bedroom design

■ The front Porch adds Country charm

■ The Deck in the rear expands living space outdoors

■ A sloped ceiling and an arched window highlight the secondary Bedroom

■ The design elements used add dimension to the Great Room

■ A whirlpool tub makes the Master Bath special

■ No materials list is available for this plan

Main floor - 1,990 sq. ft.
Basement - 1,338 sq. ft.
Garage - 660 sq. ft.
Porch - 212 sq. ft.

MAIN FLOOR

Versatility and Charm

Design by Studer Residential Design, Inc.

■ Total living area 1,998 sq. ft. ■ Price Code C ■

No. 92628

■ **This plan features:**

— Three bedrooms

— Two full baths

■ The spacious Great Room has a corner fireplace and tall transom windows

■ The formal Dining Room allows for easy entertaining

■ An optional Study/Bedroom provides flexibility for this home

■ A large island snack bar and Breakfast Bay Area expand the Kitchen

■ The Master Bedroom has a Luxurious Bath with a walk-in closet

■ No materials list is available for this plan

First floor — 1,998 sq. ft.
Garage — 488 sq. ft.
Basement — 1,863

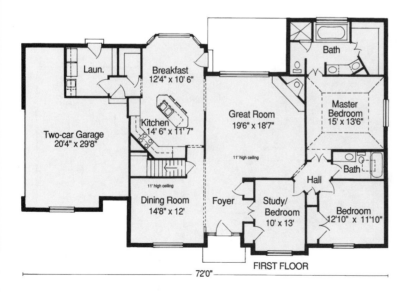

Design by Ahmann Design, Inc.

Beautiful and Functional

■ *Total living area 2,007 sq. ft.* ■ *Price Code D* ■

No. 97151   BL

■ This plan features:

— Three bedrooms

— Two full baths

■ The gracious, keystone arch Entry opens to the formal Dining Room and the Great Room

■ The spacious Great Room features a fireplace surrounded by windows and topped by a cathedral ceiling

■ The Kitchen/Nook layout is ideal for busy household with easy access to the Deck, the Dining Room, the Laundry and the Garage

■ The corner Master Bedroom offers privacy, a double vanity Bath and a huge walk-in closet

■ No materials list is available for this plan

Main floor — 2,007 sq. ft.
Garage — 748 sq. ft.

WD. DECK
12'0" X 12'0"

BR. #2
12'0" X 11'8"

GRT. RM.
CATHEDRAL CLG.
16'0" X 20'0"

NK.
10'6" X 12'0"

KIT.
10'6" X 12'0"

MBR.
16'0" X 13'0"

PAN.

BR. #3
12'0" X 11'0"

E.
11' 1-1/8"
CEILING HGT.

DIN.
TRAY CEILING
12'0" X 13'0"

3 CAR GAR.
34'0" X 22'0"

53'0"

61'0"

MAIN FLOOR PLAN

Attractive Facade

Design by The Garlinghouse Company

No. 24259

■ This plan features:

— Three Bedrooms

— Two full Baths

■ This design has a Great Room with a fireplace and a built-in entertainment center

■ The private Master Bedroom has a luxurious Bath and walk-in closet

■ The Dining Room has a Butler Pantry

■ Two additional Bedrooms share a full Bath in the hall

Main floor — 2,010 sq. ft.
Basement — 2,010 sq. ft.

Total living area 2,010 sq. ft. • Price Code D

MAIN FLOOR

56'-4"

Stately Arched Entry

Design by Donald A. Gardner Architects, Inc.

© 1998 Donald A. Gardner, Inc.

No. 98011

■ **This plan features:**

— Three bedrooms

— Two full and one half baths

■ The stately arched entry Porch is supported by columns

■ The Dining Room has a tray ceiling and is defined by columns

■ The Great Room has a fireplace and access to the rear Porch and Deck

■ The Kitchen is full of cabinet and counter space

■ The Master Bedroom has a bay window and a tray ceiling

■ The Master Bath features a dual vanity and two walk-in closets

■ There are two secondary Bedrooms, one of which could be used as a Study, that share a full Bath

■ A Bonus Room is located over the two-car Garage

Main floor — 2,024 sq. ft.
Bonus — 423 sq. ft.
Garage — 623 sq. ft.

Total living area 2,024 sq. ft. • Price Code F

MAIN FLOOR

Design by Donald A. Gardner Architects, Inc.

Stunning Stucco

No. 98018

This plan features:

— Three bedrooms

— Two full and one half baths

- A lovely courtyard greets your entry into this stunning stucco home

- The Dining Room boasts a dramatic eleven-foot ceiling and a curved window wall

- The Great Room includes a fireplace and a cathedral ceiling

- The U-shaped Kitchen has a center island and is open to the Breakfast Area

- The rear Deck and Porch add living space in pleasant weather

- A private Bath and dual walk-in closets compliment the Master Suite

- Two secondary Bedrooms share a full Bath located between them

- A two-car Garage completes this plan

Main floor — 2,027 sq. ft.
Garage — 565 sq. ft.

Total living area 2,027 sq. ft. ■ Price Code F

WIDTH 80'-2"
DEPTH 61'-0"

© Donald A. Gardner Architects, Inc.

FLOOR PLAN

Design by Donald A. Gardner Architects, Inc.

Relaxed Country Living

No. 96402

This plan features:

— Three bedrooms

— Two full baths

- This design is a comfortable Country home with a deluxe Master Suite, front and back Porches and a dual-sided fireplace

- The vaulted Great Room is brightened by two clerestory dormers and a fireplace shared with Breakfast Area

- The Dining Room and the front Bedroom/Study are dressed up with tray ceilings

- The Master Bedroom features a vaulted ceiling, back Porch access, and a luxurious Bath with an over-sized, walk-in closet

- The skylit Bonus Room over Garage provides extra room for family needs

Main floor — 2,027 sq. ft.
Bonus room — 340 sq. ft.
Garage & storage — 532 sq. ft.

Total living area 2,027 sq. ft. ■ Price Code F

MAIN FLOOR

© 1997 Donald A. Gardner Architects, Inc.

Spacious Design

Design by Weinmaster Home Design

Total living area 2,035 sq. ft. ■ Price Code D

MAIN FLOOR

No. 98802 [BL]

■ **This plan features:**

— Three bedrooms

— Two full and one half baths

■ A railed staircase creates an open Foyer

■ This spacious hillside design captures the view of the back yard

■ The efficient Kitchen serves the formal and informal rooms with ease

■ The Living Room includes a cozy, corner fireplace

■ The layout between the Family Room and the Nook creates an open, airy atmosphere

■ The luxurious Master Suite is accented by French doors, and includes a plush Bath

■ The Bedroom/Den is highlighted by a bay window

■ No materials list is available for this plan

Main floor — 2,035 sq. ft.
Basement — 2,021 sq. ft.
Garage — 528 sq. ft.

Details and Luxury

Design by Studer Residential Design, Inc.

Total living area 2,041 sq. ft. ■ Price Code E

FIRST FLOOR

LOWER LEVEL

No. 92688 [BL]

■ **This plan features:**

— Three bedrooms

— Two full baths

■ The covered front Porch leads into a raised Foyer framed by columns

■ The Great Room has a high ceiling, a fireplace, and views of the rear Deck

■ The large Kitchen offers plenty of counter space, and opens to the Dining Area

■ The Master Bedroom has an octagonal Sitting Area, a Dressing Area, a walk in closet, and a full Bath

■ On the opposite side of the house is another Bedroom, a Bath, and a Bedroom/Library

■ The lower level can be finished at your convenience and includes a Rec Room, a Kitchen, Storage, and much more

■ No materials list is available for this plan

Main floor — 2,041 sq. ft.
Unfinished Lower level — 1,942 sq. ft.
Garage — 547 sq. ft.

Design by Donald A. Gardner Architects, Inc.

No. 98019

■ **This plan features:**

— Three bedrooms

— Two full and one half baths

■ Built-ins flank the fireplace in the Great Room while a soaring cathedral ceiling expands the room visually

■ The Kitchen has an angled counter and opens to the Breakfast Area and the Great Room

■ The large screened Porch has access to the Great Room and the Master Suite

■ The Bonus Room stands ready for future expansion

Main floor — 2,042 sq. ft.
Bonus room — 475 sq. ft.
Garage — 660 sq. ft.
Porch — 514 sq. ft.

© Donald A. Gardner Architects, Inc.

■ *Total living area 2,042 sq. ft.* ■ *Price Code F* ■

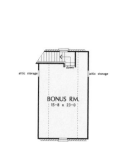

Rich Elegance

Design by Rick Garner

No. 92514

■ **This plan features:**

— Three bedrooms

— Two full baths

■ A popular split Bedroom floor plan affords maximum privacy

■ The formal Dining Room is next to the Foyer and accesses the Kitchen

■ The Great Room features a vaulted ceiling, a fireplace and built-in cabinets

■ There are two oversized secondary Bedrooms with walk-in closets and access to a full Bath

■ The Master Bedroom comes with dual walk-in closets and a comfortable Bath

■ An optional slab or crawl space foundation — please specify when ordering

Main floor — 2,045 sq. ft.
Garage — 541 sq. ft.

■ *Total living area 2,045 sq. ft.* ■ *Price Code D* ■

MAIN FLOOR

French Influenced One-Story

Design by Donald A. Gardner Architects, Inc.

© 1990 Donald A. Gardner Architects, Inc.

■ *Total living area 2,045 sq. ft.* ■ *Price Code F* ■

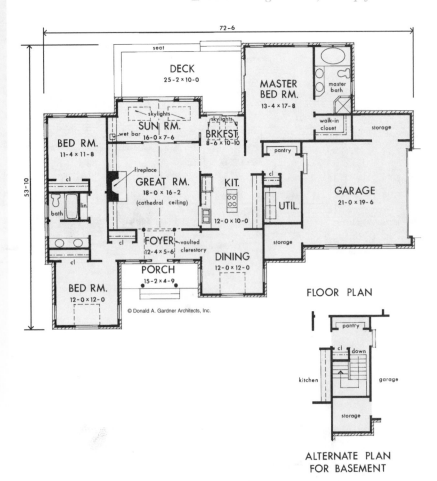

FLOOR PLAN

© Donald A. Gardner Architects, Inc.

ALTERNATE PLAN
FOR BASEMENT

No. 96421

■ This plan features:

— Three bedrooms

— Two full baths

■ Elegant details like, arched windows, stately columns, and a rich brick veneer create curb appeal

■ An arched clerestory window in the Foyer introduces natural light to the spacious Great Room

■ The Great Room adjoins a skylighted Sun Room with a wet bar which then opens onto a expansive Deck

■ The Kitchen has a cooking island with easy access to a large Pantry, and Utility Room

■ The large Master Bedroom opens to the Deck and features a private Bath with a garden tub, a separate shower, and a dual vanity

Main floor — 2,045 sq. ft.
Garage & storage — 563 sq. ft.

Contemporary Dream Home

No. 96465

This plan features:

– Three bedrooms

– Two full baths

■ Gables, a center front dormer, and a touch of brick combined with desirable amenities create an efficient floor plan

■ Dormer floods the Foyer with sunlight and intrigue, while a cathedral ceiling enlarges the Great Room

■ The Kitchen and Breakfast Area are punctuated by interior columns

■ Tray ceilings and arched windows are featured in the Dining Room and the Living Room

■ Two additional Bedrooms share a large full Bath with a double vanity in one wing, while the luxurious Master Suite enjoys privacy in another wing

Main floor — 2,050 sq. ft.
Bonus — 377 sq. ft.
Garage — 503 sq. ft.

■ *Total living area 2,050 sq. ft.* ■ *Price Code F* ■

WIDTH 68'-2"
DEPTH 56'-4"

FLOOR PLAN

Split Bedroom Plan

No. 98427

This plan features:

– Three bedrooms

– Two full baths

■ The Dining Room is crowned by a tray ceiling

■ The Living Room/Den is accessed by double doors, and enhanced by a bay window

■ The Kitchen includes a walk-in pantry and a corner double sink

■ The vaulted Breakfast Room adds light and space to the Kitchen

■ The Master Suite is topped by a tray ceiling, and offers a full Bath plus two walk-in closets

■ Two roomy, additional Bedrooms share a full Bath in the hall

■ An optional basement, slab or crawl space foundation — please specify when ordering

Main floor — 2,051 sq. ft.
Basement — 2,051 sq. ft.
Garage — 441 sq. ft.

■ *Total living area 2,051 sq. ft.* ■ *Price Code D* ■

WIDTH 56'-0"
DEPTH 60'-0"

MAIN FLOOR

Grace and Style

© 1997 Donald A. Gardner Architects, Inc.

B. NATHAN

■ *Total living area 2,057 sq. ft.* ■ *Price Code F* ■

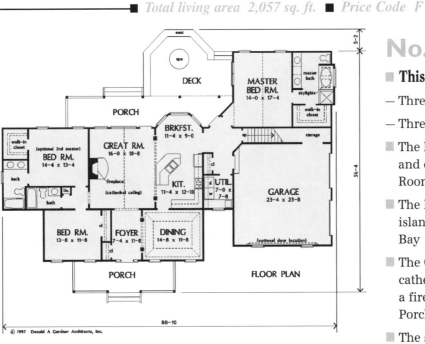

© 1997 Donald A. Gardner Architects, Inc.

(optional handicapped accessible bath)

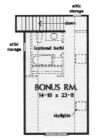

No. 96483

■ **This plan features:**

— Three bedrooms

— Three full baths

■ The Foyer is accented by columns and entry into the formal Dining Room

■ The Kitchen features an angled island and is open to the Breakfast Bay

■ The Great Room is topped by a cathedral ceiling and enhanced by a fireplace plus access to the rear Porch

■ The secluded Master Suite has a skylit Bath

■ Two secondary Bedrooms, one with a private Bath that can be altered for wheelchair accessibility, provide comfortable sleeping space

Main floor — 2,057 sq. ft.
Garage & storage — 622 sq. ft.
Bonus room — 444 sq. ft.

Design by Garrell Associates, Inc.

No. 93608 BL

This plan features:

– Three bedrooms

– Two full baths

– The graceful front Portico leads past the Foyer to the open Grand Room beyond

– Ten-foot ceilings and large windows draw light into all the rooms

– The large Kitchen with an island opens to the Breakfast Room and an optional Porch in the rear

– The split Bedroom design affords the utmost in privacy for all

– The oversized Laundry/Sewing Room is rarely seen in a home of this size

– The drive under Garage has plenty of room for three vehicles, or vehicles and a boat

– No materials list is available for this plan

Main floor — 2,060 sq. ft.
Garage — 1,000 sq. ft.

■ Total living area 2,060 sq. ft. ■ Price Code D ■

WIDTH 64'-0"
DEPTH 46'-6"

Design by Vaughn A. Lauban Designs

No. 96505 BL

This plan features:

– Three bedrooms

– Two full and one half baths

– The secluded Master Bedroom is tucked into a corner of the home, and has a full Bath and two walk-in closets

– Two additional Bedrooms on the opposite side of the home share the full Bath in the hall

– The expansive Living Room is highlighted by a corner fireplace and has access to the rear Porch

– The Kitchen is sandwiched between the bright, Eating Nook and the formal Dining Room providing ease in serving

Main floor — 2,069 sq. ft.
Garage — 481 sq. ft.

■ Total living area 2,069 sq. ft. ■ Price Code D ■

WIDTH 70'-0"
DEPTH 58'-0"

MAIN FLOOR

Four Bedrooms

Design by The Garlinghouse Company

Total living area 2,070 sq. ft. ■ Price Code D ■

MAIN FLOOR

68'-6"

52'-0"

No. 22004 BL

■ **This plan features:**

— Four bedrooms

— Three full baths

■ This plan is designed with four roomy
Bedrooms, including the Master Bedroom

■ The centrally located Family Room features
a fireplace, wet bar, and access to the Patio

■ The large Dining Room is located at the
front of the home for entertaining

■ The interesting Kitchen and Nook have an
adjoining Utility Room

Main floor — 2,070 sq. ft.
Garage — 474 sq. ft.

Charming Country Home

Design by Donald A. Gardner Architects, Inc.

©1999 Donald A. Gardner, Inc.

Total living area 2,078 sq. ft. ■ Price Code F ■

FLOOR PLAN

No. 98082 BL

■ **This plan features:**

— Three bedrooms

— Two full and one half baths

■ Bay windows expand both of the home's
Dining Areas, while the Great Room and
Kitchen are amplified by a shared cathedral
ceiling

■ The home maintains the Master Suite's
privacy while keeping close proximity to the
children's Bedrooms

■ A cathedral ceiling enhances the Master
Bedroom which includes a walk-in closet
and luxurious private Bath

■ Two additional Bedrooms, one with
cathedral ceiling, share a generous hall Bath

Main floor — 2,078 sq. ft.
Bonus — 339 sq. ft.
Garage — 523 sq. ft.

Room to Roam

■ *Total living area 2,080 sq. ft.* ■ *Price Code D* ■

No. 97242 **BL**

■ This plan features:

— Three bedrooms

— Two full and one half baths

■ The Family Room is the center of activity

■ The fireplace affords a cozy atmosphere while the Breakfast Area includes skylights and a French door to the rear yard

■ The Dining Room is accented by an elegant tray ceiling

■ The Bedroom wing includes a Master Suite with a large walk-in closet and a full Bath

■ An optional basement or crawl space foundation — please specify when ordering

■ No materials list is available for this plan

Main floor — 2,080 sq. ft.
Basement — 2,107 sq. ft.
Garage — 448 sq. ft.

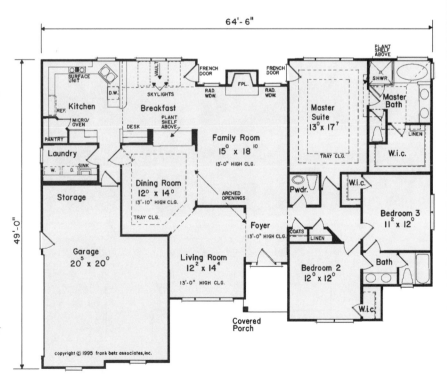

Packed with Options

No. 98559

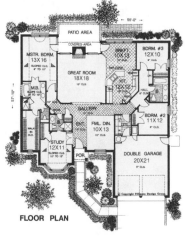

■ Total living area 2,081 sq. ft. ■ Price Code D ■

FLOOR PLAN

■ **This plan features:**

— Three bedrooms

— Three full baths

■ This home has a tiled Entry and Gallery that leads to the living space

■ The Great Room has a rear wall fireplace set between windows

■ Both Dining Areas are located steps away from the Kitchen

■ The Study has a sloped ceiling and a front bay of windows

■ The Master Bedroom has a private Bath and a galley-like walk-in closet

■ Two secondary Bedrooms are on the opposite side of the home

■ No materials list is available for this plan

Main Floor — 2,081 sq. ft.
Garage — 422 sq. ft.

Porches Expand Living Space

Design by Vaughn A. Lauban Designs

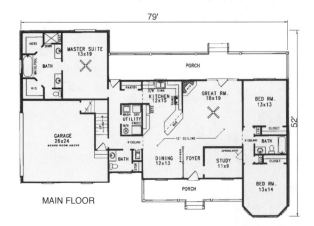

■ Total living area 2,089 sq. ft. ■ Price Code D ■

MAIN FLOOR

No. 96529

■ **This plan features:**

— Three bedrooms

— Two full and one half baths

■ Porches on the front and the rear of this home expand the living space to the outdoors

■ The rear Porch is accessed directly from the Great Room

■ The spacious Great Room is enhanced by a twelve-foot ceiling and a fireplace

■ The well-appointed Kitchen has an extended counter/eating bar and easy access to the Dining Room

■ Secondary Bedrooms have a full Bath located between the rooms

■ The Master Suite is enhanced by dual walk-in closets, a whirlpool tub, and a separate shower

■ There is a Bonus Room for future expansion

Main floor — 2,089 sq. ft.
Bonus room — 497 sq. ft.
Garage — 541 sq. ft.

Design by Donald A. Gardner Architects, Inc.

Dramatic Arched Entrance

No. 96450

This plan features:

- Three bedrooms
- Two full baths
- Stucco and tile are featured in a dramatic arched entrance
- A fireplace and built-in cabinets accent the large Great Room along with a cathedral ceiling
- The smart Kitchen with skylit Breakfast Area opens to the Great Room
- The Master Suite is highlighted by a skylit Bath and accesses the rear Deck
- Cathedral and tray ceilings plus nine-foot ceilings throughout the home add dramatic vertical proportion

Main floor — 2,090 sq. ft.
Garage — 568 sq. ft.

© Donald A. Gardner Architects, Inc.

■ *Total living area 2,090 sq. ft.* ■ *Price Code F* ■

Design by Vaughn A. Lauban Designs

Always in Style

No. 96539

This plan features:

- Four bedrooms
- Three full baths
- Flexibility is the key for the front Bedroom/Office which can easily convert to a Nursery with direct access to the Master Suite
- The split Bedroom layout affords the Master Suite privacy from the secondary Bedrooms
- Arched openings add to the custom look of the home
- Sloped ceilings and a fireplace highlight the Living Room
- No materials list is available for this plan

Main floor — 2,098 sq. ft.
Garage — 590 sq. ft.
Porch — 292 sq. ft.

■ *Total living area 2,098 sq. ft.* ■ *Price Code D* ■

WIDTH 69'
DEPTH 64'

MAIN FLOOR

Beautiful Combination

Design by The Garlinghouse Company

No. 24256

Total living area 2,108 sq. ft. ■ Price Code D

This plan features:

— Three bedrooms

— Two full baths

■ Vaulted ceilings are featured in the Living Room, Dining Room, Family Room and Eating Nook

■ An open layout between the Kitchen, Nook, and Family Room, makes the rooms appear even more spacious

■ A corner fireplace is found in the Family Room, which also has access to the Patio

■ A peninsula counter in the Kitchen doubles as an eating bar

■ The lavish Master Suite is equipped with a private Bath and walk-in closet

■ Two family Bedrooms share a full hall Bath

Main Area — 2,108 sq. ft.

Spacious Ranch

Design by Ahmann Design, Inc.

No. 97105 BL

Total living area 2,112 sq. ft. ■ Price Code D

This plan features:

— Three bedrooms

— Two full and one half baths

■ The Great Room has an eleven-foot ceiling and built-in cabinets framing the cozy fireplace

■ Arches decorate the doorways into the Breakfast Room and the Great Room

■ The Master Suite has a walk-in closet and a full Bath with a Spa tub

■ The open layout between the Kitchen, the Nook, and the Great Room encourages communication and family interaction through the rooms

■ No materials list is available for this plan

Main floor — 2,112 sq. ft.
Basement — 2,112 sq. ft.

MAIN FLOOR

Windows Add Light and Space

No. 20108

■ This plan features:

— Three bedrooms

— Two full and one half baths

■ Shutters, round-cut shingles, and an attractive porch add classic charm to the Traditional exterior of this home

■ The central Entry leads to the formal Living Room and also to the informal Family Room

■ Elegant ceiling treatment and a room-sized, walk-in closet are found in the Master Suite

■ The Kitchen has a range-top island, bump-out window and ideal location between the Family and Dining Rooms

Main floor — 2,120 sq. ft.
Basement — 2,120 sq. ft.
Garage — 576 sq. ft.

Total living area 2,120 sq. ft. ● Price Code D

MAIN FLOOR

Mid-Sized Country Style

No. 98748

■ This plan features:

— Three bedrooms

— Two full baths

■ A vaulted ceiling is featured over the Entry, Living Room, Dining Room, Family Room and Master Suite

■ A wide window bay expands the Living Room

■ A wide garden window expands the Kitchen while the cooktop, L-shaped island/eating bar adds convenience

■ A walk-in closet and a double vanity outside the Bath Area highlight the Master Suite

■ Two roomy additional Bedrooms share the full Bath in the hall

Main floor — 2,126 sq. ft.

Total living area 2,126 sq. ft. ● Price Code D

WIDTH 64'-0"
DEPTH 64'-0"

FLOOR PLAN

Rambling Ranch

Design by Donald A. Gardner Architects, Inc.

© 1994 Donald A. Gardner Architects, Inc.   B. NATHAN

■ *Total living area 2,136 sq. ft.* ■ *Price Code F* ■

FIRST FLOOR PLAN

DECK

spa

SCREEN PORCH
16-0 x 10-0

BED RM.
12-0 x 11-8

(cathedral ceiling)
GREAT RM.
20-0 x 24-10

fireplace

cabinets

BRKFST.
12-0 x 8-0

KIT.
12-0 x 13-8

BED RM.
12-0 x 12-0

FOYER
14-8 x 8-10

DINING
12-0 x 12-0

PORCH

MASTER BED RM.
14-0 x 17-4

master bath

skylights

walk-in closet

up

storage

GARAGE
23-4 x 22-8

UTIL.

skylights

64-4

76-4

© Donald A. Gardner Architects, Inc.

BONUS RM.
14-4 x 26-4

down

skylights

No. 99846

■ **This plan features:**

— Three bedrooms

— Two full and one half baths

■ The Great Room is the focal point of the home with its fireplace, cabinets and access to the Porch

■ The Master Suite is privately situated and highlighted with skylights

■ The front of the house includes the large Foyer, the Powder Room and the formal Dining Area

■ Two additional Bedrooms share a full Bath

■ The Bonus Room is complimented with skylights

Main floor — 2,136 sq. ft.
Garage — 670 sq. ft.
Bonus — 405 sq. ft.

Design by Fillmore Design Group

Established Feeling

No. 92247 BL

This plan features:

- Four bedrooms
- Two full and one half baths
- The expansive Great Room and the Breakfast Room are crowned by cathedral ceilings
- There is access to the rear Patio from the Breakfast Room and the Great Room
- A ten-foot ceiling tops the formal Dining Room
- A lavish private Bath and a vaulted ceiling highlight the Master Suite
- No materials list is available for this plan

Main floor — 2,149 sq. ft.
Garage — 465 sq. ft.

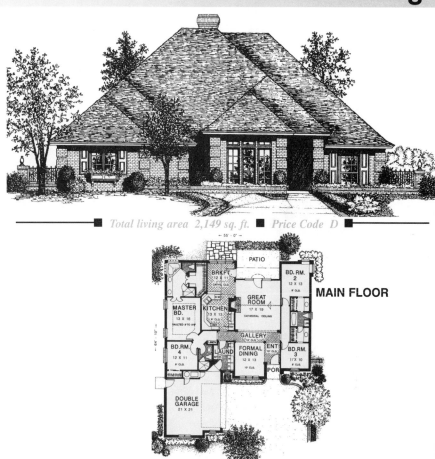

■ *Total living area 2,149 sq. ft.* ■ *Price Code D* ■

MAIN FLOOR

Sensational Floor Plan

Design by Donald A. Gardner Architects, Inc.

No. 98103 BL X

This plan features:

- Three bedrooms
- Two full and one half baths
- This home's simple footprint makes it economical to build
- Cathedral and tray ceilings add volume to the rooms
- The rear Deck expands living space to the outdoors and is accessed from the Great Room
- The Bonus Room provides for future expansion

Main floor — 2,152 sq. ft.
Bonus room — 453 sq. ft.
Garage/storage — 626 sq. ft.
Porch — 96 sq. ft.
Deck — 205 sq. ft.

© Donald A. Gardner, Inc.

■ *Total living area 2,152 sq. ft.* ■ *Price Code F* ■

Convenience and Style

Design by Frank Betz Associates, Inc.

■ Total living area 2,158 sq. ft. ■ Price Code D ■

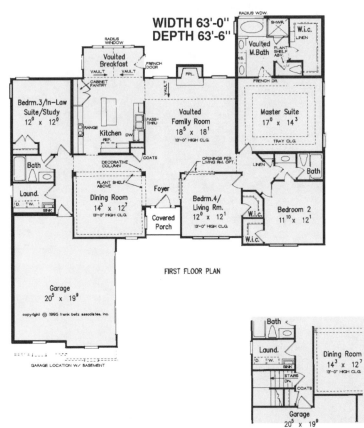

WIDTH 63'-0"
DEPTH 63'-6"

FIRST FLOOR PLAN

Opt. Basement Stair Location

No. 97294

■ This plan features:

— Four bedrooms

— Three full baths

■ The Dining Room has decorative columns at its entrance

■ The Family Room has a vaulted ceiling and a focal point fireplace

■ The Master Suite is topped by a tray ceiling

■ There is also a Private Suite at the other end of the house

■ An optional basement, slab or crawl space foundation — please specify when ordering

■ No materials list is available for this plan

First floor — 2,158 sq. ft.
Garage — 485 sq. ft.
Basement — 2,190 sq. ft.

Outstanding Family Home

■ *Total living area 2,162 sq. ft.* ■ *Price Code D* ■

No. 96504 BL ✗

■ **This plan features:**

— Three bedrooms

— Two full baths

■ A split Bedroom layout is the perfect floor plan for a family with older children

■ The Great Room includes a cozy fireplace, access to the rear Porch and an open layout with the Nook and Kitchen

■ An Extended counter in the Kitchen provides a snack bar for meals or serving

■ The Formal Dining Room directly accesses the Kitchen

■ The Bright Nook has a built-in Pantry

■ The Master Suite includes access to the rear Porch, a pampering Bath and walk-in closet

Main floor — 2,162 sq. ft.
Garage — 498 sq. ft.

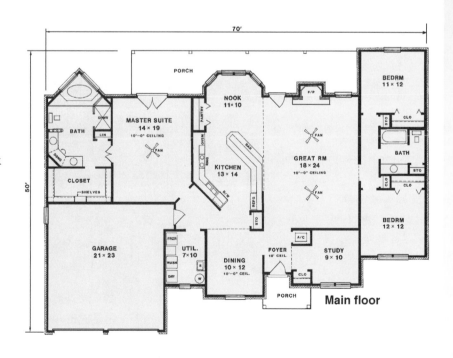

Dual Closets

No. 90484 BL ✕

■ This plan features:

— Three bedrooms

— Two full baths

■ Lovely windows grace the front of this home

■ Varied ceilings make the Master Suite special

■ Columns add interest to the living areas

■ Windows and a fireplace compliment the Great Room

■ The split Bedroom design provides the secondary Bedrooms their own wing

■ The Kitchen is a cook's delight

■ An optional basement, slab, or crawl space foundation — please specify when ordering

Main floor — 2,167 sq. ft.
Basement — 2,167 sq. ft.
Garage — 491 sq. ft.
Deck — 184 sq. ft.

■ *Total living area 2,167 sq. ft.* ■ *Price Code D* ■

MAIN FLOOR

Attractive Exterior

No. 98512 BL

■ This plan features:

— Three bedrooms

— Two full baths

■ In the gallery columns separate the space into the Great Room and the Dining Room

■ The backyard covered Patio is accessed from the Breakfast Nook

■ The large Kitchen is a chef's dream with lots of counter space and a Pantry

■ The Master Bedroom is removed from traffic areas and contains a luxurious Bath

■ A hall connects the two secondary Bedrooms which share a full skylit Bath

■ No materials list is available for this plan

Main floor — 2,167 sq. ft.
Garage — 690 sq. ft.

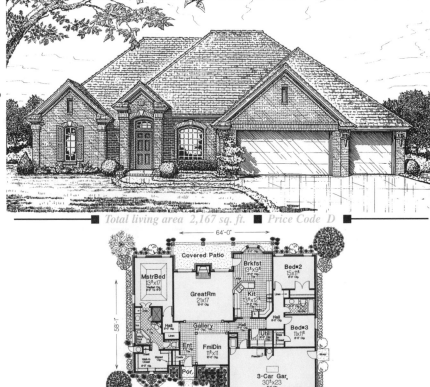

■ *Total living area 2,167 sq. ft.* ■ *Price Code D* ■

MAIN FLOOR

Attention to Detail

Design by W.D. Farmer F.A.I.B.D.

No. 94811

■ This plan features:

—Three bedrooms

—Two full baths

■ The privately located Master Suite is complimented by a luxurious Bath with two walk-in closets

■ Two additional Bedrooms have ample closet space and share a full Bath

■ The Activity Room has a sloped ceiling, a large fireplace and is accented with columns

■ The Deck is accessed through the Dining Room

■ The Kitchen and Breakfast Area have easy access to Garage for bringing in groceries

Main floor — 2,165 sq. ft.
Garage — 484 sq. ft.
Basement — 2,165 sq. ft.

Total living area 2,165 sq. ft. ■ *Price Code D* ■

MAIN FLOOR

WIDTH 65'-6"
DEPTH 57'-0"

Bold Brick

Design by Kent & Kent, Inc.

No. 92900 BL

■ This plan features:

— Three bedrooms

— Two full and one half baths

■ Tray ceilings project architectural interest in the Family Room, Master Suite and Dining Room

■ The covered Porch extends the living space to the outdoors

■ The open layout between the Family Room and the Breakfast Room allows for uninterrupted conversation

■ The lavish Master Suite includes a fireplace and a Sitting Room

■ No materials list is available for this plan

Main floor — 2,166 sq. ft.
Garage — 561 sq. ft.

Total living area 2,166 sq. ft. ■ *Price Code D* ■

MAIN FLOOR

WIDTH 56'-0"
DEPTH 76'-0"

Prepare to be Pampered

Design by Fillmore Design Group

■ *Total living area 2,169 sq. ft.* ■ *Price Code D* ■

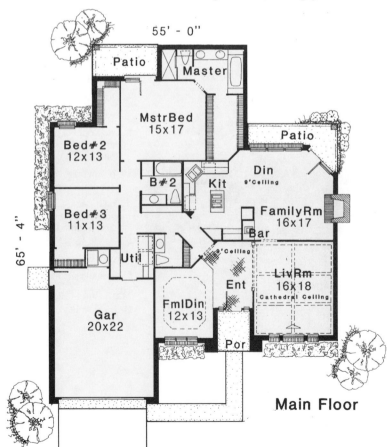

55' - 0"

65' - 4"

Patio
Master
MstrBed
15x17
Bed#2
12x13
B#2
Kit
Din
9'Ceiling
Patio
Bed#3
11x13
FamilyRm
16x17
Bar
Util
9'Ceiling
Ent
LivRm
16x18
Cathedral Ceiling
Gar
20x22
FmlDin
12x13
Por

Main Floor

No. 98500

■ **This plan features:**

— Three bedrooms

— Two full and one half baths

■ A large arched window and a cathedral ceiling highlight the Living Room

■ The open Family/Dining Room has a built-in bar and a warm brick fireplace

■ The Kitchen includes a large island and ample cabinet space

■ The large Master Suite has a private Patio and a large walk-in closet

■ No materials list is available for this plan

Main floor – 2,169 sq. ft.
Garage – 440 sq. ft.

Perfect Family Home

©1995 Donald A. Gardner Architects, Inc.

B. NATHAN

■ *Total living area 2,170 sq. ft.* ■ *Price Code F* ■

No. 96467

BL ✕ ℛR

■ **This plan features:**

– Three bedrooms

– Two full baths

■ Brick gables, picture windows, and a center front dormer combine with desirable amenities and flexible Bonus space in this home

■ A vaulted ceiling enlarges the Great Room

■ Interior columns define the Kitchen/Breakfast Room from the Great Room

■ The private Master Suite includes a skylit Bath with a garden tub

Main floor — 2,170 sq. ft
Garage/storage — 526 sq. ft.
Bonus — 1,008 sq. ft.

BONUS

MAIN FLOOR

© 1995 Donald A Gardner Architects, Inc.

Appealing Brick Elevation

Design by Design Basics, Inc.

© design basics, Inc.

■ *Total living area 2,172 sq. ft.* ■ *Price Code D* ■

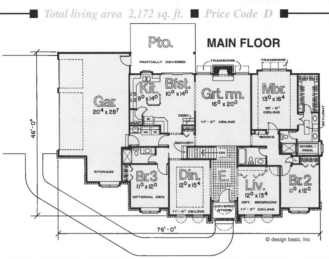

MAIN FLOOR

© design basic, Inc

No. 94971

■ **This plan features:**

— Three bedrooms

— Two full and one three quarter baths

■ The Formal Living and Dining Rooms flank the Entry

■ The Impressive Great Room is topped by an eleven-foot ceiling

■ Awing windows frame the raised hearth fireplace

■ The Attractive Kitchen/Dinette Area includes an island, desk, wrap-around counters, a walk-in Pantry and access to the covered Patio

■ The lavish Master Suite has a skylit Dressing Area, a walk-in closet, double vanity, a whirlpool tub and a decorative plant shelf

Main floor — 2,172 sq. ft.
Garage — 680 sq. ft.

Entertaining Indoors and Out

Design by National Home Planning Service

■ *Total living area 2,177 sq. ft.* ■ *Price Code D* ■

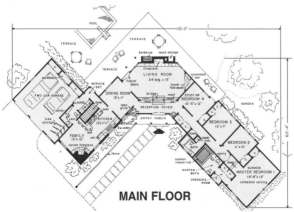

MAIN FLOOR

No. 90001 BL X

■ **This plan features:**

— Four bedrooms

— Two full and one half baths

■ Gracious double doors lead into the Foyer with a unique bridge over a moat to the Living Room

■ A huge, stone fireplace with a barbeque and wood storage on the Terrace side, a concealed bar and French doors enhance the Living Room

■ The gracious Dining Room is equipped with an open grill

■ The efficient Kitchen has an Eating Bar as part of the Family Room which has a corner fireplace

■ The sunken Master Bedroom has a decorative window topped by a cathedral ceiling, three closets and a private Bath with a Roman tub

■ The Three large Bedrooms have ample closet space and share a full Bath

Main floor — 2,177 sq. ft.

Dramatic Exterior

No. 93722

■ **This plan features:**

– Three bedrooms

– Two full and one half baths

■ The Great Room and Dining Room have high ceilings and large windows

■ The rear Porch extends living space outdoors

■ The large Kitchen has expansive counter space, a Pantry and a work island

■ An optional basement, slab or crawl space foundation — please specify when ordering

■ No materials list is available for this plan

Main floor — 2,184 sq. ft.

Total living area 2,184 sq. ft. ■ *Price Code D*

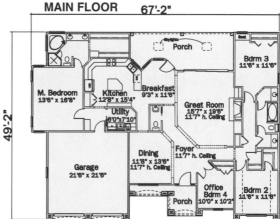

MAIN FLOOR 67'-2"

Four Bedroom Charmer

No. 91346

■ **This plan features:**

– Four bedrooms

– Two full baths

■ The vaulted ceiling is seen in the naturally lighted Entry

■ The Living Room has a masonry fireplace, large bay windows and a vaulted ceiling

■ The coffered ceiling and built-in china cabinets is featured in the Dining Room

■ The large Family Room has a woodstove alcove

■ An island cooktop, built-in Pantry and a telephone desk are found in the efficient Kitchen

■ The luxurious Master Bath has a whirlpool garden tub, walk-in closet and double sink vanity

■ The Two additional Bedrooms share a full Bath

■ The Study features a window seat and built-in bookshelves

Main floor — 2,185 sq. ft.

Total living area 2,185 sq. ft. ■ *Price Code D*

MAIN FLOOR

Options to Expand

Design by Frank Betz Associates, Inc.

Total living area 2,188 sq. ft. ■ Price Code D

No. 97278

■ **This plan features:**

— Three bedrooms

— Three full and one half baths

■ Volume ceilings and arched openings create a magnificent first impression

■ The extra special Master Suite occupies the entire left wing of the home

■ The split Bedroom layout assures privacy to the Master Suite

■ The loft above has an optional full bath, fourth Bedroom and a walk-in closet

■ The large bonus Room above the garage is ready for future expansion

■ An optional basement, slab or crawl space foundation — please specify when ordering

Main floor — 2,188 sq. ft.
Optional loft/bonus — 674 sq. ft.
Basement — 2,188 sq. ft.
Garage — 455 sq. ft.

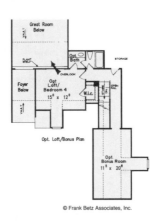

© Frank Betz Associates, Inc.

A Little Bit of Country

Design by Landmark Designs, Inc.

Total living area 2,192 sq. ft. ■ Price Code D

No. 99774

■ **This plan features:**

— Three bedrooms

— Two full baths

■ Front-facing dormers, cedar shake roofing, and a wide front Porch add a Country touch to an otherwise contemporary style

■ Vaulted ceilings heighten the sense of spaciousness in the family living areas

■ The Kitchen and the Family Room have warm, natural light from four skylights

■ A bay window in the Living Room juts out onto the wrap-around Porch

■ The Master Suite includes a walk-in closet, and a luxurious Bathroom with skylights, oversized shower, Spa tub and two vanities

■ The Two additional Bedrooms share a full hall Bath with a double vanity

Main Floor — 2,192 sq. ft.
Garage — 800 sq. ft.

MAIN FLOOR

Design by Donald A. Gardner Architects, Inc.

Designed for Today's Family

No. 99838

■ This plan features:

— Three bedrooms

— Two full baths

■ Nine-foot ceilings add elegance to a comfortable, open floor plan

■ Secluded Bedrooms are designed for pleasant retreats at the end of the day

■ The airy Foyer is topped by a vaulted dormer for plenty of natural light

■ The formal Dining Room is delineated from the Foyer by columns and is topped with a tray ceiling

■ Extra flexibility can be found in the front Bedroom or Study

■ A tray ceiling, skylights and a garden tub highlight the Master Suite

Main floor — 2,192 sq. ft.
Garage & Storage — 582 sq. ft.
Bonus — 390 sq. ft.

© 1995 Donald A. Gardner Architects, Inc.

■ *Total living area 2,192 sq. ft.* ■ *Price Code F* ■

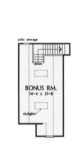

© 1995 Donald A. Gardner Architects, Inc.

Sitting Room in Master Suite

Design by Frank Betz Associates, Inc.

No. 98466

■ This plan features:

— Four bedrooms

— Three full baths

■ The Living Room could easily become the fourth Bedroom

■ High ceilings accent the Family Room and the Dining Room

■ The Master Suite boasts a tray ceiling over the Bedroom and a vaulted ceiling over the Bath

■ The expansive Kitchen opens to the Breakfast Room and includes a large central work island

■ An optional basement, slab or crawl space foundation — please specify when ordering

■ No materials list is available for this plan

Main floor — 2,193 sq. ft.
Basement — 2,193 sq. ft.
Bonus — 400 sq. ft.
Garage — 522 sq. ft.

■ *Total living area 2,193 sq. ft.* ■ *Price Code D* ■

© Frank Betz Associates, Inc.

SECOND FLOOR W/ OPT. BONUS ROOM

Stunning Family Plan

Design by Fillmore Design Group

Total living area 2,194 sq. ft. ■ Price Code D

No. 98501 [BL]

■ **This plan features:**

— Four bedrooms

— Two full and one half baths

■ Windows, brick, and columns combine to create an eye-catching elevation

■ The formal Dining Room is located just steps away from the Kitchen

■ Set on a unique angle, the Family Room has a rear wall fireplace

■ The open Kitchen has a center island, which makes for easy meal preparation

■ The three additional Bedrooms are located in their own wing of the home

■ A Patio is found in the rear of the home

■ This plan features a two-car Garage

■ No materials list is available for this plan

Main floor — 2,194 sq. ft.
Garage — 462 sq. ft.

MAIN FLOOR

Courtyard Features Pool

Design by The Garlinghouse Company

Total living area 2,194 sq. ft. ■ Price Code D

No. 10507 [BL] [X] [US]

■ **This plan features:**

— Three bedrooms

— Two full baths

■ A central Courtyard is complete with a Pool

■ The secluded Master Bedroom is accented by a skylight, a spacious walk-in closet, and a private Bath

■ The convenient Kitchen easily serves the Patio for comfortable outdoor entertaining

■ This plan features a detached two-car Garage

Main floor — 2,194 sq. ft.
Garage — 576 sq. ft.

MAIN FLOOR

Design by Ahmann Design, Inc.

No. 93190

BL ✕ 🦅

Luxury on One-Level

This plan features:

– Three bedrooms

– Two full and one half baths

■ The covered front Porch leads into the Entry and the Great Room, both with vaulted ceilings

■ The huge Great Room is perfect for entertaining or family gatherings and has a cozy fireplace

■ The arched soffits and columns surround the formal Dining Room

■ The country-sized Kitchen has a Pantry, work island, bright, eating Nook with access to the screened Porch and Laundry Room and Garage

■ The corner Master Bedroom offers a large walk-in closet and a luxurious bath with a double vanity and spa tub

■ The two additional Bedrooms have over-sized closets and share a full Bath

Main floor — 2,196 sq. ft.
Basment — 2,196 sq. ft.

■ *Total living area 2,196 sq. ft.* ■ *Price Code D* ■

MAIN FLOOR PLAN

Design by Donald A. Gardner Architects, Inc.

Elegant Brick Veneer

No. 98003

BL ✕ Я

This plan features:

– Three bedrooms

– Two full and one half baths

■ The arched and oval windows enhance the elegance of this home

■ The open, formal Dining Room is defined by columns and is topped by a tray ceiling

■ The expansive Great Room has a tray ceiling, Porch access and a cozy fireplace with windows all around

■ The curved serving counter, vaulted ceiling and bright Breakfast Area highlight the Kitchen

■ A separate Master Bedroom is accented by a vaulted ceiling, roomy walk-in closet and lavish Bath

■ The two secondary Bedrooms, close to the Laundry Area, have roomy closets and share a double vanity Bath

■ The Bonus Room offers attic storage and a cozy window seat

Main floor — 2,198 sq. ft.
Bonus room — 325 sq. ft.
Garage — 588 sq. ft.

■ *Total living area 2,198 sq. ft.* ■ *Price Code F* ■

FLOOR PLAN

© 1997 Donald A Gardner Architects, Inc.

Charming with Drama

Design by Donald A. Gardner Architects, Inc.

© 1997 Donald A. Gardner Architects, Inc.

B. NATHAN

■ Total living area 2,203 sq. ft. ■ Price Code F ■

FLOOR PLAN

© 1997 Donald A Gardner Architects, Inc.

No. 96478

■ **This plan features:**

— Four bedrooms

— Three full baths

■ Transom windows and gables enhance this design

■ Decorative columns and dramatic ceiling treatments highlight the interior

■ The Great Room and Kitchen are open to each other as well as the Breakfast Area

■ A sliding pocket door separates the Kitchen from the formal Dining Room, which is topped by a tray ceiling

■ The Master Suite has a tray ceiling and a luxurious Bath with a skylit garden tub and a walk-in closet

■ The three additional Bedrooms, including one with a private Bath that is adaptable for the physically challenged, are located on the opposite side of the home

Main floor — 2,203 sq. ft.
Bonus room — 395 sq. ft.
Garage & storage — 551 sq. ft.

Refined Country Style

Design by Donald A. Gardner Architects, Inc.

© 1993 Donald A. Gardner Architects, Inc.

B. NATHAN

■ Total living area 2,207 sq. ft. ■ Price Code F ■

FLOOR PLAN

© 1994 Donald A Gardner Architects, Inc.

No. 96447 BL X R

■ **This plan features:**

— Four bedrooms

— Two full and one half baths

■ Arched windows and interior columns add refined style to this design

■ The generous Great Room has a soaring cathedral ceiling

■ The well-planned, angled counter Kitchen has an adjoining Nook

■ The privately situated Master Bedroom has a Bath and walk-in closet

■ The large secondary Bedrooms share a full Bath

Main floor — 2,207 sq. ft.
Garage — 634 sq. ft.
Bonus — 435 sq. ft.

Design by Donald A. Gardner Architects, Inc.

Executive Home

No. 96449 BL X ʀR

■ This plan features:

— Three bedrooms

— Two full baths

■ Exciting roof lines and brick detailing are found on the exterior of this home

■ The open Kitchen assures great cooks lots of company

■ The large Deck is easily accessible from the Breakfast Area, the Great Room and the Master Bedroom

■ The Great Room has a cathedral ceiling above arched windows and a fireplace which is nestled between built-ins

■ The private Master Suite features a walk-in closet and plush Bath with twin vanities, shower and corner window tub

Main floor — 2,211 sq. ft.
Bonus room — 408 sq. ft.
Garage & storage — 700 sq. ft.

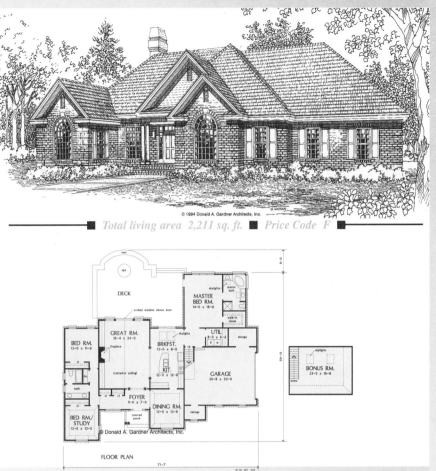

■ Total living area 2,211 sq. ft. ■ Price Code F ■

© 1994 Donald A. Gardner Architects, Inc.

Design by Sater Design Group

Turret Adds Appeal

No. 94206 BL

■ This plan features:

— Three bedrooms

— Two full baths

■ The garden Entry, with double doors leads into the open Foyer and the Great Room

■ Vaulted ceilings are seen above a decorative window in the Dining Area and sliding glass doors to the Veranda open from the Great Room

■ The private Study has double doors and turret windows

■ A large, efficient Kitchen features a walk-in Pantry, a skylit Nook, and is near the Laundry Area and Garage

■ The Master Suite has a vaulted ceiling, two huge, walk-in closets, a luxurious Bath and sliding glass doors to the Veranda

■ The two additional Bedrooms have over-sized closets and share a full Bath

■ No materials list is available for this plan

Main floor — 2,214 sq. ft.
Garage — 652 sq. ft.

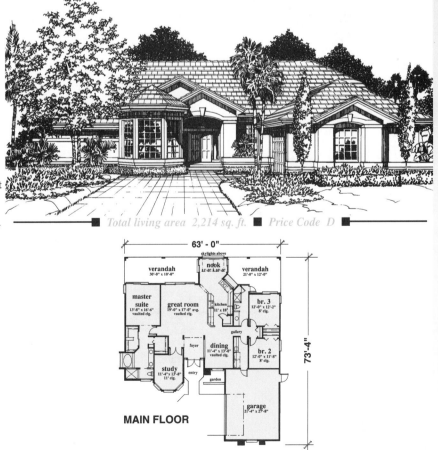

■ Total living area 2,214 sq. ft. ■ Price Code D ■

Traditional Ranch Plan

Design by Corley Plan Service

■ *Total living area 2,218 sq. ft.* ■ *Price Code D* ■

MAIN FLOOR

No. 90454

■ **This plan features:**

— Three bedrooms

— Two full baths

■ The large Foyer is set between the formal Living and Dining Rooms

■ The spacious Great Room is adjacent to the open Kitchen/Breakfast Area

■ The secluded Master Bedroom is highlighted by the Master Bath with a garden tub, a separate shower, and two vanities

■ A bay window allows bountiful natural light into the Breakfast Area

■ An optional basement or crawl space foundation — please specify when ordering

Main floor — 2,218 sq. ft.
Basement — 1,658 sq. ft.
Garage — 528 sq. ft.

A Must See Design

■ *Total living area 2,229 sq. ft.* ■ *Price Code D* ■

No. 97135 **BL**

■ This plan features:

– Three bedrooms

– Two full baths

■ The attractive, arched entrance leads into the Great Room with a wall of windows a cozy fireplace and expansive cathedral ceiling

■ The convenient Kitchen has easy access to the Nook and Dining Areas, Laundry and Garage

■ The corner Master Bedroom is enhanced by two large, walk-in closets, cathedral ceiling and private, double vanity Bath

■ The two secondary Bedrooms share a double vanity Bath

■ No materials list is available for this plan

Main floor — 2,229 sq. ft.
Basement — 2,229 sq. ft.
Garage — 551 sq. ft.

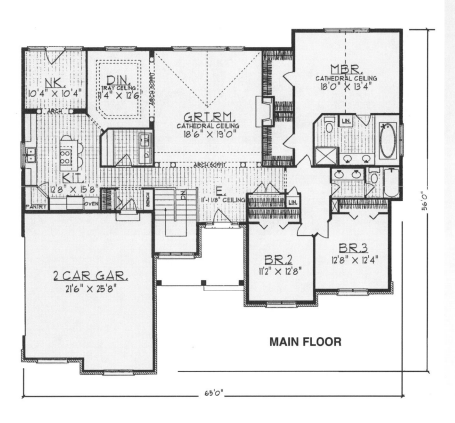

MAIN FLOOR

For The Busy Family

Design by Fillmore Design Group

No. 98521 BL

This plan features:

– Four Bedrooms

– Three full baths

The Entry opens into the Gallery, Formal Dining Area, and the Living Room is accented with a cozy fireplace

The open and efficient Kitchen easily serves the Breakfast Alcove, the Patio, and Dining Area

The corner Master Bedroom provides a huge walk-in closet and lavish Bath

Two Bedrooms, one with two closets and a window seat, share a full Bath; the fourth Bedroom has a separate Bath

No materials list is available for this plan

Main floor — 2,233 sq. ft.
Garage — 635 sq. ft.

■ *Total living area 2,233 sq. ft.* ■ *Price Code D* ■

WIDTH 63'-10"
DEPTH 56'-10"

MAIN FLOOR

Private Tropical Dreams

Design by Lifestyles Home Design

No. 98327 BL

■ *Total living area 2,235 sq. ft.* ■ *Price Code D* ■

This plan features:

– Three bedrooms

– Two full and one half baths

A highly windowed exterior allows for a terrific indoor/outdoor relationship

The Kitchen and Breakfast Area open into the Family Room

A wetbar and a fireplace highlight the Family Room

A five-piece bath and a fireplace enhance the Master Suite

No materials list is available for this plan

Main floor — 2,235 sq. ft.
Garage — 776 sq. ft.

MAIN FLOOR

Design by Frank Betz Associates, Inc.

Sprawling Ranch

No. 98424

This plan features:

- Three bedrooms
- Two full and one half baths
- The Foyer, with a 12-foot high ceiling, flows into the Dining and Living Rooms
- The Family Room in the rear of the home has a fireplace and radius windows
- The L-shaped Kitchen has a center island cooktop
- The curved Breakfast Bay Area includes a walk-in Pantry
- The Master Suite has a tray ceiling, a Sitting Area, a walk-in closet and a luxurious Bath
- The two other Bedrooms are large in size and share access to a full Bath
- An optional basement or crawl space foundation — please specify when ordering

Main floor — 2,236 sq. ft.
Basement — 2,236 sq. ft.
Garage — 517 sq. ft.

■ Total living area 2,236 sq. ft. ■ Price Code ? ■

WIDTH 63'-0'
DEPTH 67'-0"

© Frank Betz Associates, Inc.

Design by Fillmore Design Group

Splendid Single Level

No. 98544 BL

This plan features:

- Four bedrooms
- Three full baths
- A ten-foot ceiling tops the tiled formal Entrance
- The Family Room, Dinette and Kitchen are laid out in an open style for a more spacious atmosphere
- A fireplace and direct access to the covered Porch highlight the Family Room
- A skylight illuminates the five-piece bath and a large walk-in closet provides ample storage in the Master Suite
- No materials list is available for this plan

Main floor — 2,238 sq. ft.

■ Total living area 2,238 sq. ft. ■ Price Code D ■

MAIN FLOOR

Country French Home

Design by Donald A. Gardner Architects, Inc.

No. 98095

This plan features:

— Three bedrooms

— Two full and one half baths

■ The Porch leads into the Foyer which opens to the curved Dining Area and Great Room

■ An inviting fireplace is nestled between built-in shelves in the Great Room

■ A wall of glass with Deck access enhances the Great Room

■ The Country Kitchen has a cooktop island, curved Breakfast Area and easy access to the Porch and Deck

■ The comfortable Master Bedroom offers a tray ceiling, two walk-in closets and Master Bath with two vanities and a garden window tub

■ The two secondary Bedrooms, with ample closets, share a full Bath in the hall

Main floor — 2,250 sq. ft.
Garage — 565 sq. ft.

Total living area 2,250 sq. ft. ■ *Price Code F*

©1998 Donald A. Gardner Architects, Inc.

FLOOR PLAN

© 1998 Donald A Gardner Architects, Inc.

Columned Arched Entry

Design by Vaughn A. Lauban Designs

No. 96503

This plan features:

— Three bedrooms

— Two full baths

■ Keystone arches and arched transoms are situated above the windows

■ The formal Dining Room and Study flank the Foyer

■ A fireplace accents the Great Room

■ The efficient Kitchen has a peninsula counter and bayed Nook

■ The Master Suite features a step ceiling and has an interesting Master Bath with a triangular area for the oval bath tub

■ The secondary Bedrooms share a full Bath in the hall

Main floor — 2,256 sq. ft.
Garage — 514 sq. ft.

Total living area 2,256 sq. ft. ■ *Price Code E*

Main floor

Fieldstone Facade

Design by Fillmore Design Group

No. 92284

■ This plan features:

— Four bedrooms

— Two full and one half baths

■ The Gallery Entry opens to the Great Room with a focal point fireplace and Patio access

■ The formal Dining Room is conveniently located for entertaining

■ A cooktop island, built-in Pantry and a bright Breakfast Area are featured in the Kitchen

■ The secluded Master Bedroom has Patio access. A large walk-in closet and corner Spa tub

■ The three additional Bedrooms have ample closets and share a double vanity Bath

■ No materials list is available for this plan

Main floor — 2,261 sq. ft.
Garage — 640 sq. ft.

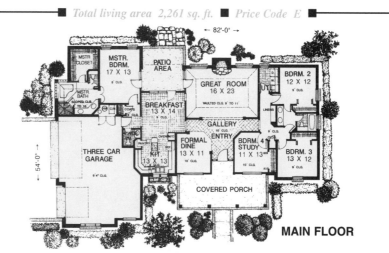

■ Total living area 2,261 sq. ft. ■ Price Code E ■

MAIN FLOOR

True Tradition

Design by Donald A. Gardner Architects, Inc.

No. 98076

■ This plan features:

— Four bedrooms

— Two full and one half baths

■ Stately columns frame the front Entry and are repeated in the home's formal Foyer

■ The generous Great Room has a fireplace between built-in shelves

■ A dramatic cathedral ceiling enhances the space in the Great Room and continues into the adjoining screened Porch

■ Dual skylights enrich the Breakfast Area

■ The Master Suite includes Deck access, a walk-in closet and a private Bath with a corner tub and dual vanities

Main floor — 2,262 sq. ft.
Bonus Room — 388 sq. ft.
Garage — 542 sq. ft.

■ Total living area 2,262 sq. ft. ■ Price Code G ■

MAIN FLOOR

Hit the Bricks

Design by Corley Plan Service

Total living area 2,271 sq. ft. ■ Price Code E

MAIN FLOOR

No. 90485

■ **This plan features:**

— Four bedrooms

— Two full baths

■ This plan features a low maintenance brick exterior

■ The sloped ceiling adds dimension to the Great Room

■ The Kitchen is well planned and executed

■ The Master Bedroom has a tray ceiling

■ The three secondary Bedrooms are located in their own wing

■ An optional basement, slab, or crawl space foundation — please specify when ordering

Main floor — 2,271 sq. ft.
Garage — 484 sq. ft.

An Exciting Mixture

Design by Donald A. Gardner Architects, Inc.

©1997 Donald A. Gardner Architects, Inc.

Total living area 2,273 sq. ft. ■ Price Code G

MAIN FLOOR

No. 98007

■ **This plan features:**

— Four bedrooms

— Two full and one half baths

■ The exterior is a mixture of brick, and siding and features a wrap around porch

■ The Dining Room has five windows for plenty of natural light

■ A fireplace with built-in shelving adds character to the Great Room

■ The U-shaped Kitchen is roomy and conveniant

■ A rear-covered Porch and a breezeway leads to the Garage

■ The Master Bedroom features a walk-in closet and private Bath

■ Lovely windows brighten all of the secondary Bedrooms

■ The Bonus Room is found over the Garage

Main floor — 2,273 sq. ft.
Bonus — 342 sq. ft.
Garage — 528 sq. ft.

Design by Atlanta Plan Source, Inc.

Traditional Ranch

No. 92404 BL ✕

■ This plan features:

— Three bedrooms

— Two full baths

■ A tray ceiling in the Master Suite is equipped with dual walk-in closets and the private Master Bath with a cathedral ceiling

■ The formal Living Room has a cathedral ceiling

■ A decorative tray ceiling is found in the elegant formal Dining Room

■ The spacious Family Room has a vaulted ceiling and a fireplace

■ The modern, well-appointed Kitchen has a snack bar and the bay Breakfast Area

■ Two additional Bedrooms, each having the walk-in closet, share a full hall bath

First floor — 2,275 sq. ft.
Basement — 2,207 sq. ft.
Garage — 512 sq. ft.

Total living area 2,275 sq. ft. ■ Price Code E

MAIN FLOOR

Design by Donald A. Gardner Architects, Inc.

Stunning Executive Home

No. 96496 BL ✕ ЯR

■ This plan features:

— Three bedrooms

— Two full and one half baths

■ This home's Traditional exterior masks an open, contemporary floor plan

■ The openness of this floor plan is accentuated by numerous special ceiling treatments

■ The versatile Bedroom/Study may be used as the formal Living Room, Home Office or the Guest Bedroom

■ The generous Bonus Room makes the great Playroom, keeping children's toys upstairs and out of sight

Main floor — 2,282 sq. ft.
Bonus — 354 sq. ft.
Garage — 572 sq. ft.

Total living area 2,282 sq. ft. ■ Price Code G

FLOOR PLAN

305

Elegant Exterior

Design by Vaughn A. Lauban Designs

No. 96530

■ **This plan features:**

— Three bedrooms

— Three full baths

■ The exterior is highlighted by a high columned Porch and many windows

■ The Receiving Room is graced by a see-through fireplace that is shared with the Great Room

■ The Great Room is spacious and opens onto the Veranda

■ The Kitchen/Dining Area adjoins the Great Room adding a spacious feeling to the home

■ A vaulted ceiling, a private whirlpool Bath and a Lounging Room are in the Master Suite

■ The two additional Bedrooms have access to a full Bath

Main floor — 2,289 sq. ft.
Garage — 758 sq. ft.

■ *Total living area 2,289 sq. ft.* ■ *Price Code E* ■

European Styling

Design by Corley Plan Service

No. 90467

■ **This plan features:**

— Three bedrooms

— Two full and one half baths

■ The large Foyer leads to the open Living and Dining Rooms

■ A large informal area includes the Kitchen, Gathering, and Breakfast Rooms

■ The Kitchen features an island bar, double sink, Pantry, desk, and a wall oven

■ The home has two fireplaces, one in the Great Room and one in the Gathering Room

■ Decorative ceilings can be found in the Dining Room, the Master Suite, and the Breakfast Nook

■ The Master Suite features dual walk-in closets and a five piece Bath

■ Two additional Bedrooms share a linen closet and a full Bath

■ An optional basement or crawl space foundation — please specify when ordering

Main floor — 2,290 sq. ft.
Basement — 2,290 sq. ft.
Bonus — 304 sq. ft.
Garage — 544 sq. ft.

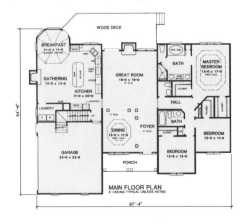

■ *Total living area 2,290 sq. ft.* ■ *Price Code E* ■

Dignified Traditional

Design by Larry E. Belk

No. 93049 BL

■ This plan features:

— Four bedrooms

— Two full and one half baths

■ Dramatic columns define the elegant Dining Room and frame the entrance to the large, spacious Great Room

■ The Breakfast Bar and work island is found in the gourmet Kitchen which also includes an abundance of counter and cabinet space

■ All Bedrooms are conveniently grouped at the opposite side of the home

■ The Master Suite has the enormous walk-in closet and the luxuriant Master Bath

■ Two additional Bedrooms have walk-in closets and share a full Bath with a double vanity

■ No materials list is available for this plan

Main floor — 2,292 sq. ft.
Garage — 526 sq. ft.

■ *Total living area 2,292 sq. ft.* ■ *Price Code E* ■

© Larry E. Belk

WIDTH 80-7

Exquisite Entrances

Design by Andy McDonald Design Group

No. 97503 BL

■ This plan features:

— Three bedrooms

— Two full baths and one half bath

■ Elegant French doors lead into the formal living areas

■ A large fireplace and direct access to the rear Porch enhance the living space

■ The informal living space continues the open airy feeling of the home

■ The split Bedroom layout makes sure that the Master Suite is secluded and private

■ This plan is not to be built in a 20 mile radius of Madisonville, LA or in Baton Rouge, LA

■ No materials list is available for this plan

Main floor — 2,310 sq. ft.
Garage — 638 sq. ft.

■ *Total living area 2,310 sq. ft.* ■ *Price Code E* ■

WIDTH 54'-6"
DEPTH 47'-7"

MAIN FLOOR

Great Details

Design by Design Basics, Inc.

No. 97404 BL ✕

■ This plan features:

– Three bedrooms

– Two full and one half baths

■ The Entry, the Great Room and the Dining Room share a ten-foot ceiling and create an open atmosphere

■ Arched windows and a pass-through wet bar/buffet highlight the Great Room

■ The corridor design offers privacy between the Master Suite and the secondary Bedrooms

■ Dual walk-in closets, the large Dressing Area, separate shower and whirlpool space in the Bath produce the stylish Master Suite

Main floor — 2,311 sq. ft.
Garage — 657 sq. ft.

■ Total living area 2,311 sq. ft. ■ Price Code E ■

MAIN FLOOR

© design basics inc.

Those Fabulous Details

Design by Frank Betz Associates, Inc.

No. 97246 BL

■ This plan features:

– Four bedrooms

– Two full and one half baths

■ The unique style created by keystone, arched windows and the entrance continues inside with arched openings

■ The hub of this home is the vaulted Family Room with French door, arched window, cozy fireplace and pass-thru to the Kitchen

■ The vaulted Breakfast Area expands the efficient Kitchen for a busy household

■ The spacious Master Suite boasts the Sitting Area with fireplace

■ This plan offers optional expansion to the second floor Bonus Room and Bath

■ An optional basement or crawl space foundation — please specify when ordering

■ No materials list is available for this plan

Main floor — 2,311 sq. ft.
Bonus — 425 sq. ft.
Basement — 2,311 sq. ft.
Garage — 500 sq. ft.

■ Total living area 2,311 sq. ft. ■ Price Code E ■

MAIN FLOOR

OPT. BONUS FLOOR PLAN

Irresistible Craftsman Style

No. 98068

This plan features:

- Four bedrooms
- Two full baths
- The Dining Room enjoys a graceful tray ceiling and multiple columns
- A cathedral ceiling expands the Great Room and the Kitchen
- A duo of double doors connects the Great Room to the back Porch
- The Master Suite has a tray ceiling, dual walk-in closets, a linen closet and bath with dual sink vanity

Main floor — 2,342 sq. ft.
Garage & Storage — 575 sq. ft.
Bonus room — 353 sq. ft.

B. NATHAN   ©1998 Donald A. Gardner, Inc.

■ *Total living area 2,342 sq. ft.* ■ *Price Code G* ■

MAIN FLOOR

© 1998 Donald A Gardner, Inc.

Homestead Happiness

No. 90478

This plan features:

- Three bedrooms
- Two full baths
- The brick exterior, columns, and dormers add to the charm of this Traditionally styled Ranch
- The Foyer leads to the Study, the Dining Room, or the Great Room
- The Great Room features a fireplace and access to the rear Deck
- The efficient Kitchen is open to the Great Room and the Breakfast Nook
- The Master Bedroom is isolated from the other Bedrooms and is quite luxurious
- Two secondary Bedrooms have ample closet space and share a full Bath
- An optional basement, slab or crawl space foundation — please specify when ordering

Main floor — 2,344 sq. ft.
Basement — 2,344 sq. ft.
Garage — 498 sq. ft.

■ *Total living area 2,344 sq. ft.* ■ *Price Code E* ■

MAIN FLOOR

For Sun Lovers

Design by The Garlinghouse Company

No. 10619

■ **This plan features:**

— Three bedrooms

— Three baths

■ This design is made for the sun lover with the front Deck and Patio

■ The sunken Living Room has three window walls and a massive fireplace

■ A hot tub in the Bath, a skylight, and a vaulted ceiling are included in the Master Suite with convenient access to the Utility Area

Main floor — 2,352 sq. ft.
Basement — 2,352 sq. ft.
Garage — 696 sq. ft.

Total living area 2,352 sq. ft. ■ *Price Code E* ■

MAIN FLOOR

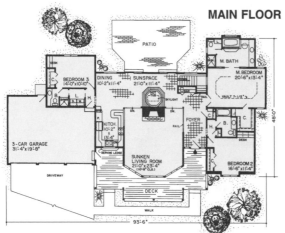

One Level Beauty

Design by Design Basics, Inc.

No. 94967

■ **This plan features:**

— Three bedrooms

— Two full and one half baths

■ From the tiled Entry one can view the terrific Great Room

■ A built-in wet bar and a three-sided fireplace, shared with the Hearth Room, highlight the Great Room

■ The Hearth Room, that has a built-in entertainment center, is open to the Kitchen and Breakfast Room

■ The sloped gazebo ceiling and a built-in hutch highlight the Breakfast Room

■ The Master Bedroom has an impressive and luxurious Bath and the walk-in closet

■ The secondary Bedrooms have private access to a full Bath

Main floor — 2,355 sq. ft.
Garage — 673 sq. ft.

Total living area 2,355 sq. ft. ■ *Price Code E* ■

MAIN FLOOR

© Larry E. Belk

Design by Greg Marquis & Associates

Convenience

No. 93440 BL

■ **This plan features:**

— Three bedrooms

— Three full baths

■ Porches in the front and rear grace this home

■ A sloped ceiling and a fireplace complete the Family Room

■ There is a snack bar in the Kitchen for meals on the go

■ The Office/Game Room could be used as the guest Bedroom

■ The Master Bedroom is zoned for privacy

■ No materials list is available for this plan

Main floor — 2,361 sq. ft.
Basement — 2,361 sq. ft.
Garage — 490 sq. ft.

Total living area 2,361 sq. ft. ■ *Price Code E* ■

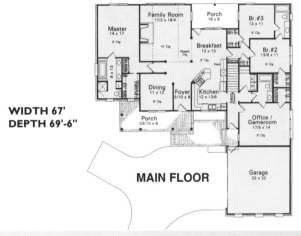

WIDTH 67'
DEPTH 69'-6"

MAIN FLOOR

Design by Rick Garner

Symmetrical and Stately

No. 92546 BL ✗

■ **This plan features:**

— Four bedrooms

— Two full and one half baths

■ A double column Porch leads into the open Foyer, the spacious Den and the Dining Room are accented by an arched window and pillars

■ A decorative ceiling crowns the Den with its hearth fireplace, built-in shelves and window access to the rear Porch

■ The large, efficient Kitchen with a peninsula serving counter, the Breakfast Area, adjoins the Utility and the Garage

■ The Master Bedroom has a decorative ceiling, two vanities and a large walk-in closet

■ Three additional Bedrooms have double closets and share a full Bath

■ An optional slab or crawl space foundation — please specify when ordering

Main floor — 2,387 sq. ft.
Garage — 505 sq. ft.

Total living area 2,387 sq. ft. ■ *Price Code E* ■

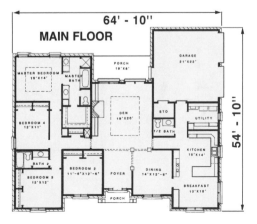

MAIN FLOOR

Easy, Step-Saving Floor Plan

Design by Fillmore Design Group

■ *Total living area 2,393 sq. ft.* ■ *Price Code E* ■

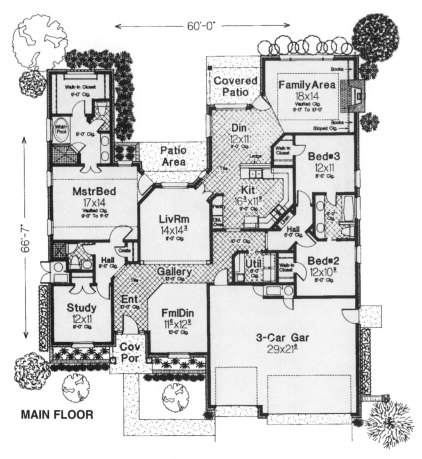

MAIN FLOOR

No. 97800 [BL]

■ This plan features:

— Three bedrooms

— Two full and one half baths

■ The tiled Entry directs traffic effortlessly into the Living Room or Formal Dining Room

■ A large fireplace in the Family Room is flanked by bookshelves

■ The Master Suite is located on the opposite side of the home from the secondary Bedrooms for privacy

■ The covered Patio off the Dining Room and the Patio off the Master Bedroom extend living space to the outdoors

■ No materials list is available for this plan

Main floor — 2,393 sq. ft.
Garage — 622 sq. ft.

Warm Southern Welcome

■ *Total living area 2,400 sq. ft.* ■ *Price Code E* ■

No. 94641 ☐BL

■ **This plan features:**

— Four bedrooms

— Two full baths

■ Four columns accentuate the warm Southern welcome alluded to by the front Porch

■ The Foyer leads to the Living Room and the Dining Room

■ The Master Bedroom is topped by a decorative ceiling treatment and is pampered by the lavish Master Bath with a whirlpool tub

■ The additional Bedrooms share a double vanity Bath in the hall

■ No materials list is available for this plan

Main floor — 2,400 sq. ft.
Garage — 534 sq. ft.

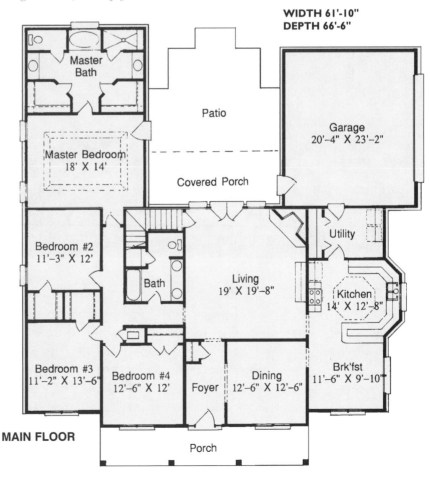

WIDTH 61'-10"
DEPTH 66'-6"

Master Bath

Patio

Garage
20'-4" X 23'-2"

Master Bedroom
18' X 14'

Covered Porch

Bedroom #2
11'-3" X 12'

Bath

Living
19' X 19'-8"

Utility

Kitchen
14' X 12'-8"

Bedroom #3
11'-2" X 13'-6"

Bedroom #4
12'-6" X 12'

Foyer

Dining
12'-6" X 12'-6"

Brk'fst
11'-6" X 9'-10"

MAIN FLOOR

Porch

Gather Around Fireplace

Design by Design Basics, Inc.

No. 94979 BL ✗ R

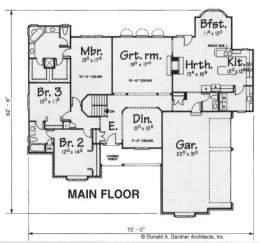

Total living area 2,404 sq. ft. ■ Price Code E

MAIN FLOOR

Mbr. 13⁰ x 17⁵ 10'-0" CEILING
Grt. rm. 19⁰ x 17⁰ 10'-0" CEILING
Bfst. 11⁴ x 12⁰
SNACK BAR
Hrth. 13⁴ x 16⁶
Kit. 12⁰ x 12⁸
Br. 3 13⁰ x 11⁶
Br. 2 12⁰ x 14³
Din. 12⁰ x 12² 9'-0" CEILING
Gar. 22⁰ x 31⁰
E.
DN
LIN.
COVERED PORCH
29' - 8"
72' - 0"
© Donald A. Gardner Architects, Inc.

This plan features:

— Three bedrooms

— Two full and one half baths

■ A see-through fireplace is situated between the Hearth Room and the Great Room

■ The open layout between the Kitchen, Hearth Room and the Breakfast Room creates a terrific informal living space

■ A built-in Pantry, work island and a peninsula counter/snack bar highlight the Kitchen

■ The Great Room is directly across the hall from the Dining Room and is at the heart of the home

■ Master Bedroom features two walk-in closets and a five-piece Bath

■ Two additional Bedrooms have private access to a full Bath

Main floor — 2,404 sq. ft.
Garage — 696 sq. ft.

Stately Elegance

Design by Larry E. Belk

No. 93095 BL ✗

Total living area 2,409 sq. ft. ■ Price Code E

WIDTH 85-8
STORAGE
DOUBLE GARAGE
COVERED PORCH
BRICK STEPS
MASTER BATH
MASTER BEDROOM 16-8 X 13-6 9' CEILING
BREAKFAST 10-0 X 11-8 8' CEILING
PWDR
UTIL
GREAT ROOM 21-4 X 17-0 9' CEILING
KITCHEN 14-8 X 13-0 8' CEILING
PAN
BEDROOM 2 12-4 X 12-0 9' CEILING
FOYER 9' CEILING
DINING ROOM 13-4 X 14-0 9' CEILING
BEDROOM 3 13-0 X 11-8 9' CEILING
BATH 2
PORCH
DEPTH 68-8
MAIN FLOOR
© Larry E. Belk

FUTURE GAME RM 16-2 X 15-0
FUTURE BEDRM 11-6 X 13-0
BONUS AREA 709 FT

This plan features:

— Three bedrooms

— Two full and one half baths

■ Elegant columns frame the entry into the Foyer and expansive Great Room

■ The efficient Kitchen, ideal for a busy cook, has a walk-in Pantry, Breakfast Area and access to the formal Dining Room, Laundry and Garage

■ The private Master Bedroom boasts a plush Bath with two huge, walk-in closets, a double vanity, and whirlpool tub

■ Two secondary Bedrooms with large closets, share a double vanity Bath

■ Staircase in Kitchen leads to expandable second floor

■ An optional slab or crawl space foundation — please specify when ordering

Main floor — 2,409 sq. ft.
Garage — 644 sq. ft.
Bonus — 709 sq. ft.

314

Perfect for a Porch Swing

■ *Total living area 2,424 sq. ft.* ■ *Price Code E* ■

No. 98744 BL ✕

■ This plan features:

— Three bedrooms

— Two full baths

■ The long Porch sweeps across most of the front facade

■ A skylight brightens the recessed Entry

■ The formal Living Room and Dining Rooms open to each other with a fireplace for partial separation

■ The Family Theater with a built-in entertainment center is accessible on either side of the wall

■ Two secondary Bedrooms share a full Bath in the hall

■ The efficient Kitchen is separated from the Nook by a peninsula counter/eating bar

Main floor — 2,424 sq. ft.
Garage — 962 sq. ft.

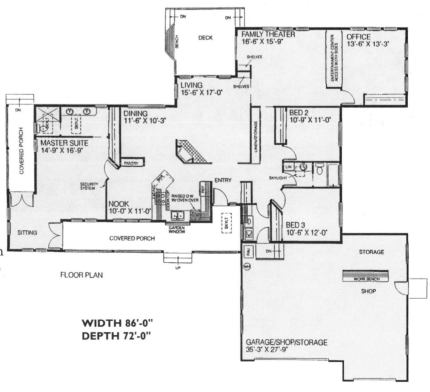

WIDTH 86'-0"
DEPTH 72'-0"

FLOOR PLAN

Lap of Luxury

Design by Fillmore Design Group

No. 98511

- **This plan features:**
- — Four bedrooms
- — Three full baths
- Entertain in grand style in the formal Living Room, the Dining Room, or under the covered Patio in the backyard
- The Family Room is crowned in a cathedral ceiling, enhanced by a center fireplace, and built-in bookshelves
- The efficient Kitchen is highlighted by a wall oven, plentiful counter space, and a Pantry
- The Master Bedroom has a Sitting Area, huge walk-in closet, Private Bath, and access to the covered Lanai
- The secondary Bedroom wing contains three additional Bedrooms with ample closet space, and two full Baths
- No materials list is available for this plan

Main floor — 2,445 sq. ft.
Garage — 630 sq. ft.

Total living area 2,445 sq. ft. • Price Code E

MAIN FLOOR

Striking Facade

Design by The Garlinghouse Company

No. 10570

- **This plan features:**
- — Four bedrooms
- — Two full baths
- A recessed entrance leads into the tiled Foyer and bright, expansive Living Room with a skylight and a double fireplace below a sloped ceiling
- The Library/Den features the Study Alcove, a storage space, a decorative window and a fireplace between built-in bookshelves
- The ideal Kitchen has a work island, a cooktop snackbar, the walk-in Pantry and the tiled Dining Area with a built-in china cabinet, skylights and wall of windows that overlooks the Deck
- The Master Bedroom has a corner fireplace, the walk-in closet and a plush Bath with two vanities and a raised, tiled tub below the skylight

Main Floor — 2,450 sq. ft.
Basement — 2,450 sq. ft
Garage — 739 sq. ft.

Total living area 2,450 sq. ft. • Price Code E

MAIN FLOOR

Design by Corley Plan Service

Columned Elegance

No. 90461

This plan features:

- Three bedrooms

- Two full baths

- This Traditional home is enhanced by elegant columns on the large front Porch

- The Study and the Dining Room both overlook the front Porch

- The Great Room has a fireplace, built-in book shelves and access to the rear Deck

- The modern Kitchen has an angled serving bar with a double sink

- The Breakfast Nook has a bright wall of windows that overlooks the rear yard

- The secluded Master Suite has dual walk-in closets, and a Bath with a Spa tub

- Two additional Bedrooms, located on the opposite side of the home, share a full Bath

- An optional basement or crawl space foundation — please specify when ordering

Main floor — 2,485 sq. ft.
Basement — 2,485 sq. ft.
Garage — 484 sq. ft.

■ *Total living area 2,485 sq. ft.* ■ *Price Code E* ■

Design by Donald A. Gardner Architects, Inc.

Sprawling Four Bedroom

No. 98060 BL

This plan features:

- Four bedrooms

- Three full baths

- A trio of dormers and the gracious front Porch adorn the facade of this home

- The spacious Great Room sports a cathedral ceiling, a fireplace and built-in shelves

- The split Bedroom layout provides privacy for homeowners

- The generous Master Suite has a tray ceiling, private Bath with a corner tub and a walk-in closet

- No material list is available for this plan

Main floor — 2,487 sq. ft.
Garage & Storage — 606 sq. ft.

■ *Total living area 2,487 sq. ft.* ■ *Price Code G* ■

Details! Details!

Design by Frank Betz Associates, Inc.

No. 97299 BL

■ **This plan features:**

– Three bedrooms

– Two full and one half baths

■ Decorative columns define the Dining Room entrance and a tray ceiling brings elegance to the room

■ The Living Room has a high ceiling and a radius window

■ The Kitchen includes a cooktop island/serving bar, the walk-in Pantry and ample work and storage space

■ The Breakfast Room and the Family Room flow into the Kitchen for a feeling of spaciousness

■ An optional basement or crawl space foundation — please specify when ordering

■ No material list is available for this plan

First floor — 2,491 sq. ft.
Bonus room — 588 sq. ft.
Basement — 2,491 sq. ft.
Bonus room — 522 sq. ft.

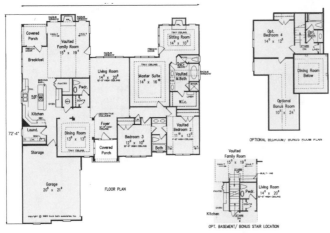

Total living area 2,491 sq. ft. ■ Price Code E

Single-Level Convenience

Design by Fillmore Design Group

No. 92254 BL

■ **This plan features:**

– Three bedrooms

– Three full baths

■ The Kitchen flows into the Dinette Area and is joined by the Family Room

■ The Family Room includes a fireplace and a cathedral ceiling

■ The split Bedroom floor plan assures the Master Suite of privacy

■ The perfect Guest Room is located near the Master Suite and has direct access to a full Bath

■ No material list is available for this plan

Main floor — 2,495 sq. ft.
Garage — 452 sq. ft.

Total living area 2,495 sq. ft. ■ Price Code E

Design by Fillmore Design Group

No. 98550

Split Bedroom Layout

2,501-3,000 sq.ft. HOME PLANS

This plan features:

– Four bedrooms

– Three full baths

■ The Master Bedroom includes a vaulted ceiling, and a private Bath with a walk-in closet and access to the Patio

■ A ten-foot ceiling enhances the Living Room

■ The informal Dining Area flows from the Kitchen and the Family Room and has access to the Patio

■ The snack bar/island, and the built-in Pantry offer added workspace and storage to the Kitchen

■ No material list is available for this plan

Main floor — 2,506 sq. ft.
Garage — 441 sq. ft.

■ *Total living area 2,506 sq. ft.* ■ *Price Code F* ■

Main Floor

Design by Landmark Designs, Inc.

No. 98732

Quality Family Living

This plan features:

– Three bedrooms

– Two full baths

■ The lovely railed Country styled, covered wrap-around Porch entrance has skylights creating a spotlight effect directly in front of the door

■ A vaulted ceiling helps the Dining and Living Rooms flow together and warmth and color is provided from a corner fireplace

■ Windows filling most of the rear wall and French doors at the center open onto the rambling Deck

■ With windows on four sides, the octagonal Nook is richly illuminated with natural light

■ An eating bar, step-in Pantry, raised dishwasher and built-in oven make the Kitchen even more efficient

■ Five skylights brighten the sumptuous Master Suite and the Sitting Area

■ No material list is available for this plan

Main floor — 2,508 sq. ft.
Garage — 772 sq. ft.

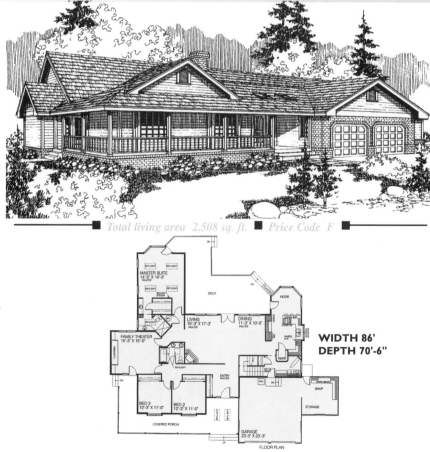

■ *Total living area 2,508 sq. ft.* ■ *Price Code F* ■

**WIDTH 86'
DEPTH 70'-6"**

FLOOR PLAN

Detailed Bricks and Arches

Design by Design Basics, Inc.

■ *Total living area 2,512 sq. ft.* ■ *Price Code F* ■

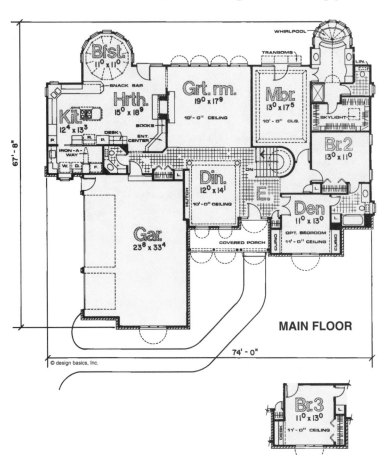

MAIN FLOOR

74' - 0"

© design basics, Inc.

67' - 8"

Br.3
11⁰ x 13⁰
11'-0" CEILING

OPT. BEDROOM

No. 94973

■ **This plan features:**

— Two bedrooms

— Two full and one half baths

■ The Master Bedroom has a vaulted ceiling, luxurious Bath, and is complimented by a skylit walk-in closet

■ The second Bedroom shares a full Bath with the Den/optional Bedroom with built-in curio cabinets

■ Columns and arched windows define the elegant Dining Room

■ The Great Room shares a see-through fireplace with the Hearth Room, which also has a built-in entertainment center

■ The gazebo-shaped Nook opens into the Kitchen with a center island, snack bar and desk

Main floor — 2,512 sq. ft.
Garage — 783 sq. ft.

Traditional Ranch

■ *Total living area 2,525 sq. ft.* ■ *Price Code F* ■

No. 93718 BL

■ This plan features:

– Three bedrooms

– Two full and one half baths

■ This home features open formal rooms with ten-foot ceilings and arched openings

■ The Family Room is open to the Breakfast Room/Kitchen and has a cathedral ceiling

■ The large Kitchen has a walk-in Pantry, built-in window seat and a large work island

■ The large Utility Room has a built-in desk

■ An optional basement, slab, or crawl space foundation — please specify when ordering

■ No materials list is available for this plan

Main floor — 2,525 sq. ft.
Garage — 462 sq. ft.

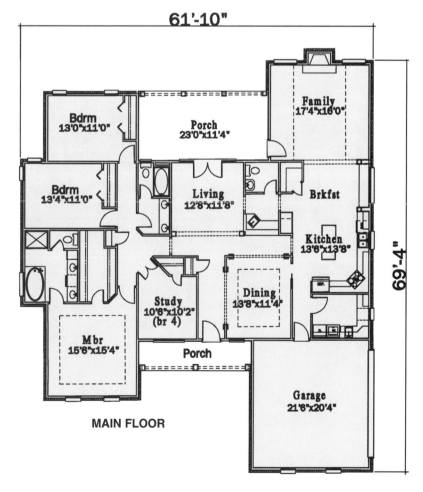

61'-10"

Bdrm
13'0"x11'0"

Porch
23'0"x11'4"

Family
17'4"x16'0"

Bdrm
13'4"x11'0"

Living
12'8"x11'8"

Brkfst

Kitchen
13'6"x13'8"

Study
10'6"x10'2"
(br 4)

Dining
13'8"x11'4"

Mbr
15'6"x15'4"

Porch

Garage
21'6"x20'4"

69'-4"

MAIN FLOOR

Stately Home

Design by Donald A. Gardner Architects, Inc.

■ *Total living area 2,526 sq. ft.* ■ *Price Code H* ■

MAIN FLOOR

No. 96435

■ This plan features:

— Four bedrooms

— Two full and one half baths

■ This home is designed with an elegant brick exterior and careful detailing

■ Light floods through the arched window in the clerestory dormer above the Foyer

■ The Great Room is topped by a cathedral ceiling and has built-in cabinets and bookshelves

■ Both the Dining Room and the Bedroom/Study have tray ceilings

■ The Master Suite includes a fireplace, access to the Deck, dual vanities, a shower and a whirlpool tub

Main floor — 2,526 sq. ft.
Garage — 611 sq. ft.

Heart of the Home

■ *Total living area 2,558 sq. ft.* ■ *Price Code F* ■

No. 94640 BL

■ This plan features:

— Three bedrooms

— Three full baths

■ The Living Room and Dining Room are to the right and left of the Foyer

■ The Dining Room has French doors that open to the Kitchen

■ The Breakfast Room includes access to the Utility Room and to the secondary Bedroom wing

■ The Master Bedroom is equipped with a double vanity Bath, two walk-in closets and a linen closet

■ A cozy fireplace and a decorative ceiling highlight the Family Room

■ No materials list is available for this plan

Main floor — 2,558 sq. ft.

Garage — 549 sq. ft.

WIDTH 63'-6"
DEPTH 71'-6"

Two-car Garage
21'-4" X 22'-2"

Storage

Utility

Bath

Master Bedroom
17'-10" X 14'

Covered Porch

Breakfast
12'-4" X 12'

Bedroom
11' X 12'-6"

Ba.

Family Room
20' X 17'-6"

Kitchen
12'-4" X 12'-6"

Ba.

Bedroom
12'-2" X 13'

Living Room
13'-4" X 14'-6"

Foyer

Dining Room
13'-4" X 12'

Bedroom
12'-1" X 12'

Porch

MAIN FLOOR

A View to the Side

■ *Total living area 2,579 sq. ft.* ■ *Price Code F* ■

No. 93708

■ This plan features:

— Three/Four bedrooms

— Three full and one half baths

■ This design is perfect for a homesite with a view to the side

■ The domed Foyer and French doors lead to the Study or Guest Bedroom with a vaulted ceiling

■ The arched Entrance and columns introduce the Dining Room

■ The sunken Great Room has a high tray ceiling, arches and columns further enhanced by a fireplace

■ The Breakfast Room opens to the Kitchen via the eating bar

■ No materials list is available for this plan

Main floor — 2,579 sq. ft.
Garage — 536 sq. ft.

Main Level Floor Plan

Extra Special Luxuries

© 1997 Donald A Gardner Architects, Inc.

■ *Total living area 2,602 sq. ft.* ■ *Price Code H* ■

No. 99820 BL ✕ ℛR

■ **This plan features:**

— Four bedrooms

— Two full and one half baths

■ The Foyer leads to the formal Dining Room on the left

■ The large Great Room includes a cathedral ceiling, a fireplace, built-ins and access to the airy Sun Room

■ The Kitchen has a center work island and accent columns at the entrance to the Great Room

■ The indulgent Master Suite has the skylit, plush Bath and a walk-in closet

■ Two additional Bedrooms share a full Bath in the hall

Main floor — 2,602 sq. ft.
Garage — 715 sq. ft.
Bonus — 399 sq. ft.

FLOOR PLAN

© Donald A. Gardner Architects, Inc.

With Room for All

Design by Fillmore Design Group

■ Total living area 2,615 sq. ft. ■ Price Code F ■

No. 92271

■ This plan features:

— Four bedrooms

— Three full baths

■ This impressive home features corner quoins, segmented arches and shutters, a fan light and side lights

■ The Kitchen/Breakfast Bay Area access the Family Room

■ A fireplace is featured in the Family Room

■ The formal Dining Room is located across the Gallery from the Kitchen which includes a Butler's Pantry

■ The Master Suite is at the opposite end of the house

■ No materials list is available for this plan

Main floor — 2,615 sq. ft.
Garage — 713 sq. ft.

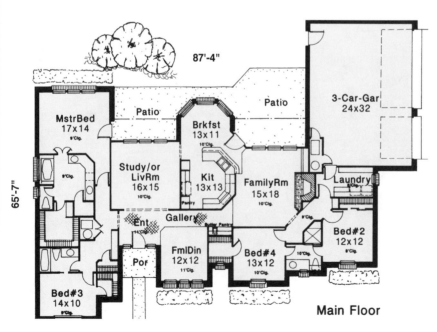

Main Floor

Open Spaces

■ *Total living area 2,618 sq. ft.* ■ *Price Code F* ■

No. 97505 BL

■ This plan features:

— Four bedrooms

— Three full and one half baths

■ The open floor plan is airy and spacious

■ The Dining and Living Rooms features elegant columns

■ A fireplace highlights the Family Room with built-ins to either side

■ The Porch has direct access from the Breakfast Bay

■ A tray ceiling decorates the Master Bedroom

■ No materials list is available for this plan

Main floor – 2,618 sq. ft.
Garage – 482 sq. ft.

br.4
11-10 X 12

porch

brkfst
11-5 X 17-7

kit
10-8 X 13-9

laundry

WIDTH 71'-0"
DEPTH 74'-0"

mbr
15-10 X 14

m bath

br.2
12 X 12

family
19 X 19

dining
11 X 14

foyer

garage
20 X 22

living
11 X 13

br.3
12 X 11-5

MAIN FLOOR

Attractive Roof Line

Design by Fillmore Design Group

■ *Total living area 2,620 sq. ft.* ■ *Price Code F* ■

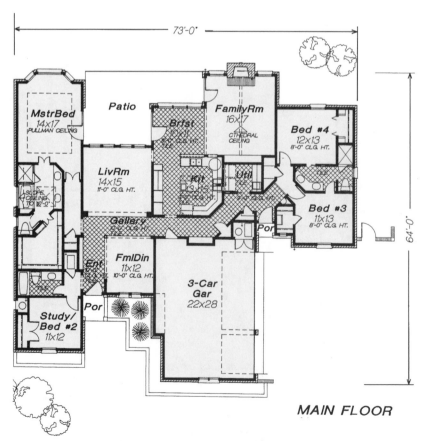

MAIN FLOOR

No. 92285 [BL]

■ **This plan features:**

— Four bedrooms

— Two full and one three-quarter baths

■ The Foyer leads into the tiled Gallery and the formal Living Room

■ An island in the center of the U-shaped Kitchen adds to the abundance of work area

■ Tiling in the Breakfast Room adds style

■ A cathedral ceiling tops the Family Room, which includes a fireplace

■ The Master Suite is positioned for maximum privacy

■ No materials list is available for this plan

Main floor — 2,620 sq. ft.
Garage — 567 sq. ft.

Delightful Detailing

■ *Total living area 2,622 sq. ft.* ■ *Price Code F* ■

No. 98426

■ This plan features:

— Three bedrooms

— Two full and one half baths

■ The vaulted ceiling extends from the Foyer into the Living Room

■ The Family Room has a vaulted ceiling and a fireplace

■ The Kitchen is equipped with an island serving bar, a desk, a wall oven, the Pantry and the Breakfast Bay

■ The Master Suite is highlighted by the Sitting Room, a walk-in closet and a private Bath with a vaulted ceiling

■ An optional basement or a crawl space foundation — please specify when ordering

Main floor — 2,622 sq. ft.
Bonus room — 478 sq. ft.
Basement — 2,622 sq. ft.
Garage — 506 sq. ft.

329

Brick Detailing

■ *Total living area 2,626 sq. ft.* ■ *Price Code F* ■

MAIN FLOOR

No. 98547

■ This plan features:

— Four bedrooms

— Three full baths

■ The tiled Entry and Gallery Area give access to the four corners of this home

■ The Living Room is to the left of the Entry and includes a bay window

■ The formal Dining Room encompasses the arched window in the front of the home

■ A vaulted ceiling tops the Master Suite which has a sloped ceiling over its Bath and the walk-in closet

■ No materials list is available for this plan

Main floor – 2,626 sq. ft.
Garage – 506 sq. ft.

Design by Larry E. Belk

Vintage Elevation

■ *Total living area 2,648 sq. ft.* ■ *Price Code F* ■

No. 93086 BL

■ This plan features:

— Four bedrooms

— Two full baths

■ Twelve-foot ceilings give the Study, Dining Room and Great Room a large, spacious appearance

■ Stately arches are featured at the entrance to the Dining Room and the Great Room

■ The Kitchen includes a cooktop work island, the Pantry and a four foot eating bar

■ The Master Suite includes dual closets and an amenity filled Bath

■ No materials list is available for this plan

Main floor — 2,648 sq. ft.
Bonus room — 266 sq. ft.
Garage — 552 sq. ft.

BONUS

FIRST FLOOR

331

Classically Styled

■ *Total living area 2,659 sq. ft.* ■ *Price Code F* ■

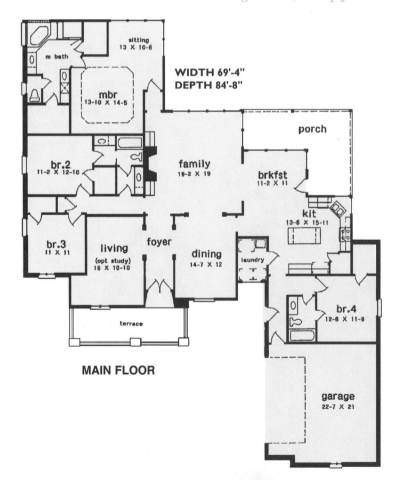

sitting
13 X 10-6

m bath

mbr
13-10 X 14-5

WIDTH 69'-4"
DEPTH 84'-8"

br.2
11-2 X 12-10

family
19-2 X 19

porch

brkfst
11-2 X 11

kit
13-6 X 15-11

br.3
11 X 11

living
(opt study)
16 X 10-10

foyer

dining
14-7 X 12

laundry

br.4
12-6 X 11-9

terrace

MAIN FLOOR

garage
22-7 X 21

No. 97507 BL

■ This plan features:

— Four bedrooms

— Three full baths

■ A fireplace and views of the rear yard accent the Family Room

■ The Breakfast Room and the Kitchen flow into each other for a spacious atmosphere

■ The Master Bedroom includes the Sitting Area, a tray ceiling, and a five-piece Master Bath

■ The fourth Bedroom, located next to the Kitchen, has its own private Bath

■ No materials list is available for this plan

Main floor — 2,659 sq. ft.
Garage — 517 sq. ft.

■ *Total living area 2,674 sq. ft.* ■ *Price Code F* ■

No. 98584 BL

■ **This plan features:**

— Four bedrooms

— Three full and one half baths

■ The Kitchen includes an island, the built-in Pantry and ample cabinet and storage space

■ A cathedral ceiling tops the Great Room, highlighted by a fireplace

■ There is access to the rear Patio and a built-in bookshelf in the Great Room

■ The Master Suite is crowned in a decorative ceiling and includes a lavish Bath

■ The Bonus Area on the second floor stands ready for expansion

■ No materials list is available for this plan

Main floor – 2,674 sq. ft.
Bonus room – 352 sq. ft.
Garage – 622 sq. ft.

FIRST FLOOR

BONUS

Outstanding Elevation

Design by Living Concepts Home Planning

■ *Total living area 2,677 sq. ft.* ■ *Price Code F* ■

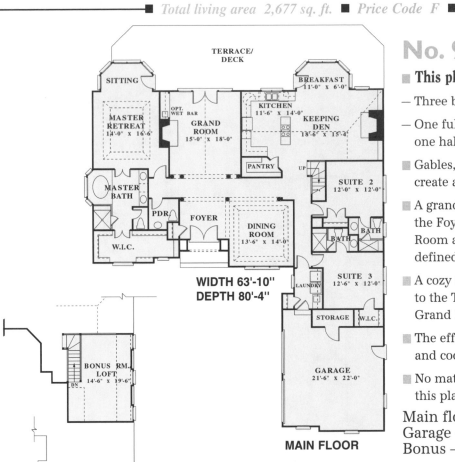

TERRACE/ DECK

SITTING

MASTER RETREAT
14'-0" x 16'-6"

OPT. WET BAR

GRAND ROOM
15'-0" x 18'-0"

KITCHEN
11'-6" x 14'-0"

BREAKFAST
11'-0" x 6'-0"

KEEPING DEN
18'-6" x 15'-3"

PANTRY

MASTER BATH

UP

SUITE 2
12'-0" x 12'-0"

PDR

FOYER

DINING ROOM
13'-6" x 14'-0"

W.I.C.

BATH

BATH

SUITE 3
12'-6" x 12'-0"

WIDTH 63'-10"
DEPTH 80'-4"

LAUNDRY

STORAGE

W.I.C.

GARAGE
21'-6" x 22'-0"

BONUS RM. LOFT
14'-6" x 19'-6"

DN

MAIN FLOOR

No. 96913

■ This plan features:

— Three bedrooms

— One full, two three-quarter and one half baths

■ Gables, keystones and arches create an appealing style

■ A grand double door entrance into the Foyer and the formal Dining Room and the Grand Room is defined by columns

■ A cozy fireplace and French doors to the Terrace/Deck enhance the Grand Room

■ The efficient Kitchen has a Pantry and cooktop island

■ No materials list is available for this plan

Main floor — 2,677 sq. ft.
Garage — 543 sq. ft.
Bonus — 319 sq. ft.

A Classic Design

Total living area 2,678 sq. ft. ■ *Price Code F* ■

No. 96600 BL

■ This plan features:

— Four bedrooms

— Two full and one half baths

■ An elegant arched opening graces the entrance of this classic design

■ The dramatic arch detail is repeated at the Dining Room entrance

■ The Kitchen, Breakfast Room and Family Room are open to one another

■ The Kitchen has amenities including a walk-in Pantry, double ovens and an eating bar

■ The Master Suite is located apart from the other Bedrooms for privacy

■ No materials list is available for this plan

Main floor — 2,678 sq. ft
Garage — 474 sq. ft.

MAIN FLOOR

WIDTH 70–2

Stone and Siding

Design by W.D. Farmer F.A.I.B.D.

■ *Total living area 2,690 sq. ft.* ■ *Price Code F* ■

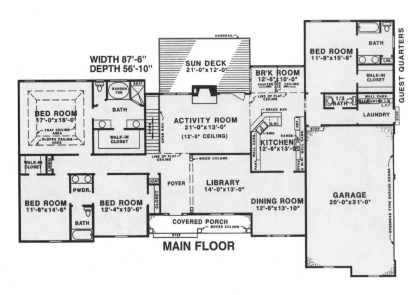

WIDTH 87'-6"
DEPTH 56'-10"

SUN DECK
21'-0"x12'-0"

HANDRAIL

BED ROOM
17'-0"x16'-0"
TRAY CEILING AREA
SLOPED CEILING AREA

BATH
GARDEN TUB
SEAT

BR'K ROOM
12'-6"x10'-0"
VAULTED CEILING
LINE OF FLAT CEILING

BED ROOM
11'-8"x15'-8"

BATH

LIN.

ACTIVITY ROOM
21'-0"x13'-0"
(12'-0" CEILING)

WALK-IN CLOSET

SNACK BAR

OPEN RAIL

WALK-IN CLOSET

WALL CABS.

1/2 BATH

WALL CABS.
WASH DRYER LN
L.T.

LAUNDRY

WALK-IN CLOSET
LINEN

KITCHEN
12'-6"x13'-0"

SINK

RANGE

REF.

D.W.

LINE OF FLAT CEILING

WOOD COLUMN

PWDR.

BED ROOM
11'-6"x14'-6"

BED ROOM
12'-4"x13'-6"

COAT
CLOSET

FOYER

LIBRARY
14'-0"x13'-0"

DINING ROOM
12'-6"x13'-10"

GARAGE
20'-0"x31'-0"

OVERHEAD TYPE GARAGE DOORS

GUEST QUARTERS

STEP

STEP

BATH

COVERED PORCH BOXED COLUMN
STEP

MAIN FLOOR

WHEELCHAIR BATH
(OPT.)

No. 94810 BL

■ This plan features:

— Four bedrooms

— Three full and one half baths

■ The attractive styling is used with a combination of stone and siding

■ The formal Foyer gives access to the Bedroom wing, Library or Activity Room

■ The Activity Room has a fireplace and direct access to the rear Deck and the Breakfast Room

■ The Breakfast Room is topped by a vaulted ceiling and flows into the Kitchen

■ A snack bar/peninsula counter is found in the Kitchen which also includes a built-in Pantry

■ The Master Suite is topped by a tray ceiling and five-piece Bath

MAIN FLOOR — 2,690 SQ. FT.
BASEMENT — 2,690 SQ. FT.
GARAGE — 660 SQ. FT.

Design by Kent & Kent, Inc.

All On One Floor

■ *Total living area 2,691 sq. ft.* ■ *Price Code F* ■

No.92901 BL

■ This plan features:

— Three bedrooms

— Three full baths

■ The design of this home gives privacy to the Bedroom Wing and an easy entrance to the Study/ Computer Room

■ The large Kitchen has two islands and the walk-in Pantry

■ Entry from Garage will cut down on tracked in dirt

■ The Dining Room is located next to the Kitchen for ease in serving

■ No materials list is available for this plan

Main floor — 2,691 sq. ft.
Garage — 611 sq. ft.
Porch — 96 sq. ft.
Patio — 366 sq. ft.

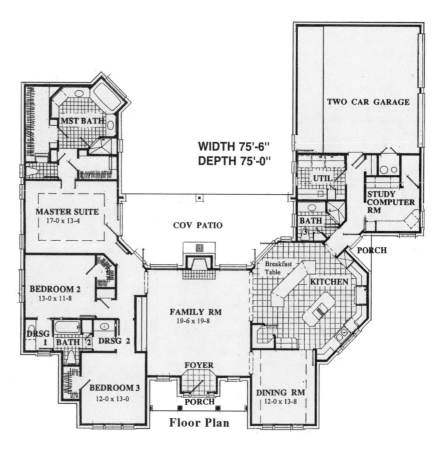

TWO CAR GARAGE

WIDTH 75'-6"
DEPTH 75'-0"

UTIL

STUDY
COMPUTER
RM

MST BATH

BATH
3

PORCH

MASTER SUITE
17-0 x 13-4

COV PATIO

Breakfast
Table

KITCHEN

BEDROOM 2
13-0 x 11-8

FAMILY RM
19-6 x 19-8

DRSG
1   BATH   DRSG 2
        2

FOYER

BEDROOM 3
12-0 x 13-0

PORCH

DINING RM
12-0 x 13-8

Floor Plan

European Style

Design by Rick Garner

■ *Total living area 2,727 sq. ft.* ■ *Price Code F* ■

No. 92501

■ **This plan features:**

— Four bedrooms

— Three full and one half baths

■ The central Foyer is between the spacious Living and Dining Rooms with arched windows

■ The hub Kitchen has an extended counter and nearby Utility/Garage entry, which easily serves the Breakfast Area and Dining Room

■ The spacious Den has a hearth fireplace with built-in shelves and sliding glass doors to the Porch

■ The Master Bedroom wing has a decorative ceiling, plush Bath and two walk-in closets

■ An optional slab or crawl space foundation — please specify when ordering

Main floor — 2,727 sq.
Garage — 569 sq. ft.

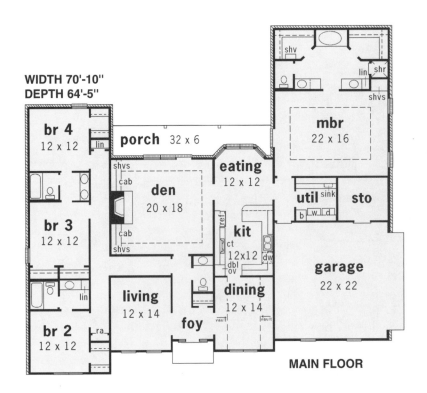

WIDTH 70'-10''
DEPTH 64'-5''

MAIN FLOOR

Extraordinary Ranch Design

■ *Total living area 2,730 sq. ft.* ■ *Price Code F* ■

No. 99162 **BL**

■ This plan features:

— Three bedrooms

— Two full and one half baths

■ This home is a Traditional Ranch with Country trimmings

■ The highly windowed Great Room is illuminated by natural light creating an airy atmosphere

■ The split Bedroom layout creates the private Master Suite

■ There is a see-through fireplace from the Master Bedroom to the Master Bath

■ With the formal Dining Room and the casual Nook, you can entertain for any occasion

■ No materials list is available for this plan

Main floor — 2,730 sq. ft.
Basement— 2,730 sq. ft.
Garage — 707 sq. ft.

MAIN FLOOR PLAN

Candid Ranch

Design by Ahmann Design, Inc.

■ *Total living area 2,731 sq. ft.* ■ *Price Code F* ■

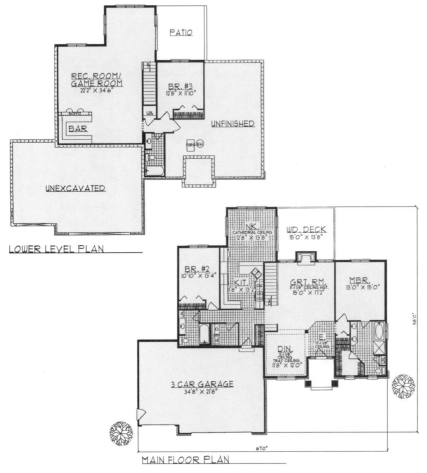

LOWER LEVEL PLAN

REC. ROOM/ GAME ROOM
22'2" x 34'6"

BAR

UNEXCAVATED

PATIO

BR. #3
12'8" x 11'0"

UNFINISHED

MAIN FLOOR PLAN

NK.
CATHEDRAL CEILING
17'8" x 13'8"

WD. DECK
15'0" x 13'8"

BR. #2
10'10" x 13'4"

KIT.
11'8" x 13'2"

GRT. RM.
9'-1 1/8" CEILING HGT.
15'0" x 17'2"

MBR.
13'0" x 15'0"

DIN.
9'-1 1/8"
TRAY CEILING
11'8" x 12'0"

3 CAR GARAGE
34'8" x 21'8"

No. 99160

■ **This plan features:**

— Three bedrooms

— Three full baths

■ The elegant formal Dining Room has a tray ceiling

■ The comfortable Great Room is equipped with a fireplace flanked by broad windows

■ The Master Bedroom has its own private Bath, walk-in closet, and linen storage

■ A cathedral ceiling accentuates the sunny eating Nook

■ On the lower level there is a great amount of room for the third Bedroom and Recreation Room

■ No materials list is available for this plan

Main floor – 1,692 sq. ft.
Lower level – 1,039 sq. ft.
Basement – 653 sq. ft.
Garage – 751 sq. ft.

Lavish Accommodations

■ *Total living area 2,733 sq. ft.* ■ *Price Code F* ■

No. 92538 BL X

■ **This plan features:**

– Four bedrooms

– Three full baths

■ The central Den includes a large fireplace, built-in shelves and cabinets and a decorative ceiling

■ Columns define the entrance to the formal Dining Room

■ The Kitchen includes a walk-in Pantry

■ The informal Breakfast Room is directly accessible from either the Kitchen or the Den

■ The Master Bedroom is enhanced by a decorative ceiling and a walk-in closet as well as the luxurious Master Bath

■ An optional slab or crawl space foundation — please specify when ordering

Main floor — 2,733 sq. ft.
Garage & storage — 569 sq. ft.

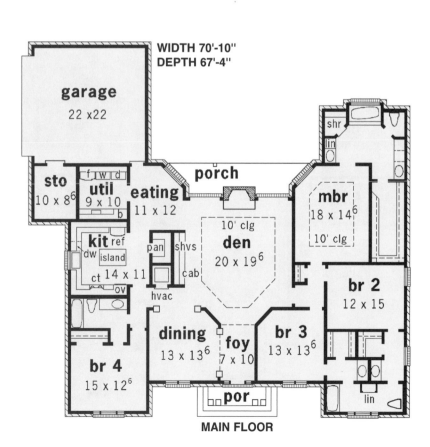

WIDTH 70'-10''
DEPTH 67'-4''

garage
22 x22

sto
10 x 8⁶

util
9 x 10

eating
11 x 12

porch

kit
14 x 11

den
20 x 19⁶

10' clg

mbr
18 x 14⁶

10' clg

br 2
12 x 15

dining
13 x 13⁶

foy
7 x 10

br 3
13 x 13⁶

br 4
15 x 12⁶

por

MAIN FLOOR

Distinctive Windows

Design by Rick Garner

■ *Total living area 2,735 sq. ft.* ■ *Price Code F* ■

No. 92550 BL X

WIDTH 68'-10"
DEPTH 67'-4"

MAIN FLOOR

- mbr 15 x 21⁴ raised clg
- porch 8 x 30⁸
- br 4 14 x 12
- sto 8⁶ x 8
- util 8⁶ x 9
- eating 13 x 11
- den 18 x 24
- br 3 14 x 12
- garage 21 x 22
- kit 13 x 13
- raised clg
- dining 14 x 12
- foy
- porch
- br 2 14 x 12
- ledge

■ **This plan features:**

— Four bedrooms

— Three full baths

■ The private Master Bedroom has a raised ceiling and private Bath with a Spa tub

■ The wing of three Bedrooms on the right side of the home share two full Baths

■ The efficient Kitchen is straddled by an Eating Nook and the Dining Room

■ The cozy Den has a raised ceiling and a fireplace that is the focal point of the home

■ The two-car Garage has the Storage Area

■ An optional slab or crawl space foundation — please specify when ordering

Main floor — 2,735 sq. ft.
Garage — 561 sq. ft.

With A European Influence

Design by Larry E. Belk

COPYRIGHT LARRY E. BELK

■ *Total living area   2,745 sq. ft.* ■ *Price Code F* ■

No. 96602 BL

■ **This plan features:**

— Four bedrooms

— Two full and one half baths

■ The Foyer opens to the well-proportioned Dining Room

■ Double French doors lead off the Living Room to the rear Porch

■ The spacious Kitchen is adjacent to the Breakfast and Family Room

■ A vaulted ceiling tops the Breakfast Room and the Family Room

■ The Master Bedroom features a tray ceiling

■ No materials list is available for this plan

■ An optional basement, slab or crawl space foundation — please specify when ordering

Main floor — 2,745 sq. ft.
Garage — 525 sq. ft.

WIDTH 69–6

COVERED PORCH

FAMILY ROOM
15-4 X 16-0
12 FT VAULTED CLG

LIVING ROOM
17-0 X 16-0
12 FT CLG

BEDRM 4/STUDY
13-4 X 14-8
10 FT CLG

MASTER BATH

MASTER BEDROOM
15-4 X 15-4
12 FT TRAY CLG

BRKFST RM
15-4 X .7-6
12 FT VAULTED CLG

42" LEDGE

UP→

KITCHEN
15-4 X 16-4
10 FT CLG

+DOWN

DINING ROOM
12-8 X 14-4
12 FT CLG

FOYER
12 FT CLG

PWDR

BATH 2

PAN

UTIL

PORCH

BEDROOM 3
12-4 X 13-6
10 FT CLG

BEDROOM 2
12-8 X 12-6
10 FT CLG

DEPTH 76-6

COPYRIGHT LARRY E. BELK

GARAGE

MAIN FLOOR

343

Especially Unique

■ *Total living area 2,748 sq. ft.* ■ *Price Code F* ■

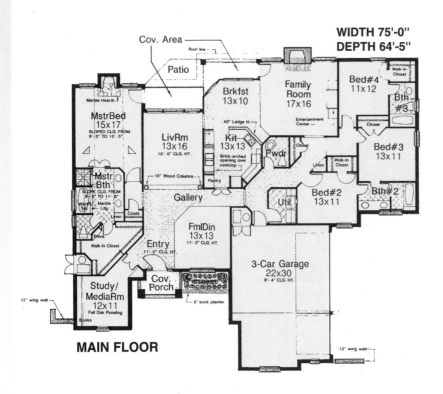

MAIN FLOOR

No. 98528

■ This plan features:

— Four bedrooms

— Three full and one half baths

■ The arch covered Entry and arched windows add a unique flair to this home

■ From the eleven-foot Entry turn left into the Study/Media Room

■ The formal Dining Room is open to the Gallery, and the Living Room beyond

■ The Family Room has a built-in entertainment center, a fireplace and access to the rear Patio

■ The Master Bedroom is isolated, and has a fireplace, a private Bath and the walk-in closet

■ No materials list is available for this plan

MAIN FLOOR — 2,748 SQ. FT.
GARAGE — 660 SQ. FT.

Just Past the Garden Gate

■ *Total living area 2,757 sq. ft.* ■ *Price Code G* ■

No. 93097 [BL]

■ This plan features:

— Four bedrooms

— Two full and one half baths

■ From the covered front Porch step through double doors into the Foyer with a ten-foot ceiling

■ There is an arched entry from the Foyer into the Dining Room

■ The Family Room and Breakfast Room are warmed by a fireplace and share a sloped ceiling

■ The Living Room has French doors that open to the rear Porch

■ The Kitchen is located in the rear of the home and conveniently accesses the Garage

■ No materials list is available for this plan

Main floor — 2,757 sq. ft.
Garage — 484 sq. ft.

MAIN FLOOR

© Larry E. Belk

COPYRIGHT LARRY E. BELK

GARAGE

UTIL

PAN

KITCHEN
15-4 X 13-8
10 FT CLG

42" LEDGE

PORCH

LIVING ROOM
17-0 X 16-4
12 FT CLG

BEDRM 4/STUDY
13-4 X 15-0
10 FT CLG

MASTER BATH
10 FT CLG

K.S.

MASTER BEDROOM
15-6 X 15-0
12 FT TRAY CLG

DEPTH 68-8

BRKFST ROOM
15-4 X 9-4
14 FT CLG

SLOPE→ ←SLOPE

FAMILY ROOM
15-4 X 14-0
14 FT CLG

FP

UP→

←DOWN

DINING ROOM
12-4 X 14-4
12 FT CLG

FOYER
10 FT CLG

PWDR

PORCH

BEDROOM 3
12-4 X 12-8
10 FT CLG

BATH 2

BEDROOM 2
12-6 X 12-8
10 FT CLG

WIDTH 69-6

Traditional-Styled Home

Design by Larry E. Belk

■ *Total living area 2,777 sq. ft.* ■ *Price Code G* ■

No. 93068 BL

■ This plan features:

— Three bedrooms

— Two full and one half baths

■ The Foyer is notable for its graceful columns and arches

■ The Kitchen, Breakfast Room and Family Room are in an open format

■ The Master Suite is separated from the secondary Bedrooms to provide privacy

■ The Study includes a bay window and a coffered ceiling

■ No materials list is available for this plan

Main floor – 2,777 sq. ft.
Garage – 501 sq. ft.

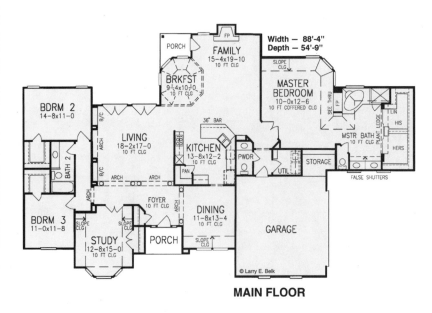

MAIN FLOOR

Brick Magnificence

■ *Total living area 2,858 sq. ft.* ■ *Price Code G* ■

No. 92243 BL

■ This plan features:

— Four bedrooms

— Three full baths

■ Large windows and attractive brick detailing using segmented arches give fantastic curb appeal

■ The convenient Ranch layout allows for step-saving one floor ease

■ A fireplace in the Living Room adds a warm ambience

■ The Family Room sports a second fireplace and built-in shelving

■ Two of the four Bedrooms include private access to a full double vanity Bath

■ No materials list is available for this plan

Main floor — 2,858 sq. ft.
Garage — 768 sq. ft.

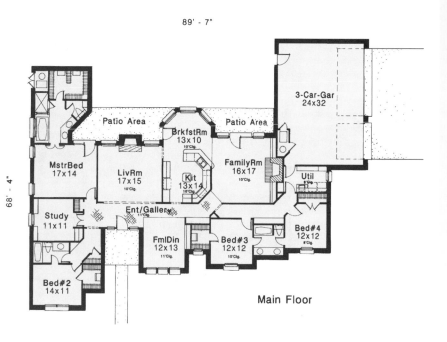

Main Floor

Lovely Rambler

Design by The Garlinghouse Company

■ Total living area 2,860 sq. ft. ■ Price Code G ■

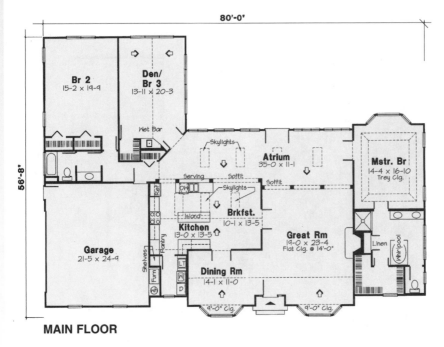

MAIN FLOOR

80'-0"

56'-8"

Br 2
15-2 x 19-9

Den/
Br 3
13-11 x 20-3

Wet Bar

Skylights

Atrium
35-0 x 11-1

Mstr. Br
14-4 x 16-10
Trey Clg.

Serving

Soffit

Skylights

Soffit

Island

Brkfst.
10-1 x 13-5

Kitchen
13-0 x 13-5

Great Rm
19-0 x 23-4
Flat Clg. @ 14'-0"

Linen

Whirlpool

Garage
21-5 x 24-9

Shelves

Pantry

Furn

Dining Rm
14-1 x 11-0

9'-0" Clg.

9'-0" Clg.

No. 24661

■ **This plan features:**

— Three bedrooms

— Two full baths

■ The Great Room is enhanced by a lovely bay window, fireplace and columns defining the skylit Atrium

■ Bay windows further enhance the formal Dining Room and Master Bedroom

■ The bright and open Kitchen/ Breakfast Area offers skylights, a built-in Pantry, a work island and serving bar for the Atrium

■ The luxurious Master Bath boasts a huge walk-in closet, double vanity and whirlpool tub

■ No materials list is available for this plan

Main floor — 2,860 sq. ft.
Garage — 558 sq. ft.

Elegant Living

■ Total living area 2,911 sq. ft. ■ Price Code G ■

No. 98569 BL

■ This plan features:

— Four bedrooms

— Three full and one half baths

■ The large walk-in Pantry is located in the Breakfast Area

■ The Master Bedroom has two walk-in closets and a luxurious Bath

■ The future Playroom on the second floor will keep children's happy noises and toys away from view and earshot

■ An optional basement or slab foundation — please specify when ordering

■ No materials list is available for this plan

Main floor — 2,911 sq. ft.
Garage — 720 sq. ft.

MAIN FLOOR

A Custom Look

■ *Total living area 2,978 sq. ft.* ■ *Price Code G* ■

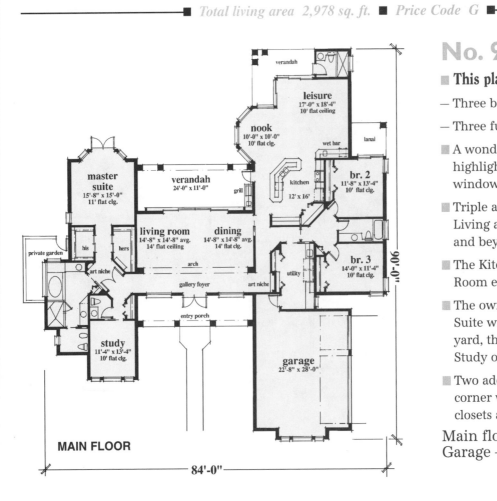

MAIN FLOOR

84'-0"

No. 94242

■ This plan features:

— Three bedrooms

— Three full and one half baths

■ A wonderfully balanced exterior is highlighted by triple arched windows

■ Triple arches lead into the Formal Living and Dining Room, Veranda and beyond

■ The Kitchen, Nook, and Leisure Room easily flow together

■ The owners' wing has the Master Suite with glass alcove to rear yard, the lavish Bath and the Study offering many uses

■ Two additional Bedrooms with corner windows and over-sized closets access a full Bath

Main floor — 2,978 sq. ft
Garage — 702 sq. ft.

Large Contemporary

■ *Total living area 2,987 sq. ft.* ■ *Price Code G* ■

No. 99784 BL ✗

■ **This plan features:**

— Four bedrooms

— Three full baths

■ Slender brick columns support the dramatic gabled Porch

■ Vaulted ceilings are featured in the Entry, Guest Suite, Living Room, Office and the Kitchen

■ A Family Theater, which is also accessible from the Utility Room, has built-in cabinets and shelves

■ Back to Back fireplaces are located in the Office and Kitchen

■ The sunny Family Kitchen has skylights and the Pantry

■ The Master Suite includes the bay windowed Sitting Area

■ The Master Bath is equipped with a Spa and an oversized shower

Main floor — 2,987 sq. ft.
Garage — 690 sq. ft.

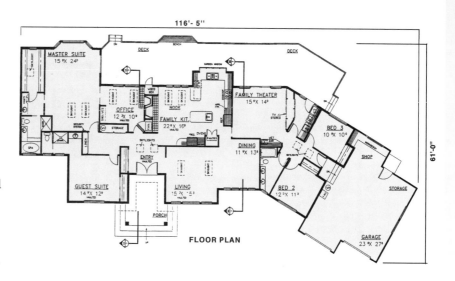

FLOOR PLAN

Impressive Entryway

Design by Sater Design Group

■ *Total living area 2,998 sq. ft.* ■ *Price Code G* ■

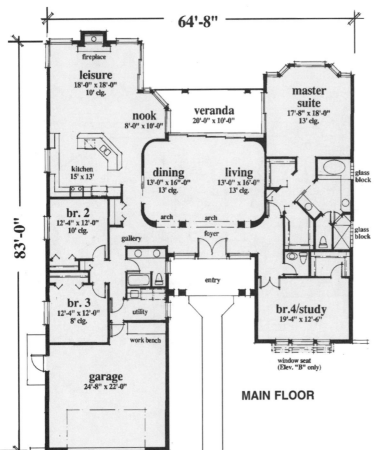

leisure
18'-0" x 18'-0"
10' clg.

nook
8'-0" x 10'-0"

veranda
20'-0" x 10'-0"

master suite
17'-8" x 18'-0"
13' clg.

kitchen
15' x 13'

dining
13'-0" x 16'-0"
13' clg.

living
13'-0" x 16'-0"
13' clg.

glass block

glass block

br. 2
12'-4" x 12'-0"
10' clg.

gallery

arch   arch

foyer

br. 3
12'-4" x 12'-0"
8' clg.

entry

utility

br.4/study
19'-4" x 12'-6"

work bench

garage
24'-8" x 22'-0"

window seat
(Elev. "B" only)

MAIN FLOOR

64'-8"

83'-0"

fireplace

No. 94243 BL

■ **This plan features:**

— Three or four bedrooms

— Two full baths

■ Double door leads into the curved
Living/Dining Area and the
Veranda beyond

■ The efficient Kitchen has an
angled serving counter/snack bar,
eating Nook and Leisure Area
with a fireplace

■ The large Master Suite has access
to the Veranda, two walk-in closets
and the deluxe Bath with two
vanities

■ French doors lead into the bright
Study/Bedroom with walk-in
closet

■ No materials list is available for
this plan

Main floor — 2,998 sq. ft.
Garage — 632 sq. ft.

Eye-Catching Elevation

■ *Total living area 3,032 sq. ft.* ■ *Price Code H* ■

No. 97511 BL

■ **This plan features:**

- Three bedrooms

- Three full baths

■ There are large, arched glass doorways into the Study, Foyer and Dining Room

■ The Keeping Room, Breakfast Area and the Kitchen Area open to each other for a terrific, informal living area

■ The Family Room is located at the heart of the home

■ The split Bedroom layout assures the Master Suite of privacy

■ No materials list is available for this plan

■ This plan is not to be built within a 20 mile radius of Madisonville, LA or in Baton Rouge, LA

Main floor — 3,032 sq. ft.
Garage — 594 sq. ft.

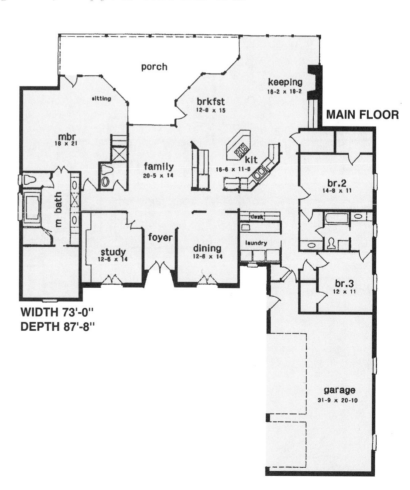

MAIN FLOOR

porch

keeping
16-2 x 16-2

sitting

brkfst
12-8 x 15

mbr
18 x 21

family
20-5 x 14

kit
16-6 x 11-8

br.2
14-8 x 11

m bath

study
12-6 x 14

foyer

dining
12-6 x 14

desk

laundry

br.3
12 x 11

WIDTH 73'-0"
DEPTH 87'-8"

garage
31-9 x 20-10

Relax on the Veranda

Design by Landmark Design, Inc.

■ Total living area 3,051 sq. ft. ■ Price Code H ■

WIDTH 90'-0"
DEPTH 82'-0"

MAIN FLOOR

No. 91749

■ This plan features:

— Four bedrooms

— Three full and one half baths

■ The Veranda wraps around this home

■ The sky-lit Master Suite has an elevated custom Spa, twin basins, a walk-in closet, and an additional vanity outside the Bathroom

■ A vaulted ceiling is featured in the Den

■ A fireplace is located in both the Family Room and the formal Living Room

■ The efficient Kitchen has a peninsula counter and a double sink

■ Two additional Bedrooms have walk-in closets and share a Bath

Main floor — 3,051 sq. ft.
Garage — 646 sq. ft.

Columned Classic

■ *Total living area 3,084 sq. ft.* ■ *Price Code H* ■

No. 96521

This plan features:

- Four bedrooms
- Three full and one half baths
- Grand columns are featured both on the front Porch and in the Entry way
- The formal Living Room has a corner fireplace
- The U-shaped Kitchen has a convenient Eating Bar
- The Master Bedroom in rear of home overlooks the Courtyard
- Three additional large Bedrooms share two and a half Baths

Main floor — 3,084 sq. ft.
Bonus — 868 sq. ft.
Garage — 672 sq. ft.

MAIN FLOOR

OPTIONAL ROOM

Future Rm

Easy Living Plan

Design by Fillmore Design Group

■ *Total living area 3,089 sq. ft.* ■ *Price Code H* ■

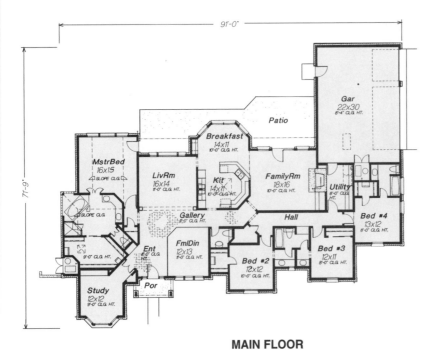

MAIN FLOOR

No. 98597

■ **This plan features:**

— Four bedrooms

— Three full and one half baths

■ The popular split Bedroom plan gives privacy to the Master Suite

■ An angled counter in the Kitchen becomes a terrific serving bar and snack bar

■ The large Patio extends living space to the outdoors and has access from the Master Bedroom and the Family Room

■ The Utility Room serves the family efficiently as the Mud Room from the Garage

■ No materials list is available for this plan

Main floor — 3,089 sq. ft.
Garage — 660 sq. ft.

With Room for All

■ *Total living area 3,121 sq. ft.* ■ *Price Code H* ■

No. 92221

■ **This plan features:**

– Five bedrooms

– Four full baths

■ The three Bedroom duplex provides privacy to the Master Suite and an abundance of storage space

■ A full Bath is located between the two roomy secondary Bedrooms

■ A fireplace and a built-in wetbar enhance the Living Room

■ The two Bedroom unit includes large rooms and a double sided fireplace adding warmth and atmosphere

■ No materials list is available for this plan

Main floor — 3,121 sq. ft.
Garage — 1,034 sq. ft.

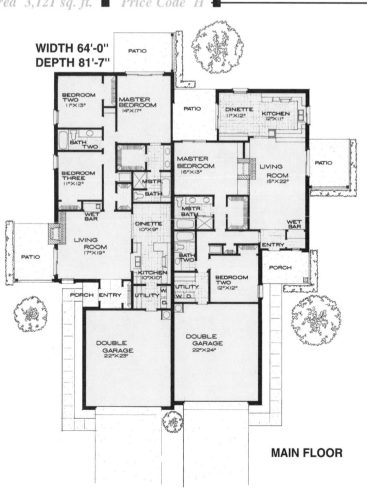

WIDTH 64'-0"
DEPTH 81'-7"

MAIN FLOOR

Sprawling Sun-Catcher

Design by Alan Mascord Design Associates

■ *Total living area 3,160 sq. ft.* ■ *Price Code H* ■

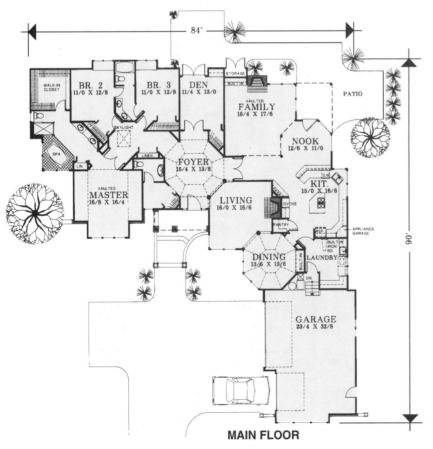

MAIN FLOOR

No. 91501

■ **This plan features:**

— Three bedrooms

— Two full and one half baths

■ The central Foyer opens to every area of the house

■ The fabulous Master Suite has a garden Spa, double vanity and a room-size walk-in closet

■ The cozy Den has French doors to the rear Patio

■ Columns separate the Living Room with fireplace from the octagonal, vaulted-ceiling Dining Room

■ The Kitchen has twin ovens and a peninsula counter

■ The eating Nook Area is open to the Kitchen

Main floor — 3,160 sq. ft.

Country-Style

■ *Total living area 3,188 sq. ft.* ■ *Price Code H* ■

No. 91750 BL ✕ R R

■ **This plan features:**

– Four bedrooms

– Three full and one half baths

■ This plan is easily adaptable for wheelchair accessibility

■ Vaulted ceilings are featured over the Entry, Living and Dining Rooms, adding elegance

■ A cozy fireplace with a built-in wood box and bookshelves is located in the Living Room

■ A walk-in Pantry, the Nook Area, cooktop island, and a corner double sink help to make this huge Kitchen efficient

■ The Family Room is brightened by three skylights

Main area — 3,188 sq. ft.
Covered porch — 560 sq. ft.
Deck — 324 sq. ft.
Garage — 705 sq. ft.

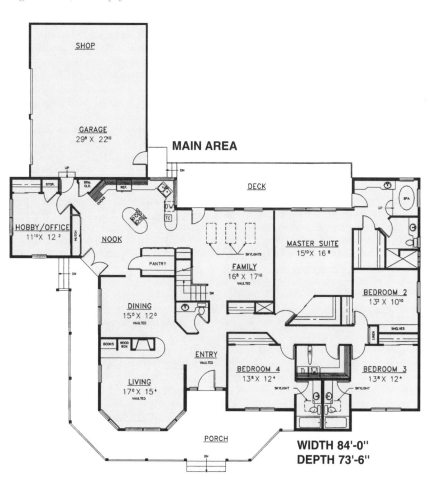

MAIN AREA

SHOP

GARAGE
29⁸ X 22⁰

HOBBY/OFFICE
11¹⁰ X 12²

NOOK

PANTRY

DINING
15⁰ X 12⁰
VAULTED

LIVING
17⁰ X 15⁴
VAULTED

ENTRY
VAULTED

DECK

FAMILY
16⁸ X 17¹⁰
VAULTED

MASTER SUITE
15¹⁰ X 16⁸

SPA

BEDROOM 2
13² X 10¹⁰

BEDROOM 4
13⁸ X 12⁴
SKYLIGHT

BEDROOM 3
13⁸ X 12⁴
SKYLIGHT

PORCH

WIDTH 84'-0"
DEPTH 73'-6"

359

■ *Total living area 3,225 sq. ft.* ■ *Price Code H* ■

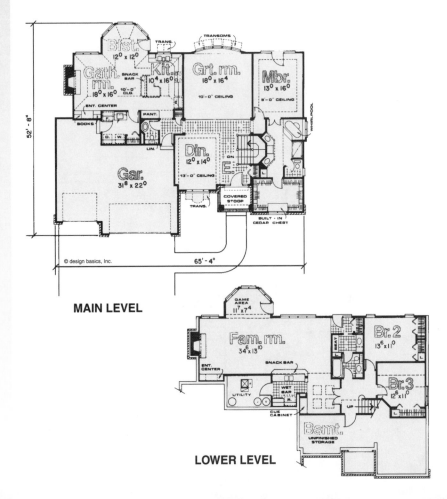

MAIN LEVEL

LOWER LEVEL

No. 97410

■ **This plan features:**

— Three bedrooms

— Two full and one half baths

■ This plan has a lower level that includes two Bedrooms

■ On the main level, the Dining Room has a towering front wall window

■ The Great Room has a rear bow window

■ The Kitchen is brightened by a window with a transom over the sink

■ The Gathering Room shares a fireplace with the gazebo-shaped Breakfast Nook

■ The Master Bedroom has a French door to the rear yard

Main level — 1,887 sq. ft.
Lower level — 1,388 sq. ft.
Basement — 549 sq. ft.
Garage — 738 sq. ft.

Design by Andy McDonald Design Group

Sprawling Yet Elegant

■ *Total living area 3,230 sq. ft.* ■ *Price Code H* ■

No. 97513 [BL]

■ This plan features:

– Three bedrooms

– Three full baths

■ Palladian windows located at the entrance to this home provide an elegant first impression

■ The Family Room includes a fireplace, as does the Keeping Room

■ There is a wetbar in the Family Room

■ The Home Office is located off the Kitchen

■ The plush Master Suite includes a lavish Bath and Sitting Area

■ No materials list is available for this plan

Main floor — 3,230 sq. ft.
Garage — 729 sq. ft.

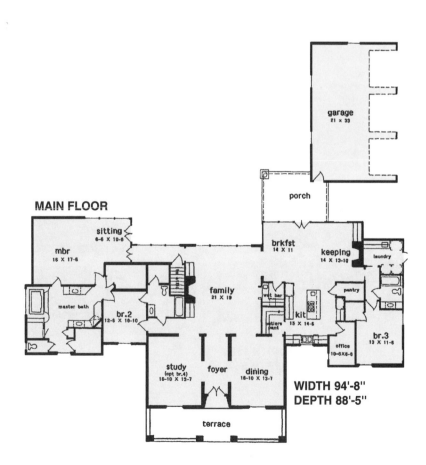

MAIN FLOOR

garage
21 X 33

porch

sitting
6-6 X 10-6

mbr
16 X 17-6

brkfst
14 X 11

keeping
14 X 13-10

laundry

master bath

family
21 X 19

wet bar

kit
15 X 14-6

pantry

br.2
12-6 X 10-10

butlers pant

office
10-6X8-6

br.3
13 X 11-6

study
(opt br.4)
16-10 X 13-7

foyer

dining
16-10 X 13-7

WIDTH 94'-8"
DEPTH 88'-5"

terrace

Rambling Ranch

Design by Fillmore Design Group

■ *Total living area 3,239 sq. ft.* ■ *Price Code H* ■

No. 98598 BL

■ **This plan features:**

— Three bedrooms

— Three full baths

■ The formal and informal rooms are perfectly situated for a busy lifestyle

■ The split Bedroom plan gives the Owner's Suite the privacy it deserves

■ The covered Patio and courtyard area take living space to the outdoors

■ The peninsula counter in the Kitchen is a perfect Eating Bar

■ No materials list is available for this plan

Main floor — 3,239 sq. ft.
Garage — 748 sq. ft.
Deck — 184 sq. ft.

MAIN FLOOR

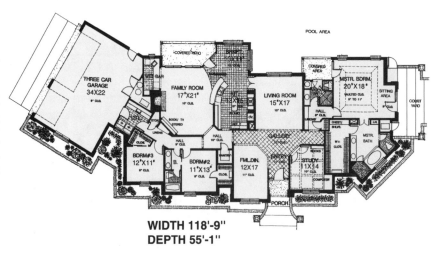

WIDTH 118'-9"
DEPTH 55'-1"

Luxurious One-Floor Living

Total living area 3,254 sq. ft.   ■   **Price Code I**   ■

No. 92273

This plan features:

- Four bedrooms

- Three full baths

- The formal Living Room, accented by a fireplace between windows, overlooks the rear yard

- A breakfast bar, work island, and an abundance of storage and counter space are featured in the Kitchen

- A bright alcove for the informal Dining and Family Rooms has access to the covered Patio and adjoins the Kitchen

- The spacious Master Bedroom has access to covered Patio, a lavish Bath and huge walk-in closet

- No materials list is available for this plan

Main floor — 3,254 sq. ft.
Garage — 588 sq. ft.

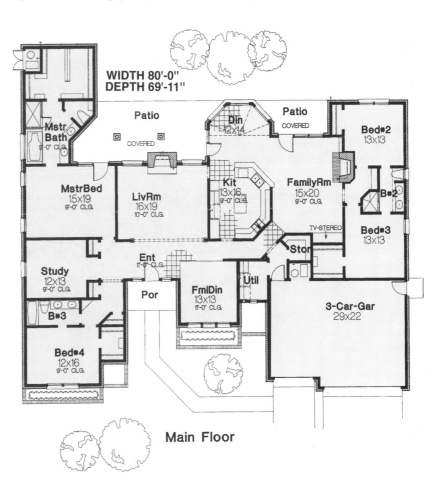

WIDTH 80'-0"
DEPTH 69'-11"

Main Floor

French Country Styling

■ *Total living area 3,352 sq. ft.* ■ *Price Code I* ■

No. 98513

■ **This plan features:**

— Three bedrooms

— Three full and one half baths

■ Brick and stone blend masterfully for an impressive French Country exterior

■ The separate Master Suite has an expansive Bath and closet

■ The Study contains a built-in desk and bookcase

■ The angled Kitchen is highlighted by a walk-in Pantry and is open to the Breakfast Bay

■ The fantastic Family Room includes a brick fireplace and a built-in entertainment center

■ No materials list is available for this plan

Main floor — 3,352 sq. ft.
Garage — 672 sq. ft.

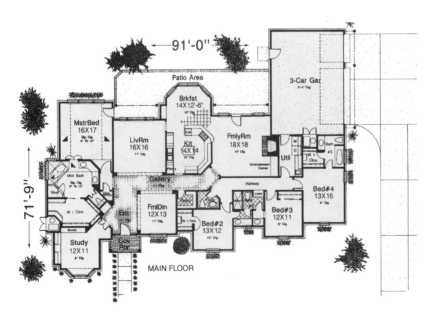

Unique V-Shaped Home

■ *Total living area 3,417 sq. ft.* ■ *Price Code I* ■

No. 99721 **BL**

■ This plan features:

- Two bedrooms

- Three full baths

■ Bookshelves, interspersed with windows, line the long hallway that provides access to the owner's wing

■ Four skylights brighten the already sunny Eating Nook in the huge country Kitchen

■ A walk-in Pantry, range-top work island, built-in barbecue and a sink add to the amenities of the Kitchen

■ A wide window bay and an entire wall of windows along its length illuminate the Living Room

■ No materials list is available for this plan

Main floor — 3,417 sq. ft.

Garage — 795 sq. ft.

WIDTH 128'-6"
DEPTH 79'-6"

MAIN FLOOR

Easy Living

■ Total living area 3,430 sq. ft. ■ Price Code I ■

MAIN FLOOR

sitting
7-2 x 9-5

master bath

mbr
17-1 x 18

solarium
20 x 9-6

brkfst
12-10 x 13-8

pantry

br.4
14-6 x 14-6

br.3
11-6 x 12-4

family
22 x 21

kit
13-6 x 15-4

laundry

butler

storage
3-6 x 16-2

br.2
12-6 x 11-6

foyer

dining

living rm
(opt. study)
11-8 x 14

garage
20-6 x 21

WIDTH 78'-9"
DEPTH 79'-4"

No. 97514

■ **This plan features:**

— Four bedrooms

— Three full and one half baths

■ The Dining Area accesses the Kitchen through the Butler's Pantry

■ The Kitchen features a work island

■ The Family Room has a fireplace with built-ins to either side

■ The Master Suite features the Sitting Area

■ No materials list is available for this plan

■ This plan is not to be built within a 20 mile radius of Madisonville, LA or in Baton Rouge, LA

Main floor — 3,430 sq. ft.
Garage — 469 sq. ft.

Design by Studer Residential Design, Inc.

Multiple Gables

■ Total living area 3,570 sq. ft. ■ Price Code J ■

No. 97714 BL

■ This plan features:

- Three bedrooms

- Three full and one half baths

■ The impressive Foyer offers dramatic view past the Dining Room

■ The gourmet Kitchen with island and snack bar combines with the spacious Breakfast Room and the Hearth Room to create a warm atmosphere

■ The Master Suite has a fireplace complemented by the deluxe Dressing Room with whirlpool tub, shower and dual vanity

■ No materials list is available for this plan

Main floor — 3,570 sq. ft.
Bonus — 2,367 sq. ft.
Basement — 1,203 sq. ft.

MAIN FLOOR

Dressing

Sitting
11'2" x 7'9"
Irregular

WALK-IN CLOSET

Master Bedroom
17'8" x 17'4"
Irregular

Great Room
19'5" x 17'8"

Breakfast
13'6" x 13'11"
Irregular

Hearth Room
22'11" x 17'1"
Irregular

Kitchen
16'10" x 17'11"
Irregular

Bath

WALK-IN CLOSET

Hall

Bedroom
13'4" x 14'0"

WALK-IN CLOSET

Bath

Foyer

Hall

Garage
21'4" x 40'11"

Dining Room
14'4" x 15'7"
Irregular

Laun.

Bedroom
13'4" x 12'3"
Irregular

Porch

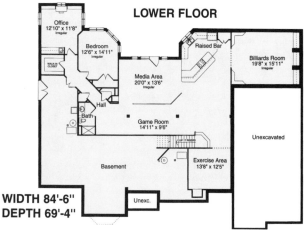

LOWER FLOOR

Office
12'10" x 11'8"
Irregular

Bedroom
12'6" x 14'11"
Irregular

Raised Bar

Billiards Room
19'8" x 15'11"
Irregular

WALK-IN CLOSET

Media Area
20'0" x 13'6"
Irregular

Hall

Bath

Game Room
14'11" x 9'6"

Unexcavated

Basement

Exercise Area
13'8" x 12'5"

WIDTH 84'-6"
DEPTH 69'-4"

Unexc.

Luxurious Masterpiece

Design by Fillmore Design Group

Total living area 3,818 sq. ft. ■ Price Code K

No. 92265 BL

MAIN FLOOR

■ **This plan features:**

— Four bedrooms

— Three full and one half baths

■ The expansive formal Living Room has a fourteen-foot ceiling and a raised hearth fireplace

■ The informal Family Room offers another fireplace, wetbar, cathedral ceiling and access to the covered Patio

■ The hub Kitchen has a cooktop island, peninsula counter/snack bar, and the bright Breakfast Area

■ The private Master Bedroom is enhanced by a pullman ceiling, lavish dual Baths, and a garden window tub in the Bath

■ No materials list is available for this plan

Main floor — 3,818 sq. ft.
Garage — 816 sq. ft.

Total living area 4,028 sq. ft. ■ *Price Code L*

No. 94224 BL

■ This plan features:

- Three bedrooms

- Three full and one half baths

■ Cascading arches frame the Foyer, Dining Room ceiling and Living Room fireplace

■ The spacious Kitchen with walk-in Pantry, efficient work island and peninsula counter serves Eating Nook with skylit atrium, and the Dining Room with ease

■ The expansive Leisure Room has a built-in entertainment center, wetbar and access to the Lanai

■ The Master Suite is enhanced by the Sitting Area, access to the Lanai, cascading arches, two walk-in closets and a plush Bath

■ No materials list is available for this plan

Main floor — 4,028 sq. ft.
Garage — 660 sq. ft.

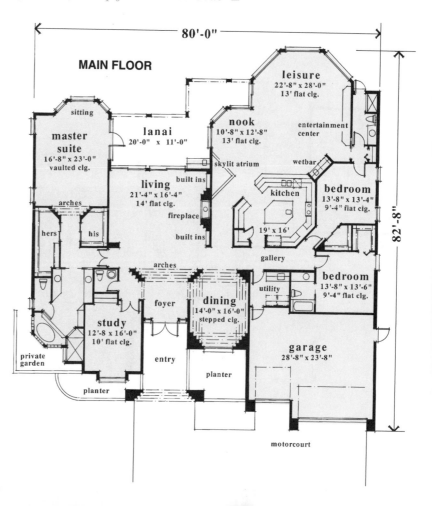

MAIN FLOOR

80'-0"

82'-8"

sitting

master suite
16'-8" x 23'-0"
vaulted clg.

lanai
20'-0" x 11'-0"

leisure
22'-8" x 28'-0"
13' flat clg.

nook
10'-8" x 12'-8"
13' flat clg.

entertainment center

arches

living
21'-4" x 16'-4"
14' flat clg.

built ins

skylit atrium

wetbar

bedroom
13'-8" x 13'-4"
9'-4" flat clg.

hers

his

fireplace

kitchen

19' x 16'

built ins

gallery

bedroom
13'-8" x 13'-6"
9'-4" flat clg.

arches

foyer

dining
14'-0" x 16'-0"
stepped clg.

utility

private garden

study
12'-8" x 16'-0"
10' flat clg.

entry

planter

garage
28'-8" x 23'-8"

planter

planter

motorcourt

Exceptional Family Living

Total living area 4,082 sq. ft. ■ Price Code L

Floor Plan

No. 98538

■ This plan features:

— Four bedrooms

— Three full and one half baths

■ A decorative dormer, a bay window and an eyebrow arched window provide for a pleasing Country farmhouse facade

■ The cozy Study has its own fireplace and a bay window

■ The large formal Living Room has a fireplace and built-in bookcases

■ The huge Kitchen is open to the Breakfast Bay and the Family Room

■ The Master Suite includes a large Bath with a unique closet

■ No materials list is available for this plan

Main floor — 4,082 sq. ft.
Garage — 720 sq. ft.

©1997 Donald A. Gardner Architects, Inc.

■ *Total living area 4,523 sq. ft.* ■ *Price Code L* ■

No. 98010

This plan features:

- Four bedrooms

- Four full and two half baths

■ Brick, gables and a Traditional hip roof always seem to be in style

■ Inside find dramatic spaces that include the Dining Room and the Great Room, both with fourteen-foot ceilings

■ The Study features a wall of built-in bookshelves

■ The Sun Room and the Breakfast Nook share a counter with the Kitchen

■ The Master Bedroom is opulent with dual Baths and closets

■ Storage space abounds with the walk-in Pantry, numerous closets, and storage space in the Garage

Main floor — 4,523 sq. ft.
Garage — 1,029 sq. ft.

Everything You Need...
...to Make Your Dream Come True!

You pay only a fraction of the original cost for home designs by respected professionals.

You've Picked Your Dream Home!

You can imagine your new home situated on your lot in the morning sunlight. You can visualize living there, enjoying your family, entertaining friends and celebrating holidays. All that remains are the details. That's where we can help. Whether you plan to build it yourself, act as your own general contractor or hire a professional builder, your Garlinghouse Co. home plans will provide the perfect design and specifications to help make your dream home a reality.

We can offer you an array of additional products and services to help you with your planning needs. We can supply materials lists, construction cost estimates based on your local material and labor costs and modifications to your selected plan if you would like.

For over 90 years, homeowners and builders have relied on us for accurate, complete, professional blueprints. Our plans help you get results fast... and save money, too! These pages will give you all the information you need to order. So get started now... We know you'll love your new Garlinghouse home!

Sincerely,

Bradford Kading
President

James D. McNair III
Chief Executive Officer

EXTERIOR ELEVATIONS

Elevations are scaled drawings of the front, rear, left, and right sides of a home. All of the necessary information pertaining to the exterior finish materials, roof pitches, and exterior height dimensions of your home are defined.

CABINET PLANS

These plans, or in some cases elevations, will detail the layout of the kitchen and bathroom cabinets at a larger scale. This gives you an accurate layout for your cabinets or an ideal starting point for a modified custom cabinet design. Available for most plans. You may also show the floor plan without a cabinet layout. This will allow you to start from scratch and design your own dream kitchen.

TYPICAL WALL SECTION

This section is provided to help your builder understand the structural components and materials used to construct the exterior walls of your home. This section will address insulation, roof components, and interior and exterior wall finishes. Your plans will be designed with either 2x4 or 2x6 exterior walls, but most professional contractors can easily adapt the plans to the wall thickness you require.

FIREPLACE DETAILS

If the home you have chosen includes a fireplace, the fireplace detail will show typical methods to construct the firebox, hearth and flue chase for masonry units, or a wood frame chase for a zero-clearance unit. Available for most plans.

FOUNDATION PLAN

These plans will accurately dimension the footprint of your home including load bearing points and beam placement if applicable. The foundation style will vary from plan to plan. Your local climatic conditions will dictate whether a basement, slab or crawlspace is best suited for your area. In most cases, if your plan comes with one foundation style, a professional contractor can easily adapt the foundation plan to an alternate style.

ROOF PLAN

The information necessary to construct the roof will be included with your home plans. Some plans will reference roof trusses, while many others contain schematic framing plans. These framing plans will indicate the lumber sizes necessary for the rafters and ridgeboards based on the designated roof loads.

TYPICAL CROSS SECTION

A cut-away cross-section through the entire home shows your building contractor the exact correlation of construction components at all levels of the house. It will help to clarify the load bearing points from the roof all the way down to the basement. Available for most plans.

DETAILED FLOOR PLANS

The floor plans of your home accurately dimension the positioning of all walls, doors, windows, stairs and permanent fixtures. They will show you the relationship and dimensions of rooms, closets and traffic patterns. The schematic of the electrical layout may be included in the plan. This layout is clearly represented and does not hinder the clarity of other pertinent information shown. All these details will help your builder properly construct your new home.

STAIR DETAILS

If stairs are an element of the design you have chosen, the plans will show the necessary information to build these, either through a stair cross section, or on the floor plans. Either way, the information provides your builders the essential reference points that they need to build the stairs.

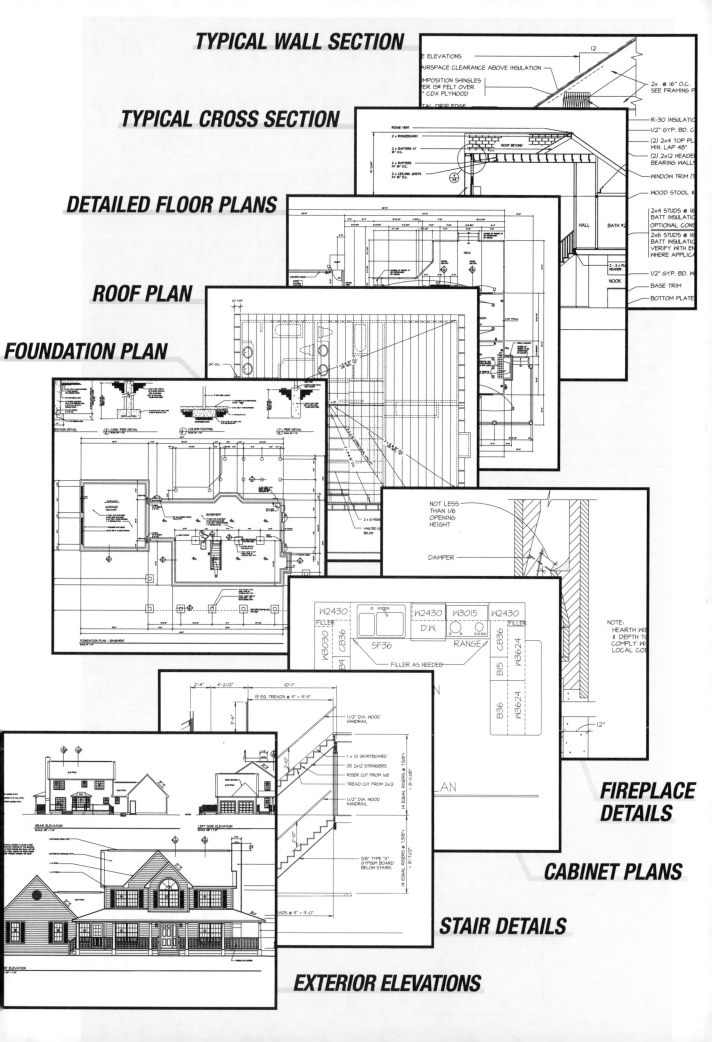

TYPICAL WALL SECTION

TYPICAL CROSS SECTION

DETAILED FLOOR PLANS

ROOF PLAN

FOUNDATION PLAN

FIREPLACE DETAILS

CABINET PLANS

STAIR DETAILS

EXTERIOR ELEVATIONS

Garlinghouse Options & Extras ...Make Your Dream A Home

Reversed Plans Can Make Your Dream Home Just Right!

"That's our dream home...if only the garage were on the other side!"

You could have exactly the home you want by flipping it end-for-end. Check it out by holding your dream home page of this book up to a mirror. Then simply order your plans "reversed." We'll send you one full set of mirror-image plans (with the writing backwards) as a master guide for you and your builder.

The remaining sets of your order will come as shown in this book so the dimensions and specifications are easily read on the job site...but most plans in our collection come stamped "REVERSED" so there is no construction confusion.

As Shown   Reversed

We can only send reversed plans with multiple-set orders. There is a $50 charge for this service.

Some plans in our collection are available in Right Reading Reverse. Right Reading Reverse plans will show your home in reverse, with the writing on the plan being readable. This easy-to-read format will save you valuable time and money. Please contact our Customer Service Department at (860) 343-5977 to check for Right Reading Reverse availability. (There is a $135 charge for this service.)

Specifications & Contract Form

We send this form to you free of charge with your home plan order. The form is designed to be filled in by you or your contractor with the exact materials to use in the construction of your new home. Once signed by you and your contractor it will provide you with peace of mind throughout the construction process.

$19.95 *per set*
(includes postage)

Remember To Order Your Materials List

It'll help you save money. Available at a modest additional charge, the Materials List gives the quantity, dimensions, and specifications for the major materials needed to build your home. You will get faster, more accurate bids from your contractors and building suppliers — and avoid paying for unused materials and waste. Materials Lists are available for all home plans except as otherwise indicated, but can only be ordered with a set of home plans. Due to differences in regional requirements and homeowner or builder preferences... electrical, plumbing and heating/air conditioning equipment specifications are not designed specifically for each plan. However, non-plan specific detailed typical prints of residential electrical, plumbing and construction guidelines can be provided. Please see below for additional information.

Detail Plans Provide Valuable Information About Construction Techniques

Because local codes and requirements vary greatly, we recommend that you obtain drawings and bids from licensed contractors to do your mechanical plans. However, if you want to know more about techniques — and deal more confidently with subcontractors — we offer these remarkably useful detail sheets. These detail sheets will aid in your understanding of these technical subjects. **The detail sheets are not specific to any one home plan and should be used only as a general reference guide.**

RESIDENTIAL CONSTRUCTION DETAILS

Ten sheets that cover the essentials of stick-built residential home construction. Details foundation options — poured concrete basement, concrete block, or monolithic concrete slab. Shows all aspects of floor, wall and roof framing. Provides details for roof dormers, overhangs, chimneys and skylights. Conforms to requirements of Uniform Building code or BOCA code. Includes a quick index and a glossary of terms.

RESIDENTIAL PLUMBING DETAILS

Eight sheets packed with information detailing pipe installation methods, fittings, and sizes. Details plumbing hook-ups for toilets, sinks, washers, sump pumps, and septic system construction. Conforms to requirements of National Plumbing code. Color coded with a glossary of terms and quick index.

RESIDENTIAL ELECTRICAL DETAILS

Eight sheets that cover all aspects of residential wiring, from simple switch wiring to service entrance connections. Details distribution panel layout with outlet and switch schematics, circuit breaker and wiring installation methods, and ground fault interrupter specifications. Conforms to requirements of National Electrical Code. Color coded with a glossary of terms.

Modifying Your Favorite Design, Made *EASY!*

Modifying Your Garlinghouse Home Plan

Simple modifications to your dream home, including minor non-structural changes and material substitutions, can be made between you and your builder by marking the changes directly on your blueprints. However, if you are considering making significant changes to your chosen design, we recommend that you use the services of The Garlinghouse Design Staff. We will help take your ideas and turn them into a reality, just the way you want. Here's our procedure!

When you place your Vellum order, you may also request a free Garlinghouse Modification Kit. In this kit, you will receive a red marking pencil, furniture cut-out sheet, ruler, a self addressed mailing label and a form for specifying any additional notes or drawings that will help us understand your design ideas. Mark your desired changes directly on the Vellum drawings. NOTE: Please use only a **red pencil** to mark your desired changes on the Vellum. Then, return the redlined Vellum set in the original box to us. **IMPORTANT:** Please **roll** the Vellums for shipping, **do not fold** the Vellums for shipping.

We also offer modification estimates. We will provide you with an estimate to draft your changes based on your specific modifications before you purchase the vellums, for a $50 fee. After you receive your estimate, if you decide to have us do the changes, the $50 estimate fee will be deducted from the cost of your modifications. If, however, you choose to use a different service, the $50 estimate fee is non-refundable. (Note: Personal checks cannot be accepted for the estimate.)

Within 5 days of receipt of your plans, you will be contacted by the Design Staff with an estimate for the design services to draw those changes. A 50% deposit is required before we begin making the actual modifications to your plans.

Once the design changes have been completed to your vellum plan, a representative will call to inform you that your modified Vellum plan is complete and will be shipped as soon as the final payment has been made. For additional information call us at 1-860-343-5977. Please refer to the Modification Pricing Guide for estimated modification costs.

Reproducible Vellums for Local Modification Ease

If you decide not to use Garlinghouse for your modifications, we recommend that you follow our same procedure of purchasing our Vellums. You then have the option of using the services of the original designer of the plan, a local professional designer, or architect to make the modifications to your plan.

With a Vellum copy of our plans, a design professional can alter the drawings just the way you want, then you can print as many copies of the modified plans as you need to build your house. And, since you have already started with our complete detailed plans, the cost of those expensive professional services will be significantly less than starting from scratch. Refer to the price schedule for Vellum costs.

IMPORTANT RETURN POLICY: Upon receipt of your Vellums, if for some reason you decide you do not want a modified plan, then simply return the Kit and the unopened Vellums. Reproducible Vellum copies of our home plans are copyright protected and only sold under the terms of a license agreement that you will receive with your order. Should you not agree to the terms, then the Vellums may be returned, **unopened,** for an exchange less a 20% restocking fee. For any additional information, please call us at 1-860-343-5977.

MODIFICATION PRICING GUIDE

CATEGORIES	ESTIMATED COST
KITCHEN LAYOUT — PLAN AND ELEVATION	$175.00
BATHROOM LAYOUT — PLAN AND ELEVATION	$175.00
FIREPLACE PLAN AND DETAILS	$200.00
INTERIOR ELEVATION	$125.00
EXTERIOR ELEVATION — MATERIAL CHANGE	$140.00
EXTERIOR ELEVATION — ADD BRICK OR STONE	$400.00
EXTERIOR ELEVATION — STYLE CHANGE	$450.00
NON BEARING WALLS (INTERIOR)	$200.00
BEARING AND/OR EXTERIOR WALLS	$325.00
WALL FRAMING CHANGE — 2X4 TO 2X6 OR 2X6 TO 2X4	$240.00
ADD/REDUCE LIVING SPACE — SQUARE FOOTAGE	QUOTE REQUIRED
NEW MATERIALS LIST	QUOTE REQUIRED
CHANGE TRUSSES TO RAFTERS OR CHANGE ROOF PITCH	$300.00
FRAMING PLAN CHANGES	$325.00
GARAGE CHANGES	$325.00
ADD A FOUNDATION OPTION	$300.00
FOUNDATION CHANGES	$250.00
RIGHT READING PLAN REVERSE	$575.00
ARCHITECTS SEAL (Available for most states.)	$300.00
ENERGY CERTIFICATE	$150.00
LIGHT AND VENTILATION SCHEDULE	$150.00

Questions?

Call our customer service department at 1-860-343-5977

"How to obtain a construction cost calculation based on labor rates and building material costs in <u>your</u> Zip Code area!"

ZIP-QUOTE!
HOME COST CALCULATOR

ZIP QUOTE
HOME COST CALCULATOR

WHY?

Do you wish you could quickly find out the building cost for your new home without waiting for a contractor to compile hundreds of bids? Would you like to have a benchmark to compare your contractor(s) bids against? *Well, Now You Can!!,* with **Zip-Quote** Home Cost Calculator. Zip-Quote is only available for zip code areas within the United States.

HOW?

Our new **Zip-Quote** Home Cost Calculator will enable you to obtain the calculated building cost to construct your new home, based on labor rates and building material costs within your zip code area, without the normal delays or hassles usually associated with the bidding process. Zip-Quote can be purchased in two separate formats, an itemized or a bottom line format.

"How does **Zip-Quote** actually work?" When you call to order, you must choose from the options available, for your specific home, in order for us to process your order. Once we receive your **Zip-Quote** order, we process your specific home plan building materials list through our Home Cost Calculator which contains up-to-date rates for all residential labor trades and building material costs in your zip code area. "The result?" A calculated cost to build your dream home in your zip code area. This calculation will help you (as a consumer or a builder) evaluate your building budget. This is a valuable tool for anyone considering building a new home.

All database information for our calculations is furnished by Marshall & Swift, L.P. For over 60 years, Marshall & Swift L.P. has been a leading provider of cost data to professionals in all aspects of the construction and remodeling industries.

OPTION 1

The **Itemized Zip-Quote** is a detailed building material list. Each building material list line item will separately state the labor cost, material cost and equipment cost (if applicable) for the use of that building material in the construction process. Each category within the building material list will be subtotaled and the entire Itemized cost calculation totaled at the end. This building materials list will be summarized by the individual building categories and will have additional columns where you can enter data from your contractor's estimates for a cost comparison between the different suppliers and contractors who will actually quote you their products and services.

OPTION 2

The **Bottom Line Zip-Quote** is a one line summarized total cost for the home plan of your choice. This cost calculation is also based on the labor cost, material cost and equipment cost (if applicable) within your local zip code area.

COST

The price of your **Itemized Zip-Quote** is based upon the pricing schedule of the plan you have selected, in addition to the price of the materials list. Please refer to the pricing schedule on our order form. The price of your initial **Bottom Line Zip-Quote** is $29.95. Each additional **Bottom Line Zip-Quote** ordered in conjunction with the initial order is only $14.95. **Bottom Line Zip-Quote** may be purchased separately and does NOT have to be purchased in conjunction with a home plan order.

FYI

An **Itemized Zip-Quote** Home Cost Calculation can ONLY be purchased in conjunction with a Home Plan order. The **Itemized Zip-Quote** can not be purchased separately. The **Bottom Line Zip-Quote** can be purchased separately and doesn't have to be purchased in conjunction with a home plan order. Please consult with a sales representative for current availability. If you find within 60 days of your order date that you will be unable to build this home, then you may exchange the plans and the materials list towards the price of a new set of plans (see order info pages for plan exchange policy). The **Itemized Zip-Quote** and the **Bottom Line Zip-Quote** are NOT returnable. The price of the initial **Bottom Line Zip-Quote** order can be credited towards the purchase of an **Itemized Zip-Quote** order only. Additional **Bottom Line Zip-Quote** orders, within the same order can not be credited. Please call our Customer Service Department for more information.

Itemized Zip-Quote is available for plans where you see this symbol. 🔲

Bottom Line Zip-Quote is available for all plans under 4,000 square feet.

SOME MORE INFORMATION

Itemized and Bottom Line Zip-Quotes give you approximated costs for constructing the particular house in your area. These costs are not exact and are only intended to be used as a preliminary estimate to help determine the affordability of a new home and/or as a guide to evaluate the general competitiveness of actual price quotes obtained through local suppliers and contractors. However, Zip-Quote cost figures should never be relied upon as the only source of information in either case. Land, sewer systems, site work, landscaping and other expenses are not included in our building cost figures. Garlinghouse and Marshall & Swift L.P. can not guarantee any level of data accuracy or correctness in a Zip-Quote and disclaim all liability for loss with respect to the same, in excess of the original purchase price of the Zip-Quote product. All Zip-Quote calculations are based upon the actual blueprints and do not reflect any differences or options that may be shown on the published house renderings, floor plans, or photographs.

IMPORTANT INFORMATION TO READ BEFORE YOU PLACE YOUR ORDER

How Many Sets Of Plans Will You Need?

The Standard 8-Set Construction Package

Our experience shows that you'll speed every step of construction and avoid costly building errors by ordering enough sets to go around. Each tradesperson wants a set — the general contractor and all subcontractors; foundation, electrical, plumbing, heating/air conditioning and framers. Don't forget your lending institution, building department and, of course, a set for yourself. * Recommended For Construction *

The Minimum 4-Set Construction Package

If you're comfortable with arduous follow-up, this package can save you a few dollars by giving you the option of passing down plan sets as work progresses. You might have enough copies to go around if work goes exactly as scheduled and no plans are lost or damaged by subcontractors. But for only $60 more, the 8-set package eliminates these worries. * Recommended For Bidding *

The Single Study Set

We offer this set so you can study the blueprints to plan your dream home in detail. They are stamped "study set only-not for construction", and you cannot build a home from them. In pursuant to copyright laws, it is _illegal_ to reproduce any blueprint.

An Important Note About Building Code Requirements:

All plans are drawn to conform to one or more of the industry's major national building standards. However, due to the variety of local building regulations, your plan may need to be modified to comply with local requirements — snow loads, energy loads, seismic zones, etc. Do check them fully and consult your local building officials.

A few states require that all building plans used be drawn by an architect registered in that state. While having your plans reviewed and stamped by such an architect may be prudent, laws requiring non-conforming plans like ours to be completely redrawn forces you to unnecessarily pay very large fees. If your state has such a law, we strongly recommend you contact your state representative to protest.

The rendering, floor plans, and technical information contained within this publication are not guaranteed to be totally accurate. Consequently, no information from this publication should be used either as a guide to constructing a home or for estimating the cost of building a home. Complete blueprints must be purchased for such purposes.

Order Form

Plan prices guaranteed until 1/1/02— After this date call for updated pricing

Order Code No. **CHP18**

Foundation _____

_____ set(s) of blueprints for plan #_____ $_____

_____ Vellum & Modification kit for plan #_____ $_____

_____ Additional set(s) @ $50 each for plan #_____ $_____

_____ Mirror Image Reverse @ $50 each $_____

_____ Right Reading Reverse @ $135 $_____

_____ Materials list for plan #_____ $_____

_____ Detail Plans @ $19.95 each   _____

_____   ❏ Construction ❏ Plumbing ❏ Electrical $_____

_____ Bottom line ZIP Quote @ $29.95 for plan #_____ $_____

Additional Bottom Line Zip Quote

@ $14.95 for plan(s) #_____ $_____

Zip Code where you are building_____

Itemized ZIP Quote for plan(s) #_____ $_____

Shipping (see charts on opposite page) $_____

Subtotal $_____

Sales Tax   (CT residents add 6% sales tax) (Not required for all states) $_____

TOTAL AMOUNT ENCLOSED $_____

Email address _____

Send your check, money order or credit card information to:
(No C.O.D.'s Please)

Please submit all United States & Other Nations orders to:

Garlinghouse Company
174 Oakwood Drive
Glastonbury, CT 06033

ADDRESS INFORMATION:

NAME: _____

STREET: _____

CITY: _____ **STATE:** _____ **ZIP:** _____

DAYTIME PHONE: _____

Credit Card Information

Charge To: ❏ Visa   ❏ Mastercard

Card # | | | | | | | | | | | | | | | | |

Signature _____ Exp. _____ / _____

ORDER TOLL FREE — 1-800-235-5700
Monday-Friday 8:00 a.m. to 8:00 p.m. Eastern Time
or FAX your Credit Card order to 1-860-659-5692
All foreign residents call 1-800-343-5977

BEST PLAN VALUE IN THE INDUSTRY!

Please have ready: 1. Your credit card number 2. The plan number 3. The order code number ⇨ **CHP18**

Garlinghouse 2001 Blueprint Price Code Schedule

Additional sets with original order $50

	1 Set	4 Sets	8 Sets	Vellums	ML	Itemized ZIP Quote
A	$350	$395	$455	$550	$60	$50
B	$390	$435	$495	$600	$60	$50
C	$430	$475	$535	$650	$60	$50
D	$470	$515	$575	$700	$60	$50
E	$510	$555	$615	$750	$70	$60
F	$555	$600	$660	$800	$70	$60
G	$600	$645	$705	$850	$70	$60
H	$645	$690	$750	$900	$70	$60
I	$690	$735	$795	$950	$80	$70
J	$740	$785	$845	$1000	$80	$70
K	$790	$835	$895	$1050	$80	$70
L	$840	$885	$945	$1100	$80	$70

Shipping — (Plans 1-54999)

	1-3 Sets	4-6 Sets	7+ & Vellums
Standard Delivery (UPS 2-Day)	$25.00	$30.00	$35.00
Overnight Delivery	$35.00	$40.00	$45.00

International Shipping & Handling

	1-3 Sets	4-6 Sets	7+ & Vellums
Regular Delivery Canada (7-10 Days)	$25.00	$30.00	$35.00
Express Delivery Canada (5-6 Days)	$40.00	$45.00	$50.00
Overseas Delivery Airmail (2-3 Weeks)	$50.00	$60.00	$65.00

Shipping — (Plans 60000-99999)

	1-3 Sets	4-6 Sets	7+ & Vellums
Ground Delivery (7-10 Days)	$15.00	$20.00	$25.00
Express Delivery (3-5 Days)	$20.00	$25.00	$30.00

Our Reorder and Exchange Policies:

If you find after your initial purchase that you require additional sets of plans you may purchase them from us at special reorder prices (please call for pricing details) provided that you reorder within 6 months of your original order date. There is a $28 reorder processing fee that is charged on all reorders. For more information on reordering plans please contact our Customer Service Department.

Your plans are custom printed especially for you once you place your order. For that reason we cannot accept any returns.

If for some reason you find that the plan you have purchased from us does not meet your needs, then you may exchange that plan for any other plan in our collection. We allow you sixty days from your original invoice date to make an exchange. At the time of the exchange you will be charged a processing fee of 20% of the total amount of your original order plus the difference in price between the plans (if applicable) plus the cost to ship the new plans to you. Call our Customer Service Department for more information. Please Note: Reproducible vellums can only be exchanged if they are unopened.

Important Shipping Information

Please refer to the shipping charts on the order form for service availability for your specific plan number. Our delivery service must have a street address or Rural Route Box number — never a post office box. (PLEASE NOTE: Supplying a P.O. Box number only will delay the shipping of your order.) Use a work address if no one is home during the day.

Orders being shipped to APO or FPO must go via First Class Mail.

For our International Customers, only Certified bank checks and money orders are accepted and must be payable in U.S. currency. For speed, we ship international orders Air Parcel Post. Please refer to the chart for the correct shipping cost.

Thank you

BL Bottom-line Zip Quote Available | Materials List Available | Zip Quote Available | **R** Right Reading Reverse | Duplex Plan

Icon key: BL = Bottom-line Zip Quote Available; ML = Materials List Available; ZQ = Zip Quote Available; RRR = Right Reading Reverse

Plan#	Page#	Price Code	Sq. Ft.	Icons
96527	261	C	1972	BL ML
96529	278	D	2089	BL ML
96530	306	E	2289	BL ML
96537	194	B	1676	BL
96539	279	D	2098	BL
96600	335	F	2678	BL
96601	244	C	1890	BL
96602	343	F	2745	BL
96902	254	A	1950	BL
96913	334	F	2677	BL
97105	280	D	2112	BL
97108	219	C	1794	BL
97124	103	A	1416	BL
97135	299	D	2229	BL
97137	120	A	1461	BL
97148	91	A	1370	BL
97151	267	D	2007	BL
97152	154	B	1557	BL
97224	88	A	1363	BL
97233	206	B	1743	BL
97242	277	D	2080	BL
97246	308	E	2311	BL
97253	241	C	1875	BL
97254	197	B	1692	BL
97256	52	A	1198	BL
97259	55	A	1222	BL
97262	121	A	1467	BL
97274	111	A	1432	BL ML
97277	251	C	1927	BL
97278	292	D	2188	BL ML
97294	284	D	2158	BL
97299	318	E	2491	BL
97404	308	E	2311	BL ML
97410	360	H	3225	BL ML
97415	216	C	1782	BL ML
97442	183	B	1650	BL ML
97445	174	B	1628	BL ML
97503	307	E	2310	BL
97505	327	F	2618	BL
97507	332	F	2659	BL
97511	353	H	3032	BL
97513	361	H	3230	BL
97514	366	I	3430	BL
97600	87	A	1361	BL
97601	118	A	1459	BL
97623	262	C	1978	BL
97702	168	B	1601	BL
97703	259	C	1963	BL
97714	367	J	3570	BL
97724	131	A	1488	BL
97730	77	A	1315	BL
97731	76	A	1315	BL
97800	312	E	2393	BL
98000	132	C	1488	BL ML RRR
98003	295	F	2198	BL ML RRR
98004	141	D	1517	BL ML RRR
98005	149	D	1542	BL ML RRR
98006	245	E	1899	BL ML RRR
98007	304	G	2273	BL ML RRR
98008	249	E	1911	BL ML RRR
98009	255	E	1954	BL ML RRR
98010	371	L	4523	ML RRR
98011	268	F	2024	BL ML RRR
98018	269	F	2027	BL ML RRR
98019	271	F	2042	BL ML RRR
98020	220	E	1795	BL ML RRR
98026	126	C	1476	BL ML RRR
98027	150	D	1544	BL ML RRR
98029	95	C	1377	BL ML RRR
98034	250	E	1918	BL ML RRR
98054	218	E	1792	BL ML
98056	229	E	1844	BL
98058	184	D	1652	BL
98059	109	C	1428	BL
98060	317	G	2487	BL
98061	251	E	1925	BL
98062	188	D	1658	BL ML
98068	309	G	2342	BL ML
98075	50	C	1182	BL ML
98076	303	G	2262	BL ML
98081	123	C	1473	BL ML
98082	276	F	2078	BL ML
98083	138	D	1511	BL ML
98086	201	D	1700	BL ML
98087	204	D	1733	BL ML
98095	302	F	2250	BL ML
98096	119	C	1460	BL ML
98097	253	E	1933	BL ML
98100	219	E	1792	BL ML
98101	231	E	1845	BL ML
98103	283	F	2152	BL ML
98238	252	C	1928	BL ML
98327	300	D	2235	BL
98337	177	B	1633	BL ML
98354	111	A	1431	BL ML
98408	235	C	1856	BL ML
98411	93	A	1373	BL ML
98412	152	B	1553	BL ML
98414	160	B	1575	BL ML
98415	110	A	1429	BL ML
98423	193	B	1671	BL ML
98424	301	D	2236	BL ML
98425	230	C	1845	BL ML
98426	329	F	2622	BL ML
98427	273	D	2051	BL ML
98430	243	C	1884	BL ML
98432	192	B	1670	BL ML
98434	82	A	1346	BL ML
98435	253	C	1945	BL ML
98441	137	B	1502	BL
98443	84	A	1359	BL
98456	203	B	1715	BL ML
98460	150	B	1544	BL
98461	51	A	1185	BL
98464	216	C	1779	BL
98466	293	D	2193	BL
98468	44	A	1104	BL
98472	133	A	1492	BL
98479	158	B	1575	BL
98498	46	A	1135	BL
98500	288	D	2169	BL
98501	294	D	2194	BL
98503	242	C	1876	BL
98511	316	E	2445	BL ZQ
98512	287	D	2167	BL
98513	364	I	3352	BL ZQ
98521	300	D	2233	BL
98522	142	B	1528	BL
98528	344	F	2748	BL ZQ
98538	370	L	4082	
98544	301	D	2238	BL
98547	330	F	2626	BL
98549	110	A	1431	BL
98550	319	F	2506	BL
98559	278	D	2081	BL ZQ
98569	349	G	2911	BL
98580	179	B	1640	BL
98584	333	F	2674	BL
98589	246	C	1902	BL
98597	356	H	3089	BL
98598	362	H	3239	BL
98732	319	F	2508	BL
98743	258	C	1958	BL
98744	315	E	2424	BL ML
98747	65	A	1280	BL ML
98748	281	D	2126	BL ML
98802	270	D	2035	BL
98804	91	A	1372	BL
98805	43	A	1089	BL
98807	130	A	1487	BL
98808	78	A	1326	BL
98814	199	B	1699	BL
98912	82	A	1345	BL ZQ
98915	54	A	1208	BL
98920	182	B	1646	BL
98936	214	C	1772	BL
99081	164	B	1590	BL
99106	134	A	1495	BL
99113	247	C	1906	BL
99115	254	C	1947	BL RRR
99152	153	B	1557	BL
99154	248	C	1907	BL
99160	340	F	2731	BL
99162	339	F	2730	BL
99163	167	B	1600	BL
99167	142	B	1537	BL
99208	227	C	1830	BL ML
99216	142	B	1521	BL ML
99303	105	A	1421	BL ML
99321	90	A	1368	BL ML
99324	72	A	1307	BL ML
99487	224	C	1806	BL ML
99503	172	B	1620	BL
99504	45	A	1127	BL
99639	89	A	1367	BL ML
99641	155	B	1567	BL ML
99657	180	B	1641	BL ML
99662	121	A	1466	BL ML
99668	188	B	1658	BL ML
99669	102	A	1412	BL ML
99721	365	I	3417	BL
99727	242	C	1876	BL ML
99774	292	D	2192	BL ML
99784	351	G	2987	BL ML
99802	161	D	1576	BL ML ZQ RRR
99803	8	E	1977	BL ML ZQ RRR
99804	12	E	1815	BL ML ZQ RRR
99805	218	E	1787	BL ML ZQ RRR
99806	61	C	1246	BL ML RRR
99807	14	E	1879	BL ML ZQ RRR
99808	18	E	1832	BL ML ZQ RRR
99809	21	C	1417	BL ML ZQ RRR
99810	24	D	1685	BL ML ZQ RRR
99811	23	D	1699	BL ML RRR
99812	96	C	1386	BL ML ZQ RRR
99813	259	E	1959	BL ML RRR
99814	221	E	1800	BL ML ZQ RRR
99815	250	E	1912	BL ML ZQ RRR
99820	325	H	2602	BL ML RRR
99826	31	C	1346	BL ML ZQ RRR
99828	70	C	1298	BL ML RRR
99830	31	C	1372	BL ML ZQ RRR
99831	200	D	1699	BL ML RRR
99833	112	C	1440	BL ML RRR
99834	160	D	1575	BL ML RRR
99835	140	D	1515	BL ML RRR
99838	293	F	2192	BL ML ZQ RRR
99840	176	D	1632	BL ML RRR
99844	205	D	1737	BL ML RRR
99845	25	E	1954	BL ML ZQ RRR
99846	282	F	2136	BL ML RRR
99849	77	C	1322	BL ML RRR
99850	32	D	1590	BL ML RRR
99854	173	D	1625	BL ML RRR
99856	75	C	1310	BL ML RRR
99857	237	E	1865	BL ML RRR
99858	62	C	1253	BL ML ZQ RRR
99860	135	C	1498	BL ML ZQ RRR
99864	108	C	1426	BL ML RRR
99868	83	C	1350	BL ML RRR
99870	88	C	1362	BL ML RRR
99871	19	D	1655	BL ML ZQ RRR
99878	26	E	1864	BL ML ZQ RRR

CREATIVE HOMEOWNER®

How-To Books for...

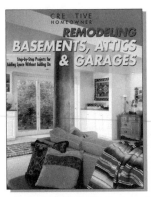

REMODELING BASEMENTS, ATTICS & GARAGES

Cramped for space? This book shows you how to find space you may not know you had and convert it into useful living areas. 40 colorful photographs and 530 full-color drawings.

BOOK #: 277680   192pp.   8½"x10⅞"

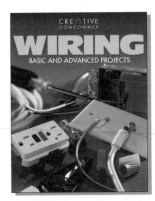

WIRING: Basic and Advanced Projects
(Conforms to latest National Electrical Code)

Included are 350 large, clear, full-color illustrations and no-nonsense step-by-step instructions. Shows how to replace receptacles and switches; repair a lamp; install ceiling and attic fans; and more.

BOOK #: 277049   256pp.   8½"x10⅞"

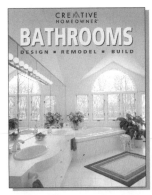

BATHROOMS: Design, Remodel, Build

Shows how to plan, construct, and finish a bathroom. Remodel floors; rebuild walls and ceilings; and install windows, skylights, and plumbing fixtures. Specific tools and materials are given for each project. Includes 90 color photos and 470 color illustrations.

BOOK #: 277053   192pp.   8½"x10⅞"

The Smart Approach to BATH DESIGN

Everything you need to know about designing a bathroom like a professional is explained in *this book*. Creative solutions and practical advice about space, the latest in fixtures and fittings, and safety features accompany over 150 photographs.

BOOK #: 287225   176pp.   9"x10"

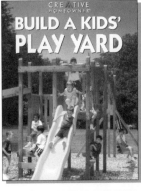

BUILD A KIDS' PLAY YARD

Here are detailed plans and step-by-step instructions for building the play structures that kids love most: swing set, monkey bars, balance beam, playhouse, teeter-totter, sandboxes, kid-sized picnic table, and a play tower that supports a slide. 200 color photographs and illustrations.

BOOK #: 277662   144 pp.   8½"x10⅞"

CABINETS & BUILT-INS

26 custom cabinetry projects are included for every room in the house, from kitchen cabinets to a bedroom wall unit, a bunk bed, computer workstation, and more. Also included are chapters on tools, techniques, finishing, and materials.

BOOK #: 277079   160 pp.   8½"x10⅞"

DECKS: Planning, Designing, Building

With this book, even the novice builder can build a deck that perfectly fits his yard. The step-by-step instructions lead the reader from laying out footings to adding railings. Includes three deck projects, 500 color drawings, and photographs.

BOOK #: 277162   192pp.   8½"x10⅞"

FURNITURE REPAIR & REFINISHING

From structural repairs to restoring older finishes or entirely refinishing furniture: a hands-on step-by-step approach to furniture repair and restoration. More than 430 color photographs and 60 full-color drawings.

BOOK #: 277335   240pp.   8½"x10⅞"

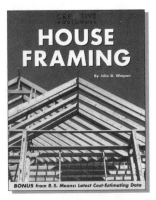

HOUSE FRAMING

Written for those with beginning to intermediate building skills, this book is designed to walk you through the framing basics, from assembling simple partitions to cutting compound angles on dormer rafters. More than 400 full-color drawings.

BOOK #: 277655   240pp.   8½"x10⅞"

the Home Planner, Builder & Owner

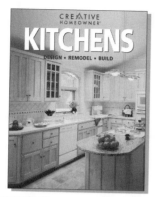

KITCHENS: Design, Remodel, Build

This is the reference book for modern kitchen design, with more than 100 full-color photos to help homeowners plan the layout. Step-by-step instructions illustrate basic plumbing and wiring techniques; how to finish walls and ceilings; and more.

BOOK #: 277065   192pp.   8½"x10⅞"

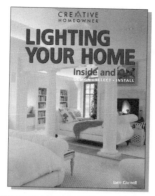

LIGHTING YOUR HOME: Inside and Out

Lighting should be selected with care. This book thoroughly explains lighting design for every room as well as outdoors. It is also a step-by-step manual that shows how to install the fixtures. More than 125 photos and 400 drawings.

BOOK #: 277583   176pp.   8½"x10⅞"

MASONRY: Concrete, Brick, Stone

Concrete, brick, and stone choices are detailed with step-by-step instructions and over 35 color photographs and 460 illustrations. Projects include a brick or stone garden wall, steps and patios, a concrete-block retaining wall, a concrete sidewalk.

BOOK #: 277106   176pp.   8½"x10⅞"

The Smart Approach to KITCHEN DESIGN

Transform a dated kitchen into the spectacular heart of your home. Learn how to create a better layout and more efficient storage. Find out about the latest equipment and materials. Savvy tips explain how to create style like a pro. More than 150 color photos.

BOOK #: 279935   176 pp.   9"x10"

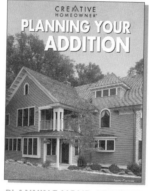

PLANNING YOUR ADDITION

Planning an addition to your home involves a daunting number of choices, from choosing a contractor to selecting bathroom tile. Using 280 color drawings and photographs, architect/author Jerry Germer helps you make the right decision.

BOOK #: 277004   192pp.   8½"x10⅞"

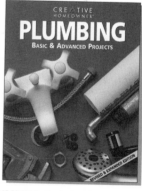

PLUMBING: Basic & Advanced Projects

Take the guesswork out of plumbing repair and installation for old and new systems. Projects include replacing faucets, unclogging drains, installing a tub, replacing a water heater, and much more. 500 illustrations and diagrams.

BOOK #: 277620   176pp.   8½"x10⅞"

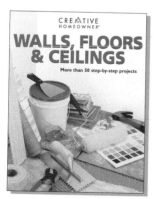

WALLS, FLOORS & CEILINGS

Here's the definitive guide to interiors. It shows you how to replace old surfaces with new professional-looking ones. Projects include installing molding, skylights, insulation, flooring, carpeting, and more. Over 500 color photos and drawings.

BOOK #: 277697   176pp.   8½"x10⅞"

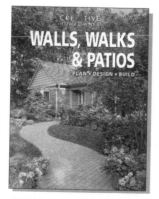

WALLS, WALKS & PATIOS

Learn how to build a patio from concrete, stone, or brick and complement it with one of a dozen walks. Learn about simple mortarless walls, landscape timber walls, and hefty brick and stone walls. 50 photographs and 320 illustrations, all in color.

BOOK #: 277994   192pp.   8½"x10⅞"

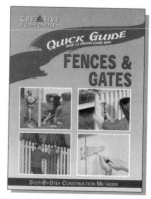

QUICK GUIDE: FENCES & GATES

Learn how to build and install all kinds of fences and gates for your yard, from hand-built wood privacy and picket fences to newer prefabricated vinyl and chain-link types. Over 200 two-color drawings illustrate step-by-step procedures.

BOOK #: 287732   80pp.   8½"x10⅞"

Place Your Order ....

WORKING WITH TILE
Design and complete interior and exterior tile projects on walls, floors, countertops, shower enclosures, more. 425 color illustrations and over 80 photographs.

BOOK #: 277540   176pp.   8½"x10⅞"

COLOR IN THE AMERICAN HOME
Find out how to make the most of color in your home. Over 150 photographs of traditional and contemporary interiors.

BOOK #: 287264   176pp.   9"x10"

The Smart Approach to HOME DECORATING
Learn how to work with space, color, pattern, and texture with the flair of a professional designer. More than 300 color photos.

BOOK #: 279667   256pp.   9"x10"

CREATIVE HOMEOWNER®

BOOK ORDER FORM   *Please Print*

SHIP TO:

Name:

Address:

City: State: Zip: Phone Number:

(Should there be a problem with your order)

Quantity	Title	Price	CH #	Cost
	375 Southern Home Plans	$9.95	277037	
	380 Country & Farmhouse Home Plans	9.95	277035	
	400 Affordable Home Plans	9.95	277012	
	408 Vacation & Second Home Plans	8.95	277036	
	508 Two-Story Home Plans	9.95	277031	
	600 Most Popular Home Plans	9.95	277029	
	Adding Value to Your Home	16.95	277006	
	Advanced Home Gardening	24.95	274465	
	Annuals, Perennials, and Bulbs	19.95	274032	
	Bathrooms: Design, Remodel, Build	19.95	277053	
	Better Lawns, Step by Step	14.95	274359	
	Bird Feeders	10.95	277102	
	Build a Kids' Play Yard	14.95	277662	
	Cabinets & Built-Ins	14.95	277079	
	Color in the American Home	19.95	287264	
	Complete Guide to Wallpapering	14.95	278910	
	Complete Guide to Water Gardens	19.95	274452	
	Complete Home Landscaping	24.95	274615	
	Creating Good Gardens	16.95	274244	
	Custom Closets	12.95	277132	
	Decks: Planning, Designing, Building	16.95	277162	
	Decorating with Paint & Paper	19.95	279723	
	Decorating with Tile	19.95	279824	
	Decorative Paint Finishes	10.95	287371	
	Drywall: Pro Tips for Hanging & Finishing	14.95	278315	
	Easy-Care Guide to Houseplants	19.95	275243	
	Fences, Gates & Trellises	14.95	277981	
	Furniture Repair & Refinishing	19.95	277335	
	Gazebos & Other Outdoor Structures	14.95	277138	
	Home Book	40.00	267855	
	Home Landscaping: California Reg.	19.95	274267	
	Home Landscaping: Mid-Atlantic Reg.	19.95	274537	
	Home Landscaping: Midwest Reg./S Can.	19.95	274385	
	Home Landscaping: Northeast Reg./SE Can.	19.95	274618	
	Home Landscaping: Southeast Reg.	19.95	274762	
	House Framing	19.95	277655	
	Kitchens: Design, Remodel, Build (New Ed.)	16.95	277065	
	Lighting Your Home Inside & Out	16.95	277583	
	Lyn Peterson's Real Life Decorating	27.95	279382	
	Masonry: Concrete, Brick, Stone	16.95	277106	
	Mastering Fine Decorative Paint Techniques	27.95	279550	
	Planning Your Addition	16.95	277004	
	Plumbing: Basic and Advanced Projects	14.95	277620	
	Remodeling Basements, Attics & Garages	16.95	277680	
	Smart Approach to Bath Design	19.95	287225	
	Smart Approach to Home Decorating	24.95	279667	
	Smart Approach to Kitchen Design	19.95	279935	

Quantity	Title	Price	CH #	Cost
	Smart Approach to Window Decor	$19.95	279431	
	Trees, Shrubs & Hedges for Home Landscaping	19.95	274238	
	Walls, Floors & Ceilings	16.95	277697	
	Walls, Walks & Patios	14.95	277994	
	Wiring: Basic and Advanced Projects	19.95	277049	
	Working with Tile	16.95	277540	
	Yard and Garden Furniture (Plans & Projects)	19.95	277462	

Quick Guide Series

Quantity	Title	Price	CH #	Cost
	Quick Guide - Attics	$7.95	287711	
	Quick Guide - Basements	7.95	287242	
	Quick Guide - Ceramic Tile	7.95	287730	
	Quick Guide - Decks	7.95	277344	
	Quick Guide - Fences & Gates	7.95	287732	
	Quick Guide - Floors	7.95	287734	
	Quick Guide - Garages & Carports	7.95	287785	
	Quick Guide - Gazebos	7.95	287757	
	Quick Guide - Insulation & Ventilation	7.95	287367	
	Quick Guide - Interior & Exterior Painting	7.95	287784	
	Quick Guide - Masonry Walls	7.95	287741	
	Quick Guide - Patios & Walks	7.95	287778	
	Quick Guide - Plumbing	7.95	287863	
	Quick Guide - Ponds & Fountains	7.95	287804	
	Quick Guide - Pool & Spa Maintenance	7.95	287901	
	Quick Guide - Roofing	7.95	287807	
	Quick Guide - Shelving & Storage	7.95	287763	
	Quick Guide - Siding	7.95	287892	
	Quick Guide - Stairs & Railings	7.95	287755	
	Quick Guide - Storage Sheds	7.95	287815	
	Quick Guide - Trim (Crown Molding, Base & more)	7.95	287745	
	Quick Guide - Walls & Ceilings	7.95	287792	
	Quick Guide - Windows & Doors	7.95	287812	
	Quick Guide - Wiring, Third Edition	7.95	287884	

Number of Books Ordered _____   Total for Books _____

NJ Residents add 6% tax _____

Prices subject to change without notice.   Subtotal _____

Postage/Handling Charges _____
$3.75 for first book / $1.25 for each additional book

Total _____

Make checks (in U.S. currency only) payable to:

CREATIVE HOMEOWNER®
P.O. BOX 38, 24 Park Way
Upper Saddle River, New Jersey 07458-9960

Please visit us at our Web site: **www.creativehomeowner.com**